AN INSTITUTIONAL INVESTOR PUBLICATION

ACTIVE ASSET ALLOCATION

STATE-OF-THE-ART
PORTFOLIO POLICIES,
STRATEGIES & TACTICS

Robert D. Arnott
Frank J. Fabozzi

E D I T O R S

PROBUS PUBLISHING COMPANY
Chicago, Illinois
Cambridge, England

ISBN 1-55738-237-9

Printed in the United States of America

BB

1   2   3   4   5   6   7   8   9   0

DEDICATION

To my wonderful son, Robin, to my wife, Bobbi, and to our forthcoming twins, all of whom help to make life a joy.

Robert D. Arnott

To my wife Dessa.

Frank J. Fabozzi

Special thanks are owing to the staff of First Quadrant Corp. who assisted us at various stages of this project.

Contents

Contributors

Keith P. Ambachtsheer, *Ambachtsheer Letter and Canadian Investment Review*

Robert D. Arnott, *First Quadrant Corporation*

Lawrence N. Bader, *Salomon Brothers Inc*

Peter L. Bernstein, *Peter L. Bernstein, Inc.*

Roger G. Clarke, *TSA Capital Management*

Charles H. DuBois, *Chancellor Capital Management, Inc.*

Jeremy J. Evnine, *Iris Financial Engineering and Systems, Inc.*

Frank J. Fabozzi, *Massachusetts Institute of Technology and Journal of Portfolio Management*

H. Gifford Fong, *Gifford Fong Associates*

Roy D. Henriksson, *Kidder Peabody, Inc.*

Roger D. Ibbotson, *Ibbotson Associates, Inc.*

Stanley Kogelman, *Salomon Brothers Inc*

Adrian J. Lee, *J. P. Morgan Investment Management, Inc., London*

Martin L. Leibowitz, *Salomon Brothers Inc*

Mark W. Riepe, *Ibbotson Associates, Inc.*

Paul Samuelson, *Massachusetts Institute of Technology*

William F. Sharpe, *Stanford University*

Laurence B. Siegel, *Ibbotson Associates, Inc.*

Meir Statman, *Santa Clara University*

SECTION ONE

The Many Dimensions of the Asset Allocation Decision

CHAPTER 1

The Many Dimensions of the Asset Allocation Decision

ROBERT D. ARNOTT
PRESIDENT AND CHIEF INVESTMENT OFFICER
FIRST QUADRANT CORP.

FRANK J. FABOZZI
VISITING PROFESSOR
SLOAN SCHOOL OF MANAGEMENT
MASSACHUSETTS INSTITUTE OF TECHNOLOGY
AND EDITOR
JOURNAL OF PORTFOLIO MANAGEMENT

Asset allocation. Everyone's talking about it, but what is it and what are people doing? One of the puzzles in asset allocation is that the asset allocation decision is *not* one decision. Much of the confusion and mystique that surrounds asset allocation stems directly from this fact. The term "asset allocation" means different things to different people in different contexts. Asset allocation can loosely be divided into three categories: *policy* asset allocation, *tactical* asset allocation, and *dynamic* strategies for asset allocation, designed to reshape the return distribution. Most of the attention in this book is focused on the first two categories, but there are many variants on each of the three themes, which deserve a brief overview.

POLICY ASSET ALLOCATION

The policy asset mix decision can loosely be characterized as a long-term asset allocation decision, in which the investor seeks to assess an appropriate long-term "normal" asset mix which represents an ideal blend of controlled risk and enhanced return. The strategies which offer the greatest prospects for strong long-term rewards tend to be inherently risky strategies. The strategies which offer the greatest safety tend to offer only modest return opportunities. The balancing of these conflicting goals is what we call "policy" asset allocation.

Even within this definition of policy asset allocation, there are many considerations which the investor must address. Policy asset allocation is the balancing of risk and reward in assessing a long-term "normal" asset mix. But *what* risks and *what* rewards are to be contemplated in this evaluation? For the investor with a short investment horizon and a need to preserve capital, the relevant definition of risk is very different from a long-horizon investor such as a pension fund or an endowment fund. Ironically, the lowest risk strategy for a short-horizon investor may be a high-risk strategy for a long-horizon investor. This somewhat surprising fact is explored from several angles throughout the opening section of the book, which focuses on policy asset allocation.

For many investors, there is more than one definition of risk which may have a bearing on the policy asset allocation decision. For example, the pension sponsor needs to be concerned with volatility of assets, volatility of liabilities, volatility of the surplus (or difference between assets and liabilities), volatility of the expense ratio or contribution rate for funding the pension plan, as well as a handful of other factors. But risk is not just volatility. Under the new pension accounting guidelines for United States-based corporations, risk also can be defined in terms of shortfall. After all, upside risk is a risk that no one fears. But downside risk is to be avoided. Notably in pension management, there is the need to avoid any risk of a net, unfunded liability. No pension officer wants to be tagged as the individual responsible for a new liability appearing on the balance sheet!

In assessing the policy asset allocation, there is even a host of different tools at the investor's disposal. Should the investor use optimization techniques? Should optimization techniques with a shortfall constraint be the basis for the policy asset mix decision? How does the suitable policy mix shift with different investor circumstances? All of these are questions which can and must be addressed in assessing the policy asset allocation decision.

DYNAMIC STRATEGIES

Some of the more intriguing and controversial strategies to emerge in recent years are the "dynamic" strategies, in which the asset mix is mechanistically shifted in response to changing market conditions. The most well publicized variant of these dynamic strategies would certainly be *portfolio insurance.* However, dynamic strategies can be used for a whole host of purposes which go well beyond simple portfolio insurance, for all of its potential merits or demerits. In essence, these dynamic strategies enable the investor to reshape the entire return distribution. By dynamically shifting the asset mix, investors can control both downside risk and surplus volatility; can directly build a "shortfall constraint" into their strategy; and in essence can reshape the return distribution as they see fit. Dynamic strategies are notable for their mechanistic nature and for their potential impact on policy asset allocation. They are mechanistic in the sense that any action in the capital markets triggers a prescribed reaction in the portfolio of assets.

Dynamic strategies have an interesting implication for the policy asset allocation decision. If a dynamic strategy is employed, it can represent a long-term policy asset allocation *response* to changing market conditions. Many advocates of portfolio insurance have also been advocates of a more aggressive asset allocation stance, leaning more heavily towards equities in response to the protection offered by portfolio insurance. Other investment practitioners have argued for the opposite strategy: selling portfolio insurance. Such a process would involve boosting equity exposure after a decline and lowering it after a rally, thereby ostensibly providing a "built-in" policy response to changing market conditions. Such strategies clearly provide greatly increased flexibility in investment management and greatly improved control over the nature of the portfolio, *if the dynamic strategy can be implemented at a reasonable cost.* This last issue has been the focal point of much of the controversy regarding dynamic strategies in the wake of the October 1987 market crash.

TACTICAL ASSET ALLOCATION

Once the policy asset allocation has been established, the investor can turn attention to the possibility of active departures from policy. If such a decision is based upon rigorous objective measures of value, it is often called tactical asset allocation (TAA). Here again things are not as simple as they would appear on the surface. Tactical asset allocation is not a single, clearly defined strategy. There are many variations and nuances involved in building a tactical allocation process.

Attention might first be paid to the whole puzzle of semantics. One of the problems in reviewing the concepts of asset allocation is that the same terms are often used for different concepts. The term "dynamic asset allocation" has been used to refer to the long-term policy decision and to intermediate-term efforts to strategically position the portfolio to benefit from major market moves, as well as to aggressive tactical strategies. Even the words "normal asset allocation" convey a stability which is not consistent with the real world. As an investor's risk expectations and tolerance for risk change, the normal or policy asset allocation may change. It is critical in exploring asset allocation issues to know what *element* of the asset allocation decision is the subject of discussion, and to know *in what context* the words "asset allocation" are being used.

Tactical asset allocation broadly refers to active strategies which seek to enhance performance by opportunistically shifting the asset mix of a portfolio in response to the changing patterns of reward available in the capital markets. Notably, tactical asset allocation tends to refer to disciplined processes for evaluating prospective rates of return on various asset classes and establishing an asset allocation response intended to capture higher rewards. In the various implementations of tactical asset allocation, there are different investment horizons and different mechanisms for evaluating the asset allocation decision. These also merit a brief review.

Tactical asset allocation can refer to either an intermediate-term or a short-term process. There are tactical processes which seek to measure the relative attractiveness of the major asset classes which seek to participate in major movements in the stock or bond markets. Other approaches are more short-term in nature, designed to capture short-term movements in the markets. The shared attributes of these tactical asset allocation processes are several:

- They tend to be objective processes, based on analytic tools, such as regression analysis or optimization, rather than relying on subjective judgment.
- They tend to be driven primarily by objective measures of prospective values within an asset class. We *know* the yield on cash, we *know* the yield to maturity on long bonds, and the earning yield on the stock market represents a reasonable and objective proxy for long-term rewards available in stocks. These objective measures of reward lead to an inherently value-oriented process.
- Tactical asset allocation processes tend to buy after a market decline and sell after a market rise. As such, they can tend to be inherently contrary. By objectively measuring which asset classes are offering the greatest prospective rewards, tactical asset allocation disciplines measure which asset classes are most out of favor. In so doing, they steer investments into unloved asset classes. These assets are priced to reflect the fact that they are out of favor and the corresponding fact that investors demand a premium reward for an out-of-favor investment. *Therein lies the effectiveness of tactical asset allocation disciplines.*

The types of tactical asset allocation disciplines cover a wide spectrum. Some are simple, objective comparisons of available rates of return. Others seek to enhance the timeliness of these value-driven decisions by incorporating macroeconomic measures, sentiment measures, volatility measures and even technical measures. In essence, the users of these more elaborate approaches would argue that, just as an undervalued stock can get more undervalued, so too an undervalued asset class can grow more undervalued. The investor who buys an asset as soon as it becomes undervalued does less well than the investor who buys that same asset class shortly before it finally rebounds.

THE ASSET ALLOCATION DECISIONS

In conclusion, we should reiterate that there is not one asset allocation decision, but several. In this book, we seek to assemble some of the best thinking in the investment world today on the subject of asset allocation. To be sure, there are many fine practitioners and theoreticians whose ideas do not appear in this volume. Regrettably, it is not possible to assemble all of the worthy asset allocation thinking in a single volume. Nonetheless, we believe we have selected some of the ideas and some of the thinkers who have been important, creative contributors to the whole field of asset allocation.

CHAPTER 2

Overview of the Total Asset Allocation Problem*

PETER L. BERNSTEIN
PRESIDENT
PETER L. BERNSTEIN, INC. AND
CONSULTING EDITOR
JOURNAL OF PORTFOLIO MANAGEMENT

Before the process of asset allocation begins — in fact, even before the definition of the related liability structure begins — investors must answer four questions. The answers to these questions are not obvious to any of us. In fact, we do not ask these questions of ourselves frequently enough. Some of us never ask them. Nevertheless, answers to these questions are essential if asset allocation is going to deliver the results expected, instead of just random surprises.

The four questions are:

1. Who is the owner of the assets and why does it matter? The owner of the assets determines the character of the liabilities that the assets are supposed to fund.

---

*This chapter is adapted from a paper that appeared in the *Financial Analysts Journal*, March/April, 1987.

2. What are the assets and why does it matter? The conventional breakdown into asset classes hides a veritable tangle of hybrid securities and disparate parts whose reality is different from their appearance and whose covariances are fluid or obscure.
3. Who are the managers and why does it matter? How closely are the owners of the assets with multimanager structures really controlling the risks of the total portfolio?
4. Is diversification itself dead and why does it matter? Portfolio insurance and other forms of dynamic hedging strategies are doing strange things to the types of orthodox diversification techniques that usually come under the heading of asset allocation.

WHO IS THE OWNER OF THE ASSETS?

Portfolio managers tend to become so fascinated with assets that they forget that assets have no reason for being except to fund liabilities. If we never had any liabilities, we would have no need for assets. As soon as we assume any kind of obligation, however, the search for appropriate assets to fund that obligation begins.

The manner in which we deploy the assets under management — the urgency for high rates of return, the consequences of loss, the time horizon that is acceptable — will therefore depend totally on the owner of those assets. Different owners have different liability structures, which means that the urgency for high rates of return, the consequences of loss, and the acceptable time horizon will vary from one owner to another.

The proverbial widow has to worry about losses, because the time horizon for recouping is short; high returns have to be a secondary consideration. A young executive on the make has the luxury of plenty of time and opportunity to recoup losses and can therefore invest aggressively. Pension funds have long time horizons, but the sponsor of a fund may worry about having to make good on losses or about covariances between asset returns and the fund's liabilities, so that some blend of these three considerations is most likely.

In many cases, the ownership of the assets is obscure rather than simple. An elderly widow may think one way, but her hungry heirs may encourage her to follow aggressive investment policies to suit their own time horizon and urgencies for high returns. The conflicts of interest between the income beneficiaries of a trust and the remaindermen are all too familiar. A young executive may have more than just a few immediate liabilities with impatient creditors acting like proxy owners of his assets.

The corporate pension fund presents even more complex questions of ownership. The debate over who owns the fund's assets continues without clear resolution, but the appropriate allocation of assets will also lack definition until we have resolved the debate over ownership.

Are the employees of the corporation the owners of the assets? Or are they simply creditors?

The employees have the senior claim on the assets. They have lent their deferred wages to the corporation and have a further contractual claim on future compensation. The assets of the pension fund are collateral to secure these claims.

Followed to its logical conclusion, this view reveals the employees as the ultimate owners of the assets in the pension fund. The sole objective of the employees is to be as certain as possible that their claims are secure. Like our proverbial widow, they will be willing to minimize return in exchange for the comfortable feeling that the plan is, first and foremost, minimizing risk.

I would argue that this view holds despite the new reality that pension funds own an increasing share of corporate sponsors themselves. This puts the employees in an odd conflict of interest with themselves, but their dominant interest must continue to be the safety of the pension fund rather than rate of return.

What about the stockholders? The stockholders own the residual interest in the pension fund, even if we can debate their ownership of the portion of the fund required to collateralize the pension obligations. As a result of the bull market of the 1980s in stocks and bonds, many of those residual interests have become substantial interests relative to the assets of the corporation as a whole.

The goal of the stockholders is to minimize pension expense and to maximize their residual interest in the fund — perhaps with a view to subsequent recapture for the corporation as a whole. This approach is the only one consistent with the stockholders' objective of maximizing the long-run value of the corporation.

In the extreme, furthermore, the stockholders have the right to put the liabilities of the pension fund to the Pension Benefit Guaranty Corporation. This means that the stockholders are perfectly willing to brush off the consequences of loss and to accept higher risks than the employees would accept: the stockholders, rather than the beneficiaries of the fund, will enjoy the fruits of the higher returns that the greater risks are expected to provide.

But there is a third guest at the party: management. The pension officer, the chief financial officer, the chief executive officer, and often the board of directors also have a stake in the performance of the fund. In addition, they — not the employees or the stockholders — make the hands-on decisions that determine the risk/reward tradeoffs in the pension fund.

These people are employees and often stockholders as well, but the pension officer and the Chief Financial Officer have separate roles to play. They know that senior management looks to the performance of the pension fund as a measure of their performance for the corporation. The future careers of the pension officer and the Chief Financial Officer brighten or dim as, calendar quarter by calendar quarter, the fund results roll in. Their time horizon is much shorter than the time horizon of the employees or the stockholders.

Management likes good results, of course. But management also wants results that are *smooth*. Surprises are jarring and raise questions that may be difficult to answer. Smooth results lead to easy and confident extrapolation. This means that high returns are nice for management but volatility is anathema. Such views lead to partiality toward portfolio insurance or broad diversification and other forms of bet-hedging, even at the expense of maximizing returns.

Who are the owners of the pension fund? How can we decide what asset allocation strategy to select until we know the answer?

WHAT ARE THE ASSETS?

Even if we think we know how to allocate the assets appropriately, how much do we know about the essential nature of what we are allocating? The conventional breakdown of stocks, bonds, and paper — now frequently expanded to include non-U.S. securities, real estate, and venture capital — is a dangerous oversimplification of reality.

The conventional taxonomy of assets is intrinsically dirty. Most assets are hybrids. As we look deeper, we find that what we call equities and bonds and short-term paper are in fact complex combinations of options — puts and calls — and zero-coupon riskless bonds. These three elements are the atoms from which we form the enormous variety of molecules to which we assign familiar names, but whose performance is going to reflect their essential natures.

For example, we can replicate the performance of put options simply by combining risky assets and risk-free assets in a systematic manner. A conventional asset class breakdown would disguise our ownership of a synthetic put. We can also go the other way. Combining risky assets with the right combination of puts and calls will mimic the performance of a risk-free asset, but our asset allocation breakdown would show no risk-free asset in the portfolio.

Consider a portfolio that consists only of equities. What do the stockholders really own? They share a claim on the assets with the creditors. The creditors have the prior claim. Therefore, the stockholders do not really own the assets. They own a put that they have purchased from the creditors — an option that gives the stockholders the right to walk away from their debts and leave the creditors holding the bag. The price that the stockholders pay for this option depends on the same variables that determine the price of any option: the strike price, the time to expiration, and the volatility of the underlying assets.

Looked at from the other side, the creditors own a call on the residual assets. Therefore, corporate bonds are in reality a riskless security plus this call option and are subject to the stockholders' exercise of their put option. This means that corporate bonds, even AAA bonds, have a significant equity element and will respond to changes in equity expectations as well as to changes in interest rates. It is no wonder, then, that stock index futures will often hedge bond portfolios more efficiently than Treasury bond futures can hedge them.

The difficulties with asset allocation classification procedures extend beyond the complexities of asset structure. Conventional breakdowns are incomplete, because they hide the covariances among asset returns that are essential to the whole process of portfolio formation. Common factor themes run right across all asset classes; inflation, fear/greed, the role of the United States in the world, and oil prices are just a few examples of such common factors.

I pointed out above that corporate bonds are a combination of a risk-free asset and equity features. The point works in reverse. Most stocks have at least some degree of interest sensitivity; many stocks have a high degree of interest sensitivity.

The essential nature of an equity is best seen when it is peeled like an onion. The outer layer is the dominating influence of the stock market itself, so that each individual stock is a microcosm of an index fund. Then come each stock's own specific responses, as well as a variety of covariances with subgroups of stocks or common economic factors. As interest rates are among the most powerful common factors that influence stock returns, each individual stock is not only a microcosm of a stock index fund, but also a microcosm of a bond index fund.

Unfortunately, the opposite is true. We have just considered asset classes that share covariances with other asset classes. Some so-called asset classes have such low covariance among their component parts that they do not deserve the name of an asset class.

We talk about international investing as though putting assets outside the United States meant depositing them in some kind of identifiable basket of stocks. A recent Salomon Brothers study of international investing shows that this is a serious misconception.[1] Independent movements among 28 national markets are more the rule than the exception More than 60 out of 784 intermarket correlations are negative and most are less than +0.10. The United States correlations with the other 27 countries range all the way from −0.03 (Thailand) to 0.64 (Canada).

We also treat real estate as a homogeneous asset class, with as little justification. A paper by Grissom, Kuhle, and Walther shows significant differences in both risk and return among office buildings, residential real estate, shopping centers, and industrial properties.[2] The same paper and a paper by Froland, Grolow, and Sampson[3] demonstrate that the real estate markets in different parts of the country also have low covariances with one another.

Even within the stock market itself, the prices are uncomfortably disparate. According to Ibbotson Associates,[4] small stock returns correlate negatively with bond returns and positively with inflation. Large capitalization stocks do the opposite. Are stocks a hedge against inflation? Small stocks had an annual standard deviation of 36.0% from 1926 through 1985, while large stocks show only 21.2%. How risky are stocks?

What are the assets? We must recognize that the conventional taxonomy of assets is intrinsically dirty.

---

[1]*International Equity Analysis*, Salomon Brothers Inc, New York, June 1987.

[2]Terry V. Grissom, James L. Kuhle, and Carl H. Walter, "Diversification Works in Real Estate, Too," *Journal of Portfolio Management*, Winter 1987, pp. 66–71.

[3]Charles Froland, Robert Grolow, and Richard Sampson, "The Market Risk of Real Estate," *Journal of Portfolio Management*, Spring 1986, pp. 12–19.

[4]Stocks, Bonds, Bills, and Inflation: 1986 Yearbook, Ibbotson Associates, Chicago, 1986, p. 32.

WHO ARE THE MANAGERS?

By this question, I mean: Who is really managing the show?

The easy answer is that the owner of the assets or the owner's designated agent — say, the pension officer — is managing the show. These people do have the *responsibility*, but do they in reality have the authority? Or, is the authority so dispersed among the individual portfolio management organizations that *no one* is managing the show? This arrangement seems to be most frequently the case.

What are all these people supposed to be doing? The goal of portfolio management is to select and arrange assets that will assure the payment of all explicit and implicit liabilities as they come due. Only minor modifications are needed to make this simple statement fit all possible kinds of investors. To the extent that investors ignore this definition and pursue different goals, those investors are probably taking either more risk than they must, or less risk than they should.[5]

Liabilities, like assets, have variable values; even nominally fixed assets and liabilities have variable real values. Therefore, the process of minimizing risk is the process of matching the variability of the assets to the variability of the liabilities. Risk begins where mismatch begins.

How closely can the owner of the assets, or the owner's agent, control for mismatch in an environment where the number of separate portfolio managers significantly exceeds one? Can there be any control at all, when each management organization is pursuing its own duration and other risk control strategies in accordance with its own assigned asset class, its own investment style, its own market expectations and its overwhelming drive to provide higher returns than its peers provide? If everybody landed on the appropriate setting of the risk dial, the coincidence would be nothing short of amazing.

For example, let us assume that stocks are relatively insensitive to interest rates at some moment in time. Does the asset owner then make certain that the fixed-income managers hold a preponderance of long-term bonds, even against the better judgment of those managers, so as to offset the lack of exposure to interest rate variability in the stock portfolio? Or, conversely, if the equity portfolio managers have composed a portfolio that has high interest sensitivity, will the total allocation

---

[5]For an emphatic and systematic defense of this view of the goals of portfolio management and the meaning of risk, see Robert H. Jeffrey, "A New Paradigm for Portfolio Risk," *Journal of Portfolio Management*, Fall 1984, pp. 33–40.

to fixed-income or the duration of the fixed-income share of the total portfolio reflect that fact?

The essence of prudent portfolio management is to hedge bets — don't put all the eggs in one basket, seek out asset groups with negative covariances. We do this with the full expectation that some baskets will provide better returns than others. Indeed, we explicitly select some assets to underperform under most likely conditions and to outperform only when our primary bets go haywire. In other words, we pray and hope that the assets that hedge our primary bets will underperform, because we will have made the wrong primary bet if the hedging asset does better.

How can the owners of the assets preserve this crucial hedging structure when they parcel out the assets to different managers, all of whom justify their very existence by aiming to outperform their competitors? Can the owners tell Manager A or Manager B to underperform, that is, to posture their share of the portfolio so that it will perform well only under low-probability outcomes? Is there a manager who would accept an account under those constraints?

In recent years, for example, both bonds and stocks have been effective hedges against disinflation. This means that you needed only one of these two assets, not both. But if both expectations and liability structures ordained a heavy overweight in common stocks for your portfolio, then how would you have protected against an outbreak of inflation? An instruction to the fixed-income managers to hold only short-term paper would do the trick. How do you tell your fixed-income manager to hang in at the short end at a time when bond returns are going through the roof?

Who are the managers? The lines of authority in the management structure are less direct than most people recognize.

IS DIVERSIFICATION DEAD?

The question perhaps overstates the issue, but let us consider the full implications for asset allocation of substituting portfolio insurance for diversification. The transformation is profound.

We employ diversification as the cornerstone of asset allocation, as I mentioned above, for reasons of prudence. We want to avoid putting all our eggs in one basket and tend to shun different baskets with identical characteristics. Put another way, diversification is an explicit sacrifice of return maximization to assure survival if something goes wrong with our primary bets.

Portfolio insurance, at first glance, appears to be a logical substitute for diversification. The goal of portfolio insurance is also to sacrifice some upside potential in order to assure survival.

Two critical differences distinguish these two risk-reducing strategies, however. First, portfolio insurance sets a minimum amount below which the insured assets or asset/liability surplus will not fall. Diversification merely promises to reduce downside risks, not to eliminate them. That is, portfolio insurance explicitly defines the risky and the riskless asset; diversification is less firm on the matter of definition, assuming simply that not all of the assets will do badly at the same time.

Second, portfolio insurance is an active strategy — or dynamic strategy, to use the popular buzzword — while diversification is passive. In theory, insured portfolios should vary their mix between the risky and the riskless asset with every market movement, no matter how small; in practice, the activity does tend to be high. Diversified portfolios, on the other hand, are much more inclined to be buy-and-hold.

As a result of these two distinctions, the underlying assumptions of the strategies are fundamentally different. The consequences for both the portfolio and the markets are also fundamentally different.

Diversification is an explicit recognition of uncertainty and makes no definite judgments about how investors are going to behave in the future. Diversification is, therefore, a probability-driven strategy.

Portfolio insurance, however, embodies a clear statement about the intentions of other investors. The owners of insured portfolios fully expect uninsured investors to oblige by holding the cash reserves of the insured investors until needed and then by providing the insured investors with those cash reserves as called upon to do so. The uninsured investors are also expected to provide the insured investors with the risky asset on demand.

For portfolio insurance to provide what it is purported to provide, the probabilities must be 100% that uninsured investors will play their proper role without hesitation. Portfolio insurance is, therefore, a certainty-driven strategy.

The consequences of these two strategies for market volatility are clear enough and too familiar to warrant repetition here. Nevertheless, in light of the distinctions that I have set forth, these consequences appear even more significant.

The more modest pretensions of diversification make it likely that diversification as a means of reducing risk will never lose its luster. As long as there are assets that covary negatively, or only slightly positively, with other assets, diversification will make sense. Asset allocation will then have to deal with a broad menu of assets.

Portfolio insurance concentrates on only two assets, carefully predetermined. To the extent that its assumptions about the behavior of uninsured investors turn out to be less than 100% correct, however, portfolio insurance can end up only chasing its own tail. The refusal of uninsured investors to play their appointed role will increase the volatility of risky assets and drive insured portfolios to sell or buy even more aggressively than they would have in the first place.

OVERVIEW OR UNDERVIEW?

Before the investor gets down to the nitty-gritty of asset allocation, a myriad of issues must be examined. Who owns the assets to be allocated and how does that owner want to structure the risk exposure? What *are* the assets intrinsically as opposed to how they are labeled? Who will manage the show and make certain the risks are hedged as they are supposed to be hedged? Are the underlying assumptions of diversification or portfolio insurance consistent with all of the above?

In short, the overview of asset allocation must begin with an underview: a thorough examination of the very guts of the matter in terms of ownership, the intrinsic nature of the assets, risk control mechanisms, and basic assumptions about market behavior. Only after settling these issues can the investor proceed to consider how to allocate the assets.

CHAPTER 3

The Role of the Liabilities: Defining and Managing Pension Fund Risk*

ROBERT D. ARNOTT
PRESIDENT AND CHIEF INVESTMENT OFFICER
FIRST QUADRANT CORP.

PETER L. BERNSTEIN
PRESIDENT
PETER L. BERNSTEIN INC.
AND EDITOR
JOURNAL OF PORTFOLIO MANAGEMENT

The way we manage risk is ultimately going to depend on how we define that risk. This is often a more complicated task than it appears to be at first glance. Risk is such a many-headed monster that focusing on the right head can be a major challenge.

---

*This chapter is an adaptation and expansion of Robert D. Arnott and Peter L. Bernstein, "The Right Way to Manage Your Pension Fund," *Harvard Business Review*, January/February 1988. Copyright 1988 by the President and Fellows of Harvard University.

Although the analysis that we offer here relates specifically to pension fund risk, the development of our argument and the issues that we raise lend themselves to broad generalizations. The precise definition of the risk we face is critically important, and risk management must be exquisitely sensitive to that definition.

Corporate executives have traditionally defined pension fund risk in terms of the trade-off between risk and return on the *assets* accumulated to fund pension obligations. Although there has been growing recognition that this focus on asset risk was too narrowly defined, there has also been strong resistance to breaking deep-seated habits.

Assets do not exist in a vacuum, seeking return and avoiding risk for their own sakes. This may seem obvious when stated in so many words, but it has taken Financial Accounting Standards Board Statement 87 (FASB 87) to bring the variability of pension fund *liabilities* to front and center. FASB 87 focuses on the pension fund *surplus* — the difference between the assets and the liabilities. This focus has been reinforced by the Omnibus Budget Reconciliation Act (OBRA) of 1987. OBRA adds legal weight to the FASB accounting guidelines by mandating pension contribution rates and Pension Benefit Guaranty Corporation (PBGC) insurance premiums which are sensitive to the pension funding ratio. The result is a belated awakening to the simple idea that the assets need to have some systematic relationship to the character of the liabilities that they fund.

Nevertheless, the implications of new notions are frequently subtle, and the response of pension fund strategies to FASB 87 and to OBRA is no exception. At most corporation, the definition of pension fund risk has shifted, but remains flawed because it remains oversimplified. This means that the restructuring of those funds may still be inappropriate in terms of the "true" risks of the pension plan. The oversimplification arises from paying too much attention to the interest sensitivity of the pension surplus, as result of FASB 87's emphasis on defining the surplus in terms of the interest sensitivity of the fund's actuarial liabilities.

These considerations are highly significant in their impact on corporate profitability and financial health. Pension fund assets have accumulated to a point where they tend to loom large relative to the total pool of assets in the corporation. Their variability and their rate of return have a meaningful influence on the company's bottom line; under FASB 87, their relationship to the liabilities of the pension fund may become visible on the published balance sheet as well.

Senior management should seek to achieve two objectives. First, the pension fund deserves as much attention as any significant operating division. Second, senior management must begin to analyze pension fund decisions in the context of potential long-term returns *measured against the true impact on corporate risk.*

THE CONVENTIONAL VIEW OF PENSION FUND RISK

As pension funds began to assume importance among corporate assets — say, over the past thirty years — pension fund management focused on the trade-off between the expected returns on their investments and the volatility of those returns. The idea was to maximize return consistent with some control over the magnitude of year-to-year, and sometimes even quarter-to-quarter, variations in the rate of return.

Volatility was of concern for three reasons:

1. First, all other things being equal, volatility tends to reduce returns over the long run. To put it simply, if you lose 50%, you have to gain 100% to break even.
2. Second, even if you believe that the assets you select can return enough to overcome the drag imposed by variability, the variability by its very nature creates uncertainty as to what the assets will be worth when the liabilities come due.
3. Finally, corporate managements tend to like smooth numbers. Irregular numbers raise questions that most people would be just as happy to avoid.

The traditional approach, therefore, was to seek the highest possible return at an acceptable level of volatility or, alternatively, to minimize volatility at any given level of expected return. This view of risk and reward was described in an array such as that shown in Exhibit 1, which plots expected asset returns on the vertical axis and variability of asset returns on the horizontal axis. The array runs from cash at the low end to stocks at the high end.

Putting all your eggs in one basket is never optimal. By employing the magic of diversification to reduce variability, you can obtain more expected return per unit of risk or reduce the risk per unit of expected return by combining assets instead of selecting just one. That process results in the curve known in investment parlance as the "efficient fron-

22   Arnott/Bernstein

EXHIBIT 1
RISK AND REWARD—THE TRADITIONAL PERSPECTIVE

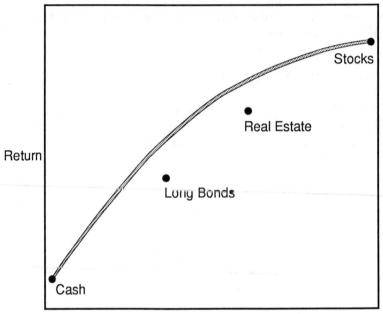

Variability of Asset Returns

tier." This curve shows the best return that can be achieved through diversification at any given level of risk.

The popularity of this approach to pension fund management rested on its simplicity, its familiarity and its convenience. It became a total expression of the culture of the pension fund world in the 1970s. The evaluation of assets based on market levels fits the intuitive idea of what investing a pension fund is all about. As Exhibit 2 suggests, other important variables — future contributions to the fund, estimated future wage growth and the discount rate used to calculate net present values were all determined by the actuary, were independent of movements in the capital markets and were changed infrequently.

This traditional view of pension risk suggests that pension plans with low tolerance for risk will tend to locate themselves toward the left-hand side of the frontier, with more in bonds and cash and less in stocks.

EXHIBIT 2
RISK AND REWARD—TRANSITION TO FASB–87

	Traditional	FASB–87
Assets	Variable: Market-Driven	Variable: Market-Driven
Asset Growth	Fixed*	Fixed*
NPV Liability Components		
Wage Growth	Fixed*	Fixed*
Discount Rate	Fixed*	Variable: Market-Driven

*Set by actuary.

Those with a greater willingness to bear risk in the search for higher returns will locate themselves toward the right, with heavier concentrations in the riskier assets like stocks and real estate.

As is evident in Exhibit 3, the slope of the efficient frontier is relatively flat in the zones where most funds position themselves. This feature of the frontier would lead us to conclude that most funds are highly tolerant of risk, because a curve with only a slight upward slope means that these funds will accept a large increase in risk for a modest increment in expected return.

This view of pension risk and reward is unrealistic for three reasons:

1. First, corporate pension fund sponsors tend to be prudent, careful investors, with risk tolerances that cover a wide range from conservative to moderately aggressive. They take their fiduciary responsibility seriously. Relatively few have risk tolerances as high as Exhibit 3 suggests.
2. Furthermore, this traditional perspective is silent on the subject of liabilities — it tells management nothing about where they should position themselves on the frontier. It provides information only on what the shape of the frontier is like. Corporations with a mature workforce or with unique business risks should hardly want to be on the same point of the frontier or at the same level of risk

EXHIBIT 3
RISK AND REWARD: THE TRADITIONAL PERSPECTIVE—
OBSERVED RISK TOLERANCE

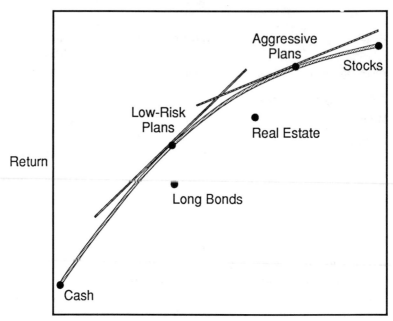

Variability of Asset Returns

tolerance as corporations with a young workforce or with stable earnings power.

3. Finally, the definition of risk here is limited to variability of expected returns on assets, with no attention given to the variability patterns of the liabilities the assets are to fund. Pension liabilities are highly sensitive to many factors, including changes in interest rates, which suggests rather a different definition of pension risk from what we see here.

THE IMPACT OF FASB 87

FASB 87 brings the liabilities into the picture by putting the focus on the *surplus* of the pension fund — the difference between the assets and the liabilities. This introduces an extra level of complexity. The value of the assets is easy enough to measure, but the liabilities are something else again. As shown in Exhibit 2, the major change induced by the accounting standard has been to mandate the use of market interest rates on long-term bonds for the calculation of the net present value of those liabilities. Projections of asset growth and wage growth remain in the domain of the actuary. (See Exhibit 4.)

The rationale for the insistence on market-determined discount rates is simple enough. Actuarial valuations tend to lag reality and aim, like many other features of corporate bookkeeping, at smooth changes. The capital markets are anything but smooth, but their view of the appropriate discount rate is immediate and inescapable. In addition, the markets are undoubtedly more accurate than the view, no matter how judicious, of a single individual or organization aiming to be conservative, avoiding frequent changes and shunning disruptive numbers.

The consequence of this redefinition of risk is profound. If the objective is to maximize the excess of assets over liabilities, while seeking to minimize the *variability* of that excess, then we have to ask which assets best match the variability pattern of the liabilities. Since FASB 87 treats the liabilities as fixed obligations, discounted at a market interest rate, this equivalent to asking, "Which assets act most like long-term bonds?" The answer is obvious. As we shall see shortly, the answer is perhaps too obvious.

The immediate implication of FASB 87 is that long-term bonds are the lowest risk asset, replacing cash in that enviable spot. Therefore, we have to redraw our chart showing the trade-off between risk and expected return. The result appears in Exhibit 5. The expected rates of return are the same, but the riskiness of the assets has changed.

In the context of the FASB 87 definition of surplus valuation, the chart tells us that any asset with variable income or whose principal value does not move closely with the bond market will be a risky asset. At the extreme, cash becomes anathema, with its low expected return and high variability of income; its much-vaunted stability of principal does no good in hedging liabilities whose principal value can vary widely over time.

The clear implication of this shift in viewpoint is that bonds provide the risk-minimizing choice for pension funds, at an attractive long-term rate of return. Other assets can still make good sense, but at a considerable increase in risk. In fact, the simplicity of the analysis presented here is so attractive that one may be sorely tempted to pronounce the problem

EXHIBIT 4
WHAT ARE FASB 87 AND THE OBRA?

FASB 87 is the ruling by the Financial Accounting Standards Board relating to pension accounting. For many corporations, FASB ruling #87 has had more impact on corporate earnings than any other ruling to date. FASB 87 mandates that:

- For both reported earnings and balance sheet calculations, pension accounting for defined benefit plans must estimate liability by applying a *market* interest rate to the expected obligations served by the pension plan, in order to determine the net present value of those obligations. This means that as market interest rates move, so too does the liability. If market rates rise, the net present value of the future obligations declines, and vice versa.
- For those defined benefit plans with an underfunded pension plan (i.e., the net present value of the liability exceeds the assets in the plan), the liability side of the balance sheet must include this unfunded pension liability.
- *Changes* in the surplus for the pension plan, if larger than 10% of plan assets or liabilities, must be reflected in the *earnings* statement in the form of operating earnings. This takes the form of an allowance for changes in pension contributions, amortized to compensate for the change in pension surplus. Whether or not the corporation chooses to actually change their pension contribution rate, FASB 87 requires the corporation to treat reported earnings as if contributions are adjusted to reflect a change in the pension surplus.

The Omnibus Budget Reconciliation Act of 1987 (OBRA) is a legislative initiative which reinforces the FASB 87 interpretation of liabilities. OBRA mandates that:

- Pension contributions for an underfunded pension plan (with an ABO funding ratio below 100%) must accelerate contributions to the pension plan. The underfunded liability must be amortized over a period of just five years.
- A pension sponsor with an ABO funding ratio in excess of 150% must cease pension contributions.
- Underfunded pension plans must pay a significantly increased insurance premium to the Pension Benefit Guarantee Corporation (PBGC). Because of a conservative definition of the discount rate used to calculate liabilities, this applies to pension plans with a funding ratio below approximately 125%.

EXHIBIT 4 *(continued)*
WHAT ARE FASB 87 AND THE OBRA?

These two sets of rulings may have a profound effect in shortening the investment horizon of the corporate pension sponsor. For the pension fund that slides from marginal funding into underfunded territory, many ills are visited upon the corporation: pension expense rises, thereby reducing reported corporate earnings; contributions to the pension plan must sharply accelerate; PBGC insurance premiums rise rapidly; and, last but not least, a new liability appears on the balance sheet. The stipulation that contributions must cease for well-funded plans will also have a potentially serious effect. Without contributions, the well-funded pension plans will gradually be forced down to ABO funding ratios which will result in some vulnerability to the adverse consequences detailed above. The net result may be a gradual but long-term shift in the direction of more conservative pension management policies in order to prevent the pension plant from adversely affecting corporate management or earnings. If this shift to conservatism takes place, it would be at the cost of reducing long-term rates of return for pension management and increasing the long-term cost of pension plans.

DEFINED BENEFIT VERSUS DEFINED CONTRIBUTION

Clearly, neither ruling applies to defined *contribution* plans which make up some 30% of all pension assets. If a corporation offers a defined contribution plan to their employees, there is no pension surplus or unfunded liability. A defined contribution plan involves a contractual commitment to contribute a certain amount of money to a pension plan, with no guarantee as to how much money will be in the plan at retirement and no guarantee as to the annual retirement benefit that the employee will receive. A defined *benefit* plan does the opposite. While it makes no guarantee as to the amount of contribution which the corporation will make, it does guarantee a defined annual retirement benefit to the employee.

In a defined contribution plan, the employee bears all market risk and captures all of the reward in the event of strong markets. In a defined benefit plan, the corporation bears the market risk: if the performance is disappointing, the corporation must suffer the penalty of increased pension contribution costs, hence increased labor costs. If results are strong, the corporation reaps the benefit in the form of reduced pension contributions, hence reduced labor costs. These new regulations have an important impact on the balance sheet and earnings statement for any company which as a defined benefit pension plan.

EXHIBIT 5
RISK AND REWARD: THE FASB–87 PERSPECTIVE—
OBSERVED RISK TOLERANCE

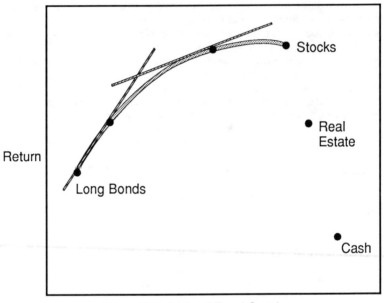

Return

Long Bonds

Stocks

Real
Estate

Cash

Variability of Fund Surplus
(assets minus present value of liabilities)

of pension fund investment solved and to turn one's attention to more pressing matters.

This is precisely the wrong conclusion to reach. FASB 87 suggests an unduly simplistic view of pension risk, which is only one step in the right direction. Compelling reasons to favor other assets exist for many funds, although not for all.

The search, and the justification for, an appropriate framework for pension management depend upon the manner in which we define pension fund risk. If pension fund risk is related solely to the variability in the discount rate used to calculate net present values, then bonds are the asset of choice. Any alternative *must* be justified only on the basis of a substantial return enhancement. When we widen the definition of risk, on the other hand, assets with variable rather than fixed-income streams can become the low-risk assets.

The critical question then becomes how to determine whether discount rate variability should be the dominant consideration in the definition of pension fund risk.

ANALYZING THE CHARACTERISTICS OF THE LIABILITIES

The attraction of bonds is greatest where the interest sensitivity of the liabilities is highest. Or, put a little differently, the attraction of bonds is greatest where the dollar amount of the liabilities, like the dollar amount of the bond coupon payments, is fixed. Under those circumstances, the only factor influencing the present value — and the ultimate obligation — of the liabilities is the relevant rate of interest.

The obligation to cover pensions for retirees meets this criterion most precisely. This is an amount that the actuaries can estimate with great accuracy. Unless the corporation assumes an obligation to protect its retirees from inflation, the retiree liability is as close to a fixed and predetermined sum as can be found in the universe of pension liabilities.

This is why the dedicated bond portfolio has attracted such a large following in recent years. Here was an opportunity to create an exact match between assets and liabilities. The primary attraction was the elimination of risk, made possible by the use of immunization and other forms of cash-matching techniques to make a perfect asset/liability match.

By "elimination of risk," we do not refer to return variability as such, but rather to the risk of giving insufficient assets to meet the obligation as it comes due. This is, indeed, the only rational definition of risk; everything else is a variation on that theme. With interest rates so high in the late 1970s and the early 1980s, the dedication of income-matched bond portfolios to meet the obligations for retired lives (and the use of annuities to permit plan termination), enabled corporate management to free up pension assets for other uses.

As it happens, the definition of the Accumulated Benefit Obligation (ABO) is remarkably similar to this retiree liability. FASB 87 defines this ABO liability as the amount to be paid to retirees and present employees assuming immediate termination of the pension plan. Essentially, this is the same as defining the size of an annuity to be purchased for these employees at retirement, with the size of the annuity to be determined on the basis of today's wages and today's "years of service."

This definition of liability, as with the liability for retirees alone, creates a fixed nominal total pension liability. The present value of the liability so defined is the Accumulated Benefit Obligation. This present value of liabilities is deducted from the value of the pension assets to determine the ABO pension surplus.

Although an important improvement over the simplistic actuarial discount rate structures of the past, this model is also unrealistic once we look beyond the Accumulated Benefit Obligation. Indeed, to some extent, it is even unrealistic within the confines of that obligation as defined under FASB 87. Three problems intervene:

1. The duration of the bond portfolio may not be as long as the duration of the liabilities. That is, the flow of coupon payments and ultimately the return of principal may arrive sooner than the time needed to fully pay off the liabilities of the ABO, which may stretch far into the future. If that incoming cash cannot be reinvested at the same or a higher rate of interest than the rate paid on the original investment, the bond portfolio will fail to cover these obligations as they come due. This risk is known as reinvestment risk.

2. Many corporations assume the responsibility of providing their retirees with at least partial protection against inflationary inroads into the purchasing power of their pensions. A pension fund invested totally in long-term bonds will clearly not address this *implicit* component of the liability.

3. Finally, and most important, the ABO contains the unrealistic assumption of immediate pension plan termination. Growth in wages and assets between the present date and retirement are ignored, and only the current years of service, rather than the years of service at retirement, are reflected in the ABO. To make matters even more unrealistic, the ABO also assumes that no new workers enter the workforce between now and the retirement of the present workforce. Implicitly, FASB 87 assumes that all of these additional obligations are addressed through future expense provisions.

THE IMPLICATIONS OF THE PROJECTED
BENEFIT OBLIGATION

Corporate managements obviously realize that their pension liability goes well beyond the ABO. Active employees are going to earn higher wages in the future, which may grow faster or slower than the actuarial assumption, and will typically receive their pensions based on final pay. Asset growth also may be greater or less than the rate assumed by the actuary. Estimates of these uncertain but critical magnitudes must be added to the ABO to derive the true total pension liability, which is known as the Projected Benefit Obligation (PBO).

Many different factors will influence the actual size of the PBO. The dominant factors on wage growth will be inflation, productivity change and the fortunes of the company in question.

Over the long run, wages tend to keep pace with changes in the cost of living, even if the match is inexact. Much of the benefit of productivity improvement has been shared between workers and stockholders, with customers receiving an additional portion in the form of lower or less rapidly increasing prices. Even with high inflation and high productivity growth, an unprofitable company will be unable to keep compensation in pace with these forces; but a highly profitable company may treat its employees even better than inflation and productivity alone would warrant.

From this viewpoint, a 100% long-term bond portfolio may not be the risk-minimizing asset for hedging against the possibility of ending up with insufficient money to fund the true pension obligations. We now must seek assets, some with fixed-income returns, but many with variable-income returns, with the variability approximating as closely as possible the variability of inflation and productivity change. In addition, we should seek assets that diversify the inherent risks of the company in question, so that the company can pay its pensioners even if it falls on ill-fortune before or during their retirement.

Exhibit 6 shows how poorly debt securities serve the purpose of keeping pace with the growth in employment costs under conditions of unexpected inflation. In the upper panel, we see the difference between total annual returns on long-term Treasury bonds and the annual percent-

EXHIBIT 6
TOTAL RETURN ON TREASURY BONDS MINUS YEAR-OVER-YEAR CHANGE IN EMPLOYEE COMPENSATION, 1954:1–1991:4

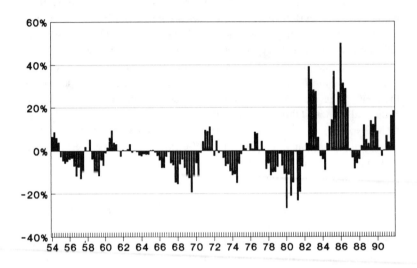

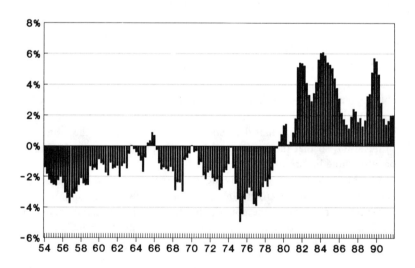

age increase in employee compensation in the nonfarm business sector; the lower panel shows the spread between short-term Treasury bill returns and the growth in employee compensation. Note that these investments failed to match the increase in employment costs by wide margins, not just in the high inflation years of the 1970s, but even during the moderate inflation years of the 1950s and 1960s. Their performance moves more firmly into positive territory only after 1981, when the inflation rate slowed dramatically.

Exhibit 7 provides an insight into how annual dividend income flows from equities and interest income flows from bonds keep pace with the growth in employee compensation. Although in some of the years before 1982 dividends failed to match the annual increases in employee compensation by wider margins than the shortfall in bond yields, dividends also grew faster than employee compensation, and by ample spreads, in 47 calendar quarters from 1954 through 1981; bond yields exceeded the growth in employee compensation only 36 quarters and even then by small margins.

But the advantage in holding equities are significantly greater than suggested by this exhibit, on two scores. The first relates to the difference in income flows, the second to the difference in the behavior of asset prices.

The income return on bonds is contractually fixed for the life of the instrument. If interest rates rise, new money can be invested at the higher rate, but the old money continues to earn the old yield. A pension fund that invested an equal amount of money in the bond market each year beginning with 1954 would have had an imbedded average yield of only 5.4% when long-term interest rates first hit double digits at the end of 1979. When a company increases its dividend, the dividend goes up on the fund's *entire* holding of that company's stock. The dividends paid on the S&P 500 increased 350% from 1954 to the end of 1979 while the pension fund's interest income rose only 113%.

The second, and more important, advantage to equities is the unlimited ceiling on their prices. Bonds have an upper ceiling because they will pay off at par at maturity; equities are a perpetuity. This difference has resulted in a huge advantage for equities in keeping up with the growth in employee compensation. Between the beginning of 1954 and the end of 1981, employee compensation increased 470%. A dollar invested in stocks over the same period of time, without regard to income, would have grown 350% — by less than the rise in compensation — but a dollar invested in bonds, without regard to income, would have *shrunk* by over

EXHIBIT 7
YEAR-OVER-YEAR DIVIDEND GROWTH VERSUS YEAR-OVER-YEAR
CHANGE IN EMPLOYEE COMPENSATION, 1954:1–1991:4

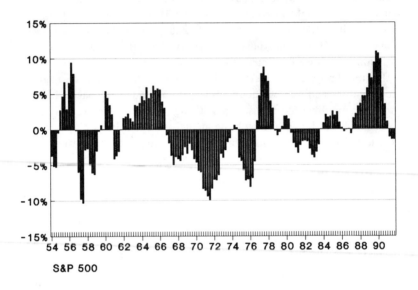

S&P 500

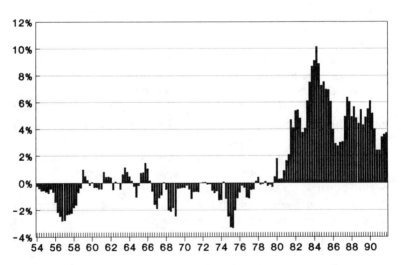

60%! By the end of 1991, with employee compensation up nearly 9 times since 1954, the equity investment was worth 16 times its original cost. Meanwhile, the dollar in the bond investment would still be at a loss, worth only 77 cents.

Although these graphs are meant only to be suggestive, their suggestions are significant. The emphasis on covariance with bond interest, as stipulated in FASB 87, becomes a dangerous oversimplification when the incremental liabilities of the Projected Benefit Obligation, above and beyond the ABO liabilities, are taken into consideration. Protection against the risk that the earnings of the pension fund will fail to cover the Projected Benefit Obligation requires a combination of assets — like equities — whose income flow is somehow related to the pressures of inflation and is also related to productivity change.

HOW TO BALANCE THE ABO AND THE INCREMENTAL PBO IN PENSION FUND RISK

Treasury bills, common stocks, and other variable return assets may do a better job than bonds in hedging the long-term risks inherent in wage growth assumptions, but they have two important disadvantages. First, their income flows are too variable to fund the retirees or the Accumulated Benefit Obligation. Second, they are only partially interest sensitive, and sometimes correlate negatively with changes in long-term interest rates, which means that they add unwanted variability to the pension fund surplus, as defined under FASB 87. A central component of that surplus is the net present value of the liabilities, which *are* highly sensitive to interest rates.

The task of senior management in determining how best to hedge pension fund risk, therefore, is to weigh as accurately as possible the relative importance of the advantages and disadvantages of each type of asset. In essence, this involves employing fixed-income assets to fund fixed-dollar obligations, where the estimate of the liability has a high degree of certainty, and employing variable-income assets to fund variable-dollar obligations, where the estimate of the liability has a high degree of uncertainty.

The best way to look at this problem is to make separate estimates of the ABO and the PBO and examine the size of the spread between the two, the incremental PBO. The more mature the plan, or the more mature the workforce, the smaller that spread is likely to be. In other words, the pension liability for a mature workforce, being by definition closer to maturity than a young workforce, lends itself more readily to certainty in the estimation process. In many such cases, the ABO can exceed 90% of the total PBO, leading to a relatively well-defined nominal liability. Mature plans, therefore, will have an incentive to favor long-term bonds at the expense of stocks or cash equivalents. Long-term bonds can provide certainty of return to cover the certainty of the liability. In addition, long-term bonds will provide maximum stability to the pension fund surplus within the definitions and reporting requirements of FASB 87.

Conversely, emerging plans, associated with younger or faster growing companies, will have a higher PBO liability relative to the ABO and therefore will have an incentive to hold a more aggressive asset mix, with a stronger relationship with future wage growth. In such a case, equities will tend to dominate.

This preference for equities is likely to hold true for reasons beyond the ability of dividends to keep pace with inflation and to reflect productivity improvements as well. Pension plans that cover young workers will start paying significant sums in pensions only in the far distant future. Reinvestment risk is minimized by matching the horizon of the liabilities. Equities can represent a good fit, because the principal is never repaid and because the cash return is expected to grow larger with the passage of time.

So far so good. Life is not quite this simple, however. We have yet to consider the conflict between the short run and the long run in pension planning, as well as the difference between variability in rates of return — essentially asset price variability — and variability in flows of income in each asset. Return variability and the short-run/long-run conflicts are interrelated.

In the short run, stability in the pension fund surplus is important because of its impact on current profitability and the balance sheet. The framers of FASB 87 knew what they were about in trying to arrive at a better definition of the influence of the pension fund on earnings and financial well-being. In the long run, on the other hand, stability of the surplus is not nearly as important as its size. The corporation would like to have something left over to accommodate reduced contributions during periods of earnings weakness. In essence, the pension plan acts as a tax-deferred savings plan, or an "IRA" for the corporation, right down to the penalty for early withdrawal.

The assets that best assure a surplus over the Projected Benefit Obligation in the long run are the riskiest in the short run, in that they add a variability to the pension fund surplus. Stocks, for example, have the clear lead for matching the attributes of the longest-term liabilities, but their short-run returns are highly variable and only weakly correlated with interest rates. At the other end of the spectrum, cash equivalents tend to have low returns that are frequently correlated negatively with returns on bonds.

A graphic display of these dilemmas appears in Exhibit 8. Here the chart relates to the Accumulated Benefit Obligation and repeats the array shown in Exhibit 5. This is essentially the short-run view of the matter. The expected rates of return are the same as in the original array in Exhibit 1. The risks, however, relate primarily to the sensitivity of asset returns to interest rates, because it is interest rates that determine the net present values of the liabilities, and we want to stabilize the relationship between the assets and the net present values of the liabilities — that is, the surplus — in the short run.

EXHIBIT 8
RISK AND REWARD—THE ABO

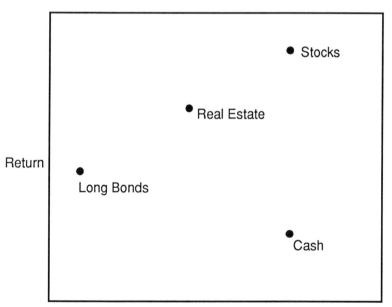

Variability of Fund Surplus
(assets minus present value of liabilities)

Exhibit 9 shows what happens when we introduce the incremental Projected Benefit Obligation into our deliberations and begin to take a longer-run view. The variable-income assets now become less risky; the fixed-income assets become riskier. In plain English, this means that the variable-income assets increase management's confidence in their ability to fund the PBO, while bonds would not be the almost "risk-free" assets that they are for the ABO.

The shift in viewpoint is critical. Now we direct our attention to the ultimate future size of the liabilities, not just to their sensitivity to interest rates, which determine only their actuarial net present values. In other words, minimizing the long-run variability of the pension fund surplus depends upon our ability to fund the PBO rather than merely minimizing the short-run variability of the ABO surplus.

Finally, Exhibits 10A and 10B demonstrate the differing choices available to mature and early growth funds. We show the location of the assets

EXHIBIT 9
RISK AND REWARD—PBO—ABO

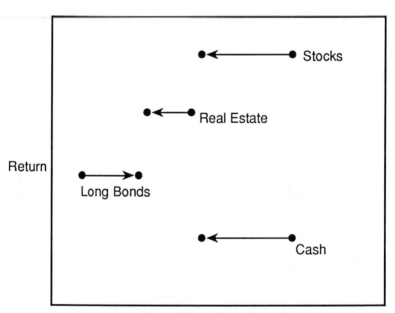

Variability of Fund Surplus
(assets minus present value of liabilities)

EXHIBIT 10A
"TRUE" RISK AND REWARD—THE MATURE PLAN (ABO DOMINATES)

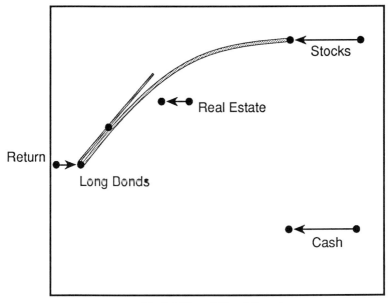

Variability of Fund Surplus
(assets minus present value of liabilities)

for the mature pension plan in Exhibit 10A and for the young plan in Exhibit 10B. Once again, we construct an efficient frontier composed of combinations of assets rather than portfolios of single assets.

The mature fund would take dangerously larger risks for each increment of return by moving very far from a bond portfolio. The fixed nature of the obligations makes anything other than fixed-income assets highly risky. The slope of the risk/return relationship is steep at the left-hand side, in the low-risk tolerance zone where this fund belongs.

In Exhibit 10B, the riskiness of variable-income assets declines as we lengthen the time horizon that is appropriate to a younger fund, while the riskiness of bonds increases. This fund has a greater appetite for riskier securities as we conventionally classify them. It will locate itself further out to the right on the efficient frontier, where the slope is flatter, as befits a fund with a higher risk tolerance. Indeed, even with the same risk tolerance (measured by the slope of the risk tolerance line) as the

EXHIBIT 10B
RISK AND REWARD—THE EARLY GROWTH PLAN (PBO » ABO)

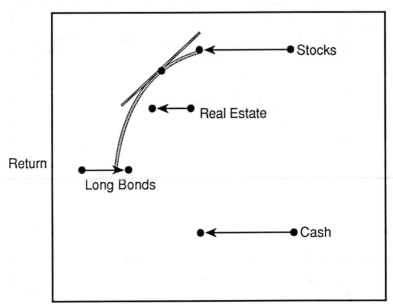

Variability of Fund Surplus
(assets minus present value of liabilities)

mature plan, the younger plan would use more stocks and real estate to match the greater sensitivity of liabilities to inflation or productivity growth.

SUMMARY

We began this analysis with the assertion that the management of risk depends critically on the manner in which we define risk. This discussion has attempted to demonstrate how inadequate or oversimplified definitions of risk have led to inappropriate asset allocation decisions for many pension funds. These inappropriate decisions have been the result of inadequate attention to the *true* nature of pension fund risk and the many forces that play upon it.

The simplest approach to pension risk analysis concentrates only on the riskiness of the assets themselves, without regard to their correlations with the riskiness of the liabilities. This has been by far the most popular approach, but it remains a most inappropriate way to approach pension fund management. We can be grateful to the Financial Accounting Standards Board for forcing the pension sponsor to weigh the assets *and* liabilities in assessing the merits of pension management strategies.

The current tendency is to put too much emphasis on the structures of FASB 87 and to look to long-term bonds to save the day. Long-term bonds are appropriate for stabilizing the surplus in the short run, where the net present value of the liabilities is the crucial consideration. In view of the definition of the Accumulated Benefit Obligation, bonds are also appropriate where the liability is estimated with a high degree of certainty, as in the case of retired lives or a pension fund for a mature workforce.

On the other hand, there is a danger in viewing all pension funds in these terms. Sometimes there is a temptation to go in that direction just because of the simplicity of relating the variability of the assets to the variability of the present values. Sometimes this temptation arises from a slavish devotion to the short run, where the desire for smoothness and consistency can easily dominate the acceptance of the variability that is inescapable in achieving high longer-run returns.

In reality, the size of the pensions that the corporation pays in future years will have relatively little to do with today's level of long-term interest rates. In reality, therefore, the future value of the pension obligation is going to be far more important than today's present value. The corporation that seeks to have a surplus in its pension fund in the future had better consider the risks likely to arise in the future, not just the immediate risks.

But that warning applies to all risk management. You do not buy life insurance on a building or fire insurance on a senior executive. You do not take out a 30-year term life policy on a 55-year-old executive or a 6-month maintenance agreement on a brand new mainframe computer. Insurance policies are matched to the nature and time horizon of the risks. The pension fund example is different from these examples only in its complexities, but then all corporations face many risks of equivalent complexity. They deserve equivalent analysis.

CHAPTER 4

Managing the Asset Mix

ROBERT D. ARNOTT
PRESIDENT
CHIEF INVESTMENT OFFICER
FIRST QUADRANT CORP.

Asset allocation has been an enormously popular topic among institutional investors in recent years. Yet, surprisingly, few of us are engaging in any systematic or deliberate asset allocation process, beyond setting a normal asset mix. If the asset allocation of a portfolio is not managed as a deliberate strategy, then it is drifting on autopilot, driven by the whims of the markets. This is the often overlooked fact of asset allocation: if we don't engage in asset allocation management on a continuous basis, the markets will do it for us. The markets will assure that we are overexposed at market highs and underexposed at market lows.

As noted in Chapter 1, while it is often thought of as one decision, asset allocation really consists of several distinct and largely independent decisions.

- Policy asset allocation is a long-term decision aimed at assessing the appropriate normal asset mix. This mix represents a careful balancing between the often conflicting desires for return and controlled risk.

43

- Tactical asset allocation represents an opportunistic strategy which seeks to enhance returns through deliberate shifts away from the normal policy allocation. The asset mix is shifted in response to the shifting patterns of return available in the markets.

- Dynamic strategies, such as portfolio insurance, represent a mechanistic attempt to reshape the return distribution. Typically, dynamic strategies are used to reduce risk in adverse markets, and to pay for that protection through lower returns in strong markets.

Many organizations invest significant time and expense to establish the appropriate long-term normal asset mix. After this mix has been established, the portfolio is often allowed to drift with the movements of the capital markets. This "drifting mix" is an important problem; it represents a significant drain both on the time of the investment officer and on investment results. It drains the time of the investment executive, because ultimately a drifting mix must be corrected. Rectifying a drifting asset mix requires a careful decision as to changes in the allocation of assets among managers. As we shall demonstrate, it also erodes investment performance.

Rule 1:
Don't Exceed the Client Risk Tolerance

One of the most important rules in asset management is to never exceed the risk tolerance of our clients. If we abide by this rule, then our clients will show due patience when, inevitably, our investment strategies are temporarily out of step. If we exceed the risk tolerance of our clients, then our clients' patience will run out before a normal dry spell runs its course.

This adage holds as true for the pension sponsor as it does for the asset manager. The principal difference is in the nature of the customer. The asset manager's customer, most typically, is the pension officer, or perhaps, the Treasurer. For the pension officer, there is a very different (and often less predictable) "customer." Ironically, the pension officer's customer is not the pension beneficiary. The pension beneficiary does not determine whether the pension officer keeps his or her job! But, the CFO and pension committee most assuredly do.

If we are not to exceed the risk tolerance of our customers, then we must understand their objectives. This is a multi-faceted problem. As

Exhibit 1 suggests, there is no single measure for risk. In essence, risk may be loosely defined as any unpleasant and unanticipated consequence of our investment strategies. This may include losing money. Or, it may include growing the assets more slowly than the liabilities (hence, losing surplus or falling underfunded). It also may include failing to adequately educate our "customers" as to the patterns of risk and reward associated with our chosen strategies.

EXHIBIT 1
WHAT RISKS MATTER?

I. **How important is portfolio volatility?**
    A. What role can be played by appraisal-based assets or "book value" assets, such as real estate or venture capital, in dampening volatility without forfeiting returns?
    B. How much volatility can be tolerated in an effort to achieve high returns?

II. **How important is volatility in the surplus (actuarial liabilities minus assets)?**
    A. Should we seek to match the duration of assets against an artificial definition of liabilities (either the actuarial or accounting definition) to constrain surplus volatility?
    B. Should we seek high returns at a cost of surplus volatility?

III. **How important is long-term business risk?**
    A. Will my "customer" (the pension committee of the board) tolerate nominal portfolio volatility or surplus volatility in a quest for the high returns? High returns can ultimately reduce pension contributions and boost long-term corporate profitability, but only at a cost of short-term volatility.
    B. What is their "threshold of pain?" How much disappointment, in either nominal returns or diminished surplus, will they tolerate in this quest?

IV. **How important is "maverick risk?"**
    A. If our asset allocation strategies and policies differ sharply from the strategies and policies of other institutional investors, our results will differ sharply from our institutional compatriots.
        1. How tolerant will my "customer" be if this "relative performance risk" goes against us?
        2. How far can we safely stray from the pack?

Understanding Risk

Before we begin to manage the asset mix, it is imperative for us to understand "risk." Risk is not just portfolio volatility. It is not just the volatility of funding ratios or pension surplus. It is not just the long-term business decision of pursuing a strategy which moderates portfolio risk at a cost of increased long-term pension cost. More fundamentally, risk could be viewed as the likelihood of "doing something wrong."

There are widespread misunderstandings about asset allocation, evident in its practice in portfolio management. These misconceptions lead to errors which would be comical, were they not so terribly costly. Managers shuffle their asset mix and churn portfolios in an emotional response to the markets. Pension sponsors hire the recently successful manager, only to see that performance falter, then terminate the manager just before results turn. This pattern seems rooted in human nature.

Each of these errors can be quite expensive. They are costly for reasons that are also inherent in human nature. People want to do what is comfortable. Human nature conditions us to believe that what has been working will continue to work and that failure heralds failure. In investments, what is comfortable is rarely profitable.

It is uncomfortable to employ a manager whose style has led to recent disappointments. It is uncomfortable to take money from a manager who has been successful. It is uncomfortable to move from the recently successful asset class into a market which has been dismal. It is uncomfortable to maintain one's own investment style in the face of disappointing results.

But, to act in a comfortable fashion diminishes results, for the simple reason that it is "comfortable." Uncomfortable and out-of-favor investments are priced low by the markets, to reflect a demand for reward. It is the uncomfortable strategies which are priced to offer superior rewards. Indeed, it is almost axiomatic that the investment world prices comfortable investments to reflect a reduced demand for reward. Those who invest conventionally, or "comfortably," reap correspondingly substandard rewards.

A Clash of Cultures

Part of the problem ironically stems from a fundamental dichotomy between the appropriate values and culture of a successful corporation and the appropriate values and culture of a successful investment manager. The successful business culture has long favored an "economic Darwinism," the survival of the fittest, depending on a pattern of aggressively rewarding success and ruthlessly punishing failure. In so doing, they grow and prosper by constantly weeding out those who cannot compete. The successful investment management operation follows essentially the opposite pattern. Investments which have performed well should typically be viewed as candidates for liquidation, while investments which have performed poorly will more typically be candidates for purchase.

One of the most common errors in asset management is the assumption that what has been profitable will continue to work and what has performed badly will continue to fail. There are many manifestations of this. There are investment managers who, when their investment style is "out of sync" with the markets, hasten to correct it. There are the pension sponsors who are notorious for hiring an investment manager just after a spectacular three- to five-year run and just before the results collapse (then firing the manager just before the strategy rebounds). There are similar ad hoc "rearview mirror" shifts in the asset mix of a portfolio.

The Fiduciary Tightrope

Pension executives face an unusual tightrope walk. As fiduciaries, they know that performance will be improved by pursuing an often unconventional, often uncomfortable strategy. However, they also know that such strategies attract scrutiny and encourage second-guessing if the strategy goes awry.

In essence, the pension executive has a "customer." That customer is not the pension beneficiary; the "customer" is the group responsible for the pension officer's livelihood. This group consists of the top financial officers of the company, as well as the pension committee of the Board of Directors. Ironically, the most profitable strategies may exceed the risk tolerance of the "customer." No one objects to risk or surprise when it is on the upside. However, any strategy that can generate favorable surprise can also generate unfavorable surprise. The unsophisticated or underinformed "customer" will be intolerant of any adverse surprise.

One of the most valuable responses to this "fiduciary tightrope" is education. The educated Board or CFO is less likely to be surprised. The educated Board is more likely to tolerate contrarian disciplines. If the Board is educated as to the importance of asset allocation, the nature of market movements, the peril of ad hoc shifts, and the impact that a few basis points can have on corporate wealth, that Board will respond to the choices that it faces in an intelligent fashion. The pension officer who fails to adequately educate the board does so at his or her peril.

What Risk Matters?

Once we understand our client, we can better understand that each of these measures of risk matters. Portfolio volatility does matter. If the portfolio is volatile, it may suffer a drop in value which exceeds the risk tolerance of our "customer." The mismatch between assets and liabilities (surplus volatility) does matter. A high volatility in surplus creates a risk that the surplus could disappear. This is a risk that most Boards of Directors would find distasteful at best.

The "maverick risk" associated with straying too far from the actions of our compatriots in the pension community is a risk which should not matter, but does. Like it or not, we are in a horserace. If our asset mix strategies lead to results which fall far behind those of other pension funds, our judgment will be called into question. This will happen even if portfolio volatility works to our benefit (i.e., good returns), and surplus volatility works to our benefit (i.e., an improved funding status). "Maverick risk" matters for an important business reason. If our pension fund offers inferior results relative to our competitors' funds, their cost of doing business will decline relative to ours. Therefore, in the short run, their competitive position will improve relative to ours.

Each element of risk is a two-edged sword. If we are willing to bear "maverick risk," we create an opportunity to outstrip the pension results of our competitors. This improves our competitive position by lowering our costs of doing business. A willingness to bear surplus volatility may give us an opportunity to choose high-return asset categories which will boost our long-term returns and lower our long-term pension costs. The same holds true for portfolio volatility.

Each of these elements of risk has a direct bearing on the interplay between long-term and short-term business risk. Those who are willing to bear short-term risk, and who bear that risk with intelligence, will find that their long-term pension costs fall and their competitive position improves.

Many corporations behave as though a dollar made in the pension fund is worth less than a dollar made in incremental operating earnings. This is patently false. Indeed, it is worth even more than a dollar of operating income, due to the tax-sheltered nature of the portfolio. So, the quest for returns in pension assets should be as important to the corporation as the quest for operating profits. Most typically, it is not. The accounting and actuarial smoothing that makes pension volatility palatable also makes pension gains forgettable. But, the pension assets are real money, with a direct bearing on the long-term competitiveness, and even viability, of the corporation.

MANAGING THE POLICY MIX

The asset allocation decision cannot be avoided. As noted previously, if we choose not to make an asset allocation decision, the markets will do it for us. Only two rational positions exist in regard to asset allocation. Either market efficiency is assumed to preclude profitable shifts in asset mix, or active shifts are assumed to add value. Only a handful of investors behave in accordance with either view! How many investors allow their asset mix to float with market impulses? This is a strategy which assures heavy exposure at market highs and low exposure at market lows. How many investors were selling bonds in 1980, 1981 and 1982, during a period of peak yields? How many were bailing out of stocks in late 1974 or immediately after the 1987 crash? Such trades are hopeless attempts to escape from losses already realized. A "drifting mix" and ad hoc "rearview mirror" shifts in asset mix are not consistent with either view of market efficiency.

For those who favor the view that markets are efficient, a simple process of rebalancing can reverse the damage done by a drifting mix. A simple mechanistic rebalancing strategy solves two problems simultaneously. First, the effort invested in choosing the appropriate long-term normal policy mix (see Exhibit 2) has not gone to waste. It does so by assuring that the normal mix is maintained in a rational manner. Second, it tends to enhance risk-adjusted performance. Clearly, it does not add value in every year, or even every market cycle. But, over the long run, it appears to add measurably to performance.

Systematic rebalancing merits consideration for many reasons:

- Simple rebalancing strategies do not require that the investor believe in "market timing."
- While an investment committee may tend to frown on active asset allocation strategies, it is far easier to persuade a committee to engage in simple rebalancing. This can be an effective way to steer

EXHIBIT 2
WHAT IS OUR "POLICY" ASSET MIX?

I. **How much exposure to illiquid or non-traditional assets is appropriate?**
    A. Real estate.
    B. Venture capital.
    C. Non-U.S. stocks, bonds, real estate.
    D. Specialty categories:
        1. Limited partnerships.
        2. Energy partnerships.
        3. Timber leases.

II. **How sensitive are we to funding ratio considerations?**
    A. Avoiding the "four ills." Newly underfunded plans face:
        1. A new liability on the balance sheet.
        2. An earnings reduction due to a rise in pension expense.
        3. A cash flow cost due to sharply accelerated pension contributions.
        4. A cash flow cost due to increased PBGC insurance premiums.
    B. If well funded, how do we stay thoro?
        1. Reduce the volatility of funding ratios?
        2. Accept funding ratio volatility in the quest for high returns, thereby sustaining the funding ratios through strong returns.
        3. What is the risk to tolerance of my "customer" (likely the pension committee of the board)? Will my customer permit a long investment horizon or not?

III. **What mixture of stocks, bonds, cash, global and illiquid assets offer the best long-term rewards, without exceeding our tolerance for risk?**

---

an organization away from the ad hoc market timing which has plagued institutional performance for many years.

- A simple rebalancing strategy is easy to implement and need not disrupt the existing managers.

- A rebalancing strategy will return control of the most important investment decision to the pension officer.

• A historical evaluation of returns indicates that a rebalancing strategy adds modest value. After compounding, this modest added value can translate into significant incremental assets.

Each of these attributes of rebalancing is important and merits a detailed examination. Suppose we are skeptical about "market timing." Then, if a particular asset mix has been judged to best meet the long-term needs of the organization, a strategy which permits a drifting asset mix (or permits ad hoc shifts in mix) simply makes no sense. A skeptical view on market timing would rule out active shifts in the asset mix, based on a tactical asset allocation discipline. However, it would also rule out shifts in asset mix based on market drift or on the whims of a pension committee. In short, a belief in the efficiency of markets would suggest a systematic strategy of rebalancing the asset mix to the target policy mix, in response to any substantive market movement.

What Do We Do About the "Temptation to Tinker?"

One of the biggest challenges in managing institutional assets is the pressure to shift the asset mix in a reactive fashion after market movement. Such pressure inevitably is in the same direction as the recent market move. If a market has slumped, there is often pressure to slash our exposure. If a market has soared, there is a temptation to boost our exposure and to chase that market. These shifts in asset mix are often misguided efforts to prevent damage which has already occurred. One of the easiest ways to convince a committee not to engage in these ad hoc asset allocation shifts is to ask that committee to adopt a long-term policy asset mix and stay with it through systematic rebalancing. In other words, rebalancing can be an easy way to convince a pension committee not to disrupt a carefully crafted long-term policy for asset mix.

Can value be added by ad hoc changes in asset mix? Surely, but history suggests that most ad hoc approaches do not add value. In 1986, Brinson, Hood and Beebower reviewed the 10-year results of 91 of the largest U.S. pension funds.[1] The results in Exhibit 3 demonstrate how the typical pension sponsor forfeited 66 basis points per annum through sloppy ad hoc shifts in asset mix. This is a huge difference; after 10 years, a $1 billion portfolio, growing at 10% per annum, would be worth $160

---

[1]Gary Brinson, Randall Hood, and Gilbert Beebower, "Determinants of Portfolio Returns," *Financial Analysts Journal*, July/August, 1986.

EXHIBIT 3
ANNUALIZED 10-YEAR RETURNS OF 91 LARGE U.S. PENSION PLANS,
1974–1983

	Average Return	Minimum Return	Maximum Return	Standard Deviation
Portfolio Total Returns				
Policy Mix	10.11%	9.47%	10.57%	0.22%
Policy Mix & Timing	9.44	7.25	10.34	0.52
Policy Mix & Selection	9.75	7.17	13.31	1.33
Actual Portfolio	9.01	5.85	13.40	1.43
Differential Active Returns				
Timing Only	(0.66)%	(2.68)%	0.25%	0.49%
Security Selection	(0.30)	(2.00)	3.60	1.36
Other	(0.07)	(1.17)	2.57	0.45
Total Active Return	(1.10)	(4.17)*	3.69	1.45*

*Column not additive.
Source: "Determinants of Portfolio Returns," *Financial Analysts Journal,* July/August, 1986.

million more without these ad hoc shifts! Historically, shifts in asset mix tended to be based on this kind of ad hoc decision process. In Brinson's study, the sponsor benefitting most added just 25 basis points from timing, while the most unfortunate forfeited 268 basis points per annum over the span of a decade.

Although a disciplined framework for rebalancing has results which, like any other facet of investing, cannot be foreseen, clients who embrace it for the long run appear to prevail in the end. Investment committees tend to unite in order to avoid the unfamiliar and the uncomfortable. Persuading them to subscribe to a simple systematic process of rebalancing indicates that they will employ an extended portfolio management structure, thus offering the chance to consistently adhere to the long-term investment policy.

Let's assume that you want to maintain a policy mix of 60% stocks and 40% bonds. With the use of derivative securities (futures and options), trading costs will be minimal. It is likely that aggregate trading costs will be less than 10 basis points each way. No other trading vehicle can be traded so efficiently and economically. Indeed, it is impractical to consider ongoing active rebalancing without the use of derivative securities.

As we can see in Exhibit 4, from 1971–1990, simple rebalancing produced an average annual return of 9.98%, 34 basis points over the results for a drifting mix. Volatility was increased somewhat. By rebalancing into the more variable-return assets in a declining market, the drifting mix stands to gain more than the portfolio.

Systematic rebalancing appears to enhance performance. But its most valuable attribute is likely to be the added control it gives over the asset mix of a portfolio. It will not add value in every year or even work in every market cycle. But it does appear to work over time. Surprisingly, this incremental return is earned with a turnover of less than 1% per month. Maintaining a policy mix on a consistent basis is supremely boring. Yet, it makes sense. A belief in market timing is not necessary; it remains consistent with the view that markets are efficient, and most importantly, can help to persuade the decision makers to stay with the policy during unfavorable periods. Once they are committed to the idea, it is realistic to expect they will remain. Remember that the average pension fund in the Brinson study forfeited 66 basis points (not the 34 basis points of our study), due to untimely ad hoc decisions to stray from a long-term policy.

Too Much Cash!

A second element of "policy mix" that deserves attention is the large cash reserves maintained in most institutional portfolios. Idle cash reserves do not bear any resemblance to the liabilities served by the pension portfolio. In this context, cash can actually be a very high-risk investment. For example, substantial drops in interest rates reduce income on cash earnings, and we miss the bond and stock rallies that typify such markets. Similarly, if real wages rise, the returns on cash simply will not keep pace with real wage boosts that come from an increase in productivity.

Yet, while the risk implications of cash are subtle, the return implications are not. Historically, the rate of return on cash equivalents has been less than that for stocks and bonds by roughly 6% and 1% per annum, respectively. To illustrate, cash equivalents will forfeit about 400 basis points annually on an average pension fund portfolio with a 60/40 stock/bond mix. Therefore, for long-term investors (and pension funds

EXHIBIT 4
VALUE ADDED BY REBALANCING VS. A DRIFTING MIX

Results for Jan. 1971 to Dec. 1990	Drifting Mix Return	Rebalancing Return	Value Added
Average Return	9.63	9.98	0.34
Max. Return	31.85	31.95	2.29
75th Percentile	20.42	20.47	0.58
Median	13.30	12.96	0.20
25th Percentile	1.81	3.18	0.05
Min. Return	−14.80	−14.46	−1.70
Standard Dev.	13.10	13.17	0.87

Trans Average   0.52% turnover/month

Summary of Annual Returns

Year	Drifting Mix Return	Rebalancing Return	Value Added
1971	13.30	13.50	0.20
1972	13.58	13.65	0.07
1973	−13.19	−12.62	0.58
1974	−14.80	−14.46	0.35
1975	22.46	24.75	2.29
1976	20.42	20.47	0.05
1977	−4.94	−4.90	0.04
1978	3.13	3.18	0.05
1979	10.09	10.01	−0.08
1980	18.01	16.32	−1.70
1981	−4.65	−4.48	−0.17
1982	29.02	30.70	1.68
1983	13.86	12.95	−0.90
1984	9.13	9.65	0.52
1985	31.85	31.95	0.09
1986	20.12	20.44	0.32
1987	1.81	3.82	2.01
1988	12.94	12.96	0.02
1989	27.02	27.76	0.74
1990	−0.43	0.05	0.48

should most assuredly be long-term investors) idle cash reserves produce low returns at a terrible cost in risk.

According to Federal Reserve data, some 11–15% of U.S. corporate pension holdings over the past decade have been cash equivalents. This means that many pension funds may have forfeited as much as 60 basis points per annum due solely to the cost of excessive idle cash reserves. Over the past decade, if U.S. pension funds were fully invested, their aggregate value would be more than $100 billion greater than today. Endowment funds, similarly, continue to sustain large cash reserves, while still attending to commitments they hope will be lasting.

Most pension officers are not even aware of the magnitude of the problem. Few admit to cash reserves above 10%, yet Federal Reserve data suggests that the average is even higher than this. The problem is simple. Cash crops up in the portfolio in many spots. Equity managers maintain idle cash reserves, as do bond managers. Cash is contributed to the portfolio and lingers pending allocation to investment managers. The pension fund maintains a modest deliberate cash reserve in order to serve near-term pension benefits. It is the combination that represents such a huge number (and such a huge drain on investment results).

These idle cash reserves are necessary. Active stock and bond managers need cash to seize opportunities in the marketplace. Cash is needed to serve near-term benefits. However, while the cash is needed in the portfolio, it doesn't have to look like cash. Futures and options can be used to synthetically create exposure to stocks or bonds, so that a portfolio can always be fully invested.

If we believe that the markets are efficient, then we cannot justify idle cash reserves; only a fully invested portfolio can be justified. Therefore, unless we choose to adopt a tactical framework for asset allocation, and unless that tactical framework suggests the use of cash in the face of vulnerable markets, then we have a responsibility to put idle cash reserves to work. Remarkably, this is more the exception than the rule, and at a terrible cost to the institutional investing community.

Exhibit 5 compares the rewards of disciplined rebalancing against the returns for a portfolio with a drifting asset mix and with 10% of the portfolio in idle cash reserves. As we have already observed, cash reserves in the average pension portfolio are larger than this. In this example, a pension sponsor, with excess idle cash and with a drifting asset mix (not even suffering from the costly ad hoc shifts which so typify pension management), realizes returns some 47 basis points per year less

EXHIBIT 5
VALUE ADDED BY REBALANCING VS. A DRIFTING MIX WITH 10% CASH

Results for Jan. 1971 to Dec. 1990	Drifting Mix Return	Rebalancing Return	Value Added
Average Return	9.51	9.98	0.47
Max. Return	29.50	31.95	4.39
75th Percentile	18.96	20.47	1.70
Median	12.43	12.95	0.51
25th Percentile	2.21	3.18	−0.42
Min. Return	−12.34	−14.46	−2.07
Standard Dev.	11.79	13.18	1.71

| Trans. Average | 0.56% turnover/month | | |

Summary of Annual Returns

Year	Drifting Mix Return	Rebalancing Return	Value Added
1971	12.39	13.44	1.05
1972	12.67	13.65	0.98
1973	−11.39	−12.62	−1.23
1974	−12.39	−14.46	−2.07
1975	20.36	24.75	4.39
1976	18.77	20.47	1.70
1977	−3.95	−4.90	−0.94
1978	3.60	3.18	−0.42
1979	10.14	10.01	−0.13
1980	17.40	16.32	−1.08
1981	−2.73	−4.48	−1.75
1982	27.02	30.70	3.68
1983	13.38	12.95	−0.42
1984	9.21	9.65	0.44
1985	29.50	31.95	2.45
1986	18.96	20.44	1.47
1987	2.21	3.82	1.61
1988	12.43	12.95	0.51
1989	25.41	27.89	2.48
1990	0.24	0.02	−0.22

than those provided by disciplined rebalancing. History suggests that the average sponsor actually does moderately worse than this.

Rebalancing and full investment of all idle cash reserves provide results which, over the long run, are measurably better than those achieved by the average pension sponsor. But, this is at the cost of somewhat more volatility. In 1974, rebalancing had us putting more and more money into a plunging equity market. Worse yet, idle cash reserves performed far better than either stocks or bonds. So, the combination of rebalancing and synthetic investment of idle cash reserves cost 207 basis points in 1974. In 1975, the opposite occurred. Investment of idle cash reserves boosted returns wonderfully in a rising market. Rebalancing also had the portfolio move progressively out of stocks, which performed badly late in the year. The combination lifted returns by 439 basis points. In short, these disciplines make sense over the course of time. They make sense because they provide an easy framework for enforcing a "buy low, sell high" asset mix into the overall portfolio process.

Tactical Asset Allocation: Panacea or Peril?

Once the policy asset allocation has been prudently established, the sponsor can turn attention to the issue of active asset allocation. Here, once again, things are not as simple as they would appear on the surface, as we can see in Exhibit 6. Active asset allocation may include portfolio insurance and surplus insurance strategies, which reduce risk in plunging markets, but do so at a considerable cost. Alternatively, tactical asset allocation may be pursued. Tactical asset allocation seeks to shift the asset mix in response to the changing patterns of reward available in the marketplace. Yet, tactical asset allocation is not a single, clearly defined strategy. There are many variations and nuances involved in the management of the tactical asset allocation decision.

Tactical asset allocation broadly refers to active strategies which seek to enhance performance by shifting the asset mix of a portfolio in response to objective measures of the reward available in various asset classes (e.g., stocks, bonds, cash, international assets, etc.). Notably, tactical asset allocation tends to refer to disciplined processes for evaluating the respective rates of return on various asset classes and establishing an asset allocation response intended to boost performance. There are several shared attributes of the various tactical asset allocation processes.

EXHIBIT 6
DO WE PERMIT ACTIVE SHIFTS IN ASSET MIX?

I.   Should we employ tactical asset allocation to shift our mix in response to changing market conditions?
  A. What confidence do we have that tactical asset allocation will add value in the long run?
  B. What latitude should we permit in the asset mix and what discipline should be used to determine the appropriate mix within that range?
  C. What are the risks?
    1. What if the process stops working?
      a. A secular shift in the nature of capital markets behavior.
      b. A change in the equilibrium relationships between markets.
    2. What if we "lose our nerve?"
      a. The total return vs. relative returns paradigm.
      b. The episodic returns of tactical asset allocation.

II. Is my customer sufficiently risk averse that a mechanistic "insurance" approach makes sense?
  A. Should we insure nominal returns for a short span of time, such as a year?
  B. Should we insure pension funding status for a longer period, such as 5 years, using surplus insurance?
  C. What are the risks?
    1. Can we tolerate the long-term costs?
    2. Will the costs be in line with our expectations?

- They tend to be objectively driven, based on analytic tools, such as regression analysis or optimization. This is in direct contrast to the market timers of the 1960s and 1970s, who relied primarily on subjective judgment.

- They tend to be driven primarily by objective measures of prospective value among asset classes. We know the yield on cash, we know the yield to maturity on long-term bonds. The earnings yield (the reciprocal of the price/earnings ratio) on the stock market or a dividend discount rate of return on the stock market represents an objective and reasonable proxy for long-term rewards available in stocks. In essence, the markets are *telling us* what rates of return are available.

- These processes tend to rely upon a "return to equilibrium." If our objective models suggest that one market is offering greater return than normal relative to alternative markets, it is the return to equilibrium that is the most powerful source of profits. For example, if bond yields are 1% higher than normal relative to stock earnings yields, then there are two sources of return for this "disequilibrium." First, we garner 1% more return than we would normally expect from bonds relative to stocks. Secondly, if the markets return to their normal relationship, this will occur through either a 1% drop in bond yields (an impressive bond rally) or a 1% rise in stock market earnings yields (a mid-sized decline in the stock market).

- Tactical asset allocation processes tend to buy after a market decline and sell after a market rally. As such, they are inherently contrarian. By objectively measuring which asset classes are offering the greatest prospective rewards, tactical asset allocation processes measure which asset classes are the most out of favor. These assets are priced to reflect the fact that they are neglected and the corresponding fact that the investment community demands a premium reward for an out of favor investment. Tactical asset allocation steers us into these unloved assets.

Tactical asset allocation processes cover a wide spectrum. Some are simple, objective comparisons of available rates of return. Others seek to enhance the timeliness of these value-driven decisions by incorporating macroeconomic measures, sentiment measures, volatility measures and even technical measures. We believe that the more sophisticated approaches are superior to pure value approaches. An undervalued stock can get more undervalued; by the same token, an undervalued asset class can grow more undervalued. The investor who buys an asset as soon as it becomes undervalued may earn attractive rewards. If an investor buys the same asset class when economic and sentiment conditions would favor a return to "fair" pricing, that investor will do even better.

The empirical evidence suggests that simple, quantitative measures of market attractiveness have impressive potential. Exhibit 7 [Arnott and von Germeten, 1983] suggests that the excess return for stocks (stock market returns minus Treasury bill returns) are strongly correlated with several simple objective measures of the risk premium. The historic evidence, while it cannot assure future success, is compelling.

EXHIBIT 7
RISK PREMIUM AND MARKET PERFORMANCE

EX = Equity Excess Return
(Expected Equity Return—Expected Bond Return)

BX = Bond Excess Return
(Expected Bond Return—Expected Cash Return)

	Equity Return—Bond Return		Equity Return—Cash Return		Bond Return—Cash Return	
	One-Month	One-Year	One-Month	One-Year	One-Month	One-Year
Stage 1: **EX**	0.21[b]	0.47[b]	0.16[a]	0.24[a]	−0.08	−0.39[b]
	−3.10	−7.40	−2.30	−3.40	1.20	6.00
Stage 1: **BX**	0.14[a]	0.04	0.22[a]	0.20[a]	0.17[a]	0.34[a]
	−2.00	−0.06	−3.20	−2.70	−2.50	−5.10
Stage 1 Prediction	0.25[b]	0.48[b]	0.27[b]	0.31[b]	0.20[b]	0.53[b]
	−3.60	−7.40	−3.90	−4.40	−2.80	−8.50

[a]Significant at 95% level.
[b]Significant at 99.9% level.
Source: Robert D. Arnott and James N. von Germeten, "Systematic Asset Allocation," *Financial Analysts Journal* (November/December, 1983).

The Theoretic Underpinnings for Tactical Asset Allocation

If tactical asset allocation offers the hope of improved long-term returns without a corresponding increase in portfolio volatility, then it might seem that we are violating finance theory. After all, we have long been taught that there is "no such thing as a free lunch!" The answer to this puzzle is found in utility theory.

As a market rises, so too does the "wealth" in a portfolio. Unfortunately, it is easy to forget that this is accompanied by a drop in prospective subsequent returns (Exhibit 8A). However, different institutional investors will exhibit different responses to changes in wealth. The ap-

EXHIBIT 8
RISK TOLERANCE AND RETURN PROSPECTS: ASSET ALLOCATION
RESPONSE

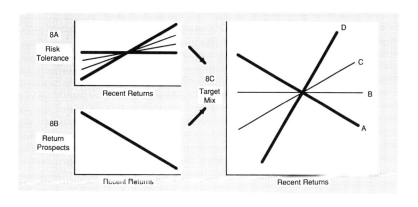

propriate asset allocation response to recent market moves differs for each of these investors.

• Exhibit 8B shows that some investors ("A") are blissfully unaffected by shifts in wealth. In other words, their tolerance for risk does not change with recent investment performance. As they become more wealthy, their tolerance for investment risk is largely unchanged. These are the long-term investors. Yet, the long-term investors who have a tolerance for risk which is relatively independent of recent results will be inclined to grasp opportunities offered by a declining market (see Exhibit 8C). These sponsors will be naturally drawn towards tactical asset allocation. The improved return prospects which come with a newly fallen market increase the attractiveness of that market. In the absence of a change in risk tolerance, the investor should buy.

• Other investors ("B") will be somewhat sensitive to recent changes in wealth. As their wealth rises, their tolerance for prospective investment risk also rises slightly. The sponsors with slight sensitivity to market movements will find that a market drop reduces their tolerance for risk, but only slightly. For these investors, the newly improved return prospects for equities are just large enough to justify a return to a static mix. These are the "natural" candidates for a simple rebalancing process.

- Yet another class of investors ("C") shows somewhat more sensitivity to recent market behavior. Their aversion to investment risk rises sharply as the wealth of the portfolio declines. The "optimal" strategy for these risk-sensitive sponsors in category "C" will be to permit their asset mix to drift with the movements of the market. As the market falls, so too does their tolerance for risk. However, as the market falls, so too does their exposure to risky markets. So, these investors may find their tolerance for risk and their exposure to risk falling in parallel, so no trades are needed. These investors will permit their mix to drift with the whims of the market.

- Lastly, we have the investors ("D") who react strongly to recent behavior. If the market rises, their tolerance for risk soars. If the market falls, their tolerance for risk plunges. As a result, a market decline triggers a desire to bail out of the falling market. The investors with a high sensitivity to recent market moves are natural candidates for insurance strategies.

Therefore, we have natural candidates for portfolio insurance or surplus insurance, for a drifting asset mix, for simple rebalancing to a static mix, and for tactical asset allocation. Tactical asset allocation is not right for everyone, for the simple reason that an improvement in long-term returns does not necessarily signal an improvement in "utility," in the satisfaction of the natural human desires for both return and comfort. Tactical asset allocation historically has improved returns without increasing risk. Theoretically, it can continue to do so. But it does not offer the long-sought "free lunch." It succeeds because total return and investor utility are not one and the same. When their wealth is declining, most investors seek the comfort of lower risk. Tactical asset allocation increases risk when it is uncomfortable to do so. It may enhance long-term returns without increasing risk, but at a cost of lower comfort, hence lower utility.

The recent work by Sharpe is a real addition to our understanding of asset allocation.[2] It provides an equilibrium framework, in which tactical asset allocation can and should enhance returns without increasing portfolio risk. This improvement in returns, without a corresponding increase

---

[2]William Sharpe, "Investor Wealth Measures and Expected Return," *Quantifying the Market Risk Premium*, ICFA, September 1989.

in risk, can only hold true if tactical asset allocation is an uncomfortable strategy which certain investors will find unacceptable. We already know this to be true. Few investors were rushing to buy bonds during the peak yields of 1980, 1981 or 1982. Still fewer were buying stocks in late 1974 or immediately after the market crashed in 1987.

What Are the Risks?

The risks for tactical asset allocation can be divided into two categories. First is the risk that the discipline may stop working. Second is the risk that a temporary period of disappointment may cause us to "lose our nerve."

Tactical asset allocation can stop working if our objective measures of prospective return are ill-conceived. For example, an equity risk premium which is based on the difference between the earnings yield on the stock market and the yield available in bonds, may sow the seeds of danger. If earnings soar, the earnings yield can rise, even as the market is rising. A secular shift in the earnings power of the market, in the relative risk of stocks and bonds, or of the normal tolerance for stock or bond risk in the investment community can all lead to an extended "dry spell."

These secular shifts in the nature of capital markets behavior are rare. It has often been said that the five most costly words in the investment world are, "Things are different this time." That statement is uttered far more often than it is true.

A more common risk in tactical asset allocation is that the equilibrium relationship between markets may change. In the 1950s, it was normal for equities to be priced at a dividend yield in excess of bond yields. This was to compensate stock market investors for their fear that the Great Depression could recur. The gap between earnings yields and bond yields were still larger. As the fear of a renewed depression dissipated, so too did the normal risk premium between stock earnings yields and bond yields.

A tactical asset allocation process which is predicated on a comparison of current market conditions with "long-term" normal relationships runs the risk of being out of step for an extended period of time. For example, the 20-year average gap between the earnings yield of the stock market and long-term bond yields will not change quickly in response to a shift in the equilibrium relationships.

Conversely, strategies which seek to respond more rapidly to changes in equilibrium relationships may be vulnerable to "whipsaw." If the equity risk premium soars, as it did in 1987 with the stock market crash, we run the risk of mistaking the jump in risk premium for a shift in the equilibrium risk premium. If we do that, we may buy stocks in response to the renewed opportunity, but may reverse those positions sooner (as many tactical asset allocation practitioners did in 1988 and 1989) as the markets return to their long-term normal relationships. History suggests that a "whipsaw" from seeking to adapt to a changing world is less than the risk of falling out of step for a long period of time when equilibrium relationships change. Nonetheless, it is a risk which damaged many tactical asset allocation managers in 1989.

The more dangerous risk in tactical asset allocation may be the risk that we "lose our nerve." This risk is inherent in the contrarian nature of the process. Tactical asset allocation sells as the market rises. As a result, it is almost inevitably out of step for at least the final weeks or months of a bull market. The opposite occurs at the end of a bear market. This makes the strategy profoundly uncomfortable at market turning points.

Tactical asset allocation objectively measures prospective rates of return and encourages purchase of the out of favor market. That market is priced to offer superior returns because it is out of favor, because it is uncomfortable. As a result, the temptation will always exist, particularly at market turning points, to "second guess" the tactical asset allocation process.

The temptation to give up on tactical asset allocation will be greatest as we approach market turning points. This holds true for any contrarian strategy, but perhaps more so for tactical asset allocation. One of the problems with tactical asset allocation is that its "episodic returns" will challenge our patience. Common sense and history tell us that it is very difficult to outpace a rising market with asset mix shifts.

If an equity manager is hired, we might reasonably hope that, in a falling market, our stocks will fall less than the market, and in a rising market, our stocks will rise more than the market. This pattern of reward might be termed an "index plus alpha" strategy. It is tempting to view any active strategy in this same context. But tactical asset allocation cannot readily outpace a strong market, and it cannot readily underperform a falling market.

Tactical asset allocation is best viewed as a total return strategy. It is tempting to view it as an "index plus alpha" strategy, but its performance is very different. If tactical asset allocation keeps pace with two out of every three rising markets, and keeps the institutional investor out of a like proportion of falling markets, then value will be added in the context of reduced risk.

The returns for tactical asset allocation are episodic. This will cause us to question whether the merits of the discipline have disappeared. We will be puzzling over this question precisely as market turning points approach and as the model will have been out of step for some weeks or months. Such is the nature of a contrarian process. Contrarian disciplines are uncomfortable, and so raise doubt when they fall out of step.

This is best illustrated in the series of diagrams shown in Exhibit 9. Here, we see the simulated performance of a simple stock/bond trading rule. This might be considered to be a crude form of tactical asset allocation. In this strategy, we buy stocks any time the stock market risk premium relative to bonds (earnings yield minus bond yield) has risen by more than 2% in the past year. We switch to bonds any time the risk premium has fallen by a like amount in the past year. This very crude tactical asset allocation discipline leads to surprisingly good results, as shown in Exhibit 9A. However, the rolling 12-month performance relative to a 100% stock portfolio is erratic, as shown in Exhibit 9B.

As noted previously, there are seeds of risk in tactical asset allocation. If equilibrium relationships change profoundly, if the fundamental pricing mechanism in the capital markets changes, then tactical asset allocation can underperform for extended periods of time. However, it is precisely at market turning points that we will be tempted to ask whether the process has "broken down." Such questions were asked in the third quarter of 1987, when tactical asset allocation practitioners around the country had underperformed by often large margins, and such questions recurred in late 1989 for the same reason.

It is worth repeating: tactical asset allocation is not for everyone. Long-term investors who wish to participate in a total return strategy may find the process occasionally uncomfortable but rewarding in the long term. Sharpe has demonstrated that the historic success of tactical asset allocation is not at odds with finance theory.[3] However, pension officers and, more importantly, boards of directors who are not comfortable with large residual risk (relative to a static asset mix), or who are overly inclined to focus on recent performance, will find themselves abandoning tactical asset allocation (and other contrarian disciplines) at

---

[3]Ibid

EXHIBIT 9

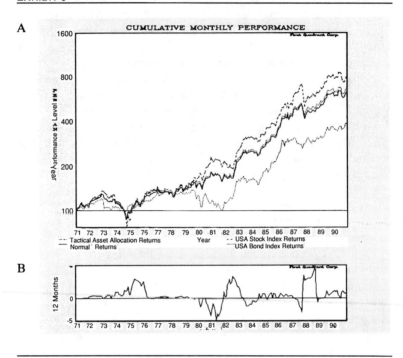

inopportune times. Such investors would be well served to adopt a persistent rebalancing strategy in order to avoid the risk of forfeiting value through inopportune shifts in asset allocation strategy.

Insurance Strategies

For the few institutional investors without the nerve to "stay the course" on something as practical as rebalancing, insurance may make sense. Here, the key questions are those summarized in Exhibit 1 and reviewed earlier in the chapter: What risk matters? How averse is the pension committee to declining markets? Will they tolerate nominal losses? How averse are they to funding shortfall? If liabilities rise faster than assets, will they exhibit patience? How much can our fund differ from the "average fund" without bearing a risk of an unacceptable shortfall relative to the competition?

All of these questions are important. The beauty of a rebalancing process is that it provides a mechanism for restraining the natural (but terribly costly) impulses to bail out after disappointment or to chase a rising market. If the Board is insufficiently disciplined, and cannot tolerate that risk, then an insurance strategy may make sense. Several points should be noted:

- An insurance strategy carries a cost. Just as all insurance companies charge a fee, the capital markets exact a cost (and a fair cost) for synthetic insurance strategies designed to prevent unacceptable consequences. This could arguably reduce long-term returns by 1–3% per annum.

- In addition to the implicit cost of an insurance strategy, there is also an explicit trading cost, which must be paid to affect the strategy. This could arguably cut long term returns 1% in addition to the cost of the insurance policy.

- These strategies yield a median return which is dramatically lower than unprotected strategies. As an offset to protecting against unacceptable negative returns, the returns in rising markets can be clobbered, to the tune of 4–8% per annum.

For certain institutional investors, these consequences are quite acceptable. Suppose that an insurance strategy is deemed a prerequisite for significant equity market exposure. Then the net consequence may be improved long-term results. Suppose the board has shown a remarkable aptitude for pulling the plug after market declines and for chasing rising markets. Then insurance may be a way to dissuade (or at least moderate) these counterproductive moves. Better still, the "floor" (the minimum nominal return or minimum funding ratio, which forms the basis for the "insurance policy") can be adjusted from time to time. After a market decline, it might be lowered to permit reinvestment back into the market. Ironically, this can provide an ad hoc solution to the problem of ad hoc judgmental asset allocation shifts.

What Are the Risks in Insurance?

Insurance strategies are not without their own special set of risks. Let us first suppose that portfolio insurance and surplus insurance can be effected with negligible trading costs. If this is true, then we must still pay the "insurance premium." Just as an insurance company charges its customer a fee for bearing the risk of loss, so too do these strategies. For the very conservative customer, wishing to eliminate the risk of loss in any calendar year, the cost may be high. For such an investor, the long-term returns on the portfolio might be penalized by 2% to prevent that risk, as median returns fall 6–8%. A 2% cost, assessed against total portfolio value each year, is huge! The cost of funding a pension plan with 2% lower returns can, for many companies, be 50–100% higher as a result! Even a moderate insurance strategy, designed to penalize long-term returns by just 50 to 100 basis points, can substantially raise the cost of funding pension benefits over a long period of time.

Even so, these insurance strategies are useful for some investors. Notably, if the Board of Directors is intolerant of risk, and if the adoption of an insurance strategy can be used as a basis for boosting the overall aggressiveness of the fund, then it may have merit for some institutions. Such strategies must be adopted with a full recognition that the cost of insurance (whether portfolio insurance or surplus insurance) is high. Mean and median returns are lower than the returns for a more conventional investment strategy. The median return is actually lower than that of an immunized portfolio, and can be 4–8% below the median returns for a more conventional approach.

A second risk in insurance strategies is the implementation risk. Can it be implemented with negligible trading costs? The answer is probably "no." The reason for this is that insurance strategies buy after a market rise and sell after a market rally. When the market is rising, it is difficult to buy without further moving the market. If the market is plunging, it is difficult to sell without further depressing the market. Trading costs are not negligible, even if they are effected through the use of futures and options. The academics who have designed portfolio insurance (and now surplus insurance) dismiss some critical variables. The markets do not provide endless liquidity. Trading costs with a "trend-following" strategy, such as portfolio insurance, are not inconsequential. At times, such as the crash of 1987, the other side of the trade may not even be available.

Given these costs, surplus insurance is still an intuitively appealing product. It promises to prevent funding ratio shortfalls, while permitting participation in rallying stock markets. It accomplishes this objective at a modest projected cost. The crash in October of 1987 showed us that the cost of effecting insurance strategies can be several hundred basis points greater than expected. However, in more normal markets, the cost can be manageable. Nonetheless, it is a cost which will be reflected in pension contributions year after year after year.

With recent regulatory and accounting changes, which heighten corporate sensitivity to funding ratios, it is likely that surplus insurance will become increasingly popular. On balance, the cost of surplus insurance is likely to exceed that estimated by its vendors, but not dramatically. Even though its intuitive appeal makes it almost certain to gain acceptance in the marketplace, it is not the right vehicle for most pension investors. Even a modest reduction in performance, compounded over many years, tremendously boosts the cost of funding a pension fund. Those who have disciplined Boards, with the wisdom to look to the long-term, will find the costs associated with these strategies to be too large relative to the comfort that the strategy affords.

CONCLUSION

One of the most dangerous, and regrettably common, misconceptions about asset allocation is that the asset mix decision is a singular decision. Indeed, it is not. The appropriate asset mix for today is dependent not only on current market opportunities, but also on our strategies for the long term.

The first critical step is the assessment of the appropriate policy for asset mix. What mix of stocks, bonds, cash, international assets and illiquid assets such as real estate or venture capital represents the best balance between the desire for return and the desire for containment of risk?

Once this decision has been made, using whatever tools and wisdom can be brought to the decision process, we can turn our attention to active management of the asset mix. The two principal categories of active asset allocation — namely, tactical asset allocation and dynamic strategies such as portfolio insurance — pose different objectives and risks. However, one risk common to both forms of active asset allocation is the risk of having results far afield from the results of the average sponsor. As always, there is symmetry to risk. A risk of underperforming due to an inappropriate active mix carries with it the corresponding opportunity to outperform our competitors. Indeed, without some kind of disciplined framework for asset allocation, it becomes very difficult to outperform our competitors. Why is this important? If we can have results for the total pension fund which are better than the competitors in our industry, then pension costs will drop, pension contributions will drop, corporate profitability will improve, and competitive positioning (along with the ability to price products competitively) will improve.

One often neglected reality is that a dollar made in the pension fund is worth at least a dollar of operating earnings. Arguably, it may be worth more because of the tax sheltered nature of the accumulation of assets. All too often, corporations act as if this is not so. The Pension Officer's role is a staff function, frequently with little promotion opportunity. The irony is all too clear. Pension funds often have assets approaching or even exceeding corporate net worth. As a result, a 100 basis point improvement in the return on plan assets can be worth as much as a 100 basis point improvement in corporate return on equity. Yet, companies that would move heaven and earth to add 1% to the ROE are not similarly motivated to add 1% to investment portfolio returns.

There is no element of the investment decision process that has a greater impact on long-term aggregate plan results than the policy asset mix decision. This decision must be made with all of the skill and wisdom that we can draw upon. History suggests that active asset allocation may offer opportunities to add measurably to portfolio returns. To do so, the active shifts in mix must be handled in a contrarian fashion.

Mechanistic insurance strategies for protecting against adverse markets are generally not devised to enhance returns. Indeed, as with an insurance policy, they exact a relatively predictable cost. The good thing about these kinds of strategies is that this cost can be softened by a more aggressive normal exposure to the high-return markets, such as equities. However, such strategies should not be undertaken without careful evaluation of the long-term consequences of the insurance cost. Just as an individual or corporation may choose to self insure, and thereby reduce costs, so too a pension plan can follow such a policy. The long-term costs of forfeiting just 100 basis points in total return can be startling.

For each element of the asset mix decision, there is no single "right" answer. Some investors should bear the risk of an aggressive asset mix policy. Others may jeopardize the competitive position of the corporation by doing so. Some organizations, particularly those with a willingness to focus on the long-term, may be in a position to seek enhanced returns through active management of the asset mix. Others may have a Board of Directors which is sufficiently risk averse, so that costly portfolio insurance strategies are necessary. The intent of this chapter has not been to provide answers, but to provide a roadmap which may be useful for pension sponsors to find their own answers.

CHAPTER 5

Risk and Return: Implications for the Asset Mix

Laurence B. Siegel
Managing Director
Ibbotson Associates, Inc.

Roger G. Ibbotson
Professor in the Practice of Finance
Yale School of Management
and President
Ibbotson Associates, Inc.

Mark W. Riepe
Senior Consultant
Ibbotson Associates, Inc.

The asset mix decision evolves from the interaction of two sets of factors: the investment objective (such as building wealth or funding an obliga-

The authors thank Linda Knight and Gary Perlin of Federal National Mortgage Association (Fannie Mae) for their helpful comments. Fannie Mae provided support for some of the research contained herein.

tion stream) and the characteristics of the assets themselves. This chapter addresses both factors, but focuses on the asset characteristics.

First, we present historical returns on the principal asset classes of the U.S. economy in the risk-premium or "building block" framework originally set forth by Ibbotson and Sinquefield.[1] Second, we use the historical data to form conclusions about the rewards (in the form of return) for taking systematic risks. These conclusions are shaped into probabilistic forecasts of return distribution for assets taken alone and for asset mixes (portfolios). Third, we note the dilemma faced by investors when simultaneously pursuing multiple investment objectives, and discuss the role of asset allocation in that dilemma. Finally, we address the impact of risk and return on the asset allocation decision throughout the chapter, as the various issues unfold.

HISTORICAL AND FORECAST ASSET RETURNS

Stocks, Bonds, Bills, and Inflation

The historical returns presented here are not only interesting in themselves, but have broad implications for forecasting, which is the essence of the asset allocation process. Specifically, the expected return on an asset is seen to be related to its risk.

Return data were collected for 1926–1990 on the principal asset classes for the U.S. economy — common stocks (represented by the Standard & Poor's 500, or S&P for short); small-company stocks; long-term government bonds; Treasury bills; and consumer goods (inflation).[2] Exhibit 1 graphically depicts the growth of a dollar invested at year-end 1925 in each of the asset classes; yearly changes in the index levels translate to annual returns. Exhibit 2 presents summary statistics of the returns used to generate Exhibit 1.

---

[1]Roger G. Ibbotson and Rex A. Sinquefield, *Stocks, Bonds, Bills, and Inflation,* 1989 edition, Dow Jones-Irwin, Homewood, IL, 1989. First book edition, 1977. First publication, *Journal of Business,* January 1976 (historical returns) and *Journal of Business,* July 1976 (forecasts of the future).

[2]The data in Exhibit 1, 2, and 3 are from Ibbotson and Sinquefield (op. cit.), updated in *Stocks, Bonds, Bills, and Inflation: 1991 Yearbook,* Ibbotson Associates, Inc., Chicago, 1991. The Yearbook also contains series for corporate bonds and intermediate-term government bonds, including monthly and annual total returns and return indices, component and inflation-adjusted series, statistical analysis, and methodology.

EXHIBIT 1
S&P 500 FUTURES VS. S&P 500 INDEX (MARCH–MAY 1991)

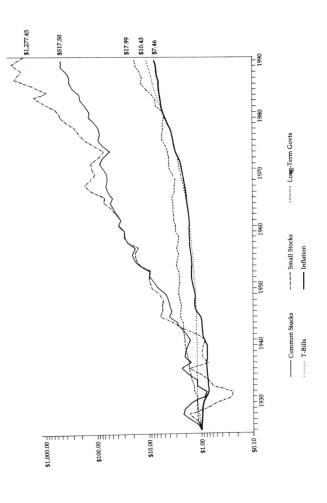

EXHIBIT 2
BASIC SERIES: SUMMARY STATISTICS OF ANNUAL RETURNS 1926–1990

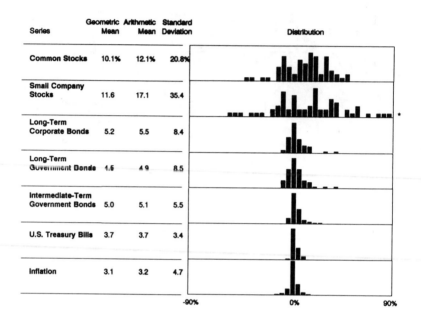

Series	Geometric Mean	Arithmetic Mean	Standard Deviation	Distribution
Common Stocks	10.1%	12.1%	20.8%	
Small Company Stocks	11.6	17.1	35.4	
Long-Term Corporate Bonds	5.2	5.5	8.4	
Long-Term Government Bonds	4.5	4.9	8.5	
Intermediate-Term Government Bonds	5.0	5.1	5.5	
U.S. Treasury Bills	3.7	3.7	3.4	
Inflation	3.1	3.2	4.7	

Note: The symbol * (to the right of the small company histogram) represents the 1933 small company total return of 142.9%.

Source: *Stocks, Bonds, Bills, and Inflation: 1991 Yearbook,* Ibbotson Associates, Inc., Chicago, 1991.

The equity series (S&P stocks and small-company stocks) have the highest average returns but are the most variable, or risky. The fixed income series (government and corporate bonds and Treasury bills) have lower returns and are less risky.

Analyzing Asset Returns: A Risk Premium or "Building Block" Approach

By taking the difference between the means of two return series, we can derive the mean risk premium realized from taking a given incremental risk. Exhibit 3 presents four differences of asset mean returns, each representing a risk premium. The equity risk premium, for example, represents the average additional return, or reward, earned by investors in S&P stocks for taking the incremental risk of stocks relative to Treasury bills. Because investors conform their expectations to that which proves over time to be realizable, this equity risk premium is a good estimate of the forward-looking risk premium in the traditional version of the Capital Asset Pricing Model (CAPM).[3] We show differences of *arithmetic* means, as contrasted with *geometric* means, because they represent the best estimate of the future value of the risk premium.

We regard the Sharpe-Lintner form of the CAPM model as primarily useful for estimating a stock's short-term expected return. We estimate the long-term expected return using a similar method, but the current long-term Treasury yield is taken as the riskless rate, and historical yield (not total returns) on long-term Treasury bonds are taken as the historical riskless return series for calculating both the equity risk premium and the stock's beta.[4]

Asserting that long-term bonds are riskless requires some elucidation. Long-term bonds, of course, fluctuate in price over time. However, they are riskless to the holder whose time horizon matches the payments of principal and coupons (if any) on the bond.[5] Such holders form the likely

---

[3]The CAPM was originally set forth in William F. Sharpe, "Capital Asset Prices: A Theory of Market Equilibrium Under Conditions of Risk," *Journal of Finance*, September 1964; and John Lintner, "The Valuation of Risk Assets and the Selection of Risky Investments in Stock Portfolios and Capital Budgets," *Review of Economics and Statistics*, February 1965. Many variants have appeared since the CAPM was first presented.

In the traditional or Sharpe-Lintner CAPM, the stock's beta is multiplied by the equity risk premium to arrive at a stock's expected return in excess of the current short-term riskless yield. The beta of a stock, in this context, is the slope parameter from regression of a stock's excess returns on the market's excess returns.

[4]The historical yield is preferable because it is an unbiased measure of market expectations. Historical bond returns are known to be biased downward; bondholders suffered a capital loss over 1926–1990. This loss must have been unanticipated since bondholders would not have invested with the expectation of suffering a loss.

[5]To the long-horizon investor, bills are risky because their yields fluctuate. This risk is called reinvestment risk.

EXHIBIT 3
RISK PREMIA: DIFFERENCES OF ARITHMETIC MEANS OF
ANNUAL TOTAL RETURNS ON PRINCIPAL ASSET CLASSES
1926–1990

Risk Premium	Difference of Means
Equity Risk Premium (stocks–bills)	8.4%
Small Stock Premium (small stocks–common stocks)	5.0
Default Premium (LT corps–LT govts)	0.6
Horizon Premium (LT govts–bills)	1.2

Source: *Stocks, Bonds, Bills, and Inflation: 1991 Yearbook*, Ibbotson Associates, Inc., Chicago, 1991.

(or highest-bidding) clientele for these bonds, and are thus likely to be the price-determining investors for them. The fact that the yield curve slopes upward on average, after controlling for anticipated changes in inflation, suggests that investors with short horizons (who regard long bonds as risky) outnumber investors with long horizons.

This "long-horizon" form of the CAPM is applicable to investors with long time horizons. One such example is a pension fund. In addition, firms contemplating a long-term investment in a project or business unit can use the CAPM to evaluate the cost of capital by examining the expected rates of return on publicly traded firms involved in similar lines of business.

Other rewards for taking risk are evident from Exhibit 3. Small-company stocks have systematically rewarded investors for taking the additional risk of small (relative to large) stocks.[6] Likewise, corporate bonds

[6]Risks that are consistently rewarded on average over time by higher returns are known as *systematic*. In the traditional CAPM framework, only beta risk is systematic; all other risks can be eliminated by diversification and are thus unsystematic and unrewarded. We believe that a variety of risks are systematic.

provide a return incremental to that of default-free Treasury bonds. Treasury bonds, in turn, provide a return incremental to that of Treasury bills, which are also free of price fluctuation risk.

Given these observations, we can construct a simple model of expected return and risk on practically any asset or mix of assets. For example, the expected return on a long-term corporate bond is the sum of the expected inflation rate, real riskless rate, horizon premium and default premium. Because in this approach the expected return on an asset is the sum of several numerical parts, the approach may be characterized as "building block" approach.[7]

FORECASTING THE MARKET

Using Historical Data to Estimate Probability Distributions of Asset Returns

The expected return on an asset is the *mean* of the probability distribution of future returns on the asset. It is just as important, or even more so, to know the *distribution* of possible future returns.

An example of such a probabilistic forecast is provided in Exhibit 4. The one-year return on the stock market is modeled as the one-year Treasury-bill yield (regarded as certain), plus an uncertain risk premium that has an arithmetic mean return of 8.4% and a standard deviation of 20.7%. (The standard deviation, like the mean, is estimated using annual data over 1926–1990.) Since historical equity risk premia have been distributed roughly lognormally, a lognormal distribution is assumed for the future also.[8] The percentiles in Exhibit 4 indicate the probability of the stock market performing worse than the indicated return. For example, the 95th percentile return is +51.0%; this indicates that the market has a 95% probability of returning 51% or less in the next year, and a 5% probability of returning more.

Estimation of probability distributions for asset returns can be carried over multiple years, as shown in the rightmost two columns of Exhibit 4, which give return and wealth distributions over a 20-year horizon.

---

[7]For an elaboration, see Roger G. Ibbotson, "How to Forecast Long-Run Asset Return," *Investment Management Review,* September/October 1988.

[8]A lognormal distribution is one in which the natural logarithms of the return relatives are distributed normally. The return relative is equal to one plus the return. That is, for a return of 15%, or 0.15, the return relative is 1.15.

EXHIBIT 4
FUTURE DISTRIBUTIONS OF STOCK MARKET (S&P 500)
TOTAL RETURNS FORECASTED AS OF DECEMBER 31, 1990

Percentile of Market Performance	One-Year Forecasts		Twenty-Year Forecasts	
	Compound Annual Return	Future Value of $1 Invested Today	Compound Annual Return	Future Value of $1 Invested Today
95th	51.0%	$1.51	21.5%	$49.31
90th	41.4	1.41	19.7	36.74
75th	26.6	1.27	16.8	22.44
50th (median)	12.1	1.12	13.7	13.00
25th	−0.8	0.99	10.6	7.53
10th	−11.1	0.89	7.9	4.60
5th	−16.8	0.83	6.3	3.43

Source: *Stocks, Bonds, Bills, and Inflation: Forecast Edition* (1991–2010), Ibbotson Associates, Inc., Chicago, 1991.

Notice that the distribution of compound annual rates of return *tightens* as one goes from few to many years, while the distribution of ending wealth value broadens.

These estimated rates of return, or forecasts, are of course not intended to beat the market. Rather, they are estimates of what the market itself is expecting or forecasting – in a sense, "market consensus forecasts."

Asset Allocation Basics: Probability Distribution of Returns for Asset Mixes

The method used to forecast distributions of asset returns in the foregoing section can also be used for asset *mixes*. The mean of the distribution for a mix of stocks and bonds, for example, is simply the weighted average of the mean for stocks and the mean for bonds, where the proportion of each asset in the mix is used as the weight. However, the standard deviation of returns is a function of not only the assets' individual standard deviations and weights in the mix, but also of the *correlation coefficient* between the two assets. Specifically, the lower the correlation between the assets, the greater the reduction in the standard deviation below the weighted average of the assets' individual standard deviations. This reduction of portfolio standard deviation is known as the gain from diversification.

Exhibit 5 shows the probability distribution of one-year returns for stocks, bonds and portfolio mixes containing both assets. At the most elementary level, one can choose which of the six portfolios shown best fits one's tolerance for risk and desire for return. The results shown in Exhibit 5 are typical of those provided by the asset allocation tools currently in use.[9]

ACHIEVING MULTIPLE INVESTMENT OBJECTIVES

The Institutional Investor's Policy Dilemma

The primary asset classes of the economy — stocks, bonds, cash, real estate, and so forth — meet the needs of the investor who has one specific objective. If the objective is to fund an obligation stream, matching of cash flows to obligations can be approximately achieved with bond dedication and/or immunization. For taxable corporations sponsoring tax-exempt pension plans, such strategies also have the advantage of arbitrating against the tax code.[10]

Most institutional investors, however, do not have such clearly defined goals. Let's consider the pension fund sponsor's peculiar objective. The sponsor must not permit the fund to fall below the amount needed to pay benefits, but must also make money in the market to provide for the future growth of obligations. Since it is impossible to fully meet both investment objectives at the same time, a compromise must be made. The two extreme positions with respect to this compromise are the tra-

---

[9]Most asset allocation software, including that available from Ibbotson Associates, also contains a mean-variance (Markowitz) optimizer, which identifies asset mixes lying on the efficient frontier. In our simplified example (where the only assets are stocks and bonds), all of the portfolios shown are on the efficient frontier. In the real world, however, with multiple assets, these same portfolios are not necessarily efficient.

[10]As was pointed out in Fischer Black, "The Tax Consequence of Long-Run Pension Policy," *Financial Analysts Journal,* July/August 1980 and Irwin Tepper, "Taxation and Corporate Pension Policy," *Journal of Finance,* March 1981, a corporation can borrow (with tax deductible interest) to buy bonds for its pension fund (with tax exempt interest). A riskless tax arbitrage is thus achieved. We would point out that the corporation need not specifically borrow for the purpose of buying bonds. It need only be indebted. In that sense, the Black-Tepper arbitrage is almost universally, if unwittingly, used.

EXHIBIT 5
FUTURE DISTRIBUTIONS OF ONE-YEAR TOTAL RETURNS
ON STOCK/BOND PORTFOLIO MIXES FORECASTED AS OF
DECEMBER 31, 1990

Percentile of Market Performance		*Portfolio Mixes*					
	% Stocks:	*100*	*80*	*60*	*40*	*20*	*0*
	% Bonds:	*0*	*20*	*40*	*60*	*80*	*100*
95th		51.0%	42.3%	34.4%	27.5%	22.8%	21.5%
90th		41.4	34.8	28.6	23.2	19.3	18.1
75th		26.6	23.1	19.6	16.4	13.8	12.5
50th (median)		12.1	11.3	10.3	9.3	8.0	6.6
25th		−0.8	0.6	1.8	2.6	2.5	1.0
10th		−11.1	−8.2	−5.4	−3.1	−2.2	−3.8
5th		−16.8	−13.0	−9.4	−6.4	−5.0	−6.5

Note: Stocks are represented by the S&P 500. Bonds are represented by U.S. government bonds with approximately 20 years to maturity.
Source: *Stocks, Bonds, Bills, and Inflation: Forecast Edition* (1991–2010), Ibbotson Associates, Inc., Chicago, 1991.

ditional approach and the augmented balance sheet approach. In practice, a blend of the two approaches is likely to be used.

The traditional approach to pension management is a blend of trust law, bankruptcy law, and actuarial science. (The prudent-person rule is a part of trust law; bankruptcy law is the basis of ERISA.)[11] Because the two streams of legal tradition have areas of conflict, the behavior of the pension sponsor is not clearly prescribed. However, some standards can be identified. The pension plan is managed exclusively for the benefit of the employee: there is a *sacred trust* between the fiduciary and the

---

[11]It is interesting that the two guiding legal principles of pension management are so greatly separated in time. Judge Samuel Putnam first enunciated the prudent-man (sometimes now called prudent-person) rule in 1824; ERISA clarified it (to include diversification) in 1974.

employee.[12] The fiduciary is held to a higher standard of conduct than practically any other business or financial agent.

The contribution of actuarial science to the traditional approach is chiefly in the way that funding decisions are made. Funding decisions are made relative to an actuarial estimate of the present value of future benefit obligations, even where this departs materially from the economic present value of future benefit obligations.

An almost diametrically opposite approach to pension management is summarized by saying that the pension management is just another company project. The pension assets are just more corporate assets, and the pension liabilities are just more liabilities. This concept is formalized as an *augmented balance sheet*.[13] The ABS has the general form:

Corporate Assets	Corporate Liabilities (Bonds, etc.)
Pension Assets	Pension Liabilities
	Common Stock
Total Assets	Total Liabilities and Net Worth

Invoking the Miller-Modigliani separation principle, no asset is "tied" to a particular liability; the assets, including the pension assets, should be managed in a unitary fashion to maximize shareholder value.

---

[12]Of course, the employees do not own the pension fund. If the employees owned the pension fund, they would receive all of the surplus. Yet, surplus does not belong to the shareholders either. Shareholders can capture it only upon pension plan termination or reversion, a practice which is severely restricted.

This has implications when selecting the plan's level of risk. Zvi Bodie ("Shortfall Risk and Pension Asset Management," *Financial Analysts Journal*, May/June 1991) has pointed out that when the payoff for risk is fair for equity holders who are positioned to capture the full upside, it is less than fair for equity holders who are not. In a defined-benefit plan, the upside does not go directly to the risktakers. This suggests that the pension plan should be invested in low-risk assets.

This argument is flawed because corporations do not have to terminate the plan to capture the benefits of high returns. The benefits show up as reduced or eliminated pension contributions. For pension plans that have a long time horizon (such as those with a young workforce), the risk of holding equities dampens; the sponsoring corporation does not have to be able to capture the maximum possible benefit from equities in order that it be motivated to hold them.

[13]Jack L. Treynor, William W. Priest, and Patrick J. Regan, *The Financial Reality of Pension Funding under ERISA*, Dow Jones-Irwin, Homewood, IL, 1976.

Viewing the pension fund from this perspective leads to two conclusions:

1. Since diversification minimizes the risk of a portfolio of company projects, the pension assets should be selected to diversify away some of the risk of the firm's *other projects*. For example, if the firm's assets are interest-rate sensitive, the pension plan should not hold any long-term bonds. Stocks, real estate, and short-term bonds or cash (the mix depending on the risk desired) are appropriate for such a plan.

2. A safety net of low-risk assets is needed in the pension fund *only* if no such safety net exists in the rest of the company. Thus, if the pension fund is small relative to the company, and the rest of the company has a supply of safe assets from which to refresh the pension in case of poor returns, the risk of the pension assets can be high. Likewise, if the plan is large or the company has a lot of risky projects, the risk of the pension assets should be minimized.

This approach does not mean that the pension plan should be managed without regard for the beneficiaries. On the contrary, the beneficiaries are likely to be helped by any management technique that maximizes the probability of corporate survival and hence continued employment.[14] In addition, the plan sponsor may wish to enrich the beneficiaries beyond the minimum specified in the defined benefit plan, to compensate for high inflation rates or other circumstances. The sponsor is only in a position to do so if it has earned a surplus in the market, presumably by taking the risks associated with high returns.

Asset Allocation Principles for Pension Plans

What do these confusing and conflicting messages sent by the traditional and ABS approaches to pension management mean for the asset mix? One compromise that was popular in the mid-1980s was portfolio insurance. By giving up a portion of the upside performance of the stock market (while capturing much of it), one could purchase a "floor" below which the portfolio value was unlikely to go. Although portfolio insur-

---

[14]Robert A. Haugen, "Pension Investing and Corporate Risk Management," in Frank J. Fabozzi, ed., *Managing Institutional Assets,* Harper & Row, New York, 1990.

ance became unpopular after the crash of October 19, 1987, because the supposedly inviolable floor had been violated, insured portfolios generally outperformed all-equity portfolios by a large margin on the crash day. As with any kind of insurance, it could not pay off in full when the catastrophe insured against was of great magnitude.

Portfolio insurance seems to mesh almost perfectly with the utility functions of many pension plan sponsors. Both the need to make money and the need to protect existing assets are, in the ideal case, met. But portfolio insurance is perceived, rightly or wrongly, to have failed in practice. The closest that one can come to the portfolio insurance payoff diagram by using primary assets is a stock-fixed income mix. In fact, the 60-40 stock-bond mix found in many pension plans can be understood as an attempt to replicate the portfolio insurance payoff structure that seems to fit pension sponsor's needs so well.

In the absence of portfolio insurance, then, the fixed-income portion of the mix provides the floor. If the duration of the fixed-income component is short, the floor is quite rigid. The stock portion provides the wealth-generating potential.

The economic insight provided by the ABS approach should be used, if not in totality then partially, to vary the asset policy mix according to characteristics of the non-pension assets of the sponsor company. Plans that can afford to take the risk of a high equity exposure should usually do so. Companies that expose employees to a particular risk in their jobs should not expose them to more of the same risk in their pension; for example, a real estate developer should not invest its pension plan in real estate. A company selling its products in Europe, and whose profits rise and fall with the European economy, should consider some Asian equities for its international stock portfolio. These kinds of diversification across the sponsor's corporate and pension assets, considered as a unit, tend to benefit not only the shareholders, but the pension plan participants, to the extent that the interests of the company and its employees are aligned.

Asset Allocation Principles for the General Investor

When the peculiarities of investing for more than one goal are removed, the implications of risk and return for the asset mix can be much more clearly specified. The asset allocation decision must be informed by an understanding of the tradeoff between a portfolio's risk and its expected return. This is a natural consequence of the fact that investors prefer more money to less and are risk-averse. In order for all assets to be held, those that present the investor with the greatest possibility of loss must also be priced so as to provide the investor with the greatest opportunity for gain.

The historical record was presented earlier for what it reveals about the future, not the past. We expect that the risk-return tradeoff observed over the past 65 years will be repeated, not in an exact mimicry of the past, but in the general sense that risk-taking will be rewarded with higher actual returns. We believe that investors conform their expectations of future return to that which can be realized in the market. As a consequence, the magnitude of the payoff for risk (called the price of risk) that was achieved over the last 65 years is probably a good forecast of the payoff which investors expect and should achieve over the long run.

CHAPTER 6

Integrating Business Planning with Pension Fund Planning*

KEITH P. AMBACHTSHEER
PUBLISHER
AMBACHTSHEER LETTER
CANADIAN INVESTMENT REVIEW

In the beginning, employer pensions were unfunded gratuities. In the last few decades, they have evolved into legal-funded property. In more recent years, the dollar value of this pension property has mushroomed, often elevating the pension plan into one of the largest "businesses" of the employer. This chapter looks at the implications of this development for the plan sponsor. Specifically, the chapter examines the financial connections between plan sponsors, pension plans and plan members. The nature of these financial connections have a good deal to say about

*This chapter is the most recent update of the author's views on this topic. They were first articulated in his book, *Pension Funds and the Bottom Line* (Dow Jones-Irwin, 1986), then updated in "In Defense of a 60-40 Asset Mix for Pension Funds," *Financial Analysts Journal*, September/October 1987, and since in the author's own pension finance and investments advisory publication, *The Ambachtsheer Letter*.

how pension fund asset mix policy should be established. This is demonstrated by the cases of ALPHA Corporation, a private sector employer, and the Public Sector Retirement System, a pension plan sponsored by a public sector entity. Trustees for both pension plans make asset mix policy decisions in this chapter, in each case keeping the legitimate interests of plan members *and* the plan sponsor in mind.

PENSION AS GRATUITIES

The concept of employer pensions has been around since the beginning of this century. But until relatively recently, pensions were gratuities, pure and simple. That is, they represented unilateral decisions by employers to bestow financial benefits on long service employees *without any legal obligation to do so.* Slowly, over time, these "gratuity" arrangements started to be codified and to evolve into contractual arrangements between employers and their (current and former) employees.

According to Paul Halbrecht, here's where things stood in the 1950s:[1]

Pension plans contain inherent limitations on the security they offer:

- the liability is limited to the size of the fund...and the degree of funding varies widely;
- the employer has the right to unilaterally modify or terminate the plan;
- actually receiving a pension is often dependent on restrictive conditions not clearly communicated to plan members;
- employees have no say in any governance or administrative matters related to the plan.

[*Halbrecht concludes*]...taken together, these provisions leave the employee very much dependent on the continued solvency and good will of the employer for any actual pension benefits.

Legislation during the 1960s and 1970s[2] did much to enhance the property rights of plan members through a standardization of vesting

---

[1]Paul Halbrecht, *Pension Funds and Economic Power*, The Twentieth Century Fund, New York, 1959.

[2]The federal and provincial Pension Benefits Acts were written in the mid-1960s in Canada. The Employee Retirement Income Security Act (ERISA) was enacted by the U.S. Congress in 1974.

requirements, funding requirements, disclosure requirements and a government guaranty that a minimum benefit would be paid.

PENSION AS PROPERTY

Both the economic evolution of employer/employee total compensation arrangements and the aforementioned legislation has led to an ability to categorize pension arrangements today into one of three categories:

1. *Asset-based Pension Arrangements.* The employer agrees to contribute a regular amount (usually a fixed percentage of current pay) into an employee investment account. The employee's pension is based on the size of the life annuity that the accumulated value of the pension investment account can purchase on retirement. This is sometimes called a "defined contribution" pension plan.
2. *Pure Defined Benefit Pension Arrangements.* The employer agrees to pay a defined pension (usually based on earnings and years of service) regardless of how the pension fund performs. Such arrangements are usually non-contributory. If the employee is required to contribute, it is at a fixed rate which will not vary with subsequent pension fund investment performance.
3. *Shared Risk Defined Benefit Pension Arrangements.* The employer agrees to pay a defined pension, but the employee agrees to pay a proportionate share of the contributions required to help finance ultimate benefits. Here *both* the employer and employee contribution rates will vary with pension fund investment performance.

   Alternatively, the plan is non-contributory and the pension benefit has a defined floor, but the ultimate value to the pension paid depends on such factors as the amount of asset surplus in the plan and the financial health of the plan sponsor.

Most plan members in North America are covered by arrangements that are legally pure defined benefit plans, although defined contribution plans are growing in popularity. While relatively few are *explicitly* covered under shared risk defined benefit arrangements, many private sector and public sector employment plans implicitly operate on this basis.[3] In this chapter we look at the asset allocation implications of both the "pure" and "shared risk" defined benefit pension arrangements.

There is an important aspect of pure defined benefit pension plans that the legislation of the 1960s and the 1970s did *not* address. This aspect continues to be a major impediment to the formulation of focused, unambiguous pension fund asset mix policies under this type of pension arrangement. The reality of this type of plan is that there are, at any point in time, not one but *two* legitimate pension liabilities. We refer to them as the "legal termination liability" and the "economic going-concern liability."

TWO LEGITIMATE LIABILITY DEFINITIONS

The reason why there are two legitimate liability definitions in defined benefit employer pension plans is simple. Once a plan exists, the employer has the option to either continue the plan, or to terminate it. And in that option lies a great anomaly in corporate and public finance. Why? Because for a typical defined benefit pension plan, *the "best estimate" continuation liability at any point in time has a much greater value than the termination liability.*

Recently, Ippolito provided a vivid example of the potential value disparity between the two liabilities.[4] He estimated that for a typical

---

[3]The most common implicit understanding in pure defined benefit plans is for the employer to provide post-retirement inflation protection on a "best efforts" basis. Over the last 10 years, this has typically meant inflation related updates of about 50% of the increase in the CPI. Some observers argue that, at some point, this regular *"ad hoc-ing"* eventually becomes an obligation to continue to do so. All this raises some interesting questions with respect to accounting treatment as well. FASB Statements 87 and 88 and CICA Handbook Section 3460 set out how defined benefit pension plans are to be treated in corporate financial statements in the U.S.A. and Canada respectively. Their appearance has created somewhat of a dilemma for many chief financial officers: do you let accounting rules drive the economics of your pension plan, or do you make the economics drive the rules? CFOs making the latter choice are finding there are ways to make the rules (and the accountants who wrote them) fit the economics *where the CFO has thought through the economics.* This chapter endeavors to contribute to that thinking-through process.

[4]Richard A. Ippolito, "The Economic Burden of Corporate Pension Liabilities," *Financial Analysts Journal*, January/February 1986. His book, *Pensions, Economics, and Public Policy* (Dow Jones-Irwin 1986), further elaborates on the distinction between what Ippolito calls "true" and "legal" pension liabilities.

55-year-old worker the "economic going-concern" pension liability might be at least 2.7 times the value of the "termination" liability. Similarly, Ezra and Ambachtsheer reported a median 3:1 ratio between these two liability levels in a sample of 146 defined benefit plans.[5]

The reason for the disparity is simple. The "economic going-concern" liability reflects an assumption that the pension benefits accruing will actually be paid out over time and that the nominal dollar value of the benefit payments over time will reflect actual inflation experience over time. By contrast, the "termination" liability simply reflects the price of a basket of fixed dollar current and deferred life annuities. These annuities, priced at current interest rates, would be just sufficient to discharge pension obligations earned to date based on today's compensation rates.

This chapter does not examine the economic, legal and even moral issues surrounding the going-concern/termination value disparity.[6] It simply takes this disparity as a "given" and focuses instead on the *investment implications* of these two possible views of pure defined benefit pension liabilities.

THE TERMINATION VIEW OF PURE DEFINED BENEFIT PENSION LIABILITIES

Much of the recent literature on balance sheet management in the context of defined benefit pension plans focuses on the investment implica-

---

[5]D. Don Ezra and Keith P. Ambachtsheer, "Pension Funds: Rich or Poor?" *Financial Analysts Journal,* March/April 1985.

[6]Ippolito, for example, argues that if workers forego the present value-equivalent of ongoing rather than termination benefits as the non-current portion of total compensation package, there is an implicit contract to provide ongoing benefits (see also footnote 3). Terminated employees and/or their unions have made this argument in a number of court cases arising out of plan terminations. In a recent case in Ontario where an employer had already received the termination surplus, the court ordered the money to be returned to the trustees until it ruled on the merits of the employees' case. An out-of-court settlement resulted with the employer and plan members splitting the termination surplus 50-50. The recent Blessit vs. Dixie Engine decision by the United States Court of Appeals suggests the courts are also starting to change their thinking on termination pension benefits. A series of recent articles by Zvi Bodie of Boston University continue this debate. See, for example, Zvi Bodie, "Shortfall Risk and Pension Fund Asset Management," *Financial Analysts Journal,* May/June 1991, and our rejoinder, "Would the Real Investment Policy Please Stand Up?" in the same issue.

tions of taking the *termination* view of pure defined benefit pension liabilities.[7]

The logic of a pension fund asset allocation framework with a "termination liabilities" focus proceeds from two critical assumptions:

1. The pension liability relevant for making asset allocation decisions is the plan "termination liability."
2. The plan "termination liability" is fixed in nominal terms.

Making these two assumptions is not without merit. After all, regulations require trusteed pension funds to be managed "...solely in the interest of plan beneficiaries...." Taken literally, this means the only role to the pension fund is to insure there is enough money available to pay the accrued pension debt if, for some reason, the plan sponsor either can't or no longer wants to. And if the plan sponsor can't or no longer wants to pay, the plan is clearly in a termination situation.

As for the "termination liability" being fixed in nominal terms, this is still the standard legal and accounting interpretation of what is owed in plan termination. That is, that there is no legally enforceable obligation to provide a termination *quid pro quo* for any explicit or implicit understanding that the plan, as a going-concern, was to provide inflation-related benefits.[8]

THE INVESTMENT IMPLICATIONS OF THE TERMINATION VIEW OF PENSION LIABILITIES

A nice feature of the "termination liabilities" formulation of the pension fund asset allocation problem is that there is a "risk-free" asset. This risk-free asset is likely to be a long duration, default free, fixed rate bond

---

[7]See, for example, Martin L. Leibowitz, "The Dedicated Bond Portfolio in Pension Funds — Part I: Motivations and Basics," *Financial Analysts Journal*, January/February 1986; Martin L. Leibowitz, "The Dedicated Bond Portfolio in Pension Funds — Part II: Immunization, Horizon Matching, and Contingent Procedures," *Financial Analysts Journal*, March/April 1986; Martin L. Leibowitz, "Total Portfolio Duration: A New Perspective on Asset Allocation," *Financial Analysts Journal*, September/October 1986; Martin L. Leibowitz, "Pension Fund Asset Allocation through Surplus Management," *Financial Analysts Journal*, March/April 1987; and Martin L. Leibowitz, "Liability Returns: A New Look at Asset Allocation," *Journal of Portfolio Management*, Winter 1987. For an updated view, see Chapter 10 by the same authors.

[8]But see footnote 6. It might be unwise to assume that the current status of the plan termination surplus ownership issue is permanent.

portfolio. Why? Fixed dollar pension plan termination liabilities can be discharged with the purchase of a portfolio of current and deferred annuities. Depending on the mix of active and retired lives and their respective age distributions, the duration of such a portfolio might be somewhere between 10 and 15 years.[9]

Liabilities with this duration are well within the duration reach of an asset portfolio of zero-coupon bonds. By matching asset and liability durations, any existing "termination surplus" (plan assets in excess of the plan "termination liability") can be locked in. In the "termination" framework, both short-term debt securities and stocks are risky. Both have far too little nominal interest-rate sensitivity. In addition, stock prices move up or down for reasons totally unrelated to changes in interest rates.

Zvi Bodie goes even further.[10] He argues that in pension plans where the ongoing pension "deal" is effectively to pay at least the termination benefit, but more if there are excess assets from which to pay more, it makes no sense to ever have excess assets. Ergo, it makes no sense to have an investment policy which might produce excess assets. He concludes that a 100% bond asset mix policy is the only way to go.

PENSION PLAN SPONSORS AND THE "TERMINATION LIABILITY" FRAMEWORK

Despite the logic of the "termination" view of pension liabilities, very few pension funds have 100% bond asset mix policies. The fact that actual pension fund asset mixes deviate significantly from the risk-free portfolio suggests that the "termination liability" framework can be explained by one of two reasons:

1. Plan sponsors use the "legal termination liability" framework but willingly assume considerable balance sheet risk in framing their asset mix policies.
2. Plan sponsors don't use the "nominal termination liability" framework in framing their asset mix policies.

---

[9]Leibowitz calculates duration of about 6 years for retireds and 13 years for actives in the sample pension plan he uses. See Martin Leibowitz, "Liability Returns: A New Look at Asset Allocation," *Journal of Portfolio Management,* Winter 1987.

[10]Zvi Bodie, "Shortfall Risk and Pension Fund Asset Management," *Financial Analysts Journal,* May/June 1990.

Reason #1 doesn't strike us as very plausible. We don't perceive pension plan sponsors in aggregate to be aggressive risk takers in managing pension plan balance sheets.

Reason #2 seems more plausible. That is, plan sponsors rightly or wrongly don't accept the two critical assumptions about "time" (i.e., finite-life pension liabilities — and hence assets) and "the nature of the pension promise" (i.e., nominal rather than inflation-sensitive) behind the "termination" view of pension liabilities. A variation on this theme is that many (especially public sector) employers believe they do not in fact have the (moral, if not legal) right to unilaterally terminate an in-place defined benefit plan.

Reason #2 is supported by a study by Malley and Jayson.[11] Their surveys and interviews with financial executives indicated much more of a "going-concern" mentality rather than a "termination" mentality among respondents making fund and investment policy decisions.

Further support for the second interpretation comes from the fact that the funding process focuses on ongoing rather than termination pension benefits. Given going concern pension liabilities require one and one-half to two times as much money to fund as termination liabilities, plan assets tend to exceed termination liabilities in the typical plan by those same multiples. Thus for most plans, solvency is not the central issue. Instead, *the central issue is to earn a high long-term rate of return* on a pool of assets, the value of which easily matches that of some of the plan sponsor's mainline businesses.[12]

---

[11]Susan L. Malley and Susan Jayson, "Why Do Financial Executives Manage Pension Funds the Way They Do?," *Financial Analysts Journal*, November/December 1986. In my book (*Pension Funds and the Bottom Line,* Dow Jones-Irwin 1986), I also make the fundamental assumption that employer pension plans are "going-concern" financial entities, and should be managed that way. I continue to believe that today.

[12]Michael W. Peskin of Morgan Stanley has recast this objective in a contribution rate minimization form. He argues persuasively that this form permits the plan sponsor to deal more realistically with asymmetries in the tax rules which force accelerated funding if plan assets fall below the termination liability, and which impose a tax on withdrawals of excess assets from pension plans. Further, the costs and benefits of alternate asset mix policies (i.e., their impacts on future plan sponsor cashflows) should be present valued using the plan sponsor's own borrowing rate as the discount rate. See, for example, Michael W. Peskin, "Financial Analysis of Investment Strategy for Corporate Defined Benefit Pension Plans," Seventh Annual *FIM* Conference, New York, September 1991.

PENSION PLAN SPONSORS, "TIME," AND "THE PENSION PROMISE"

What happens to the asset allocation question when ongoing rather than termination assumptions are made about "time" and "the nature of the pension promise"? The assumptions now become:

1. The pension liability relevant for making pension fund asset allocation decisions is *not* the "legal termination liability," but the "economic, going-concern liability."
2. The plan "economic, going-concern liability" is *not* fixed in nominal terms. It is highly inflation-sensitive.

With these assumptions, the pension fund is much more likely to be viewed as a *permanent* tax exempt capital pool, on which the return can be used to help discharge pension debt when it falls due. As to what direction the answer to the asset allocation question might now take us, there are five considerations. We list them as questions a plan sponsor might ask:

- How do we view long-term capital market prospects?
- Is it clear that risk-related return gains in the pension fund indeed do translate into reduced employer contributions?
- While a plan termination is not expected, how would we "settle" with our current and former employees if it did occur?
- How concerned are we about shorter-term fluctuations in the economic and/or accounting values of plan assets and plan liabilities, and hence the plan surplus (economic and/or accounting) positions?[13]
- To what degree are we prepared to/can we integrate the main business and the pension plan balance sheet for capital structure and tax planning purposes?

---

[13]This question highlights the issue of whether economics will drive accounting or accounting will drive economics. We have already conceded that there will be cases where the economics dictate a "termination" rather than "going-concern" view of the world. In these latter cases, shorter term fluctuations in the value of the plan termination surplus are likely to be important. Hence, paying a premium to insure its value becomes a potentially attractive economic proposition.

We expand on these five questions for asset allocation against "economic, going-concern pension liabilities" in Exhibit 1.

PENSION PLAN SPONSORS AND THE "ECONOMIC GOING-CONCERN LIABILITY" FRAMEWORK

When the pension investment problem shifts from a termination context to a long-term, ongoing context, some interesting things happen. "Risk" measured by the exposure of the "termination surplus" (plan assets in excess of the plan termination liability) to changes in long-term bond yields (i.e., the "termination" formulation) is no longer relevant.

"Risk" now is related to *anticipated* real return experience. On a 3% real return, a 16% payroll contribution rate might be needed to support plan benefit payments equal to 70% of final earnings, and maintained in real terms over the life of the pensioner. But if a 6% real return is earned, the required contribution rate might be halved — into the 8% area. Thus, real return uncertainty translates directly into "contribution rate risk."

Who bears this "contribution rate risk"? That depends very much on what the pension "deal" is between the employer and the employees. In a fully indexed, non-contributory "pure" defined benefit plan, which is being funded with, say, a 16% of payroll contribution rate, "contribution rate risk" is fully borne by the employer.

If the pension fund earns a 3% real rate of return, there will be a long-term balance between plan assets and plan (economic, going-concern) liabilities. If the fund earns more, assets grow faster than liabilities and the contribution rate can fall below 16%. If the fund earns less, assets grow slower than liabilities, and the contribution rate must rise above 16%.[14]

WHAT IS THE "GOING-CONCERN PENSION DEAL"?

What about more typical private sector cases where, for example, a final earnings formula (possibly up to 50% of final pay) ensures pre-retirement indexation, but post-retirement indexation is *"ad hoc"* and is not explic-

---

[14]This leverage of the long-term real return on assets on the required contribution rate reflects the long duration of "economic going-concern" pension liabilities: duration in excess of 20 years is not uncommon. The numbers used are illustrative only. PC-based pension liability valuation systems now exist to do such calculations for specific plans in minutes, if not seconds.

EXHIBIT 1
FIVE ASSET ALLOCATION CONSIDERATIONS

Consideration	*Commentary*
1. Long-Term Capital-Market Prospects	• Are there reasons to believe the historical structure of risk premiums will/will not be paid in the future? How do our views on this impact our choice of normal asset mix policy?
2. The "Going-Concern Deal"	• How are pension fund gains (i.e., return in excess of the risk-free long-term liability discount rate) to be distributed between the plan sponsor and plan beneficiaries? What about pension fund losses (i.e., return shortfalls)? • What do the answers to these questions tell us about how aggressive an asset mix policy to adopt?
3. The "Termination Deal"	• While we plan to run the business and the fund as going-concerns, there are a number of possible windup scenarios (i.e., conversion to a money purchase plan, corporate takeover/reorganization, bankruptcy). Will we *really* only pay plan members the absolute legal minimum? Or do we have a contract (explicit or implicit) to pay more? • How does this "more" manifest itself? As the absolute legal minimum plus a share of the termination surplus? As an expected inflation-related or "excess interest"-related increment to the legal minimum?
4. Fluctuations in the Value of Plan Assets and Liabilities	• Are shorter-term fluctuations in the economic (i.e., "real") value of plan assets and plan liabilities of major concern to us? If yes, why? What about fluctuations in the *accounting* value of assets and liabilities? If yes, why?
5. Degree of Business and Plan Integration	• We realize that full integration would have the pension fund invested in the most heavily taxed securities, with whatever offsets are needed on the main business balance sheet to give us the integrated asset/liability structure we want. • Are we prepared to live with the potential consequences of full integration (i.e., strange-looking non-integrated main business and pension balance sheets, possibly inquiries from the tax authorities and rating agencies)?

itly being pre-funded? Is the amount by which pensions are updated now dependent on pension fund performance? If there *is* a connection, you have a risk-sharing situation between the plan sponsor and plan members.

What about arrangements where the employer and the employees have agreed to split contributions, say 50%/50%, regardless of whether they amount to 5%, 10%, or 20% of pay? Now a risk-sharing situation exists *explicitly*. Thus, the plan member's risk exposure, like that of the plan sponsor, could also be in the form of contribution rate uncertainty, or it could be more direct in the form of real benefit payments uncertainty.[15]

This discussion on the nature of the pension "deal" is not peripheral, but in fact central to the pension fund asset allocation question. Probably the most fundamental requirement in the investment management profession is the "Know Your Client" rule. The obvious extension of this rule in the case of employer pension plans is to identify the financial risks and rewards inherent in any defined benefit pension arrangement and how they are to be shared by stakeholders.

From the perspective of framing an asset mix policy, there is ideally only one stakeholder: either the plan sponsor (i.e., the pure defined benefit plan case) or the plan member (i.e., the asset-based plan case). With either, it is clear who the "client" is. If the "pension deal" involves some sharing of investment and inflation-related gains and losses between these two parties, the determination of an appropriate asset mix policy must reflect this reality.

AN ASSET ALLOCATION CHECKLIST

To systematically analyze the sometimes conflicting forces impacting on long-term pension fund asset allocation, a checklist is useful. The checklist in Exhibit 2 addresses four of the five key going-concern asset allocation questions we posed above. For the sake of realism, both a private sector plan sponsor and a public sector plan sponsor are repre-

---

[15]Once one begins to study what actual pension "deals" exist between specific employers and their current and inactive employees, the popular notion that there are only two possible "deals" between them (i.e., pure defined benefit or pure defined contribution) shatters very quickly. There are in fact many "deals." Unfortunately, employers and employees don't always have the same view of what the "deal" is. Even more unfortunately, rather than solving disputes through arbitration or even the courts, politicians are sometimes brought into these disputes. If this involvement ends up constraining the range of compensation formula options open to employers and employees by law, economic efficiency will suffer. This problem is compounded because the government is typically not only the lawmaker, but also a large employer itself.

EXHIBIT 2
ASSET ALLOCATION CHECKLIST

I. THE "GOING-CONCERN DEAL"

ALPHA

- benefit accruals formally indexed, pre-retirement up to 50% of final pay . . . "*ad hoc*" post-retirement (60% of CPI is target) updates . . . no explicit tie between pension fund performance and inflation updates

- the plan is non-contributory and is being funded on a 7.5%/6.0% basis (investment return/wage growth), leading to an 8% "normal" contribution rate . . . inflation updates do not increase the contribution rate unless the updated funding target exceeds the value of plan assets . . . contribution rate reduced if plan assets exceed funding target by a certain percentage

PSRS

- benefit accruals formally indexed, pre-retirement up to 70% of final pay . . . post retirement updates tied to pension fund performance (return in excess of 3% becomes inflation update subject to a 100% of CPI upper bound and a 0% of CPI lower bound)

- the plan is contributory (50%/50%), and is being funded on a 3.0%/1.5% (investment return/wage growth) basis, leading to a 20% "normal" contribution rate . . . this contribution rate is adjusted up or down depending on plan economic funded status (i.e., plan assets at market, plan liabilities estimated on a 3.0%/1.5% return/salary increase basis)

II. THE "TERMINATION DEAL"

ALPHA

- in a voluntary plan termination situation, ALPHA would offer plan members the better of two calculations—the present value of projected benefits calculated on a 7.5% basis for inactive liabilities and a 7.5%/6.0% basis for actives . . . the alternative calculation for actives is the accumulated value of contributions, credited the risk-free rate of interest . . . ALPHA would own any asset surplus or owe any asset deficiency

PSRS

- this situation has not been explicitly contemplated . . . any termination settlement would have to be negotiated between the government and the unions involved (such negotiations would likely lead to a settlement based on the 3.0%/1.5% experience assumptions basis, with any asset surplus or deficiency split 50%/50%)

EXHIBIT 2
ASSET ALLOCATION CHECKLIST *(continued)*

III. ASSET AND LIABILITY VALUE FLUCTUATIONS

ALPHA

- ALPHA recognizes that on a going-concern economic basis, it should include a 2.5% (i.e., 60% of 4%) inflation factor, implying the use of 5.0%/3.5% experience assumptions to estimate the going-concern economic liability . . . plan assets will fluctuate depending on their sensitivity to changes in economic expectations and capital market psychology

- ALPHA's management is satisfied that the new accounting rules can be employed in such a way that the financial status of its retirement system can be represented in an unbiased way, and that through the available smoothing mechanisms no year-to-year surprises will be encountered

PSRS

- calculated on a 3.0%/1.5% basis, the going-concern liability will progress smoothly over time . . . plan assets will fluctuate depending on their sensitivity to changes in economic expectations and capital market psychology

- the new private sector accounting rules are irrelevant to the PSRS situation . . . however, asset value smoothing will be used for disclosure and contribution rate calculation purposes

IV. MAIN BUSINESS/PENSION PLAN PLANNING AND BALANCE SHEET INTEGRATION

ALPHA

- ALPHA wants to focus on "cashflow integration" rather than "tax structure integration"—in other words, it does not want to have to make extra contributions when it is least able to do so (i.e., liabilities rising faster than expected as the value of plan assets and corporate earnings are falling)

PSRS

- Government is interested in the correlation between tax revenues and the required pension plan contribution . . . it wants to avoid the need to make extra contributions at a time when tax revenues are falling (i.e., as tax revenues are falling, and plan assets are falling, plan liabilities are rising faster than expected)

EXHIBIT 2
ASSET ALLOCATION CHECKLIST (*continued*)

- ALPHA understands the tax arbitrage argument but has decided not to "plan" it—in other words, it has decided not to reshuffle corporate and pension assets and liabilities between the main business and pension plan balance sheets, mainly because such activity would signal the corporation is engaged in a not-easy-to-explain form of gaming the tax authorities and because it believes financial analysts and rating agencies mi ht misinterpret such moves

- the tax arbitrage consideration is irrelevant in the PSRS context unless the issuance of tax-exempt bonds is a realistic option

sented: the former on behalf of the ALPHA Corporation pension plan (a
pure defined benefit case), the latter on behalf of the PSRS (Public Sector
Retirement System, a shared risk defined benefit case).[16] Neither plan
sponsor is real, but their situations are realistic. We address the "capital
market prospects" question separately later in the chapter.

The Checklist Responses: Implication for Asset Mix Policy

The checklist responses contain strong messages for asset mix policy. If
the ALPHA and PSRS responses are representative for private and public
sector plan sponsors,[17] the implications are:

1. The long-term nature of pension fund investing is confirmed in
    the sense that the primary planning mode is "ongoing," rather than
    "termination." A corollary is that any segmentation of the liabilities
    into "retired lives" and "actives" is unnecessary and possibly even
    misleading.[18]
2. Investment risk, whether viewed in its "ongoing" or "termination"
    dimensions, has a "real" rather than "nominal" focus because pen-
    sion benefits have a "real" rather than a "nominal" focus:
    a. in its "ongoing" dimension, risk relates to the impact of low or
        negative real returns on future contribution rates
    b. in its "termination" dimension, risk relates to the volatility of
        the market value of pension assets in relation to the settlement
        value of the pension liability...this liability will *not* necessarily

---

[16]Readers wanting more detail on ALPHA Corporation are referred to my book *Pension
Funds and the Bottom Line*. We believe its pension "deal" to be quite reflective of many actual
U.S. and Canadian private sector pension "deals." The reason for introducing a public sector
employer separately is to show that this pension "deal" may be quite different than in the
private sector. While the actual "deal" described is hypothetical, it in fact reflects that of at
least two large Canadian public sector employer pension plans quite closely.

[17]We have already indicated that we believe they are. See footnotes 10 and 15.

[18]Active lives/retired lives segmentation was of course central to the "retired lives immunization" wave that swept the pension industry in the mid-1980s. For "retired lives immunization" to make economic sense, one of two conditions must hold: (1) the plan sponsor must
be willing to discharge its obligation to inactive plan members through the purchase of
annuities, or (2) the plan sponsor must be certain that pensions-in-pay will never be adjusted
for actual inflation experience. In fact, while we are not aware of precise statistics on the
prevalence of these conditions, the vast majority of plan sponsors have *not* bought their way
out of their retired lives obligations, and the vast majority of plan sponsors *do* provide
inflation-related updates to pensions-in-pay.

be sensitive to changes in nominal interest rates, depending on the nature of the "termination" deal

c. in either dimension, risks may be *shared* rather than borne by either the plan sponsor or the plan members

3. Despite the long-term nature of pension fund investing, shorter term changes in the economic going-concern balance sheet matter because:

a. such changes trigger changes in contribution rates and hence the disposition of future stakeholder (i.e., plan sponsor, plan member, or both) cashflows

b. such changes affect the value of the plan sponsor's own securities and hence its cost of debt and equity capital

c. if there *is* a plan termination, settlement could be related to the economic rather than the legal termination liability.

4. There is a strong basis for looking at the relationship between the nature and source of sponsor cashflows and pension fund returns. For example, if sponsor cashflows are negatively affected by changes in the inflation rate, that is all the more reason to invest in inflation hedges in the pension fund. Conversely, if sponsor cashflows are more negatively impacted by economic recession, more emphasis should go to putting recession hedges in the pension fund.

CAPITAL MARKETS PROSPECTS

Capital market prospects matter in the "economic going-concern" planning context because this context recognizes that ongoing pension benefit payments can come from only two sources: (1) contributions into the pension funds and (2) investment earnings on those contributions. Further, the more there is of the latter, the less there has to be of the former. We suggest above, for example, that an incremental 300 basis points of pension funds return could *halve* required contribution rate for a typical defined benefit pension plan. For a well-funded plan, the impact can be even more dramatic.

What *are* reasonable long-term capital market prospects today? Answers to this question always reflect a blend of historical experience, the structure of capital markets yields and prices at the point in time the question is posed, and any forward-looking judgments the forecaster is prepared to make at that point in time. The numbers in Exhibit 3 reflect "equilibrium" long-term capital markets prospects in the spirit of the work done by Ibbotson, Siegel, Brinson, Diermeier, Schlarbaum, et. al. We have been updating long-term return projections of this type for a number of years now. The Exhibit 3 figures come from our most recent study.[19]

Capital Market Prospect Implications

On a prospective returns basis, equity-oriented investments should permit a pension plan to meet its obligations with the lowest contribution rate over the long run. However, we noted above that in a going-concern mode, downdrafts in pension plan asset values still matter. Such downdrafts can lead to higher contribution rates, can affect the value of plan sponsor securities (and hence its cost of capital) and decrease the benefit security of plan members.

EXHIBIT 3
LONG-TERM REAL RETURN PROSPECTS

	Long-Term Real Return Implications
1. *Common Stocks* are not likely to repeat their extraordinary performance from the mid-1920s to the early 1990s, with dividend yields today averaging 3.0%. With these yields and real GNP growth averaging 2.5%, a realistic prospect is:	5.5%
2. *Long Bonds* by contrast offer, with 8% yields and a realistic 4% inflation expectation, historically high real return prospects:	4%
3. *Bills,* with relatively high global capital demands and relatively disciplined monetary policies, also offer historically high real return prospects:	1.5%

[19]For a fully developed set of capital markets expectations using this history/current prices/forward-looking judgments blend, see Gary P. Brinson, Jeffrey J. Diermeier, and Gary G. Schlarbaum, "A Composite Portfolio Benchmark for Pension Plans," *Financial Analysts Journal,* March/April 1986; and Roger Ibbotson and Laurence Siegel, "The World Market Wealth Portfolio," *Journal of Portfolio Management,* Winter 1983. The Exhibit 3 figures come from *The Ambachtsheer Letter #47,* February 1991.

When are diversified portfolios of equity investments most likely to suffer material downward revisions in value? Possibly during periods of high stock valuation followed by a major decline in economic activity; likely a time when inflation rates are falling, long-term interest rates on high quality bonds are falling and hence the prices of those bonds are rising. *Thus, in a going-concern mode, the rationale for high-quality bonds is not immunization, but to fund capital value and create income protection during periods of sharply falling equity values and equity-related earnings.*

For example, $1 invested in stocks at the beginning of 1929 would have been worth about 50 cents five years later (including the reinvestment of all dividends).[20] Over the same five-year period, $1 invested in long Treasury bonds would have increased to $1.20. Consumer prices fell 23% over the same time period. Thus despite the terrible fall in stock prices, a diversified stock-bond investment policy (say 50-50, or even 60–40) would have kept a pension fund whole in real terms over the 1929–1933 period.

BONDS AND INFLATION RISK

While bonds can save a pension fund during unanticipated major declines in economic activity, they can seriously undermine the real value of pension assets and income during prolonged bouts of rising price inflation. For example, $1 invested in long Treasury bonds at the beginning of 1977 was worth 90 cents five years later. But with the CPI rising 62% over the same time period, the loss in real terms was far greater than just 10 cents. While stocks did considerably better than bonds over the high inflation 1977–1981 period, they too earned a negative real return over this five-year period (–2.0% annualized versus –11.1% for bonds).

It was this experience that led pension funds to investigate and begin to invest in such direct inflation-hedge investments as real estate, oil and

---

[20]All return and inflation data came from the Ibbotson Associates database.

gas, gold and venture capital. Of course, the 1980s have demonstrated such investments do not perform nearly as well in disinflationary times.[21]

A FORWARD-LOOKING ASSET MIX POLICY

It has been observed that those who do not learn from history are bound to repeat it. In our context, that means understanding that while it is important to identify the capital market environment most likely to shape prospective stock, bond, and bill returns, that is not enough. It is also necessary to ask what could go wrong. The answer is that in modern economies, there is always the potential for achieving too little output over extended periods of time, or of experiencing too much inflation. In this regard, the 1929–1933 and 1977–1981 five-year episodes have much to teach us.

Exhibit 4 sets out what we believe to be realistic stock, bond, and bill real return prospects for the next five years. It does so not only for what we believe to be the dominant economic theme in the first half of the 1990s, namely "Degearing," but also for the other two possibilities: "Deflation" and "Reinflation." In addition to the three 100% policies, we also show the real return implications for 60-40-0, 50-50-0, 40-40-20 stocks-bonds-bills policies.[22]

EXHIBIT 4
REAL RETURN PROSPECTS IN THE 1990s

	"Degearing"	"Deflation"	"Reinflation"
Stocks	5.5%	−8.0%	−2.5%
Bonds	4.0%	8.8%	−4.5%
Bills	1.5%	1.0%	1.5%
60-40-0	4.9%	−1.3%	−3.3%
40-40-20	4.1%	0.5%	−2.5%

[21]Our observations, of course, relate to the underlying covariance structures of real rates of return. If covariance structures shift with changes in economic eras (from a period of rising inflation to deflation, for example), covariance statistics generated over periods which include more than one such era will have no predicted content. We believe that much can be learned by carefully studying actual capital markets behavior within pre-defined periods of economic history and, conversely, by studying the economic environment during pre-defined periods of capital markets history.

[22]These projections come from "The Capital Markets of the 1990s as History," and "The Capital Markets of the 1990s: Two Rough Roads We Might Travel," *The Ambachtsheer Letter*, issues #47 and #48, February and March 1991.

Exhibit 4 prompts the following observations:

1. Against a benchmark real return of 3%, bills offer the least return uncertainty. However, they are not likely to produce the 3% benchmark real rate of real returns.
2. Stocks and bonds will likely do better than 3% in the base "Degearing" case. However, stocks will do very poorly in "Deflation" and bonds will do very poorly in "Reinflation."
3. Long Treasury bonds will likely be good hedges in "Deflation." Thus, only a 10 percentage point shift of stocks to bonds (i.e., from 60-40-0 to 50-50-0) moves the projected "Deflation" real return into positive territory.
4. Neither stocks nor bonds are expected to do well in a "Reinflation" scenario. Naturally, investing part of the fund in bills helps, but at a potentially high opportunity cost should "Reinflation" not come to pass. This provides strong motivation to search for "Reinflation" protection with a lower opportunity cost. There is no shortage of possibilities. The UK and now the Canadian governments issue real return bonds. These issues are currently priced to produce real (local currency) returns in the 4–5% range. Domestic stocks could be tilted towards inflation protection stocks. Both the stock and bond holdings could be diversified internationally, thus hedging against a domestic-only "Reinflation" scenario. Modest exposures to real estate and gold could be maintained. With a carefully researched and planned program it is not unrealistic to expect that the "Reinflation" real return outcome can also be raised above zero.[23]
5. Effectively then, it would appear that in real return terms the realistic asset mix choices lie between 60-40-0 and 40-60-0, implying about a 5% prospective real return in "Degearing" and zero to marginally positive real returns in "Deflation" and "Reinflation." Where a sponsor chooses to be in that range (and also what mix of specific assets the sponsor selects) will depend on such factors as the assessed respective likelihoods of "Deflation" and "Reinflation," the sponsor's own likely economic condition through each of these two scenarios, the perceived inflation-sensitivity of the economic going-concern pension liabilities, and the

---

[23]Each of these possibilities has been examined in various issues of *The Ambachtsheer Letter* over the course of 1992.

potential accounting and funding consequences of the chosen asset mix policy.

Where will the ALPHA Corporation Pension Plan and the Public Service Retirement System position themselves in the 60-40-0 to 40-40-20 asset mix policy range? We turn to this question next.

DELIBERATIONS AT ALPHA CORPORATION

ALPHA's plan is a pure non-contributory defined benefit pension plan. Appropriately then, plan governance is under the control of ALPHA Corporation, with its management required to behave prudently and to have due regard for their obligation to maintain plan solvency. Exhibit 5 details their asset mix policy deliberations

EXHIBIT 5
ALPHA CORPORATION PENSION PLAN

The Asset Allocation Checklist

I.   *The "Going-Concern Deal"*
   - The plan as a "final earnings"-based benefit formula and ALPHA have a long history of providing *ad hoc* inflation updates averaging 60% of CPI. These two factors together suggest ALPHA should look at risk and return in real terms on the asset side of the balance sheet.
   - The plan is non-contributory, and there is no ambiguity that good investment results lead directly to lower plan contributions by the employer, just as bad investment results will lead to higher contributions by the employer.
II. *The "Terminal Deal"*
   - In any plan termination other than corporate bankruptcy, the "settlement value" of accrued pensions would be above the "legal termination liability" and would not fluctuate in line with fluctuations in long bond values and yields. The probability of plan termination is judged to be very low.
III. *Asset and Liability Value Fluctuations*
   - ALPHA management deems the "economic going-concern" balance sheet to be the one which will guide their asset mix policy decision. The plan now has about a 15% "going-concern" asset cushion (of course, its "legal termination" asset cushion is considerably larger). ALPHA policy is to increase the corporate contribution rate if the "going-concern" cushion goes negative.

EXHIBIT 5
ALPHA CORPORATION PENSION PLAN (*continued*)

- ALPHA management is well aware that it might be appropriate or even necessary to report different asset and liability numbers to the regulatory authorities and in its financial statements. These numbers will likely be a smoothed blend of the "legal termination" and "economic going-concern" balance sheets.

IV. *Degree of Main Business/Pension Plan Decisions Integration*
- The key question for management here is whether ALPHA's main business would fare worse in the deflation or rising inflation scenario (if one was decidedly worse for ALPHA than the other, it would be logical to "buy" protection against it in the pension fund). After considerable deliberation, they decided the main business would be equally hurt by deflation or rising inflation—assuming the latter brought with it significant increases in real labor costs. Also, they decided they were not prepared to guess whether one scenario was more likely to occur than the other. In conclusion, they decided they would *not* bias their asset mix policy decision due to either consideration.
- Management also decided not to engage in any pension plan tax arbitrage by reshuffling main business and pension plan assets and liabilities in an attempt to reduce corporate taxes payable.

V. *Capital Markets Prospects*
- The projected long-term incremental return from equity investments in relation to long-term debt investments is currently modest by historical standards.
- Reasonable protection against "Deflation" and "Reinflation" can be engineered through the intelligent use of alternate domestic and non-domestic asset classes.

The Asset Mix Policy Decision

Despite its going-concern focus and a healthy "going-concern" balance sheet, Alpha Corporation pension plan trustees do not believe equity investments currently promise sufficient long-term rewards to favor them heavily over long-term debt investments in the pension fund asset mix policy. This is confirmed by projecting the pension plan balance sheet forward and examining the funding and accounting consequences of alternate asset mix policies in the three scenarios. Accordingly, the chosen policy asset mix is 50-50-0. The trustees devote considerable research resources to see how best to ensure the fund earns positive real rates of return in the "Deflation" and "Reinflation" scenarios as well.

AT THE PUBLIC SECTOR RETIREMENT SYSTEM

Unlike the ALPHA Corporation situation, investment risks and rewards are shared in the Public Sector Retirement System. They are shared by the taxpaying public, active public sector employees and inactive/retired public sector employees. The composition of the Board of Trustees reflects this risk-sharing reality. Exhibit 6 sets out their asset mix policy deliberations.

EXHIBIT 6
PUBLIC SECTOR RETIREMENT SYSTEM

THE ASSET ALLOCATION CHECKLIST

I. *The "Going-Concern Deal"*
   - The pension plan has a "final earnings"-based formula. The plan also has a post-retirement inflation update formula tied to pension fund performance (return in excess of 3% becomes the inflation update subject to a 100% of CPI upper bound and a 0% of CPI lower bound). Thus, risk and return should be analyzed in both nominal and real terms on the asset side of the balance sheet.
   - Plan contributions are shared 50%/50% by the employer and active employees. Thus, through the contribution formula and through the link between inflation updates and pension fund performance, all stakeholders share in both good and poor investment performance.

II. *The "Terminal Deal"*
   - There is no formal agreement in place as to what would happen in case of a plan termination. But with the best estimate of the "going-concern" liability outstripping the value of plan assets by 30%, negotiations would surely focus on how much the "settlement value" of the benefits exceeded the value of plan assets. But with no intent on the part of the employer to terminate, all this is very hypothetical.

III. *Asset and Liability Fluctuations*
   - With the liability being calculated on a 3% discount rate basis, it will progress smoothly (assuming a steady-state plan membership size and composition) over time. The plan asset value in relation to this "economic going-concern" liability value is material because the gap between the two affects the contribution rate. The "normal" contribution rate is 16% of pay. But the *actual* current contribution rate is 20% (10% each for the employer and the employees) of pay, reflecting the amortization of the sizable unfunded past service liability. Poor investment experience would widen the asset-liability gap further, further increasing the required contribution rate for the employer and active employees.

EXHIBIT 6
PUBLIC SECTOR RETIREMENT SYSTEM *(continued)*

- Poor investment experience also affects pensioners. If the nominal fund return is below 3%, pensioners get no inflation update regardless of what the actual inflation rate was over the measurement period. Pensions-in-pay are updated for inflation experience by the amount fund returns exceed 3%, up to a maximum of 100% of CPI. Thus, possible asset mix policy choices have to be tested for impact on inflation updates to pensioners.*

IV. *Degree of Government/Pension Plan Decisions Integration*
- In assessing if deflation and rising inflation would be equally problematic "bad news" scenarios for the government (i.e., the plan sponsor in this case), the decision was "No." Deflation would decidedly be the worst of these two bad worlds. In this scenario, the government would be faced with falling tax revenues and rising demands in its financial resources, while still being obliged to make interest payments on its outstanding high-coupon long-term debt.
- While active employees feel they would be equally hurt by a rising contribution rate in the two "bad news" outcomes, pensioners fear the rising inflation scenario more. It is in this scenario they run the risk that pension fund returns won't be adequate to protect the real value of their pension.

V. *Capital Markets Prospects*
- While the prospective long-term 6% real rate of return associated with the 100% equity-oriented policy is very attractive, the consequences of a deflation outcome with this policy are unacceptable to the employer (i.e., the government). The government believes the plan has to trade off some long-term return for better deflation protection by lowering equity exposure and increasing long bond exposure.

---

*There is an interesting debate in progress on this question of how to best provide formal inflation protection for retired plan members. One school would tie the formula directly to the CPI. The other would, as in the PSRS example, tie it to capital market returns. The argument here is that pensioners should also bear at least some of the risk associated with formally (as opposed to *ad hoc*) providing inflation protection.

The Asset Mix Policy Decision

After some simulation with alternate asset mix policies in the three economic scenarios, the trustees of PSRS judge the respective interests of active plan members, retired plan members and taxpayers are best balanced with a 60-40-0 mix, with two caveats. First, of the 60% in equity-oriented investments, at least 20% should be devoted to maximizing the probability that a positive return is achieved should the "Reinflation" scenario unfold. Second, the "normal" duration of the bond portfolio should be as long as possible. The expectation is that with this policy, the required contribution rate will eventually settle well below the "current service cost" contribution rate of 16% calculated on a 3% real return basis. At the same time, PSRS will be able to ride out bouts of the kind of adverse performance that a "Deflation" or "Reinflation" scenario would bring.

ASSET ALLOCATION DECISION DETAILS

There is more to ALPHA's and PSRS's asset mix policy decisions than appears in Exhibits 5 and 6. For example, the degree of "give" in the policies will have to be decided, with special emphasis on whether any attempt is to be made to shift the asset mix based on shorter-term market anticipations. If the answer is "Yes," the double question, "Who will do it and with how much money," will require a lot of careful study. Other chapters in this book study these questions in detail.[24]

Another important consideration is the plan's likely evolving liquidity needs. Even in a "going-concern" mode, material changes in the size and composition of plan membership, and in the relationship between money flowing into the plan and out of the plan, can take place. Such potential changes also need careful study. It is not acceptable for a pension plan to have the perfect long-term asset mix policy but not to be able to write checks when it has to because it has no cash!

THE IMPORTANCE OF INTEGRATION

This chapter has placed pension fund asset allocation in a broader economic context. This context forces consideration of the nature of the

---

[24]Much has been written about the distinction between the establishment of a "normal" asset mix policy (the subject of this chapter) and tactical asset allocation or market timing. See, for example, Chapters 3, 4 and 7. The point made here is that market timing should not be confused with deciding on target asset mix policy weights in the context of investing against "economic going-concern" pension liabilities.

pension "deal" between the employer and its current and former employees. It also forces a decision as to which of the two possible planning modes, "termination" or "going-concern" is to dominate the asset mix policy decision.

In a "termination" planning mode, a classic bond immunization strategy is a feasible policy option. Interestingly, such a strategy, on a different level, also immunizes any possible economic interaction between a plan sponsor's main business and its pension "business."

A "going-concern" planning mode recognizes that, unless the pension plan really *is* shut down, the pension fund is an ongoing "money spinner" which helps to finance pension obligations when they fall due. As this chapter has shown, pension fund asset allocation decisions in this latter context become, for plan sponsors, important *financial policy decisions*. Hence, they can no longer be made in isolation. They *must* be integrated into the plan sponsor's overall financial strategy.

CHAPTER 7

Policy Asset Mix, Tactical Asset Allocation, and Portfolio Insurance*

WILLIAM F. SHARPE
TIMKEN PROFESSOR EMERITUS OF FINANCE
GRADUATE SCHOOL OF BUSINESS
STANFORD UNIVERSITY

Previous chapters in this section have discussed methods for choosing a policy asset mix. Such procedures, sometimes termed "strategic asset allocation," have been used for well over a decade. Section Three of this book deals with approaches to tactical asset allocation. These, too, have been in use for several years (initially, under the title "market timing models"). Section Two discusses surplus management, optimization, and portfolio insurance methods, the most recent in the list of procedures for asset allocation.

This chapter is intended to help the reader understand the similarities and differences among these methods. It does so by providing an over-

*Much of this chapter is taken from William F. Sharpe, "Integrated Asset Allocation," *Financial Analysts Journal*, September/October 1987. I am grateful to the Financial Analysts' Federation for permission to publish it here.

view of a general approach to asset allocation — one that subsumes the traditional procedures as special cases. We begin with a description of the overall approach, termed *Integrated Asset Allocation*. Next we discuss alternative objectives for asset allocation analyses. Since many studies are limited to two asset classes, we treat such cases in some detail. Finally, we describe the three traditional types of asset allocation analysis.

INTEGRATED ASSET ALLOCATION

Exhibit 1 shows the major steps involved in asset allocation. Boxes on the left are concerned with the capital markets. Those on the right are specific to an investor. Those in the middle bring together aspects of the capital markets and the investor's circumstances to determine the investor's asset mix and its performance. The process begins at the top and proceeds downward. Then it begins all over again.

Box I1 shows the things that matter to an investor — the current values of assets and liabilities and, by implication, net worth. An individual investor's net worth is his or her *wealth*; a pension fund's net worth is the plan *surplus*.

Net worth will generally determine an investor's current tolerance for risk, shown in box I3. The relationship between the investor's circumstances (box I1) and risk tolerance (box I3) can be portrayed by a *risk tolerance function*. It is shown in box I2.

Box C1 shows the current state of the capital markets. Included are such things as current and historic levels of stock and bond indices and past and projected dividends and earnings. Such information provides major inputs for predictions of the expected returns and risks of various asset classes and the correlations among their returns (shown in box C3). Some procedure must be used to translate capital market conditions (box C1) into predictions about asset returns (box C3). It is shown in box C2.

Given an investor's risk tolerance (box I3) and predictions concerning asset expected returns, risks and correlations (box C3), an *optimizer* can be employed to determine the most appropriate asset mix (box M2). Depending on such things as the number of assets, the optimizer (shown in box M1) could be a simple rule of thumb, a mathematical function, or a full-scale quadratic program.

Box M3 shows actual returns. Given the investor's asset mix at the *beginning* of a period (box M2), the asset returns during the period (box

EXHIBIT 1
INTEGRATED ASSET ALLOCATION

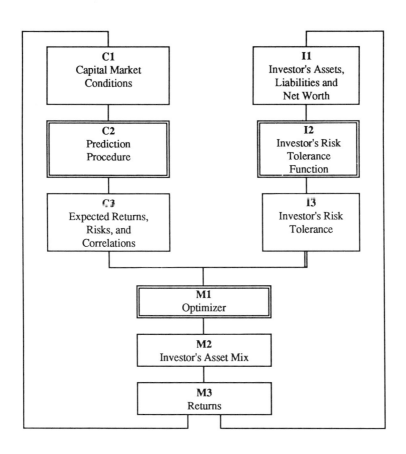

M3) determine the values of the investor's assets at the beginning of the *next* period. And, given the nature of the investor's liabilities at the beginning of a period, changes in capital markets (including returns on fixed-income obligations) and accrual of new obligations determine the investor's liabilities at the beginning of the next period. Returns in one period thus influence the investor's assets, liabilities and net worth at the beginning of the next period, as shown by the "feedback loop" from box M3 to box I1.

Returns during a period also constitute part of the overall capital market conditions at the beginning of the next period. This is shown by the feedback loop from box M3 to box C1. As these loops show, the process is a continuing one, with decisions from one period affecting those of the next.

From period to period, any (or all) of the items in boxes C1, C3, I1, I3, M2 and M3 may change. However, items in boxes C2, I2, and M1 should remain fixed, since they contain *decision rules* (procedures). Thus the investor's risk tolerance (box I3) may change, but the risk tolerance *function* (box I2) should not. Predictions concerning returns (box C3) may change, but not the *procedure* (box C2) for making such predictions. The optimal asset mix (box M2) may change, but not the *optimizer* (box M1) that determines it.

Many investors make some or all of the decisions shown in boxes I2, C2 and M1 "by hand" (and/or heuristically). However, in an increasing number of organizations some or all of these procedures have been automated, with decision rules specified in advance, then followed routinely. Portfolio insurance procedures fall clearly in this category, as do certain process-driven tactical asset allocation methods.

Key decisions that must precede any asset allocation analysis concern the choice of asset classes. How many will be considered? How will each be defined? How will current holdings be related to the selected classes? And how will recommended changes in asset holdings be implemented?

In principle, such decisions should be considered as part of the overall design of an asset allocation procedure. In practice, they are often made first, and taken as given when the procedure is designed.

ASSET ALLOCATION OBJECTIVES

To find an optimal asset mix, an optimizer must have an explicit *objective function*. Typically this involves the risk and expected value of some key attribute. In an integrated asset allocation analysis, the attribute is the investor's *net worth* at some future date. Optimization thus deals with *expected future net worth* and the *standard deviation of future net worth*.

Traditional analyses also concentrate on the value of the investor's *assets* at some point in the future. So, optimization also deals with the *expected return* and *standard deviation of return* on current *assets*.

The nature of the objective function must also be reflected in the measure of risk tolerance, which indicates the investor's willingness to accept greater risk in order to obtain a greater expected reward. In many analyses, risk tolerance is typically concerned with the tradeoff between expected return and standard deviation of return. In an integrated asset allocation analysis, it measures the investor's willingness to take on added *net worth risk* in order to increase *expected net worth*.

TWO-ASSET ALLOCATION

"Asset only" analyses can be considered special cases of integrated asset allocation in which liabilities equal zero (or are positive, but not subject to uncertainty). The remainder of this chapter will focus on the "asset only" analyses. Many asset allocation analyses conform to these restrictions, and we will discuss such approaches in this context. The chapter appendix analyzes conditions for an optimal asset mix under the general conditions in which multiple asset classes and liabilities are considered.

When only two assets are involved, the relationship between the inputs and the optimal asset mix is particularly simple. Let the assets be S (e.g., stocks) and B (e.g., bonds or bills). As shown in the appendix, the optimal (dollar) amount to be invested in S can be computed as:

$$D_S = k_0 W + k_1 ART$$

where k_0 and k_1 are parameters, W is the investor's current net worth, and ART is his or her *absolute risk tolerance*.

To determine the proportion of assets invested in stocks, both sides of the equation can be divided by W, giving:

$$\frac{D_S}{W} = k_0 + k_1 \frac{ART}{W}$$

The latter ratio is termed the investor's *relative risk tolerance*. Representing this by *RRT*, and using the standard notation X_s to represent the relative amount invested in stocks, gives:

$$X_S = k_0 + k_1 RRT$$

If asset B is riskless, the value of k_0 becomes zero, giving:

$$D_S = k_1 ART$$

and

$$X_S = k_1 RRT$$

The appendix shows that the values of k_0 and k_1 depend on the expected returns and risks of the assets and on the estimated correlation between their returns. Of particular importance is the fact that k_1 is proportional to the difference in expected returns on the two assets:

$$k_1 = \frac{E_S - E_B}{k_2}$$

where k_2 depends (as does k_0) solely on the risks of the two assets and on the estimated correlation between their returns.

To avoid excess notation, no indication of time has been included in the equations. Each value is assumed to be relevant for the single period over which a decision is to be made. As will be seen, traditional approaches to asset allocation make different assumptions concerning the constancy of various aspects of these relationships over time.

CHOOSING A POLICY ASSET MIX

Previous chapters have described key aspects associated with the choice of a policy asset mix. Here, we outline the steps involved in traditional formal approaches to such a decision. Exhibit 2 portrays a typical strategic or policy asset allocation analysis in terms comparable to those used for the more general Integrated Asset Allocation.

Strategic asset allocation studies are usually done episodically (perhaps once every three years). Relatively few asset mixes are considered (e.g., bond/stock combinations with 0%, 10%, 20%, . . . 100% invested in stocks). An analysis (typically using Monte Carlo simulation) is performed to determine the likely range of outcomes associated with each mix. Typical outcomes analyzed are pension contributions over the next five years, pension surplus five years hence, and so on. When the analysis is complete, the investor is asked to examine the ranges of outcomes

EXHIBIT 2
STRATEGIC ASSET ALLOCATION

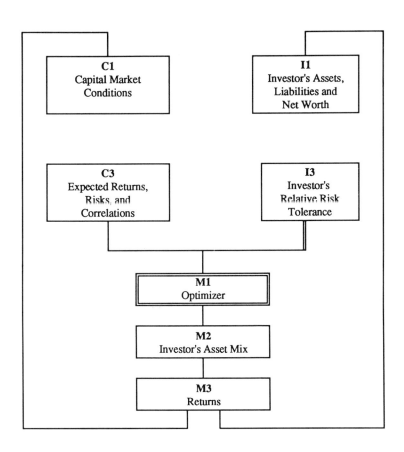

associated with each of the mixes, then choose the preferred one. This constitutes the "policy," "long-run," or "strategic" asset mix.

In the vast majority of such analyses, each mix is expressed in terms of the percentage of total value invested in each asset class. Such an approach can be termed a *constant mix strategy*. It differs from a "buy-and-hold" strategy in that transactions are required to periodically rebalance the mix after market moves change relative asset values. Although liabilities are usually included in the simulation results, no explicit attempt is made to alter the asset mix to take the nature of the liabilities into account.

Policy studies almost always employ "long-run" capital market conditions. In particular, asset expected returns, risks and correlations remain constant throughout the simulation. This is portrayed by the absence of a connection between boxes C1 and C3 in Exhibit 2. Changing capital market conditions from period to period do not influence predictions concerning asset returns.

In the case of two assets, if predictions are constant, the parameters k_0 and k_1 in our equations will remain the same from period to period. Letting the subscript t denote the time period, the equation for the proportion invested in stocks can be written as:

$$X_t = k_0 + k_1 RRT_t$$

For each set of simulations in such a study, the percentage asset mix is held constant. In the case of two assets, this implies that X_t remains the same from period to period. As the equation shows, this can only be optimal if the investor's *relative risk tolerance* is unchanged. This is portrayed by the absence of a connection between boxes I1 and I3 in Exhibit 2 and by the use of the term *relative* risk tolerance in box I3. Changing circumstances from period to period do not influence the investor's (relative) attitude toward risk.

Each of the possible strategies considered in a policy study can be represented by a different level of relative risk tolerance. The smaller the tolerance for risk, the more conservative the asset mix. The analysis is framed in terms of asset mix. However, by selecting one of the constant asset mixes, the investor provides important information about his or her risk tolerance.

TACTICAL ASSET ALLOCATION

Tactical procedures, described in the chapters of Section Three, are applied routinely, as part of continuing asset management. Their goal is to take advantage of inefficiencies in the relative prices of securities in different asset classes. Early tactical asset allocators switched funds between bonds and stocks. Many now use bonds, stocks and cash equivalents, and a few employ multiple asset classes as well as global diversification. Examples can be found in Section Three.

Exhibit 3 portrays a typical tactical asset allocation analysis in terms comparable to those used earlier. Explicitly or implicitly, tactical procedures assume that the investor's relative risk tolerance is unaffected by changes in his or her circumstances. As in Exhibit 2, this is portrayed by the absence of a connection between boxes I1 and I3 and by the use of the term *relative* risk tolerance in box I3.

Tactical changes in asset mix are driven by changes in predictions concerning asset returns. In simpler systems, only predictions of expected returns on stocks and bonds change. In more complex systems, predicted expected returns, risks and even correlations change.

In "two-way" systems, the percent invested in stocks is related linearly to the spread between the expected returns of stocks and bonds. This can be seen to follow directly from the assumed conditions. Given constant estimates of risks and correlation, the parameters k_0 and k_2 in our equations remain the same from period to period. Assuming constant relative risk tolerance, and letting the subscript t denote time, gives:

$$X_{st} = k_0 + \frac{RRT}{k_2} (E_{st} - E_{bt})$$

In practice, tactical asset allocation systems are often "contrarian" in nature. Typically, the expected return on stocks is based on the relationship between the current level of a stock market index and projections of dividends for its component stocks. Variations in projected dividends are usually smaller than the corresponding variations in stock prices. Thus expected returns tend to fall when prices rise, leading to a decrease in stock holdings.

Changes in asset expected returns, risks and correlations would take place in even the most efficient security markets. However, tactical asset allocation procedures typically operate on the assumption that markets overreact to information. In this sense, they base decisions on deviant beliefs, rather than those of the consensus of investors.

PORTFOLIO INSURANCE

Portfolio insurance procedures are described in the chapters in Section Two. They are generally applied routinely, as part of continuing asset management. In principle, they are intended to better adapt long-run results to an investor's objectives, without attempting to "time" the mar-

EXHIBIT 3
TACTICAL ASSET ALLOCATION

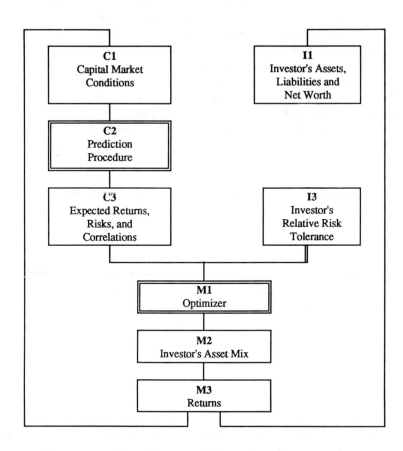

ket. In practice, they are sometimes used for "closet" market timing. We focus here on the principle. Exhibit 4 portrays an insured asset allocation procedure in the terms used earlier.

The earliest forms of portfolio insurance involved dynamic changes in asset allocation designed to replicate effects obtainable with certain option positions. For example, one might replicate the outcomes obtained by holding a portfolio plus a one-year put option written on that portfolio.

EXHIBIT 4
INSURED ASSET ALLOCATION

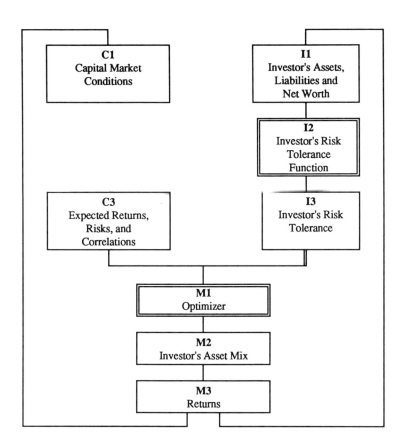

Equivalently, one might replicate the outcomes obtained by holding a one-year Treasury bill plus a one-year call option on the portfolio. In either case, the strike price of the option would represent a floor below which the value of the investor's assets at the specified horizon date should not fall. Such procedures are described in detail in Section Two. We will term an approach of this type *option-based portfolio insurance.*

Most portfolio insurance strategies allocate assets between two major classes (e.g., stocks and Treasury bills). In essence, such an approach provides a rule which relates the appropriate asset mix to the excess of the current value of the investor's net worth over a desired *floor*. The relationship is similar to that shown in Exhibit 5. The horizontal axis plots the current value of the "cushion" (asset value minus floor value) and the vertical axis the dollar amount to be invested in the risky asset (e.g., stocks). In an option-based insurance procedure, the floor at any given time is the present value of the desired floor at the horizon date. When assets fall to that value, nothing is invested in the risky asset. As asset value increases, the amount invested in the risky asset can increase, reaching the total value of the assets as an upper limit.

Option-based portfolio insurance strategies require the amount invested in the risky asset to be a function of both the current value of the asset cushion and the time remaining before the horizon (i.e., the option's expiration date). As the horizon date approaches, the curve relating asset

EXHIBIT 5
OPTION-BASED PORTFOLIO INSURANCE

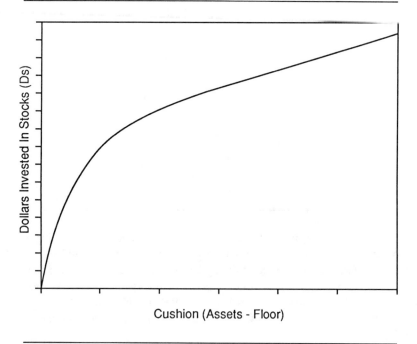

Dollars Invested In Stocks (Ds)

Cushion (Assets - Floor)

mix to the cushion moves. It reaches an extreme just before the horizon in which assets are invested entirely in one class or the other, depending on whether assets are equal to the floor or above it.

Many have objected to this *time-variant* nature of option-based portfolio insurance strategies. In particular, such a characteristic seems inappropriate for an ongoing pension fund with a very long (or infinite) horizon. More recent approaches to portfolio insurance are *time-invariant*. In particular, the curve relating the amount invested in the risky asset to the size of the cushion remains stationary from period to period.

For an important example of a time-invariant approach, see Black and Jones.[1] The foundation on which the approach is based was provided by Merton.[2] Following Perold[3] we will term the approach *constant proportion portfolio insurance* (CPPI). CPPI uses a simple rule of the type shown in Exhibit 6: the dollar amount invested in the risky asset should equal a constant times the size of the cushion (asset value minus floor value), with the constant greater than 1.

Formally, portfolio insurance approaches assume that asset expected returns, risks and correlations remain the same over the period during which the insurance is "in force" (although some *ad hoc* procedures have been developed to deal with unexpected changes in risk). This is portrayed by the absence of a connection between boxes C1 and C3 in Exhibit 4.

While portfolio insurance strategies are normally analyzed in terms of a relationship such as that shown in Exhibit 6, they are motivated by a relationship of the type shown in Exhibit 7. As before, the horizontal axis plots the level of the asset cushion, but the vertical axis now indicates the investor's absolute risk tolerance. Risk tolerance is zero when assets reach the minimum value at which the floor can be assured. As asset value increases, so does the investor's risk tolerance.

The relationship between the decision rule (see Exhibit 6) and the investor's underlying risk tolerance function (see Exhibit 7) is especially

[1]Fischer Black and Robert Jones, "Simplifying Portfolio Insurance," *Journal of Portfolio Management* (Fall 1987).

[2]Robert C. Merton, "Optimum Consumption and Portfolio Rules in a Continuous Time Model," *Journal of Economic Theory*, 3 (1971).

[3]André F. Perold, "Constant Proportion Portfolio Insurance," Harvard Business School, August 1986.

EXHIBIT 6
CONSTANT PROPORTION PORTFOLIO INSURANCE

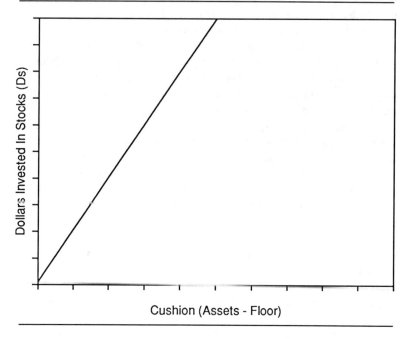

Cushion (Assets - Floor)

straightforward when one of the two assets is riskless. As shown earlier, in such a case:

$$D_S = k_1 ART$$

Thus Exhibits 6 and 7 differ only by the "scaling factor" k_1, since:

$$ART = \frac{D_S}{k_1}$$

Exhibit 7 plots the basis for constant proportion portfolio insurance: the investor's one-period absolute risk tolerance is assumed to be proportional to the size of the asset cushion. Merton[4] showed that such a policy is optimal if the investor's overall utility function displays linear

[4]Merton, "Optimum Consumption and Portfolio Rules in a Continuous Time Model," *Journal of Economic Theory*, 3, 1971.

EXHIBIT 7
A LINEAR RISK TOLERANCE FUNCTION

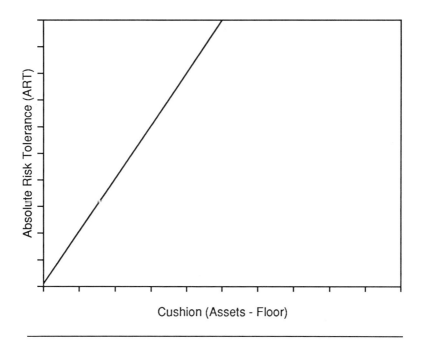

Cushion (Assets - Floor)

absolute risk tolerance relative to wealth at a specific horizon date or relative to consumption at many dates.

Different portfolio insurance approaches imply different relationships of the type shown in Exhibit 7. Some are time-variant; some are not. Some give linear relationships; some do not. However, all can be viewed as implicit specifications of the investor's *risk tolerance function*.[5]

CONCLUSIONS

As shown throughout this book, asset allocation is typically the most important task an investor undertakes. Other chapters document the ex-

---

[5]Further analysis of such relationships is provided in André F. Perold and William F. Sharpe, "Dynamic Strategies for Asset Allocation," *Financial Analysts Journal,* January/February 1988.

tensive effort devoted to the development and application of procedures for policy, tactical, and insured asset allocation. However, much of this work has been unnecessarily limited in scope.

As understanding of the interrelationships in this crucial area increases, the somewhat fragmented analyses can be expected to give way to a more complete approach. Investors, investment managers and those who provide investment services share one goal: to *integrate* all aspects of asset allocation.

APPENDIX: CONDITIONS FOR AN OPTIMAL ASSET MIX

Assume that an investor's utility is related to net worth at the end of a relatively short decision period by the function:

$$U = f(W)$$

where W represents net worth at the end of the period.

Pratt[6] defines *absolute risk aversion* as:

$$ARA = -\frac{d^2U/dW^2}{dU/dW}$$

The reciprocal is termed *absolute risk tolerance:*

$$ART = -\frac{dU/dW}{d^2U/dW^2}$$

Since the time period is short, the range of possible values of W will be small. And, over a small range of values of W, the investor's actual utility function can be adequately approximated by another function displaying constant absolute risk tolerance. Such a function can be written as:

$$U = 1 - e^{-cW}$$

with:

$$ART = \frac{1}{c}$$

Since the time period is short, changes in net worth can typically be assumed to follow a normal distribution without excessive loss of precision.

Following Von Neumann and Morgenstern,[7] assume that the investor's objective is to maximize expected utility of wealth. As shown by Lint-

---

[6]John W. Pratt, "Risk Aversion in the Small and in the Large," *Econometrica,* January–April, 1964.

[7]J. Von Neumann and O. Morgenstern, *Theory of Games and Economic Behavior,* 3rd Ed. Princeton University Press, 1953.

ner,[8] if returns are normally distributed and the investor has constant absolute risk tolerance, expected utility can be written as:

$$EU = -e^{-c(E_w - \frac{c}{2}V_w)}$$

To make this as large as possible, one should maximize:

$$E_w - \frac{c}{2}V_w$$

or:

$$E_w - \frac{1}{2ART}V_w$$

where E_w and V_w are the expected value and variance of end-of-period wealth, respectively.

Assume that the investor's current wealth is W_0. Let R_i be asset i's *value-relative:* the ratio of end-of-period value to current value. Let D_i represent the current (dollar) value of asset or liability i (since a liability is a "negative asset," it will have a negative value of D_i). Clearly, end-of-period wealth will equal:

$$W = \sum_i D_i R_i$$

Since the sum of the D_i values must equal W_0, optimality requires that an additional dollar invested in asset i must contribute as much to the objective function as an additional dollar invested in asset j. That is:

$$\frac{\partial E_w}{\partial D_i} - \frac{1}{2ART}\frac{\partial V_w}{\partial D_i} = K \text{ for all assets i}$$

Substituting equations for the partial derivatives gives:

$$E_i - \frac{1}{2ART}\sum_j D_j \sigma_i \sigma_j \rho_{ij} = K \text{ for all assets i}$$

---

[8]John Lintner, "The Market Price of Risk, Size of Market and Investor's Risk Aversion," *Journal of Business,* April, 1968.

where:

E_i = the expected value of R_i
σ_i = the standard deviation of R_i
ρ_{ij} = the correlation between R_i and R_j

Note that although the equations hold only for assets, the summation (over j) includes assets and liabilities.

In case of two assets (S and B), this implies:

$$D_S = k_0 W_0 + k_1 ART$$

where:

$$k_0 = \frac{V_B - C_{BS}}{V_S + V_B - 2C_{BS}}$$

$$k_1 = \frac{E_S - E_B}{V_S + V_B - 2C_{BS}}$$

and:

$$V_B = \sigma_B^2$$

$$V_S = \sigma_S^2$$

$$C_{BS} = \sigma_B \sigma_S \rho_{BS}$$

Note that in the text the value of W is written without a subscript, since the distinction between beginning and end-of-period values does not need to be emphasized there.

CHAPTER 8

Asset Allocation Optimization Models

H. Gifford Fong
President
Gifford Fong Associates

Frank J. Fabozzi
Visiting Professor
Sloan School of Management
Massachusetts Institute of Technology
and Editor
Journal of Portfolio Management

In this chapter we shall describe several asset allocation models. We begin with the two-asset class problem and introduce the notion of an efficient portfolio and an efficient frontier (or efficient set). The asset allocation model with more than two asset classes is then explained and extended to (1) provide supplementary measures of risk, which we refer to as the *risk-of-loss*, (2) multiple scenarios, and (3) short-term/long-term asset allocations.

The basic inputs for the asset allocation models discussed are the expected returns, expected yields, risk estimates, and correlations (or

135

covariances) for each asset class included in the analysis. The appropriate source for these inputs is the asset manager, since he is most directly concerned with these factors on a day-to-day basis. Additional insights can be achieved by using historical estimates, either from a lengthy past period or from more recent experience. The objective is to use the proxy that will best represent the future horizon of interest.

Typically, the asset manager will use his own return expectation in conjunction with historical risk measures based on the variance and covariance from a historical series. Of course, other inputs may include constraints such as target minimum or maximum concentration constraints of individual or group-of-asset types and corresponding yield constraints on part or all of the portfolio.

TWO-ASSET CLASS ALLOCATION MODEL

In order to introduce the concept of an efficient set (frontier), let us consider the asset allocation model when funds are to be allocated between only two asset classes, stocks and bonds. Exhibit 1 summarizes the expectational inputs (expected return, variance, standard deviation and correlation of returns). Exhibit 2 presents the formulas for calculating the portfolio expected return and variance of a two-asset class portfolio. When the two assets are combined to form a portfolio, the expected return for the portfolio is simply the weighted average of the expected return for the two asset classes. The weight for each asset class is equal to the dollar value of the asset class relative to the dollar value of the portfolio. The sum of the two weights, of course, must equal one. Unlike the portfolio's expected return, the portfolio's variance (standard deviation) is not simply a weighted average of the variance (standard devia-

EXHIBIT 1
EXPECTATIONAL INPUTS FOR TWO ASSET CLASSES

Asset Class	Expected Return	Variance	Standard Deviation
Stocks	.13	.0342	.185
Bonds	.08	.0036	.060

Correlation between stocks and bonds = .20

EXHIBIT 2
FORMULAS FOR EXPECTED RETURN AND VARIANCE FOR A TWO-ASSET CLASS PORTFOLIO

Portfolio expected return

$$E(R_p) = W_1 E(R_1) + W_2 E(R_s)$$

where

$E(R_p)$ = expected return for the portfolio
$E(R_1)$ = expected return for asset class 1
$E(R_2)$ = expected return for asset class 2
W_1 = percentage of the portfolio invested in asset class 1
W_2 = percentage of the portfolio invested in asset class 2

and

$$W_1 + W_2 = 1$$

Portfolio variance

$$Var(R_p) = W_1^2 \, Var(R_1) + W_2^2 \, Var(R_2) + 2W_1 W_2 \, Covar(R_1,R_2)$$

where

$Covar(R_1,R_2)$ = covariance between the returns for asset classes 1 and 2
$Var(R_1)$ = variance of return for asset class 1
$Var(R_2)$ = variance of return for asset class 2

In terms of correlation:

$$Var(R_p) = W_1^2 \, Var(R_1) + W_2^2 \, Var(R_2) \\ + 2W_1 W_2 \, Std(R_1) Std(R_2) \, Corr(R_1,R_2)$$

where

$Corr(R_1, R_2)$ = correlation between asset classes 1 and 2
$Std(R_1)$ = standard deviation of asset class 1
$Std(R_2)$ = standard deviation of asset class 2

tion) of the two asset classes. Instead, the portfolio variance depends on the correlation (covariance) between the two asset classes.

The portfolio expected return, variance, and standard deviation for different allocations of funds between the two asset classes using the input in Exhibit 1 and the formulas in Exhibit 2 are shown in tabular form in Exhibit 3. Exhibit 4 graphically portrays the portfolio expected return and standard deviation presented in Exhibit 3. With respect to Exhibit 4, the following should be noted.

1. Every point on XYZ denotes a portfolio consisting of a specific allocation of funds between stocks and bonds. Not all of the portfolios are shown in Exhibit 3. We filled in the gaps when we plotted the results.

EXHIBIT 3
PORTFOLIO EXPECTED RETURN, VARIANCE, AND STANDARD
DEVIATION FOR DIFFERENT ALLOCATIONS OF FUNDS
BETWEEN STOCKS AND BONDS*

Allocation		Expected Return	Variance	Standard Deviation
W_1	W_2	$E(R_p)$	$Var(R_p)$	$Std(R_p)$
.0	1.0	.080	.0036000	.0600000
.1	.9	.085	.0036570	.0604769
.2	.8	.090	.0043820	.0661978
.3	.7	.095	.0057740	.0759872
.4	.6	.100	.0078330	.0885054
.5	.5	.105	.0105596	.1027600
.6	.4	.110	.0139532	.1181240
.7	.3	.115	.0180141	.1342160
.8	.2	.120	.0227421	.1508050
.9	.1	.125	.0281375	.1677420
1.0	.0	.130	.0342000	.1849320

* Asset class 1 = stocks.
  Asset class 2 = bonds.
  See Exhibit 1 for the expectational inputs for these two asset classes.

EXHIBIT 4
INVESTMENT OPPORTUNITY SET AND EFFICIENT SET FOR TWO-ASSET CLASSES (STOCKS AND BONDS)

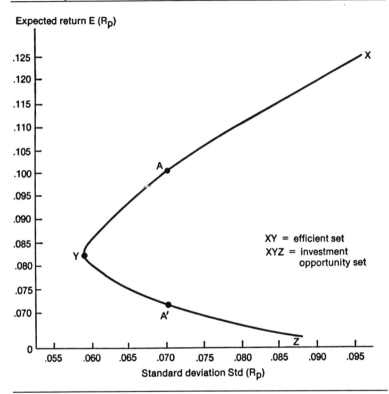

2. XYZ represents all possible portfolios consisting of these two security classes. XYZ is therefore called the *investment opportunity* or the *feasible set.*[1]

3. It would never be beneficial for an investor to allocate funds between stocks and bonds to produce a portfolio on that portion of XYZ between Y and Z (excluding portfolio Z).[2] The reason is

---

[1]The portfolios on XYZ include portfolios in which there is short selling of either asset class.

[2]The portfolio represented by point Y is the minimum variance that can be obtained by holding these two asset classes in any combination.

that for every portfolio on segment YZ there is a portfolio that dominates it on the XY segment of the investment opportunity set. By *dominates,* we mean that for a given portfolio standard deviation (risk level), an investor can realize a higher portfolio expected return. This can be seen on Exhibit 4 by examining portfolios A and A'. Portfolios A and A' have the same portfolio standard deviation; however, the expected return for portfolio A is greater than that for portfolio A'. Consequently, all portfolios on XY of the investment opportunity set dominate the portfolios on YZ of the investment opportunity set. XY, therefore, is called the *efficient set* or *efficient frontier.* We use these two terms interchangeably. A portfolio in the efficient set is said to be an *efficient portfolio* or an *optimal portfolio.*

The efficient set indicates the expected trade-off between return and risk (standard deviation) faced by the investor. Just which portfolio in the efficient set the investor selects depends on the investor's preference.

To see the impact of the correlation on the efficient set, Exhibit 5 shows in tabular form the expected return, variance, and standard deviation for portfolios consisting of stocks and bonds for various assumed correlation of returns. The efficient set for each assumed correlation is plotted on Exhibit 6. As can be seen, the lower the correlation of returns, the better off the investor is. That is, for a given set of expected returns and standard deviations for the two asset classes, the investor will be exposed to a lower level of risk (standard deviation) for a given portfolio if the correlation of returns is lower. Notice that, if the correlation is 1, the efficient set is a straight line and the portfolio standard deviation is therefore a weighted average of the standard deviations of the two asset classes.

N-ASSET CLASS ALLOCATION MODEL

The principles we have discussed for the efficient set for the two-asset class allocation model can easily be extended to the general case of *N*-asset classes. The formulas for the portfolio expected return and variance are shown in Exhibit 7.

Graphically, the efficient set of portfolios in the *N*-asset class case can be portrayed in the same manner as in the two-asset class case.

EXHIBIT 5
PORTFOLIO EXPECTED RETURN AND STANDARD DEVIATION FOR
DIFFERENT CORRELATIONS BETWEEN THE TWO ASSET CLASSES
(STOCKS AND BONDS)*

Weight for Each Asset Class		Expected Return	Portfolio Standard Deviation If the Correlation Is:				
W_1	W_2	$E(R_p)$	0.2	0.0	0.2	0.5	1.0
0.0	1.0	.080	.0600000	.0600000	.0600000	.0600000	.0600000
.1	.9	.085	.0534654	.0570789	.0604769	.0667560	.0724932
.2	.8	.090	.0544230	.0605970	.0661978	.0761736	.0849865
.3	.7	.095	.0625295	.0695845	.0759872	.0873967	.0974797
.4	.6	.100	.0755168	.0822679	.0885054	.0998180	.1099730
.5	.5	.105	.0913258	.0972111	.1027600	.1130430	.1224660
.6	.4	.110	.1087330	.1135250	.1181240	.1268210	.1349590
.7	.3	.115	.1270820	.1306980	.1342160	.1409900	.1474530
.8	.2	.120	.1460200	.1484320	.1508050	.1554430	.1599460
.9	.1	.125	.1653440	.1665470	.1677420	.1701070	.1724390
1.0	0.0	.130	.1849320	.1849320	.1849320	.1849320	.1849320

*Asset class 1 = stocks.
Asset class 2 = bonds.

Exhibit 8 shows all possible portfolios for the N-asset class case. This exhibit is analogous to Exhibit 4. The difference is that the investment opportunity set in the two-asset class case does not include points (portfolios) in the interior of XYZ. In the N-asset class case, interior points are also feasible portfolios. However, as in the two-asset class case, the portfolios represented by the segment XY dominate portfolios in the interior of the investment opportunity set.

Although the efficient set for the simple two-asset class case can be easily determined, the computation of the efficient set when funds are to be allocated to more than two asset classes becomes more difficult. Fortunately, the efficient set of the n-asset class problem can be solved using a mathematical programming technique called quadratic program-

EXHIBIT 6
COMPARISON OF EFFICIENT SET FOR DIFFERENT CORRELATIONS
BETWEEN TWO ASSET CLASSES (STOCKS AND BONDS)

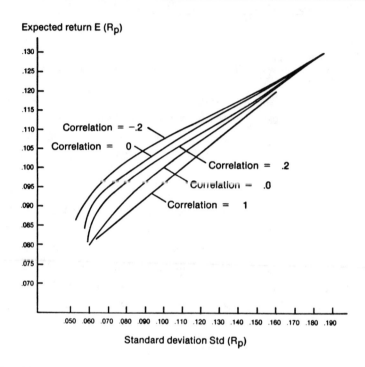

Expected return E (R$_p$)

Correlation = −.2
Correlation = 0
Correlation = .2
Correlation = .0
Correlation = 1

Standard deviation Std (R$_p$)

ming. This algorithm can also accommodate other constraints that might be imposed, such as limitations on the concentration of funds in a given asset class.

Let us now illustrate the three-asset class allocation model. Assume that an investor wishes to allocate available investment funds among the following three asset classes: stocks, bonds, and Treasury bills. Exhibit 9 presents the annual expected return, expected yield, standard deviation, and correlations for the three asset classes for two scenarios. (We will discuss the two scenarios later.) The expected yield component of the expected return is the amount of the return attributable to dividends in the case of stocks, and interest payments in the case of bonds. The difference between the expected return and expected yield is therefore the return attributable to capital appreciation.

EXHIBIT 7
FORMULAS FOR EXPECTED RETURN AND VARIANCE FOR AN *N*-ASSET
CLASS PORTFOLIO

Portfolio expected return

$$E(R_p) = \sum_{i=1}^{N} E(R_i)W_i$$

where

$$E(R_i) = \text{expected return for asset class i}$$
$$W_i = \text{percent of the portfolio invested in asset class i}$$

and

$$\sum_{i=1}^{N} W_i = 1$$

Portfolio variance

$$Var(R_p) = \sum_{i=1}^{N} W_i^2\, Var(R_i) + \sum_{i=1}^{N} \sum_{\substack{j=1 \\ \text{for } i \neq j}}^{N} W_i W_j\, Covar(R_i,R_j)$$

In terms of correlation:

$$Var(R_p) = \sum_{i=1}^{N} W_i^2 Var(R_i) + \sum_{i=1}^{N} \sum_{\substack{j=1 \\ \text{for } i \neq j}}^{N} W_i W_j Std\,(R_i)\, Std(R_j)\, Corr(R_i,R_j)$$

Using quadratic programming, the efficient set can be determined. The results for scenario 1, assuming a one-year horizon and no constraints, are shown in Exhibit 10 while the results for scenario 2 are shown in Exhibit 11. For each identified level of portfolio expected return, the corresponding standard deviation, yield component of total return, and minimum risk concentrations (weights) of each class are

EXHIBIT 8
INVESTMENT OPPORTUNITY SET AND EFFICIENT SET IN AN N-ASSET CLASS PORTFOLIO CASE

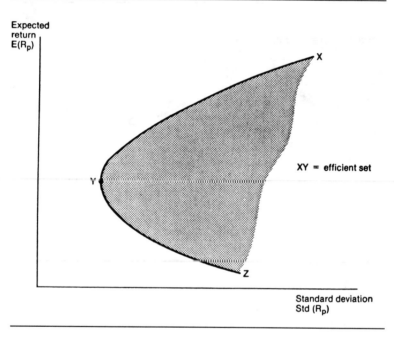

shown on both exhibits. The columns under the heading *Probability of Annual Return of Less Than* will be explained shortly.

To make sure you understand the two exhibits, let's interpret one of the results. For scenario 1, the minimum risk (standard deviation) that the investor will be exposed to if he seeks a 9% return for the 12-month period is 6.552%. There is no other allocation producing a 9% return with a standard deviation less than 6.552%. The asset mix associated with this efficient or optimal portfolio is 24.8% in stocks, 64.2% in bonds, and 10.9% in Treasury bills. (The total does not equal one because of rounding.) The annual expected return of 9% will have an expected yield of 7.04%. Therefore, 1.96% of the total annual expected return will be attributable to capital appreciation.

EXHIBIT 9
EXPECTATIONAL INPUTS FOR THREE-ASSET CLASSES
FOR TWO SCENARIOS

Asset Class	Expected Return	Expected Yield	Variance	Standard Deviation
Scenario 1:				
Stock	.13	.05	.034200	.185
Bonds	.08	.08	.003600	.060
Treasury bills	.06	.06	.000016	.004
Scenario 2:				
Stock	.15	.05	.034200	.185
Bonds	.08	.08	.003600	.060
Treasury bills	.05	.05	.000016	.004

	Correlations for Both Scenarios		
	Stocks	Bonds	Treasury bills
Stocks	1.00	.20	−.15
Bonds	.20	1.00	−.12
Treasury bills	−.15	−.12	1.00

EXTENSION OF THE ASSET ALLOCATION MODEL TO RISK-OF-LOSS

In the portfolio risk-minimization process, the variance (standard deviation) of returns was the proxy measure for portfolio risk. As a supplement, the probability of not achieving a portfolio expected return can be established. This type of analysis would be useful in determining the most appropriate mix from the set of optimal portfolio allocations.

We refer to this analysis as the *risk-of-loss*. A technical description of the analysis is described in Appendix A. The columns under the heading *Probability of Annual Return of Less Than* in Exhibits 10 and 11 show the results of the risk-of-loss analysis for four annual return levels. The interpretation of the results for the 9% expected return for scenario 1

EXHIBIT 10
OPTIMAL ASSET ALLOCATION FOR SCENARIO 1: SAMPLE PORTFOLIOS IN THE EFFICIENT SET (12-MONTH HORIZON)

Annual Expected Return	Annual Standard Deviation	Annual Expected Yield	Probability of Annual Return of Less than				Minimum Risk Asset Mix		
			0.0%	5.0%	7.0%	10.0%	Stocks	Bonds	T-Bills
6.00%	0.400%	6.00%	0.9%	0.9%	99.1%	100.00%	0.0%	0.0%	100.0%
6.04	0.389	6.02	0.0	0.5	99.0	100.0	0.3	1.0	98.7
6.50	1.097	6.18	0.0	9.7	66.7	99.8	4.1	10.9	84.9
7.00	2.174	6.35	0.1	19.2	50.0	90.0	8.3	21.7	70.0
7.50	3.271	6.52	1.3	23.5	44.3	76.0	12.5	32.4	55.1
8.00	4.368	6.70	3.8	25.8	41.5	66.4	16.6	43.1	40.3
8.50	5.462	6.84	6.6	27.3	39.9	60.0	20.7	53.7	25.6
9.00	6.552	7.04	9.3	28.3	38.8	55.6	24.8	64.2	10.9
9.50	7.649	7.09	11.6	29.0	38.1	52.4	30.4	69.6	0.0
10.00	8.918	6.79	14.1	30.0	37.7	50.0	40.5	59.5	0.0
10.50	10.356	6.48	16.5	31.0	37.7	48.2	50.5	49.5	0.0
11.00	11.895	6.19	18.8	31.9	37.8	46.9	60.5	39.5	0.0
11.50	13.497	5.89	20.8	32.7	37.9	46.0	70.4	29.6	0.0
12.00	15.142	5.59	22.5	33.3	38.0	45.2	80.3	19.7	0.0
12.50	16.813	5.29	24.0	33.9	38.2	44.6	90.2	9.8	0.0
13.00	18.500	5.00	25.2	34.4	38.3	44.2	100.0	0.0	0.0

EXHIBIT 11
OPTIMAL ASSET ALLOCATION FOR SCENARIO 2: SAMPLE PORTFOLIOS IN THE EFFICIENT SET (12-MONTH HORIZON)

Annual Expected Return	Annual Standard Deviation	Annual Expected Yield	Probability of Annual Return of Less than				Minimum Risk Asset Mix:		
			0.0%	5.0%	7.0%	10.0%	Stocks	Bond	T-Bills
5.00%	0.400%	5.00%	0.0%	50.1%	100.0%	100.0%	0.0%	0.0%	100.0%
5.06	0.389	5.03	0.0	44.3	100.0	100.0	0.3	1.0	98.7
5.50	0.784	5.24	0.0	27.2	96.5	100.0	2.8	7.9	89.3
6.00	1.501	5.47	0.0	26.3	73.5	99.3	5.5	15.7	78.7
6.50	2.248	5.70	0.2	26.3	58.3	92.6	8.3	23.5	68.2
7.00	3.003	5.94	1.2	26.4	50.0	82.3	11.0	31.2	57.7
7.50	3.757	6.17	2.6	26.4	45.0	73.1	13.8	38.9	47.3
8.00	4.509	6.40	4.3	26.5	41.8	65.9	16.5	46.6	36.9
8.50	5.258	6.63	5.9	26.5	39.5	60.4	19.2	54.2	26.6
9.00	6.005	6.85	7.4	26.5	37.8	56.1	21.9	61.8	16.3
9.50	6.750	7.08	8.8	26.6	36.5	52.7	24.6	69.4	6.0
10.00	7.505	7.13	10.0	26.6	35.5	50.0	29.1	70.9	0.0
10.50	8.374	6.91	11.5	26.9	34.9	47.8	36.4	63.6	0.0
11.00	9.345	6.69	13.0	27.4	34.6	46.1	43.6	56.4	0.0
11.50	10.386	6.48	14.5	28.0	34.4	44.8	50.7	49.3	0.0
12.00	11.478	6.26	15.9	28.5	34.4	43.7	57.8	42.2	0.0
12.50	12.605	6.05	17.3	29.0	34.4	42.9	64.9	35.1	0.0
13.00	13.756	5.84	18.5	29.5	34.4	42.2	72.0	28.0	0.0
13.50	14.927	5.63	19.6	29.9	34.5	41.6	79.1	20.9	0.0
14.00	16.109	5.42	20.5	30.3	34.5	41.1	86.1	13.9	0.0
14.50	17.302	5.21	21.4	30.6	34.6	40.7	93.0	7.0	0.0
15.00	18.500	5.00	22.2	30.9	34.7	40.4	100.0	0.0	0.0

(Exhibit 10) is as follows: there is a 9.3% probability that the annual return will be negative, a 28.3% probability that the annual return will be less than 5%, a 38.8% probability that the annual return will be less than 7%, and a 55.6% probability that the annual return will be less than 10%.

EXTENSION OF THE ASSET ALLOCATION MODEL TO MULTIPLE SCENARIOS

In Exhibit 9, the expected return and expected yield are shown for two assumed scenarios. Each assumed scenario is believed to be an assessment of the asset performance in the long run, over the investment horizon. If a probability can be assigned to each scenario, an efficient set can be constructed for the composite scenario. Appendix B explains the procedure for computing the optimal asset allocation when there are multiple scenarios which are discrete or mutually exclusive and each scenario can be assigned a probability of occurrence.

Assuming a probability of 50% for each of the two scenarios in Exhibit 9, Exhibit 12 displays the optimal asset allocation for the composite scenario for a 12-month investment horizon. Exhibit 13 provides the minimum risk portfolio for specified return levels for the composite scenario results for a 60-month horizon. In both exhibits, the risk-of-loss analysis results are also shown.

Let's take a closer look at these results to see how useful they can be in the asset allocation decision. Exhibit 14 is an illustration of the optimal mixes for the 12-month horizon for the composite scenario. The vertical height of each of the three lines represents the amount that would be allocated to an asset for a given expected return level shown on the horizontal axis. For example, Exhibit 14 has the optimal concentrations for an expected return of 8% of about 17% stocks, 45% bonds, and 38% Treasury bills, corresponding to the results shown in Exhibit 12 of 16.6% stocks, 45.2% bonds and 38.3% Treasury bills. (As noted earlier, the optimal mix may not equal one because of rounding.)

The yield component of the optimal mixes is shown for each scenario and the composite scenario in Exhibit 15. As explained earlier, the yield is the amount of return attributable to dividends and interest payments for the range of optimal portfolios. For the 8% expected return level, Exhibit 15 indicates that the yield component is 6.55%, which leaves 1.45% as the return attributable to capital appreciation.

EXHIBIT 12
OPTIMAL ASSET ALLOCATION FOR COMPOSITE SCENARIO: SAMPLE PORTFOLIOS IN THE EFFICIENT SET (12-MONTH HORIZON)

Annual Expected Return	Annual Standard Deviation	Annual Expected Yield	Probability of Annual Return of Less than					Minimum Risk Asset Mix		
			0.0%	5.0%	7.0%	10.0%		Stocks	Bonds	T-Bills
5.50%	0.422%	5.50%	0.0%	24.8%	99.5%	100.0%		0.0%	0.0%	100.0%
5.55	0.412	5.53	0.0	21.8	99.4	100.0		0.3	1.1	98.6
6.00	0.918	5.71	0.0	16.7	82.4	100.0		3.3	9.2	87.5
6.50	1.777	5.92	0.0	21.3	59.9	96.3		6.6	18.3	75.1
7.00	2.666	6.13	0.6	23.8	49.7	84.8		10.0	27.3	62.8
7.50	3.560	6.34	2.1	25.2	44.5	73.9		13.3	36.2	50.5
8.00	4.452	6.55	4.1	26.2	41.5	65.8		16.6	45.2	38.3
8.50	5.342	6.75	6.3	26.8	39.5	59.9		19.8	54.0	26.1
9.00	6.228	6.96	8.3	27.3	38.1	55.6		23.1	62.9	14.0
9.50	7.113	7.16	10.0	27.6	37.1	52.4		26.3	71.7	2.0
10.00	8.063	6.98	11.8	28.1	36.4	49.8		33.9	66.1	0.0
10.50	9.168	6.73	13.7	28.7	36.1	47.8		42.3	57.7	0.0
11.00	10.377	6.48	15.6	29.5	36.0	46.4		50.7	49.3	0.0
11.50	11.655	6.23	17.4	30.2	36.0	45.2		59.0	41.0	0.0
12.00	12.981	5.98	19.0	30.8	36.1	44.3		67.3	32.7	0.0
12.50	14.338	5.73	20.5	31.4	36.2	43.6		75.5	24.5	0.0
13.00	15.715	5.49	21.7	31.9	36.3	43.1		83.7	16.3	0.0
13.50	17.110	5.24	22.9	32.3	36.4	42.6		91.9	8.1	0.0

EXHIBIT 13
OPTIMAL ASSET ALLOCATION FOR COMPOSITE SCENARIO: SAMPLE PORTFOLIOS IN THE EFFICIENT SET (60-MONTH HORIZON)

Annual Expected Return	Annual Standard Deviation	Annual Expected Yield	Probability of Annual Return of Less than					Minimum Risk Asset Mix		
			0.0%	5.0%	7.0%	10.0%		Stocks	Bonds	T-Bills
5.50%	0.422%	5.50%	0.0%	23.7%	100.0%	100.0%		0.0%	0.0%	100.0%
5.55	0.412	5.53	0.0	17.3	100.0	100.0		0.3	1.1	98.6
6.00	0.918	5.71	0.0	4.0	95.3	100.0		3.3	9.2	87.5
6.50	1.777	5.92	0.0	4.5	70.2	100.0		6.6	18.3	75.1
7.00	2.666	6.13	0.0	5.8	49.4	98.8		10.0	27.3	62.8
7.50	3.560	6.34	0.0	6.8	38.0	92.3		13.3	36.2	50.5
8.00	4.452	6.55	0.0	7.7	31.6	81.8		16.6	45.2	38.3
8.50	5.342	6.75	0.0	8.3	27.6	71.3		19.8	54.0	26.1
9.00	6.228	6.96	0.1	8.8	25.0	62.4		23.1	62.9	14.0
9.50	7.113	7.16	0.2	9.2	23.1	55.3		26.3	71.7	2.0
10.00	8.063	6.98	0.4	9.7	21.9	49.6		33.9	66.1	0.0
10.50	9.168	6.73	0.7	10.6	21.4	45.2		42.3	57.7	0.0
11.00	10.377	6.48	1.2	11.5	21.3	41.9		50.7	49.3	0.0
11.50	11.655	6.23	1.8	12.4	21.3	39.4		59.0	41.0	0.0
12.00	12.981	5.98	2.6	13.2	21.4	37.5		67.3	32.7	0.0
12.50	14.338	5.73	3.3	14.0	21.6	36.0		75.5	24.5	0.0
13.00	15.715	5.49	4.1	14.7	21.7	34.8		83.7	16.3	0.0
13.50	17.110	5.24	4.9	15.4	21.9	33.9		91.9	8.1	0.0

EXHIBIT 14
RISK-OF-LOSS ANALYSIS: MINIMUM-RISK CONCENTRATIONS

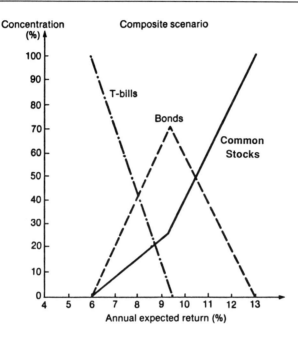

Exhibit 16 depicts the risk-of-loss or probability of not achieving the specified return benchmarks of 0%, 5%, 7%, and 10% over a one-year horizon for the composite case. From the expected return range on the horizontal axis, the probability of not achieving a given benchmark can be determined by proceeding vertically to the return benchmark curves. For example, if the 8% expected return optimal portfolio were assumed, there would be a 4% probability of not achieving a positive percent return over the next year (probabilities on the vertical axis). From Exhibit 12 the tabular results reveal the more precise value of 4.1%. Exhibit 17 graphically characterizes the risk-of-loss for the composite scenario for the five-year horizon results shown in Exhibit 13.

The comparison between Exhibit 16 and Exhibit 17 is particularly interesting. The influence of the passage of time is illustrated by comparing the 12-month horizon of Exhibit 16 and the 60-month horizon of Exhibit 17. The most striking difference is the significant downward shift of all risk-of-loss curves for the longer time horizon. This is consistent

EXHIBIT 15
RISK-OF-LOSS ANALYSIS: YIELD OF MINIMUM-RISK PORTFOLIOS

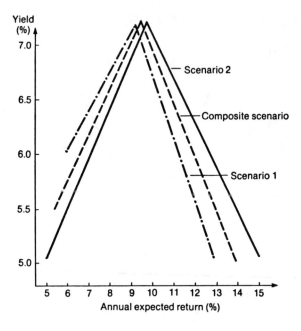

Composite scenario
five-year projection

with the return increasing at a greater rate than risk over time. The greater
the time horizon, the greater the incentive to seek higher expected re-
turn/higher expected risk portfolios. The effect of the high risk associated
with high return portfolios is most significant during short time horizons.
If the risk exposure over short horizons is important, it is apparent that
lower return portfolios are appropriate. In other words, if the investor is
concerned with near-term portfolio fluctuation, a portfolio consisting
entirely of common stock (highest expected return and risk class in our
example) is clearly not fitting. As the relevant horizon increases, however, a higher proportion of stocks is possible — and even desirable — to
achieve higher return.

In practice, there probably will be a trade-off between short-term risk
tolerance and long-term return desirability. How much short-term risk is
tolerable may therefore control the proportion of higher return assets

EXHIBIT 16
RISK-OF-LOSS ANALYSIS: PROBABILITY OF LOSS FOR
MINIMUM-RISK PORTFOLIOS

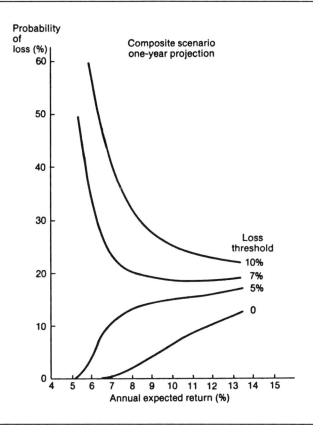

and, hence, the expected return attainable. Using formats such as Exhibit 16 and Exhibit 17 and their supporting tables, Exhibits 12 and 13, can assist the investor in choosing the most desirable return/risk trade-off.

As an alternative to visual inspection of the return/risk trade-off, the mathematically best trade-off in terms of the most return per unit of risk can be calculated. This procedure involves the evaluation of a chosen risk-of-loss curve for the point along the curve where the second derivative of the curve is zero (i.e., where its slope is steepest). This provides the greatest decrease in risk-of-loss for an increment of expected return.

EXHIBIT 17
RISK-OF-LOSS ANALYSIS: PROBABILITY OF LOSS FOR
MINIMUM-RISK PORTFOLIOS

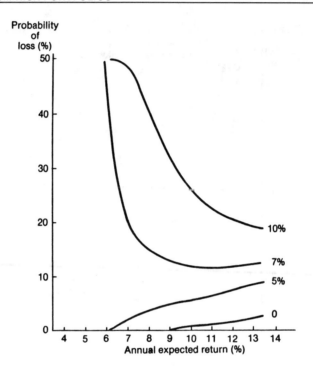

EXTENSION OF THE ASSET ALLOCATION MODEL TO SHORT-TERM/LONG-TERM ASSET ALLOCATION

In the multiple scenario case just described, it was assumed that the investor has certain expectations about the performance of the asset classes in terms of expected returns, expected yields, standard deviations, and correlations of return for each scenario. These values are used to assess, under various scenarios, the asset class performance in the long run, over the investment horizon.

It is often the case, however, that the investor expects a very different set of values to be applicable in the short run, say the next 12 months. For example, the investor may estimate the long-term expected annual return on stocks at 12%, but over the next year his expected return on stocks is only 5%. The investment objectives are still stated in terms of the portfolio performance over the entire investment horizon. The return characteristics of each asset class, however, are described by one set of values over a short period and another set of values over the remainder of the horizon.

In such a case, the investment strategy may involve investing in one portfolio over the short period and another portfolio over the remaining horizon. Naturally, the investor is mostly interested in the short-term portfolio since this addresses the current task of asset allocation. It is necessary to take into consideration the subsequent allocation as well, since both relate to the total horizon investment objectives.

To explain this point further, suppose that the investor wants to achieve a certain level of return, say 10%, with minimum risk over a five-year horizon. The 10% expected overall return may be accomplished by being very conservative in the first year and more aggressive over the remaining four years, or aggressive in the first year and more conservative thereafter. For the asset allocations in the two periods, there is a spectrum of choices that would produce the same 10% overall expected return. Not all of these choices, however, would have the same overall risk, as measured by the standard deviation of total returns. As a matter of fact, there would be one combination of the asset allocations over the first and the second periods that would have the minimum risk and overall expected return of 10%. Such a strategy represents a point on the overall efficient set. By varying the required total expected return, one can generate the whole efficient set for the investment horizon.

A procedure to identify the overall efficient frontier and characterize the investment strategies which comprise it has been developed by Gifford Fong Associates. Notice that in this context we refer to optimal strategies, rather than optimal asset allocations, because each strategy consists of two asset allocations over the two separate periods of the horizon.

This extension of basic asset allocation has considerable flexibility. It allows an investor to specify different values, both for the short period and the remainder of the horizon, for any of the basic data required in the asset allocation model. The investor can also specify different portfolio constraints in the two periods. In fact, it is even possible to consider different asset classes in two periods comprising the horizon.

The techniques involved in the generation of the efficient strategies and their characterization in terms of return and risk, as well as probabilities of meeting threshold returns (risk-of-loss analysis), for the horizon and the two subperiods are fairly complex. Since the model simultaneously optimizes over two periods, quadratic programming alone is no longer sufficient. A detailed description of the computational procedure is beyond the scope of this chapter. Briefly, the approach used is as follows. For a given level of the total expected return, the overall standard deviation is expressed as a function of the first period expected return. This is possible since a value of the first period expected return determines the second period expected return necessary to generate the given overall return expectation required. Two separate quadratic algorithms give the two one-period minimum standard deviations corresponding to the one-period returns. These standard deviations are then combined by an appropriate formula to provide the overall standard deviation. Once the total standard deviation is expressed as a function of the first period return expectation, this function is minimized to obtain a point on the overall efficient set.[3] The above process is repeated for different values of the total expected return in the feasible range to generate the whole efficient set. The optimal asset allocation strategies are obtained in the process. No assumptions beyond serial independence of returns are necessary for the calculation of the mean/variance efficient strategies. Lognormality of the return distributions is assumed for calculation of the probabilities of exceeding threshold returns.

To illustrate this extension of the asset allocation model, the following are assumed:

1. There are six asset classes over which funds are to be allocated. They are: (1) government/agencies, (2) intermediate-term industrials, (3) long-term corporates, (4) S&P 500 stocks, (5) AMEX stocks, and (6) Treasury bills.
2. The investment horizon is 60 months.
3. The investor has expectations for a 12-month horizon that differs from the 60-month horizon.
4. The basic expectational values for the 60-month (long-term) and 12-month (short-term) horizons are shown in Exhibits 18 and 19, respectively.
5. Minimum and maximum concentration constraints are imposed for each subperiod as shown in Exhibits 18 and 19.
6. The minimum yield for both subperiods is set at 6%.

---

[3]The method used for the minimization of this function is the three-point Newton iteration method.

EXHIBIT 18
LONG-TERM/SHORT-TERM ASSET ALLOCATION: LONG-TERM SPECIFICATIONS (60-MONTH PERIOD)

Name	Annual Expected Return	Annual Expected Yield	Annual Standard Deviation	Correlation with					
				G/A	ITI	LTC	S&P500	AMEX	T-bills
G/A	8.00%	8.00%	4.00%	1.000					
ITI	9.00	9.00	6.00	0.974	1.000				
LTC	10.00	10.00	12.00	0.965	0.965	1.000			
S&P500	15.00	5.00	16.00	0.353	0.401	0.387	1.000		
AMEX	20.00	5.00	25.00	0.281	0.356	0.327	0.845	1.000	
T-bills	6.00	6.00	1.00	0.611	0.560	0.508	-0.032	-0.097	1.000

Constraints:

	G/A	ITI	LTC	S&P500	AMEX	T-bills
Minimum concentration (percent)	20.00	0.0	0.0	0.0	0.0	0.0
Maximum concentration (percent)	100.00	100.00	100.00	80.00	80.00	60.00
Minimum yield (percent)	6.00					

Key: G//A = government/agencies
 ITI = intermediate term industrials
 LTC = long-term corporates
 S&P500 = Standard & Poor's 500
 AMEX = American Stock Exchange Index
 T-bills = U.S. Treasury bills

EXHIBIT 19
LONG-TERM/SHORT-TERM ASSET ALLOCATION: SHORT-TERM SPECIFICATIONS (12-MONTH PERIOD)

Name	Annual Expected Return	Annual Expected Yield	Annual Standard Deviation	Correlation with					
				G/A	ITI	LTC	S&P500	AMEX	T-bills
G/A	15.00%	8.00%	4.00%	1.000					
ITI	13.00	9.00	4.00	0.965	1.000				
LTC	25.00	10.00	6.00	0.972	0.970	1.000			
S&P500	10.50	5.00	10.00	-0.200	-0.200	-0.300	1.000		
AMEX	5.00	5.00	12.00	-0.100	-0.200	-0.200	0.848	1.000	
T-bills	7.00	7.00	0.0	0.0	0.0	0.0	-0.0	-0.0	1.000

Constraints:

	G/A	ITI	LTC	S&P500	AMEX	T-bills
Minimum concentration (percent)	20.00	0.0	0.0	0.0	0.0	0.0
Maximum concentration (percent)	100.00	100.00	100.00	80.00	80.00	100.00
Minimum yield (percent)	6.00					

Key: G/A = government/agencies
ITI = intermediate term industrials
LTC = long-term corporates
S&P500 = Standard & Poor's 500
AMEX = American Stock Exchange Index
T-bills = U.S. Treasury bills

Exhibit 20 displays the optimal strategies for the 12-month horizon. Exhibit 21 shows the optimal strategies for the residual term horizon of 48 months. The optimal composite statistics for the 60-month horizon based on the optimal strategies shown in Exhibits 20 and 21 are displayed in Exhibit 22.

APPLICATION FOR INVESTMENT STRATEGY

Implicit in the use of the model in making strategy decisions is the capability of providing capital market expectations with greater precision than using a historical average. Along with expected return judgments, it is assumed that the risk estimates are also capable of refinement. For example, over periods of less than a year the normal relationship between return and risk for the highest expected return assets will be masked by the magnitude of their expected risk (variance). Hence, unless this risk can be specified to be much lower than the historical average, the model will consistently choose the lowest-return, lowest-risk asset mixes for the short horizons. This is intuitively proper, since, if a short-term perspective is important and there is no insight as to expected return and risk other than a historical average, the lower return and risk allocation would be most appropriate for this time horizon from a risk-of-loss standpoint.

Multi-outlook analysis is especially important concerning capital market expectation. While the individual scenario distributions of return may narrow, the prospect of alternative cases may become apparent and even compelling.

Over the short run, confident return projections are extremely difficult, especially for the high expected return assets. On the other hand, if the projection is not expressed with strong conviction in the form of a relatively small expected risk, the allocation process will consistently call for low-risk allocations. Therefore, a multi-scenario projection allows a range of outcomes to be evaluated, and the probability-weighted composite provides a consensus outcome. The important result is the sensitivity of the outcome under alternative assumptions. A more effective perspective for decision-making is consequently achieved.

In the context of setting strategy for a pension fund that already has a long-term policy established, the value of the probability of loss for the desired return benchmark over the long-term horizon can be used as the maximum value for the short term. For example, if the long-term

EXHIBIT 20
LONG-TERM/SHORT-TERM ASSET ALLOCATION: OPTIMAL INITIAL STRATEGY (12-MONTH PERIOD)

Strategy	Annual Expected Return	Annual Standard Deviation	Annual Expected Yield	Probability of Annual Return Less than					Minimum Risk Asset Mix					
				0.0 Percent	8.0 Percent	10.0 Percent	12.0 Percent	20.0 Percent	G/A	ITI	LTC	S&P500	AMEX	T-Bills
1	8.66%	0.784%	7.17%	0.0%	20.0%	95.7%	100.0%	100.0%	20.0%	0.0%	0.0%	1.6%	0.0%	78.4%
2	10.10	1.214	7.34	0.0	4.0	46.9	94.1	100.0	20.0	0.0	7.5	4.2	0.0	68.2
3	12.49	1.938	7.66	0.0	0.9	9.9	40.4	100.0	20.0	0.0	20.2	7.3	0.0	52.5
4	14.92	2.680	7.98	0.0	0.4	3.1	13.7	96.9	20.0	0.0	33.1	10.4	0.0	36.5
5	17.41	3.440	8.32	0.0	0.2	1.3	5.5	77.6	20.0	0.0	46.3	13.6	0.0	20.1
6	19.96	4.216	8.66	0.0	0.1	0.7	2.6	51.1	20.0	0.0	59.8	16.9	0.0	3.3
7	21.69	4.861	9.15	0.0	0.1	0.6	2.0	37.0	20.0	0.0	71.0	8.0	0.0	0.0
8	23.00	5.581	9.60	0.0	0.2	0.7	2.1	30.1	20.0	0.0	80.0	0.0	0.0	0.0
9	23.00	5.581	9.60	0.0	0.2	0.7	2.1	30.1	20.0	0.0	80.0	0.0	0.0	0.0
10	23.00	5.581	9.60	0.0	0.2	0.7	2.1	30.1	20.0	0.0	80.0	0.0	0.0	0.0
11	23.00	5.581	9.60	0.0	0.2	0.7	2.1	30.1	20.0	0.0	80.0	0.0	0.0	0.0
12	23.00	5.581	9.60	0.0	0.2	0.7	2.1	30.1	20.0	0.0	80.0	0.0	0.0	0.0
13	23.00	5.581	9.60	0.0	0.2	0.7	2.1	30.1	20.0	0.0	80.0	0.0	0.0	0.0
14	23.00	5.581	9.60	0.0	0.2	0.7	2.1	30.1	20.0	0.0	80.0	0.0	0.0	0.0
15	23.00	5.581	9.60	0.0	0.2	0.7	2.1	30.1	20.0	0.0	80.0	0.0	0.0	0.0
16	23.00	5.581	9.60	0.0	0.2	0.7	2.1	30.1	20.0	0.0	80.0	0.0	0.0	0.0
17	23.00	5.581	9.60	0.0	0.2	0.7	2.1	30.1	20.0	0.0	80.0	0.0	0.0	0.0
18	23.00	5.581	9.60	0.0	0.2	0.7	2.1	30.1	20.0	0.0	80.0	0.0	0.0	0.0
19	23.00	5.581	9.60	0.0	0.2	0.7	2.1	30.1	20.0	0.0	80.0	0.0	0.0	0.0
20	23.00	5.581	9.60	0.0	0.2	0.7	2.1	30.1	20.0	0.0	80.0	0.0	0.0	0.0
21	23.00	5.581	9.60	0.0	0.2	0.7	2.1	30.1	20.0	0.0	80.0	0.0	0.0	0.0
22	23.00	5.581	9.60	0.0	0.2	0.7	2.1	30.1	20.0	0.0	80.0	0.0	0.0	0.0
23	23.00	5.581	9.60	0.0	0.2	0.7	2.1	30.1	20.0	0.0	80.0	0.0	0.0	0.0
24	23.00	5.581	9.60	0.0	0.2	0.7	2.1	30.1	20.0	0.0	80.0	0.0	0.0	0.0

EXHIBIT 21
LONG-TERM/SHORT-TERM ASSET ALLOCATION: OPTIMAL RESIDUAL STRATEGY (48-MONTH PERIOD)

Strategy	Annual Expected Return	Annual Standard Deviation	Annual Expected Yield	Probability of Annual Return Less than					Minimum Risk Asset Mix					
				0.0 Percent	8.0 Percent	10.0 Percent	12.0 Percent	20.0 Percent	C/A	ITI	LTC	S&P500	AMEX	T-Bills
1	6.80%	2.023%	6.80%	0.0%	88.5%	99.8%	100.0%	100.0%	40.0%	0.0%	0.0%	0.0%	0.0%	60.0%
2	6.86	2.031	6.78	0.0	87.2	99.8	100.0	100.0	39.2	0.0	0.0	0.6	0.1	60.0
3	6.91	2.042	6.76	0.0	86.1	99.8	100.0	100.0	38.8	0.0	0.0	0.8	0.4	60.0
4	6.95	2.056	6.75	0.0	85.0	99.8	100.0	100.0	38.3	0.0	0.0	1.0	0.7	60.0
5	6.99	2.072	6.74	0.0	83.8	99.8	100.0	100.0	37.9	0.0	0.0	1.2	0.9	60.0
6	7.03	2.091	6.73	0.0	82.7	99.8	100.0	100.0	37.5	0.0	0.0	1.4	1.1	60.0
7	7.26	2.246	6.66	0.0	75.2	99.3	100.0	100.0	35.2	0.0	0.0	2.4	2.4	60.0
8	7.58	2.589	6.56	0.0	63.6	97.0	100.0	100.0	31.9	0.0	0.0	3.8	4.3	60.0
9	8.19	3.415	6.72	0.0	46.9	86.1	98.7	100.0	41.7	0.0	0.0	5.3	6.2	46.7
10	8.80	4.266	6.99	0.0	36.8	72.6	93.6	100.0	56.8	0.0	0.0	6.5	7.7	29.0
11	9.41	5.125	7.27	0.0	30.6	60.9	85.3	100.0	71.9	0.0	0.0	7.7	9.1	11.3
12	10.02	5.997	7.38	0.0	26.6	51.9	76.1	99.9	79.2	0.0	0.0	9.5	11.3	0.0
13	10.63	6.951	7.24	0.1	24.1	45.3	67.5	99.6	69.3	3.7	0.0	12.1	14.5	0.0
14	11.24	7.946	7.36	0.2	22.4	40.4	60.3	98.6	41.2	28.2	0.0	14.4	16.3	0.0
15	11.85	8.956	7.39	0.3	21.3	36.8	54.5	96.7	20.0	44.7	0.0	16.5	18.8	0.0
16	12.47	10.018	7.14	0.5	20.5	34.1	49.8	93.9	20.0	38.5	0.0	18.0	23.5	0.0
17	13.08	11.134	6.89	0.8	20.1	32.1	46.1	90.4	20.0	32.2	0.0	19.6	28.3	0.0
18	13.70	12.290	6.63	1.1	19.9	30.7	43.2	86.6	20.0	25.9	0.0	21.1	33.0	0.0
19	14.31	13.474	6.38	1.5	19.8	29.5	40.9	82.7	20.0	19.6	0.0	22.7	37.7	0.0
20	14.93	14.682	6.13	2.0	19.8	28.7	39.0	79.0	20.0	13.2	0.0	24.3	42.5	0.0
21	15.55	15.917	6.00	2.4	19.8	28.1	37.5	75.5	20.0	10.0	0.0	19.1	50.9	0.0
22	16.16	17.217	6.00	3.0	20.0	27.7	36.4	72.2	20.0	0.0	8.0	12.7	59.3	0.0
23	16.78	18.573	6.00	3.6	20.3	27.5	35.5	69.2	20.0	0.0	8.0	0.4	71.6	0.0
24	16.80	18.613	6.00	3.6	20.3	27.5	35.5	69.1	20.0	0.0	8.0	0.0	72.0	0.0

EXHIBIT 22
LONG-TERM/SHORT-TERM ASSET ALLOCATION: COMPOSITE STATISTICS (60-MONTH HORIZON)

Strategy	Annual Expected Return	Annual Standard Deviation	Annual Expected Yield	Probability of Annual Return Less Than					
				0.0 percent	8.0 percent	10.0 percent	12.0 percent	20.0 percent
1	7.17%	1.848%	6.87%	0.0%	84.7%	100.0%	100.0%	100.0%
2	7.50	1.903	6.89	0.0	72.8	99.8	100.0	100.0
3	8.00	2.024	6.94	0.0	50.8	98.6	100.0	100.0
4	8.50	2.182	7.00	0.0	31.2	93.9	100.0	100.0
5	9.00	2.368	7.05	0.0	17.7	83.3	99.8	100.0
6	9.50	2.573	7.11	0.0	9.9	67.7	98.5	100.0
7	10.00	2.847	7.16	0.0	6.0	51.2	94.4	100.0
8	10.50	3.268	7.17	0.0	4.5	37.8	85.4	100.0
9	11.00	3.859	7.30	0.0	4.2	29.3	73.1	100.0
10	11.50	4.518	7.52	0.0	4.3	24.1	61.5	100.0
11	12.00	5.214	7.74	0.0	4.5	20.8	52.1	100.0
12	12.50	5.941	7.82	0.0	4.7	18.6	44.8	99.7
13	13.00	6.751	7.71	0.0	5.2	17.3	39.5	99.0
14	13.50	7.607	7.81	0.0	5.7	16.6	35.6	97.4
15	14.00	8.484	7.83	0.0	6.1	16.1	32.7	94.8
16	14.50	9.412	7.63	0.0	6.7	15.8	30.5	91.5
17	15.00	10.390	7.43	0.0	7.3	15.8	29.0	87.6
18	15.50	11.405	7.23	0.1	7.9	15.9	27.8	83.6
19	16.00	12.448	7.03	0.1	8.5	16.1	27.0	79.6
20	16.50	13.511	6.82	0.2	9.1	16.3	26.3	75.9
21	17.00	14.599	6.72	0.4	9.7	16.6	25.9	72.4
22	17.50	15.744	6.72	0.5	10.3	16.9	25.6	69.2
23	18.00	16.937	6.72	0.8	11.0	17.4	25.5	66.4
24	18.01	16.973	6.72	0.8	11.0	17.4	25.5	66.3

policy has a 15% probability of loss for 0% return, the mix may be changed over the short run, as long as the probability of loss of the new mix has a maximum of 15%. Therefore, by taking advantage of short-term expectations to maximize return, the integrity of the long-term policy is retained.

A floor or base probability of loss is therefore established that can provide boundaries within which strategic return/risk decisions may be made. As long as the alteration of the portfolio mix does not violate the probability of loss, increased return through strategic judgment can be pursued. Ultimately, the value of the judgment must be reviewed, but the mechanism for translating the judgment into decision-making boundaries is served through an asset allocation framework.

APPENDIX A: RISK-OF-LOSS ANALYSIS FOR ASSET ALLOCATION

In the process of locating points on the efficient frontier for the asset allocation optimization model we described in this chapter, the standard deviation of the optimal portfolio at each point can also be obtained. These values form the basis for determining the probabilities of loss associated with these mixes. In this appendix we shall explain this process which we called *risk-of-loss analysis*.

If the optimal mixes associated with M values of R are called χ_m (m = 1,2, . . . , M), associated with R_m, the corresponding minimum standard deviations can be called σ_m. Using matrix notation, these are related according to

$$R_m = r'\chi_m$$

and

$$\sigma_m = \sqrt{\chi'_m \Sigma \chi_m}$$

Thus R_m and σ_m represent the total expected return and total standard deviation, respectively based on the individual components r and Σ given for a single time period.

The probability of not achieving the expected return level L with the constrained optimal portfolio with an expected return of R_m,

$$Q = \Pr\{R \leq L \mid \chi_m\},$$

may now be determined.

This computation requires some assumption about the shape of the distribution of periodic returns R.

Assume that the periodic portfolio returns are lognormally distributed with mean R_m and variance so that the variable z given by

$$z = \ln(1 + R)$$

will be normally distributed with mean

$$\mu_{zm} = \ln(1 + R_m)$$

and variance

$$\sigma_m = \ln \left[\frac{\sigma_m^2 + (R_m + 1)^2}{(R_m + 1)^2} \right]$$

Under this assumption, the probability of loss for this optimal mix (expected return R_m) with the loss threshold L may then be obtained as follows:

$$Q_m = PR\{z_m \equiv \ln(1 + R) \le \ln(1 + L) \mid \chi_m\}$$

$$= \frac{1}{2} + \frac{1}{2} \, \text{erf} \left[\frac{\ln(1 + L) - \mu_{z_m}}{\sqrt{2}\sigma_{z_m}} \right]$$

where "erf" is the error functional defined as

$$\text{erf}(x) = \int_0^x e^{-t^2} \, dt$$

The probability of loss of t time periods can be obtained using the random walk assumption discussed in this chapter. It will be

$$Q_m(t) = \frac{1}{2} + \frac{1}{2} \, \text{erf} \left[\frac{\ln(1 + L) - \mu_{z_m}t}{\sqrt{2}t \, \sigma_{z_m}} \right]$$

which represents the probability of not achieving at least the total return L in t time periods using the optimal mix χ_m, which has a total expected return R_m (or tR_m for t time periods) and standard deviation σ_m (or $\sigma_m \sqrt{t}$).

APPENDIX B: MULTIPLE SCENARIO EXTENSION FOR ASSET ALLOCATION MODEL

In this chapter, we described how the basic asset allocation model could be extended to multiple scenarios. In this appendix, we shall describe this approach.

Suppose the forecast of the course of future events is to be expressed in terms of N possible scenarios, which are discrete or mutually exclusive and to each of which a probability of occurrence, P_n, $n = 1, 2, \ldots, N$, is assigned. Suppose, in addition, that the joint distribution of asset returns under each of these possible scenarios is given by $f_n(z)$, where z is the vector of future returns of the J assets over the time period of the forecast. Just as in the case of a single scenario, the expected return of the nth scenario, $\hat{R}_n$, given its occurrence, will be

$$\hat{R}_n = E_n(R(z)) = \int\int \ldots \int x'zf_n(z)dz_1dz_2 \ldots dz_j$$

$$= x'E_n(z)$$

and its standard deviation will be

$$\hat{\sigma}^2_{R_n} = E_n[(R(z) - \hat{R}_n)^2] = \int\int \ldots \int (R_n(z) - R_n)^2 f_n(z)dz_1dz_2\ldots dz_j$$

$$= x'\Sigma_n x$$

where x is a column vector whose elements are the allocation of the portfolio to security i, and where Σ_n is the covariance matrix among the J assets given the occurrence of the *nth* scenario. Consider the unconditional distribution (i.e., without knowledge of which scenario will occur), which can be called the composite distribution and identified with the scenario subscript denoted by an asterisk (*). Since the scenarios are assumed to be mutually exclusive, the composite joint distribution may be written merely as a superposition of the joint distributions of the individual scenarios:

$$f_*(z) = \sum_n P_n f_n(z)$$

This immediately yields the unconditional (or composite) expected return:

$$\hat{R}_* = \int\int ... \int x'z \left[\sum_n f_n(z)\right] dz_1 dz_2 \, ... \, dz_j$$

$$= \sum_n P_n \hat{R}_n$$

The variance of the composite distribution requires slightly more effort but may be reduced to

$$\hat{\sigma}_*^2 = E[(R - R_*)^2]$$

$$= \int\int ... \int \left(\sum_{j-1}^{J} x_j z_j - \hat{R}_*\right)\left(\sum_{k-1}^{J} x_k z_k - \hat{R}_*\right)$$

$$\times \left[\sum_n f_n(z)\right] dz_1 dz_2 \, ... \, dz_j$$

$$= \sum_n P_n \sum_{j=1}^{J} \sum_{k=1}^{J} x_j x_k \left[cov_n(z_j, z_k) - (\hat{z}_{jn} - \hat{z}_{j*})(\hat{z}_{kn} - \hat{z}_{k*})\right]$$

where $cov_n(z_j, z_k)$ represents the conditional covariance between the assets j and k given the occurrence of scenario *n*. $\hat{z}_{jn}$ represents the mean return for the *jth* asset with the *nth* scenario, and $\hat{z}_{j*}$ is the mean return of the *jth* asset with the composite scenario, or

$$\hat{z}_{j*} = \sum_n P_n \hat{z}_{jn}$$

The quadratic form $\hat{\sigma}_*^2$ may now be minimized to obtain the constrained optimal mixes at each return level of the composite scenario just as for a single scenario.

The unconditional probability of loss may be readily estimated if the assumption that the distribution of total portfolio returns for each scenario is lognormal is again made. Since the scenarios are mutually exclusive, the distribution of portfolio returns will be the sum of the conditional distributions weighted by the probability of occurrence of each:

$$g_*(z) = \sum_n P_n g_n(z)$$

It follows immediately from the expressions derived for the individual scenarios that the probability of not achieving at least the total return L in t time periods using the optimal mix (for the composite scenario) χ_{m^*}, which has a total expected return $t R_{\bullet m}$ and standard deviation $\sigma_{*m}\sqrt{t}$, will be

$$Q_{*m}(t) - \frac{1}{2} + \frac{1}{2} \sum_n P_n \mathrm{erf}\left[\frac{1n(1 + L) - \mu_{nz_m} t}{\sqrt{2t}\ \sigma_{nz_m}}\right]$$

where

$$\mu_{nz_m} = 1n(1 + \hat{R}_{nm})$$

and

$$\sigma_{nz_m} = 1n\left[\frac{\hat{\sigma}_{nm}{}^2 + (\hat{R}_{nm} + 1)^2}{(\hat{R}_{nm} + 1)^2}\right]$$

$\hat{R}_{nm}$ represents the portfolio expected return level for the *nth* scenario assumptions using the mth optimal mix for the composite portfolio and $\hat{\sigma}_{nz_m}$ the corresponding portfolio return standard deviation.

CHAPTER 9

Asset Performance and Surplus Control — A Dual-Shortfall Approach

MARTIN L. LEIBOWITZ
MANAGING DIRECTOR
SALOMON BROTHERS INC

STANLEY KOGELMAN
VICE PRESIDENT
SALOMON BROTHERS INC

LAWRENCE N. BADER
VICE PRESIDENT
SALOMON BROTHERS INC

INTRODUCTION

This chapter presents an asset allocation methodology for constructing portfolios that strikes a balance between asset performance and maintenance of acceptable levels of downside risk in *both* asset and surplus

The authors wish to express their appreciation for the helpful comments and suggestions from Keith Ambachtsheer, Allan Emkin, Michael Granito, and William Sharpe.

contexts. In the real world, pension fund sponsors do not have the luxury of being able to pursue a single well-defined goal. Rather, they must contend with a complex set of multiple objectives. These include achieving market-related returns on assets when the market does well and attaining at least some minimum return when the market does poorly. At the same time, sponsors are expected to maintain or improve their funding status relative to a variety of liability measures.

Even when the plan's funding status is not considered, the strategic asset allocation decision is not easy. The fundamental issue is how to capture the risk premium of equity while avoiding excessively high levels of volatility. Through a combination of mean-variance analysis and tradition, most funds have settled on a long-term strategic allocation target of a 50–60% investment in equity-like assets, with the balance primarily in fixed-income securities. The fixed income component tends to be regarded as a single asset class whose characteristics reflect the bond market as a whole. This characterization leads to a duration that is representative of the investment grade bond market—currently about 4.64 years.[1] In essence, when stripped of the (usually token) investments in other asset classes, many allocation studies really lead to a single decision: the percentage to be allocated to equity.

Unfortunately, the resulting 60% stock/40% bond portfolio has far less interest rate sensitivity than a pension plan's accumulated benefit obligation (ABO), which typically has a duration of about 10 years. Thus, the standard allocation leads to significant surplus volatility, because the pension fund is vulnerable both to poor equity returns when the stock market weakens, and to high liability returns when the bond market rallies. In recent years, particularly with the advent of the Financial Accounting Standards Board Statement 87 (FASB 87), there has been a growing interest in models that set the allocation problem in a liability framework.[2] However, these new asset/liability models generally have problems of their own.

At one extreme, an "immunized" portfolio minimizes surplus risk by matching the duration of a 100% bond portfolio to the duration of the liability. While "immunization" may be useful in the short-term manage-

[1]Over the past seven years the effective duration of the Salomon Broad Investment Grade Bond (BIG) Index has ranged from a low of 3.87 years to a high of 4.69 years. On April 1, 1991, the duration was 4.64 years.
[2]For example, see Martin L. Leibowitz, *A New Perspective on Asset Allocation,* The Research Foundation of The Institute of Chartered Financial Analysts, December 1987.

ment of the ABO under unusual circumstances, a dynamic ongoing fund has a far more complex liability structure than can be represented by the ABO alone. Thus, immunizing against the ABO (or indeed, against any single liability measure) tends to foreclose the growth opportunities and inflation protection needed for the long-term benefit of plan sponsors and participants alike.

However, there are more general surplus-based models that treat bonds as a "variable asset class" with duration/volatility values that range from Treasury bills up to risk levels that far exceed that of domestic equities. In contrast to asset-only models that essentially prescribe only an equity percentage, these generalized surplus-based models tend to characterize allocations in terms of the equity percentage *and* a duration target for the bond component. These models move beyond immunization and can accommodate significant equity holdings. However, surplus optimizations almost invariably push the duration to extremes by forcing the dollar duration of the bond component to match the dollar duration of the liabilities. The resulting bond durations of 15 years or longer may make sense from a narrowly defined surplus-only vantage point, but they entail extraordinary levels of asset volatility.[3]

For these reasons, surplus optimization models have not proven productive in generating allocations that most funds would find viable. To achieve a reasonable balance between asset and surplus shortfall risks, this chapter presents a methodology for applying simultaneous shortfall constraints on both the asset performance *and* the fund surplus. As an example of this methodology, we construct a new portfolio with the same asset-only shortfall risk as the 60/40 benchmark portfolio but with a more stringent limit on the surplus shortfall. One surprising finding is that modest adjustments to the bond duration and equity percentage are often sufficient to satisfy both constraints. This finding contrasts with surplus optimization approaches that tend to suggest unpalatably long durations. Thus, our dual-shortfall approach avoids the problem of extreme portfolios to which single-objective optimizations are notoriously prone. By design, this approach can develop allocations that are better crafted for the more realistic situation where the fund faces conflicting goals.

---

[3]For one approach that avoids many of these problems, see William F. Sharpe and Lawrence G. Tint, "Liabilities – A New Approach," *Journal of Portfolio Management*, Winter 1990.

THE ASSET-ONLY FRAMEWORK

To analyze the risk/return characteristics of stock/bond portfolios with
bonds of varying durations, we must make assumptions regarding expected returns, volatilities and the stock/bond correlation (see Exhibit 1).
We assume that the one-year expected return for the BIG index is 8.0%,
and that U.S. equity provides a 5% risk premium over bonds. The one-
year volatility of U.S. equity is taken as 17%, interest rate volatility is
1.5%, and the stock/bond correlation is 0.35. Under these assumptions
the bond asset class will have a volatility of approximately 7.0%.[4] For
later reference, Exhibit 1 also shows the expected return and standard
deviation of the benchmark portfolio.

The volatilities and expected returns of portfolios consisting of varying proportions of stocks and the BIG Index plot along a curve in a
risk/return diagram, as illustrated in Exhibit 2. As equity is added to the
bond portfolio, the portfolio return increases proportionately. The volatility of the portfolio returns also changes with the additional equity.
However, because the correlation is fairly low, diversification may initially lead to a decrease (or very gradual increase) in volatility.

We now broaden our discussion of asset allocation by varying the
duration of the fixed-income component of the portfolio. To clarify the
impact of duration, we use an artificial "flat yield curve" model that
makes two assumptions: 1) Bonds of all maturities provide the same 8%

EXHIBIT 1
ASSUMPTIONS ON STOCK AND BOND RETURNS
(STOCK/BOND CORRELATION = 0.35)

Asset	Expected Return	Standard Deviation
Equity	13.0%	17.0%
BIG Index	8.0	7.0
60% Stock/40% BIG Index (Benchmark)	11.0	11.5

---

[4]Because the duration of the BIG Index is fairly stable, we estimate the return volatility by
multiplying the 4.64-year duration by the 1.5% interest rate volatility. In this chapter, we make
the simplifying assumption that the interest rate volatility is the same at all points along the
yield curve.

EXHIBIT 2
THE RISK/RETURN TRADE-OFF FOR STOCKS/BOND PORTFOLIOS
(DURATION = 4.64 YEARS)

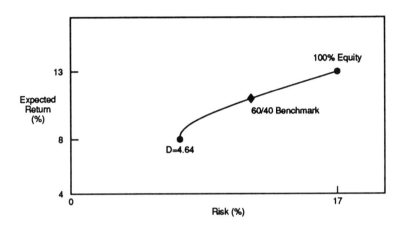

yield; and 2) the *expected return* is equal to the yield. The "cash" asset is taken to be 1-year Treasury STRIPS that have an initial duration of 1 year and a zero volatility at the end of the 1-year holding period. As the duration of bonds increases, so does the return volatility. This is shown in Exhibit 3, where we have indicated a range of fixed-income portfolio durations along a horizontal line at an 8% expected return.

In Exhibit 4, we have drawn a diagonal line from the cash point to the 100%-equity point. This line represents the risk/return characteristics of the full range of cash/equity portfolios. These portfolios plot on a straight line because all the portfolio risk is due to the proportion of equity. At any given level of risk, by moving vertically in the risk/return diagram, we see that the cash/equity portfolio provides a higher return than a portfolio of stocks and 4.64-year-duration bonds. This results from the zero volatility of cash, which permits a higher proportion of equity for a given portfolio volatility.

In Exhibit 4, we have also added the risk/return curve for portfolios containing 12-year-duration bonds. The "efficient" portfolios are located on the upper portion of this curve. The deep "bubble" to the left reflects the fact that the benefits of diversification are more pronounced for these long-duration, high-volatility bonds.

EXHIBIT 3
THE FLAT YIELD CURVE

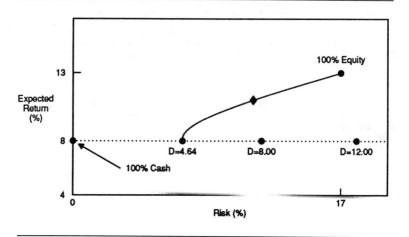

EXHIBIT 4
EFFICIENT STOCK/BOND FRONTIER FOR VARYING BOND DURATIONS
(STOCK/BOND CORRELATION = 0.35)

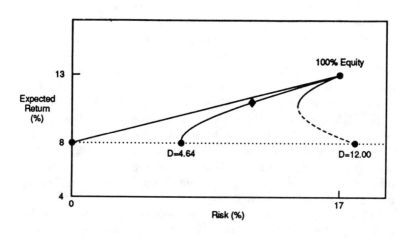

More generally, every point in the risk/return diagram represents a unique stock/bond portfolio that is characterized by the equity percentage and the duration of the fixed-income component. With our simplistic assumption of a flat yield curve and a positive stock/bond correlation, the portfolio that provides the highest return for a given level of risk will always be a cash/equity portfolio. In this sense, cash/equity portfolios dominate all other stock/bond portfolios. If the yield curve is not flat, there may be mixes of cash, bonds and equities that dominate the cash/equity portfolios. In addition, it should be noted that although the stock/bond correlation tends to be positive over long time periods, there are occasional periods when correlation is negative. During such periods, longer-duration bonds may provide significant diversification benefits even if the yield curve is flat.[5]

THE RETURN DISTRIBUTION FOR THE BENCHMARK PORTFOLIO

To gain some perspective on the expected performance of the benchmark portfolio, we assume that both stock and bond returns over a one-year horizon are normally distributed. In Exhibit 5, we illustrate the 60/40 benchmark portfolio return distribution. It can be shown that this 60% stock/40% bond portfolio has an expected return of 11% and a standard deviation of 11.5%. For any normal distribution, there is a 16% probability that returns will fall more than one standard deviation below the mean (that is, below −0.5% = 11.0% − 11.5%), and there is a 10% probability that returns will be more than 1.28 standard deviations below the mean (that is, below −3.7% = 11.0% − 1.28 x 11.5%). The region to the left of −3.7% is shaded and will be referred to as the *10% shortfall region*. A return of −3.7% will be referred to as the *threshold return*.

The −3.7% threshold return represents the implicit shortfall risk inherent in the benchmark portfolio. We will assume that the plan sponsor is comfortable with this level of asset-only risk. Consequently, any new

---

[5]See Martin L. Leibowitz, Roy D. Henriksson, William S. Krasker, *Portfolio Optimization Utilizing the Full Yield Curve: An Improved Approach to Fixed Income as an Asset Class,* Salomon Brothers Inc, October 1987.

EXHIBIT 5
THE RETURN DISTRIBUTION FOR THE BENCHMARK PORTFOLIO

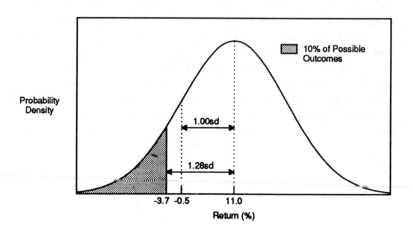

sd = Standard deviation.

allocation that offers a higher expected return but the same shortfall risk as the benchmark portfolio will be viewed as a portfolio improvement.[6]

Because the tenth percentile return is 1.28 standard deviations below the mean, it always takes 128 basis points of added expected return to compensate for 100 basis points of incremental risk. As a consequence, as we have shown in previous papers, all portfolios with equivalent shortfall risk plot along a straight line with slope 1.28 in a risk/return

[6]We utilize the indicated measure of shortfall risk because it is intuitively appealing and easy to apply. However, the shortfall probability we have defined is an incomplete measure ot risk. It fails to provide any indication of how bad the shortfall will be in the event that one should occur. For a more fully developed theory of shortfall analysis that incorporates these "higher" considerations, see W.V. Harlow and R. Rao, "Asset Pricing in a Generalized Mean-Lower Partial Moment Framework: Theory and Evidence," *Journal of Financial and Quantitative Analysis,* September 1989; and V. Bawa and E.B. Lindenberg, "Capital Market Equilibrium in a Mean, Lower Partial Moment Framework," *Journal of Financial Economics,* November 1977.

diagram.[7] In Exhibit 6, we have constructed a 10% shortfall line through the benchmark portfolio point. Note that this line intersects the (vertical) expected return axis at –3.7% — the threshold return point. All points along the shortfall line represent portfolios for which the expected return offsets the portfolio volatility sufficiently to insure a 90% probability that the one-year return will exceed –3.7%. For example, a portfolio with a standard deviation of 12.5% (100 basis points greater than the bench-mark portfolio volatility) and an expected return of 12.28% (128 basis points greater than the benchmark portfolio return), will have a tenth percentile return of –3.7% (12.28% – [1.28 x 12.5%]).

Portfolios above the shortfall line have a higher expected return for a given risk than do portfolios on the line. Consequently, all portfolios above the line have a *greater* than 90% probability that the one-year return will exceed –3.7%. Conversely, portfolios below the shortfall line have inferior shortfall performance.

EXHIBIT 6
THE IMPLICIT SHORTFALL CONSTRAINT FOR THE BENCHMARK PORTFOLIO

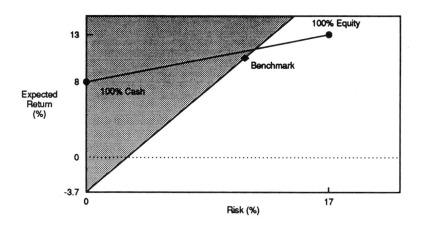

[7]See, for example, Martin L. Leibowitz, Stanley Kogelman and Thomas E. Klaffky, *A Shortfall Approach to Duration Management,* Salomon Brothers Inc, April 1990, and Martin L. Leibowitz and Stanley Kogelman, "Asset Allocation Under Shortfall Constraints," *Journal of Portfolio Management,* Winter 1991.

The shortfall line in Exhibit 6 can be shown to intersect the cash/equity line at a point representing a portfolio with 70% stocks and 30% bonds. This portfolio has the same shortfall risk as the benchmark portfolio, but it has an expected return of 11.5%. Thus, by moving to the 70/30 portfolio, the fund manager can pick up 50 basis points in expected return while maintaining the same level of asset shortfall risk.

MODELING THE LIABILITY

Our analysis focuses on the relatively well defined ABO. The ABO is the value of benefits earned to date by retirees, former employees with vested rights, and current employees. It approximates the termination liability of the plan. Thus, a comparison of the ABO with the current value of plan assets indicates the deficit or surplus that would exist if the plan were terminated.

The ABO is also the basis for a balance sheet liability under FASB 87, and a proxy for the "current liability" used under ERISA to determine whether plan contributions are currently required from the employer. Because the future events reflected in the ABO are primarily demographic (mortality, age at retirement), rather than economic (salary increases), the ABO benefit stream may be regarded as essentially fixed for investment purposes. Consequently, the ABO can be modeled as if it were a fixed-income security. The benefit payments associated with more comprehensive measures of liability, such as the projected benefit obligation (PBO), reflect future economic events and have a more complex structure.

The ABO duration is plan-specific, depending on the mix of active and retired plan participants, their ages, the assumed retirement ages of active employees, and the benefit formula. Most plans have ABO durations in the range of 9–12 years.

In computing the ABO, FASB 87 directs the use of a discount rate equivalent to that at which plan benefits could be "settled," for example by an annuity purchase. The yield on high-quality fixed-income investments (8% in our examples) is suggested as a suitable guide for this settlement rate. This rate may also be interpreted as the expected "liability return." In other words, the ABO is expected to grow at 8%, apart from benefit payments and adjustments for the additional benefits that employees earn each year (that is, the "service cost").

In Exhibit 7, we illustrate the position of a 10-year duration ABO liability in the risk/return diagram of Exhibit 4. Note that the benchmark portfolio point and the liability point are quite far apart; that is, the risk/return characteristics of the benchmark portfolio differ markedly from those of the ABO liability. We should, therefore, expect considerable variations in the pension fund surplus over time.[8]

THE SURPLUS RETURN

The pension fund surplus is the difference between the current value of the assets and the present value of the liability.[9] Over time, as the value

EXHIBIT 7
A TEN-YEAR-DURATION ABO LIABILITY

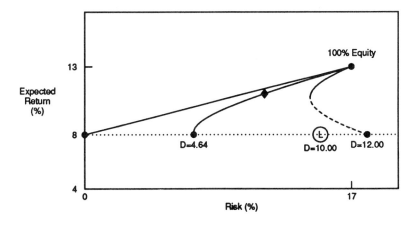

ABO = Accumulated Benefit Obligation. L = Liability.

---

[8]Our approach can easily be extended so that a performance benchmark is viewed as a "liability" against which "surplus" returns are measured. Thus, the dual-shortfall approach can be viewed as simultaneously controlling both the absolute risk and the risk relative to a designated performance benchmark.

[9]For a discussion of the application of the shortfall approach to managing an insurance company's surplus, see Alfred Weinberger and Vincent Kaminski, *Asset Allocation for Property/Casualty Insurance Companies: A Going-Concern Approach,* Salomon Brothers Inc, June 1991.

of assets and liabilities changes, so will the surplus. There are a number of ways to define a "surplus return" measure. Since the surplus itself is commonly expressed as a percentage of the liability, we define our surplus return as follows:[10]

$$\text{Surplus Return} = \frac{\text{Change in Surplus}}{\text{Initial Value of Liabilities}}.$$

For example (see Exhibit 8), suppose that the initial liability is $100 million and the initial assets are $140 million. Then the funding ratio is 140% ($140 million/$100 million) and the surplus is $40 million. If the liability increases by 8% to $108 million, and the assets increase by 11% to $155.4 million, the surplus will have increased by $7.4 million to $47.4 million ($155.4 million – $108.0 million). This surplus increase is 7.4% of the initial liability.

Exhibit 8 also shows how the value of the surplus return depends on the initial funding ratio. In general, if two pension plans have the same asset and liability returns, the plan with the greater funding ratio will have the greater surplus return. For example, if the funding ratio is 100%, the assets and liabilities will be equal and the surplus is zero. In this case, 11% asset growth leads to a surplus return of 3%. If the funding ratio is less than 100%, the assets will be less than the liability and the surplus may decrease even though the asset return is greater than the liability return. For a 60% funding ratio, for example, the surplus return is –1.4%, despite the 11% asset growth.

We will now focus on the distribution of surplus returns when the funding ratio is 140% and the assets are represented by our benchmark portfolio. Because both the asset and liability returns are assumed to be normally distributed, the surplus returns are normally distributed as well. Under our assumptions, the expected surplus return is 7.4% and the standard deviation of surplus returns is 14.7% (see Appendix for details). As indicated earlier, for any normal return distribution there is a 10% probability that the return will be 1.28 or more standard deviations below the 7.4% mean. Thus, there is a 10% probability of a surplus decline of

---

[10]The surplus could just as easily have been measured against the current value of assets. For example, see William F. Sharpe, "Asset Allocation," *Managing Investment Portfolios,* Second Edition, edited by John L. Maginn and Donald L. Tuttle, Warren, Gorham & Lamont, 1990. Our results can be converted to surplus returns relative to the current asset value by dividing by the funding ratio. Also, our results can be converted to dollar surplus changes by multiplying by the initial liability value.

at least 11.5% (–11.5% = 7.4% – 1.28 x 14.7%). In Exhibit 9, we summarize the return and shortfall characteristics from both asset and surplus perspectives. The last column in the figure shows target tenth percentile returns that will be discussed in subsequent sections.

THE SHORTFALL CURVE FOR THE SURPLUS RETURN

Pension fund sponsors who wish to achieve stability in the plan's surplus can do so with a bond portfolio that matches the liability in present value, duration, and other volatility characteristics. Such an "immunized portfolio" will preserve the surplus within some reasonable range of interest rate changes. Most sponsors, however, do not require this degree of safety. Typically, a sponsor with a 140% funding ratio might be willing to sustain some surplus risk provided the portfolio had substantial upside potential. However, there usually will be some limit to the surplus loss that a sponsor can comfortably sustain. This loss limit will depend on a variety of factors, including the current funding ratio, the fund's performance over prior years, and the level of funding needed to avoid a balance-sheet liability or sustain a contribution holiday. To quantify surplus return risk, we focus on the tenth percentile surplus return and somewhat arbitrarily impose the following *surplus shortfall condition:*

> *There should be no more than a 10% probability that the surplus return will be less than –7%. That is, we require 90% assurance of a surplus return in excess of –7%.*

In an earlier section of this chapter, we showed that an asset shortfall constraint that was similar to the above surplus constraint could be represented by a straight line in a risk/return diagram. The surplus constraint pattern is far more complicated, and it is represented by an "egg-shaped" convex curve (see Appendix for a theoretical discussion).

In Exhibit 10, we illustrate the surplus shortfall curve for a pension fund with a 140% funding ratio and a 10-year duration liability. Each point within the "egg" represents an asset portfolio that fulfills the surplus shortfall condition. We have also included the benchmark portfolio and the immunizing portfolio points for reference. The immunizing portfolio is an all-bond portfolio that has the same dollar sensitivity to interest rate changes as the liability. The duration of the immunizing portfolio is 7.1 years (that is, the 10-year liability duration divided by the 140%

EXHIBIT 8
A LIABILITY-BASED SURPLUS RETURN EXAMPLE (DOLLARS IN MILLIONS)

Funding Ratio		Initial Value	Final Value	Liability or Asset Return	Surplus Return
	Liability	$100.0	$108.0	8.0%	
140%	Assets	140.0	155.4	11.0	7.4%
	Surplus	40.0	47.4		
100	Assets	100.0	111.0	11.0	
	Surplus	0.0	3.0		3.0
60	Assets	60.0	66.6	11.0	
	Surplus	(40.0)	(41.4)		(1.4)

EXHIBIT 9
PERFORMANCE SUMMARY FOR THE BENCHMARK PORTFOLIO

	Current Expected Return	Current Standard Deviation	Current 10th Percentile Return	Target 10th Percentile Return
Asset-Only Performance	11.0%	11.5%	(3.7)%	(3.7)%
Surplus	7.4	14.7	(11.5)	(7.0)

EXHIBIT 10
THE SURPLUS SHORTFALL CURVE (FUNDING RATIO = 140%)

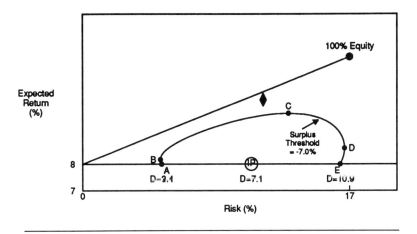

IP = Immunizing Portfolio.

funding ratio). To see why this is so, we first observe that if the liability is $100 million, the assets are $140 million. If interest rates decline by 1%, the liability, with its 10-year duration, will grow by 10% or $10 million (10% of $100 million). At the same time, the assets will increase by 7.1% (the 7.1-year duration multiplied by 1%). In dollar terms, this also represents a $10 million increase (7.1% of $140 million).

To develop an intuitive understanding of the shortfall curve, we first observe that point A in Exhibit 10 represents a 100% bond portfolio with a 3.4-year duration. This is the shortest-duration all-bond portfolio for which there is at most a 10% probability that the surplus return will be –7% or less. For any all-bond portfolio with shorter duration, the gap between the bond duration and the immunizing portfolio is too large, and the shortfall probability will exceed 10%.

As we move to the right of portfolio A, we encounter all-bond portfolios with durations that are closer to the 7.1-year immunizing duration. Consequently, such portfolios will have better shortfall performance than portfolio A. Ultimately, we reach portfolio E, which has a 10.9-year duration. Because the durations of portfolios A and E are equidistant from the 7.1-year immunizing duration, both of these portfolios have the same duration gap and therefore the same –7% surplus shortfall threshold. Portfolios to the right of portfolio E have longer durations than E and will not meet the shortfall constraint.

We now consider the impact of adding equity to portfolio A. Since equity provides a 5% expected return premium over fixed income, the portfolio return will increase as the equity percentage increases. In addition, the low correlation between equity and the liability at first causes the surplus volatility to increase more slowly than the surplus return. Consequently, the initial additions of equity actually *reduce* the surplus shortfall probability, and the shortfall curve bubbles slightly to the left as we move upward from A. However, a point (B) is reached where further equity additions cause the surplus volatility to increase very rapidly. To compensate for this equity-related volatility, the bond duration must be increased so as to bring the asset portfolio duration closer to the immunizing duration

Under the assumptions of our example, each point along the shortfall curve represents a unique portfolio characterized by the percentage of equity in the portfolio and the duration of the fixed-income component. Portfolio C is the maximum equity portfolio that fulfills the shortfall constraint. It consists of 47% stocks and 53% bonds. From a surplus perspective, portfolio C looks very attractive because of its high expected return. However, the long duration (close to 10 years) of the fixed-income portion of the portfolio leads to high volatility from an asset-only perspective.[11]

Portfolios that lie on the portion of the shortfall curve from C to E can be understood by applying logic similar to that used for portfolios from A to C. It suffices to note that these points correspond to very long duration portfolios consisting of a decreasing percentage of equity.

All portfolios that fall on or within the shortfall "egg" will meet or exceed the surplus shortfall condition. Because the benchmark portfolio "diamond" falls outside the shortfall curve, it fails to meet the surplus shortfall condition. The portion of the "egg" between portfolios B and

---

[11]The flatness of the shortfall egg near portfolio C indicates that a very small reduction in equity holdings permits a very large decrease in the bond duration without violating the surplus constraint. A fund with significant equity holdings may therefore choose a bond duration that is far from the surplus-optimal duration while obtaining surplus protection that is only slightly suboptimal. For a discussion of this insensitivity to bond duration, see Martin L. Leibowitz, Stanley Kogelman, Lawrence N. Bader, *Risk-Adjusted Surplus: A New Measure of Pension Fund Risk*, Chapter 10. For a given surplus shortfall threshold, Point C is the point at which the total portfolio duration is the immunizing duration. The total portfolio duration concept is introduced in Martin L. Leibowitz, "Total Portfolio Duration," *Financial Analysts Journal*, September/October, 1986.

C can be thought of as a "shortfall efficient frontier" because, among all portfolios meeting the surplus constraint, these portfolios offer the most favorable risk/return trade-off. However, from an asset-only perspective, some of these portfolios will have greater shortfall risk than the benchmark portfolio. In the next section, we show how the asset and surplus shortfall constraints can be jointly managed.

BALANCING ASSET AND SURPLUS SHORTFALL REQUIREMENTS

We have observed that the benchmark portfolio lies outside the surplus shortfall curve corresponding to a minimum surplus return of –7%. This is consistent with the earlier observation that the tenth percentile surplus return for the benchmark portfolio was –11.5%. Thus, meeting the surplus constraint will require restructuring the asset portfolio so that the new portfolio lies on or within the surplus shortfall curve (see the shaded portion of Exhibit 11). In choosing this new portfolio, we must be careful that the asset-only constraints are also maintained. In Exhibit 11, we observe that to meet the surplus shortfall constraint, no more than 36% of the portfolio can be allocated to equity if the bond duration is 4.6

EXHIBIT 11
PORTFOLIOS THAT MEET A –7% SURPLUS SHORTFALL
CONSTRAINT (FUNDING RATIO = 140%)

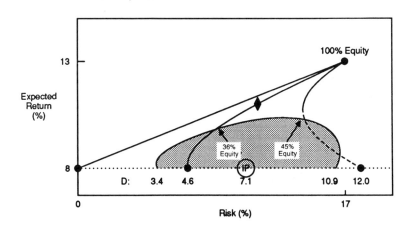

years. If the bond duration is 12 years, the maximum equity allocation is 45%.

Under the assumption that the plan sponsor finds the asset-only risk of the benchmark portfolio to be acceptable (that is, a –3.7% asset-return threshold), we now construct a portfolio that maintains that level of asset-only shortfall *and* meets the surplus constraint. In Exhibit 6, we observed that all portfolios that met the asset constraint were located on or above the shortfall line drawn through the benchmark portfolio. In Exhibit 12, we superimpose this region on the surplus shortfall region of Exhibit 11. The region above the asset shortfall line but inside the "egg" consists of all portfolios that meet both the asset and surplus shortfall requirements. The indicated point of intersection between the shortfall line and the surplus "egg" corresponds to the portfolio with the highest expected return that meets both shortfall requirements. This "dual-shortfall" portfolio consists of 44% stocks and 56% bonds with a 6.6-year duration.

In comparison to the benchmark portfolio, the reduced equity allocation in the dual-shortfall portfolio leads to an 82-basis-point reduction in expected return, from 11.00% to 10.18%. This reduction can be interpreted as the "cost" of bringing the surplus shortfall risk to an acceptable level. On the other hand, the dual-shortfall portfolio has a significantly

EXHIBIT 12
A PORTFOLIO THAT MEETS BOTH ASSET-ONLY AND SURPLUS SHORTFALL CONSTRAINTS

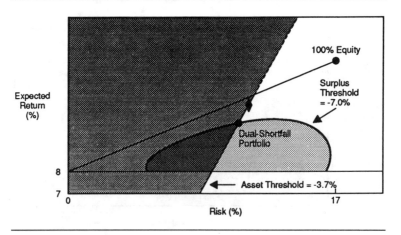

higher expected return and about the same volatility as the immunizing port-folio.[12]

Thus, even in this simple case, the dual-shortfall solution provides for more acceptable return/risk characteristics than either the original 60/40 benchmark portfolio (which has too great a surplus risk) or the immu-nizing portfolio (which guarantees low asset return *and* high asset vol-atility).

It should be noted that these results strongly depend on the one-year investment horizon assumed in our analysis. The one-year time frame allows a relatively short period in which to reliably capture the equity risk premium. Over longer horizons, reasonable surplus shortfall con-straints can be achieved with substantially higher equity allocations and with more moderate duration shifts.

THE IMPACT OF CHANGES IN THE SHORTFALL THRESHOLD

In the previous sections, we arbitrarily imposed a −7% threshold on the surplus return and assumed that the −3.7% asset-only threshold should be maintained. More often, however, the problem is determining the appropriate balance between asset-only and surplus risks. After assessing the implicit shortfall risks in the portfolio, the plan sponsor may decide that the current portfolio structure is satisfactory. If that is not the case, the sponsor must decide whether the current risk posture should be modified in either an asset-only context, a surplus context, or both. In contrast to our earlier example, this assessment might lead to a tightening of the asset constraint, while allowing for greater surplus variability.

In order to better understand the available options for portfolio re-structuring, we first review the shortfall characteristics of our benchmark portfolio with a 140% funding ratio and 10-year duration liability. Recall that in Exhibit 6, we constructed an implicit shortfall constraint for the benchmark portfolio. To that figure, we now add the surplus shortfall curve corresponding to the benchmark portfolio's implicit −11.5% sur-plus return threshold. The benchmark portfolio with the shortfall line and the "−11.5% egg" are shown in Exhibit 13. Note that at a −11.5%

---

[12]See Martin L. Leibowitz and Terence C. Langetieg, "Shortfall Risks and the Asset Allo-cation Decision: A Simulation Analysis of Stock and Bond Risk Profiles," *Journal of Portfolio Management,* Fall 1989, and Martin L. Leibowitz and Stanley Kogelman, "Asset Allocation Under Shortfall Constraints," *Journal of Portfolio Management,* Winter 1991.

threshold, the surplus shortfall requirement is so weak that it is met by almost all stock/bond portfolios. If we had set −14% as the surplus threshold, the "egg" would have been still larger and would have begun to merge with the cash/equity line.

Every portfolio on the "egg" in Exhibit 13 will have a 10% probability of a surplus decline of 11.5% or more. In addition, every portfolio on the asset shortfall line will have a 10% probability of an asset decline of 3.7% or more. Both of these conditions are fulfilled at the point of intersection of the shortfall line and shortfall curve (the benchmark in this case).[13]

Changes in the asset threshold return requirement can be viewed as parallel shifts of the shortfall line. In Exhibit 14, we illustrate the effect of moving the threshold return to a less stringent −6% and to a more stringent −1%. As we increase the threshold return, we move to the left

EXHIBIT 13
IMPLICIT SHORTFALL CONSTRAINTS IN AN ASSET-ONLY AND SURPLUS CONTEXT

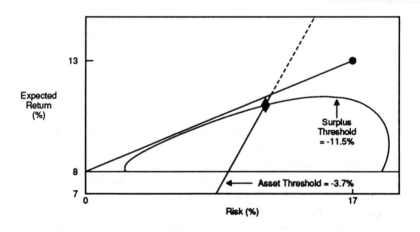

---

[13]For simplicity, we are treating the two shortfall conditions separately. We require that *each* shortfall probability is 10%; that is, we require a 90% assurance of satisfying the asset shortfall and a 90% probability of meeting the surplus requirement. Note that this is *not* equivalent to a 90% probability that all shortfall requirements are satisfied.

EXHIBIT 14
CHANGING THE ASSET RETURN THRESHOLD

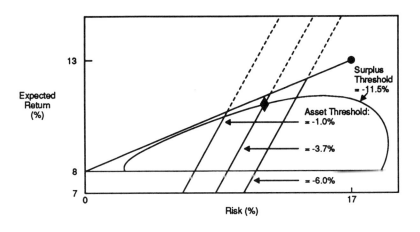

along the "egg" and must accept a lower expected return in order to meet the same surplus shortfall condition. By contrast, as we lower the threshold return, we move to the right along the "egg" and can achieve higher expected returns and the same −11.5% surplus shortfall threshold.

Raising the surplus return threshold will shrink the "egg" and significantly reduce the range of acceptable asset portfolios. As an example, in Exhibit 15, we show the surplus "eggs" corresponding to 10th percentile surplus returns of −7% (our example from the last section) and −3%.

In effect, we can think of the entire risk/return diagram as being covered by a grid of shortfall lines and shortfall curves (see Exhibit 16). Within this grid, the portfolio manager must select an appropriate surplus shortfall curve and a suitable asset shortfall line. The highest intersection point of the line and the curve represents a balanced portfolio that meets the dual-shortfall condition. For example, the most stringent surplus threshold (−3%) would require a portfolio with only 26% stocks, with the balance invested in 6.9-year-duration bonds to meet the surplus requirement and still have the same asset shortfall characteristics as the benchmark (see the "square" in Exhibit 16). When no intersection point exists, either the asset or the surplus shortfall requirement (or both) must be relaxed before a suitable portfolio can be found.

EXHIBIT 15
CHANGING THE SURPLUS RETURN THRESHOLD

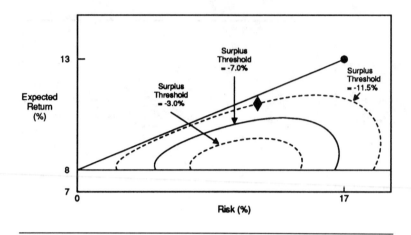

THE IMPACT OF THE FUNDING RATIO

To this point, our examples have focused on pension funds for which the funding ratio is 140%. In actuality, individual funds may have disparate goals in terms of surplus preservation. For example, of two funds having the same high funding ratio, one may desire to lock in the surplus

EXHIBIT 16
THE SHORTFALL GRID

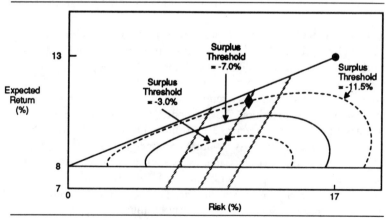

and therefore adopt a more conservative surplus threshold. In contrast, the second fund may feel that its ample surplus allows room to sustain additional surplus risk in order to reach for higher returns.

Thus, funds with the same funding ratios may use very different surplus constraints. If the funding ratios are different, we should not be surprised to encounter an even greater range of allocation choices. In fact, it turns out that the allocation trade-offs are radically altered at different funding ratios, even when the surplus constraints are kept the same.

To better understand this "funding ratio effect," we will maintain a −7% surplus threshold while varying the funding ratio.[14] In Exhibit 17, we compare the shortfall "eggs" for funding ratios of 140%, 110% and 80%. At a 140% funding ratio, the shortfall "egg" covers a wide swath of portfolios having reasonable performance characteristics and also satisfying the asset-only shortfall constraint. As the funding ratio declines, the "eggs" get smaller and move to the right. This means that as the funding ratio declines, the choice of asset portfolios becomes increas-

EXHIBIT 17
CHANGING THE FUNDING RATIO (SURPLUS THRESHOLD = −7%)

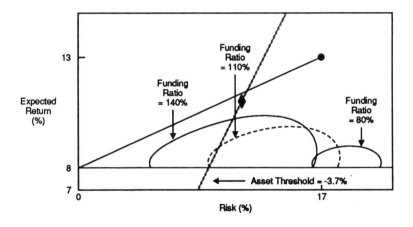

---

[14]The degree to which a plan is vulnerable to surplus shortfall risk can be analyzed in terms of changes in the funding ratio rather than surplus returns.

ingly limited, and the duration of the fixed-income portfolio is forced to more closely approximate an even longer immunizing duration. At a funding ratio of 110%, the 9.1-year immunizing duration (10 years divided by 1.1) is almost the same as the 10-year liability duration. The "egg" is now considerably smaller and has a less desirable location in terms of asset volatility. The asset-only shortfall line passes through the "egg," but the set of relatively low-return portfolios that satisfies both constraints is very restricted.

At a funding ratio of 80%, no portfolios meet the dual-shortfall conditions. In the case of such low funding ratios, there is no easy solution. An immunizing portfolio will simply lock in a negative surplus return by eliminating surplus volatility. Moreover, from an asset-only perspective, immunization would create a very volatile bond portfolio with a 12.5-year duration. As duration is decreased, asset risk decreases but the surplus risk increases and the expected surplus return remains negative. Our methodology does not provide a solution to the underfunding problem, but it does offer a convenient process for assessing the trade-offs in this very difficult environment.

More generally, this analysis shows that a fund's initial funding ratio and its tolerance for surplus risk will significantly affect the optimal target duration. Consequently, one would expect the plan sponsor to find that a more customized fixed-income benchmark is better suited to the plan's goals than any broad market benchmark such as the BIG Index. Fortunately, the diversity of the fixed-income markets naturally allows for the construction of a wide range of such customized indexes.[15]

SUMMARY AND CONCLUSION

This chapter represents a blend of three themes presented in earlier works: 1) surplus management, 2) shortfall constraints, and 3) the expansion of fixed income from a single asset class to a full continuum of available duration points. With our simple flat "return curve" assumption, cash/equity portfolios dominate all other bond/equity portfolios in terms of asset-only performance. In a surplus context, however, the picture changes dramatically. Cash/equity portfolios have considerable surplus volatility and will be inferior to portfolios where the bond component has a reasonable duration.

---

[15]See *Salomon Brothers Fixed-Income Indexes*, Salomon Brothers Inc, July 1989.

In a standard risk/return diagram, the asset-only shortfall constraint is represented by a simple diagonal line. In contrast, the surplus shortfall constraint requires a far more complex "egg-shaped" curve that is roughly centered on top of the immunizing portfolio point. By overlaying these two constraint patterns, it becomes clear how a relatively modest adjustment to the duration and equity percentage can bring the surplus shortfall to within reasonable limits. The trick is to do this without violating restrictions on the asset shortfall.

By extending the process, an asset and surplus shortfall grid can be created that enables the plan sponsor to quickly assess the trade-offs that must be made between asset-only performance and surplus control. The nature of this grid pattern is highly dependent on the initial funding ratio. Moreover, for two funds with the same funding ratio, the choice of an acceptable allocation will depend critically on the plan sponsor's risk tolerance, both in absolute and in relative terms. Consequently, one would expect the optimal portfolio duration target to vary markedly from plan to plan. It would be a rare plan that would find, by happenstance, that its duration target coincided with the duration of a broad market index. Thus, this dual-shortfall approach offers a promising technique for sponsors who are willing to break away from the traditional benchmarks and pursue allocations that are truly based on their own fund's needs and objectives.

APPENDIX

The Surplus Return Distribution

For any pension fund, the surplus is defined to be the excess of the market value of the assets over the present value of the liability. We will assume that the liability discount rate is the yield on high-quality fixed-income instruments.

Because the values of the assets and the liabilities change with changing market conditions, so will the value of the surplus. To model the surplus distribution, we assume that the values of the assets and liabilities are normally distributed. Symbols for the relevant variables are introduced in Exhibit A1.

The initial values of the surplus and funding ratio are

$$S_O = A_O - L_O \tag{1}$$
$$F_O = A_O/L_O. \tag{2}$$

After one year the values of the assets, liabilities and surplus will have changed to $\tilde{A}$, $\tilde{L}$ and $\tilde{S}$ according to the following:

$$\tilde{A} = (1 + \tilde{r}_A)A_O$$
$$\tilde{L} = (1 + \tilde{r}_L)L_O$$
$$\tilde{S} = \tilde{A} - \tilde{L}$$
$$\tilde{S} = (1 + \tilde{r}_A)A_O - (1 + \tilde{r}_L)L_O$$
$$\tilde{S} = (A_O - L_O) + \tilde{r}_A A_O - \tilde{r}_L L_O.$$

In the above equation, the first term on the right is S_O. Hence,

$$\tilde{S} - S_O = L_O[\tilde{r}_A(A_O/L_O) - \tilde{r}_L]. \tag{3}$$

Because S_O may be zero, it is necessary to define a convenient base against which surplus changes can be measured. The natural choice for this base is either A_O or L_O. We choose L_O, because it is the base against which the surplus usually is measured. After dividing both sides of equation (3) by L_O and replacing A_O/L_O by F_O (see equation [2]), the surplus return can be expressed as follows:

$$\tilde{r}_S \equiv \frac{\tilde{S} - S_O}{L_O}$$

$$\tilde{r}_S = F_O \tilde{r}_A - \tilde{r}_L . \tag{4}$$

If we think of $F_O \tilde{r}_A$ as an "adjusted-asset return," equation (4) states that the surplus return is the difference between the adjusted-asset return and the liability return.

The mean of the surplus return distribution can be found by calculating the expected value of both sides of (4).

$$\mu_S = E[\tilde{r}_S] = E[F_O \tilde{r}_A - \tilde{r}_L]$$

$$\mu_S = F_O \mu_A - \mu_L . \tag{5}$$

By definition, the variance of the surplus return distribution is

$$\sigma_S^2 = E[(\tilde{r}_S - \mu_S)^2].$$

By using equations (4) and (5), we derive the following formula for the surplus variance:

$$\sigma_S^2 = E[\{F_O(\tilde{r}_A - \mu_A) - (\tilde{r}_L - \mu_L)\}^2]$$
$$= (F_O \sigma_A)^2 + (\sigma_L)^2 - 2(F_O \sigma_A)\sigma_L \rho_{AL} .$$

The standard deviation of the surplus return distribution is

$$\sigma_S = \sqrt{(F_O \sigma_A)^2 + \sigma_L^2 - 2(F_O \sigma_A)\sigma_L \rho_{AL}} . \tag{6}$$

Allocation Variables

In the previous section, we showed that the volatility of surplus returns depends on both the volatility of the portfolio and the asset/liability correlation. Both these variables depend on the composition of the asset portfolio. Thus, we must derive a formula for σ_A and ρ_{AL} in terms of the relevant asset variables and their respective allocation weights. A summary of symbols for the asset variables is provided in Exhibit A2.

EXHIBIT A1
DEFINITION OF ASSET, LIABILITY AND SURPLUS VARIABLES

Variable	Initial Value	Random Value	One-Year Return	Mean Return	Standard Deviation of Returns	Correlation of Returns with Asset Return
Assets	A_O	$\tilde{A}$	$\tilde{r}_A$	μ_A	σ_A	1.0
Liabilities	L_O	$\tilde{L}$	$\tilde{r}_L$	μ_L	σ_L	ρ_{AL}
Surplus	S_O	$\tilde{S}$	$\tilde{r}_S$	μ_S	σ_S	—

EXHIBIT A2
DEFINITION OF ASSET VARIABLES

Asset	Percent of Portfolio	One-Year Return	Mean Return	Standard Deviation of Returns	Correlation of Returns with Equity Return	Correlation of Returns with Liability Return
Equity	w	$\tilde{r}_E$	μ_E	σ_E	1.0	ρ_{EL}
Bonds	$1-w$	$\tilde{r}_B$	μ_B	σ_B	ρ_{EB}	ρ_{BL}

Because the asset portfolio consists of only stocks and bonds, its return is the weighted average of the stock and bond returns. That is,

$$\tilde{r}_A = w\tilde{r}_E + (1 - w)\tilde{r}_B . \tag{7}$$

Likewise,

$$\mu_A = w\mu_E + (1 - w)\mu_B . \tag{8}$$

Also, from the definition of the standard deviation and the correlation coefficient, it follows that

$$\sigma_A = \sqrt{[w\sigma_E]^2 + [(1 - w)\sigma_B]^2 + 2w(1 - w)\sigma_E\,\sigma_B\,\rho_{EB}} \tag{9}$$

To find ρ_{AL}, we must first find the asset/liability covariance, σ_{AL}. By definition,

$$\sigma_{AL} = E[(\tilde{r}_A - \mu_A)(\tilde{r}_L - \mu_L)]. \tag{10}$$

After utilizing (7) and (8) in (10), we find that

$$\sigma_{AL} = wE[(\tilde{r}_E - \mu_E)(\tilde{r}_L - \mu_L)] + (1 - w)E[(\tilde{r}_B - \mu_B)(\tilde{r}_L - \mu_L)]. \tag{11}$$

The first expectation in (11) is the equity/liability covariance, σ_{EL}, and the second expectation is the bond/liability covariance, σ_{BL}. Thus, σ_{AL} is the weighted-average covariance,

$$\sigma_{AL} = w\sigma_{EL} + (1 - w)\sigma_{BL} . \tag{12}$$

In general, the covariance between two random variables is the product of the correlation coefficient and the two standard deviations. Thus, (12) can be rewritten as follows:

$$\sigma_A\,\sigma_L\,\rho_{AL} = w\sigma_E\,\sigma_L\,\rho_{EL} + (1 - w)\sigma_B\,\sigma_L\,\rho_{BL}$$

or,

$$\rho_{AL} = [w\sigma_E\,\rho_{EL} + (1 - w)\sigma_B\,\rho_{BL}]/\sigma_A .$$

If we assume that $\rho_{BL} = 1$, and the return distributions are normal, then $\rho_{EL} = \rho_{EB}$ and

$$\rho_{AL} = [w\sigma_E \, \rho_{EB} + (1 - w)\sigma_B \,]/\sigma_A \,. \tag{13}$$

As an example of the use of the formulas we have developed, we consider the assets and liabilities given in Exhibit A3.

We observe that the asset portfolio is 60% stocks/40% bonds and use equations (8) and (9) to find μ_A and σ_A.

$$\mu_A = 0.6 \times 13.0\% + 0.4 \times 8.0\% = 11.0\%$$
$$\sigma_A = \sqrt{(0.6 \times 0.17)^2 + (0.4 \times 0.0696)^2 + 2 \times (0.6 \times 0.4) \times (0.17 \times 0.0696) \times 0.35}$$
$$= 11.47\%.$$

Turning our attention to the pension fund surplus, we first observe that the funding ratio is 140% ([84 + 56]/100). Then, according to equation (5)

$$\mu_S = (1.4 \times 11.0\%) - 8.0\% = 7.4\%.$$

We now use equation (13) to find ρ_{AL}, and equation (6) to compute σ_S.

$$\rho_{AL} = [(0.60 \times 0.17 \times 0.35) + (0.4 \times 0.0696)]/0.1147 = 0.554$$

and

$$\sigma_S = \sqrt{(1.4 \times 0.1147)^2 + (0.15)^2 - 2 \times (1.4 \times 0.1147) \times 0.15 \times 0.554}$$
$$= 14.7\%.$$

EXHIBIT A3
A PENSION FUND EXAMPLE (DOLLARS IN MILLIONS)

Asset or Liability	Initial Value	Expected Return	Standard Deviation of Returns	Correlation with Bonds
Equity	$84.0	13.0%	17.00%	0.35
Bonds	56.0	8.0	6.96	1.00
Liability	100.0	8.0	15.00	1.00

The Surplus Shortfall Constraint

We wish to locate all stock/bond portfolios whose risk/return characteristics are such that there is a probability k that the surplus return $\tilde{r}_S$ will
exceed some minimum threshold S_{MIN}. This requirement can be expressed
as follows:

$$P[\tilde{r}_S \geq S_{MIN}] = k. \tag{14}$$

The above requirement is equivalent to

$$P[(\tilde{r}_S - \mu_S)/\sigma_S \geq (S_{MIN} - \mu_S)/\sigma_S] = k. \tag{15}$$

Because the quantity to the left of the inequality in (15) is a standard
normal variate, there is a positive value z_k (assuming $k > 0.5$), such that
the shortfall constraint (14) is satisfied when

$$(S_{MIN} - \mu_S)/\sigma_S = -z_k$$

or, equivalently, when

$$\mu_S = S_{MIN} + z_k \sigma_S. \tag{16}$$

As an example, we note that $z_k = 1.282$ when $k = 0.90$, because there
is a 90% probability that a standard normal variable will exceed -1.282.

Equation (16) looks deceptively simple, because it is expressed in
surplus terms. To locate the asset portfolios that fulfill equation (16), we
must express μ_S and σ_S in terms of asset variables by making use of the
various equations in this Appendix. Although the resulting mathematical
relationship between μ_A and σ_A is complicated, the portfolios that fulfill
that relationship can readily be graphed in a risk/return diagram. The
"shape" of the relationship between μ_A and σ_A for portfolios that satisfy
the surplus shortfall condition can best be described as "egg-like." Examples of these surplus shortfall "eggs" are provided in the body of this
chapter.

CHAPTER 10

Risk-Adjusted Surplus: A New Measure of Pension Fund Risk

Martin L. Leibowitz
Managing Director
Salomon Brothers Inc

Stanley Kogelman
Vice President
Salomon Brothers Inc

Lawrence N. Bader
Vice President
Salomon Brothers Inc

INTRODUCTION

When describing a pension plan's status, one generally speaks in terms of a surplus measure defined by the excess of the market value of

The authors appreciate the helpful comments of Keith Ambachtsheer, Don Ezra, Robert Ferguson, and Jeremy Gold. This chapter has been adapted from a Salomon Brothers research report with the same title, first published August 1991. Used by permission.

assets over the measured liability cost.[1] A pension plan with an asset-to-liability ratio of 140% usually is considered to reflect an ample funded status with the happy prospect of several years of reduced contributions. This statement of "raw" surplus does not leave any room for a capital cushion or for any required reserve that compensates for the riskiness embodied in the fund's portfolio. Thus, the plan will continue to be regarded as 140% funded, even when the portfolio is based on a relatively consistent long-term strategic asset allocation that intentionally embraces a high level of volatility.

In most asset/liability contexts — for example, banks, insurance companies and broker/dealers — there is a clear concept of the capital reserve that is *required* to "back up" a given book of business. This required reserve naturally depends on the risk levels of the assets and the liabilities. For example, a block of Treasury bills would require less capital than a comparable amount of long Baa corporate bonds. Different regulators use different terminology — such as risk-weighting, "haircutting" or security valuation reserves — to describe formalized procedures for computing the required reserve needed for a given risk category of assets. An institution is deemed to have "excess capital" only to the extent that its nominal surplus exceeds the required level.

The trend toward increasingly explicit reserve requirements is exemplified by the banking industry, where capital requirements have been made more stringent through the promulgation of the Bank for International Settlements (BIS) risk-weighting rules. In contrast, corporate pension funds and public retirement systems do not use any such risk-reserving procedures. Although asset (and liability) risk is reflected in sophisticated allocation and actuarial models, there appears to be no

---

[1]The methodology of this chapter is applicable to a broad range of liability structures; however, for purposes of illustration, we have chosen to deal with a simple liability that behaves like a bond and confine our analysis to the effect of investment risk on surplus measurement. Other authors have addressed different elements of surplus management. For example, see D. Don Ezra, "Asset Allocation by Surplus Optimization," *Financial Analysts Journal,* January/February 1991; William F. Sharpe and Lawrence G. Tint, "Liabilities — A New Approach," *Journal of Portfolio Management,* Winter 1990; Richard O. Michaud, "Economic Surplus and Pension Asset Management," *Pension Executive Review,* January 1989; and Keith P. Ambachtsheer, *Pension Funds and the Bottom Line,* Dow Jones-Irwin, 1986.

standard method for risk-adjusting either the funding ratio or the surplus — the key "front line" numbers used to gauge the health of a pension fund.

At a time when pension funds and their sponsors are hard-pressed to minimize the strain of contributions, it becomes all the more important that any assessment of funding status incorporate some sense of risk. In this report, we define a "risk-adjusted surplus" based on the notion that some type of insurance cushion is needed to compensate for the downside risk in a volatile portfolio. With this approach, the funding ratio is reduced from its "raw" value to a "zero-risk" equivalent.[2] While such reductions are not a common practice in a pension fund context, the risk-adjustment procedure does provide some indication of the reserve that is appropriate for a given strategic allocation. In the final analysis, there always is an implicit reserve, and that reserve takes the form of a call on the resources of the sponsoring organization.

A SHORTFALL DEFINITION OF RISK-ADJUSTED ASSETS

We begin our study of asset reserves by considering a hypothetical pension fund for which the liability is $108 million due in one year. At an 8% discount rate, the present value of the liabilities is $100 million. If assets of $100 million are invested in "cash" at an 8% risk-free rate, the plan is certain to be fully funded. However, if the plan invests in risky assets in the expectation of achieving higher returns, its fully funded status will be at risk. To keep the probability of a shortfall within tolerable limits, we must augment the initial asset value so that the excess capital can absorb the fluctuations that accompany risky investments.

In Exhibit 1, we schematically illustrate the asset levels needed for risky portfolios to provide equal levels of protection relative to the

---

[2]Although we limit our discussion to pension funds, we believe that this technique can be customized to encompass current BIS risk-weighting rules for banks and rules that currently are under discussion for insurance companies. For a more general discussion of the management of asset and surplus shortfall risk, see Chapter 8, Martin L. Leibowitz, Stanley Kogelman and Lawrence N. Bader, *Asset Performance and Surplus Control*. The definition of surplus shortfall risk in this earlier chapter is the basis for the risk-adjusted surplus defined in the current chapter. Consequently, a given "surplus shortfall" can always be recast as a risk-adjusted surplus, and vice versa.

EXHIBIT 1
ASSET PORTFOLIOS WITH EQUIVALENT FUNDING PROTECTION
(DOLLARS IN MILLIONS)

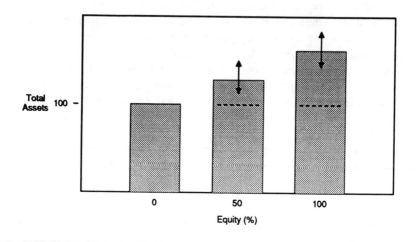

liability. If the asset portfolio is made up of "cash" assets, a funding ratio of 100% will ensure that the liability can be met. As the percentage of equity in the portfolio increases, the assets become more risky, and additional reserves are required.

To make the above intuitive discussion of capital reserves more concrete, we must formulate a measure of *risk-equivalence*. Although there are many ways to quantify a required reserve level, we define a risk-adjustment or "haircut" in terms of the shortfall measures that have been introduced in earlier publications.[3] In those publications, we measured a portfolio's "shortfall risk" by the tenth percentile return. This measure

---

[3]The shortfall approach (and its limitations as a risk measure) are discussed in Martin L. Leibowitz, Stanley Kogelman, and Thomas E. Klaffky, *A Shortfall Approach to Duration Management*, Salomon Brothers Inc, April 1990; Martin L. Leibowitz and Stanley Kogelman, "Asset Allocation Under Shortfall Constraints," *Journal of Portfolio Management*, Winter 1991; and Martin L. Leibowitz and Stanley Kogelman, "Return Enhancement from 'Foreign' Assets," *Journal of Portfolio Management*, Summer 1991.

is equivalent to taking the conservative position of gauging a fund's downside risk by the minimum level that can be promised with 90% assurance. Two portfolios will be regarded as risk-equivalent if they have equal tenth percentile returns.

To illustrate this equivalence, we consider the distribution of year-end values for a $118-million portfolio that is 100% invested in equities (see the lower graph in Exhibit 2). We assume that the expected return from equities is 13% (that is, a return premium of 5% above the 8% risk-free rate) and that the volatility is 17%. These assumptions lead to a 10% probability that the year-end value of a $118-million portfolio could fall

EXHIBIT 2
THE YEAR-END VALUE DISTRIBUTION FOR TWO PORTFOLIOS
(DOLLARS IN MILLIONS)

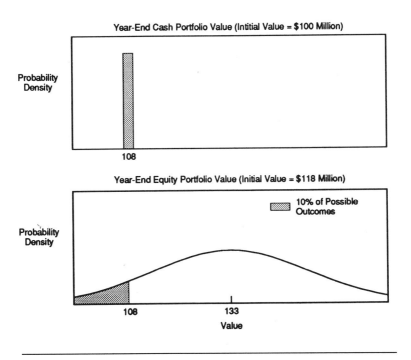

below $108 million.[4] This same year-end value could have been attained without risk by investing $100 million at 8% (see the upper graph in Exhibit 2). In essence, an all-equity portfolio with an $18-million capital cushion has a distribution that is shifted so far to the right that it provides a 90% probability of surpassing the $108-million year-end value of a $100-million cash portfolio. Thus, we can view the all-equity fund, with its risky $18-million surplus as risk-equivalent to an all-cash portfolio with a surplus of zero (that is, a 100% funding ratio).

RISK-ADJUSTED SURPLUS

The portfolio examples of the previous section illustrated the concept of a risk-adjustment. According to this concept, an all-equity portfolio with a nominal funding ratio of 118% may have a risk-adjusted funding ratio of only 100%. In other words, if a $100-million liability is funded by a 100% equity portfolio, an incremental $18 million may be *required* as a reserve to cushion the volatility of equity.

To gain a broader view of how the funding ratio risk-adjustment is related to volatility, we must have some concept as to how risk is rewarded in an investment context. In Exhibit 3, we present a traditional risk/return diagram for asset allocations consisting of varying proportions of equity and cash. All such portfolios plot along a diagonal line between these two asset classes. The horizontal axis displays the portfolio volatility. The vertical axis represents the expected return over a one-year investment horizon. As the equity allocation increases, the portfolio takes on greater levels of both expected return and volatility. The risk/return characteristics of a benchmark 60% equity portfolio are indicated by a "diamond." This portfolio has an 11% expected return and 10.2% volatility.[5]

The risk/return relationship shown in Exhibit 3 enables us to trace out how the required risk-adjustment for a $118-million portfolio changes as the equity proportion increases (see Exhibit 4). At a 0% equity allocation, there is no volatility, and no risk-adjustment is required. As the

---

[4]For simplicity, we assume that portfolio returns are normally distributed. For equities, the tenth percentile return is −8.8% (= 13% − 1.282 x 17%). The tenth percentile fund value is therefore (1 − 0.088) x 118 = 108. We assume static asset allocations in this chapter; a dynamic policy would require alterations to our model.

[5]The return premium for the 60/40 portfolio is 60% of the 5% equity risk premium, or 3%. The portfolio volatility is 60% of the 17% volatility of equities, or 10.2%.

EXHIBIT 3
THE "EFFICIENT FRONTIER" FOR CASH/EQUITY PORTFOLIOS

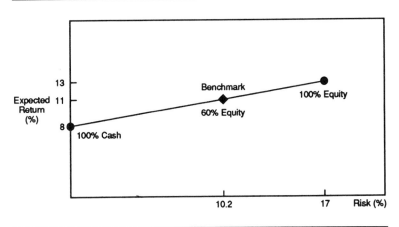

equity allocation grows, so does the volatility. The risk-adjustment increases linearly until it reaches $18 million at a 100% equity allocation.

The methodology for computing the risk-adjustment at intermediate equity allocations will be illustrated for a 60/40 portfolio. First, we

EXHIBIT 4
SURPLUS RISK-ADJUSTMENT
(FUNDING RATIO = 118%; DOLLARS IN MILLIONS)

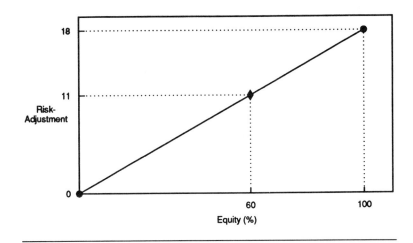

compute the tenth percentile portfolio value. For the 60/40 portfolio, the tenth percentile return is −2.1% (the 11% expected return, less 1.282 times the standard deviation of 10.2%). Thus, the tenth percentile value of a $118-million portfolio is $116 million (97.9% of 118). Next, we find that the present value of $116 million at year-end is $107 million ($116 divided by 1.08). This means that the same $116-million value could have been achieved by investing $107 million in risk-free assets. Consequently, for a 60/40 portfolio, a nominal 118% funding ratio requires an 11% risk-adjustment. This adjustment leads to a risk-adjusted funding ratio of 107%.

RISK-ADJUSTED SURPLUS WITH INTEREST-SENSITIVE LIABILITIES

In this section, we extend our methodology to liabilities that are sensitive to changes in interest rates. We introduce this generalization through an example in which the liability has a 10-year duration, all fixed-income investments have the same 8% expected return, and the initial funding ratio is 140%.[6]

In this new context, the riskless investment is an all-bond portfolio with the same interest rate sensitivity as the liability; that is, an immunized portfolio. The immunized portfolio is structured so that the dollar durations of the assets and liabilities are equal. In our example, the immunizing duration is 7.1 years (the liability duration of 10 years divided by the 140% funding ratio). All nonimmunizing portfolios are susceptible to surplus risk.

We introduce the following measure of *risk-adjusted surplus:*

The risk-adjusted surplus is the tenth percentile year-end surplus value, discounted at the risk-free rate.

---

[6]This "flat yield curve" expected return assumption is made to simplify the exposition. Our results easily can be extended to encompass a positive risk/return trade-off for fixed-income securities.

For example, if the pension fund's liability is $100 million, and $140 million is invested in 3.1-year duration bonds, the tenth percentile year-end surplus value is $32.4 million.[7] This is the same year-end surplus that can be obtained from a risk-free immunized portfolio with an 8% return and an initial value of $130 million, because the $30 million surplus will grow to $32.4 with a year's interest. Thus, one needs a risk-adjustment reserve of $10 million, or a 10% "haircut" in terms of the funding ratios. The 10% funding ratio "haircut" is attributable to the 4-year mismatch between the portfolio duration and the immunizing duration. Because a $140-million bond portfolio with a duration that is 4 years longer than the immunizing duration (11.1 years) has the same mismatch, it requires the same risk-adjustment as the 3.1-year duration portfolio. In general, the risk-adjustment for all-bond portfolios increases linearly as the duration mismatch increases (see Exhibit 5).

We now shift our attention from an all-bond portfolio to a $140-million all-equity portfolio. In this case, the funding ratio risk-adjustment can be shown to be 21.1% (see Exhibit 6). This risk-adjustment is significantly greater than it would be for all but the longest-duration bond portfolios.[8]

In Exhibit 6, we also show the risk-adjustment for portfolios with a more typical allocation of 60% stocks and 40% bonds. Observe that the risk-adjustment for the 60/40 portfolio is 16% when the 40% fixed-income component has a 0-year duration. The risk-adjustment decreases gradually to a floor of 12% at a bond duration of 11.9 years and then increases slowly.[9] The "flatness" of the risk-adjustment curve near the 11.9-year duration point indicates a low sensitivity to the choice of bond

---

[7]If annual interest rate volatility is 1.5%, the return volatilities for a 3.1-year duration bond and a 10-year liability are 4.7% (3.1 x 1.5%) and 15% (10 x 1.5%), respectively. If liability and bond returns are perfectly correlated, the surplus volatility is $8.4 million (the absolute difference between $140 x 4.7% and $100 x 15%). The expected surplus value is $43.2 million (1.08 x $40). If all distributions are normal, the tenth percentile surplus value is $32.4 million ($43.2 − 1.282 x $8.4).

[8]The surplus risk in the equity portfolio is derived from the riskiness of equity and the volatility of the liability. This risk will decrease as the correlation between equity returns and the liability returns increases. We assume that the correlation between equities and the liability is 0.35. With this correlation and our volatility assumptions for bonds and equity, it can be shown that equity has an implicit duration of 4.0 years. See Martin L. Leibowitz, "Total Portfolio Duration: A New Perspective on Asset Allocation," *Financial Analysts Journal*, September/October 1986.

[9]At a bond duration of 11.9 years, the interest-rate sensitivity of the total 60/40 portfolio equals that of the liability. See Martin L. Leibowitz, "Total Portfolio Duration: A New Perspective on Asset Allocation," *Financial Analysts Journal*, September/October 1986.

EXHIBIT 5
FUNDING RATIO RISK-ADJUSTMENT FOR ALL-BOND PORTFOLIOS
(LIABILITY DURATION = 10 YEARS; FUNDING RATIO = 140%)

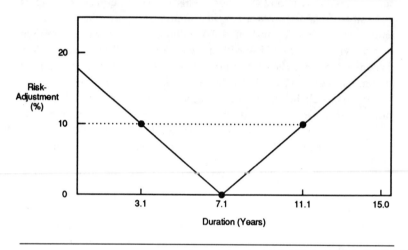

EXHIBIT 6
RISK-ADJUSTMENT FOR VARYING EQUITY ALLOCATION

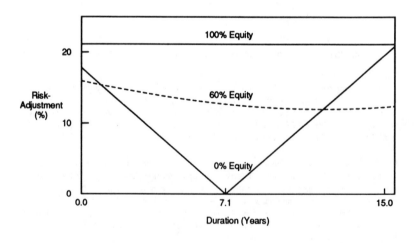

duration. This insensitivity reflects the fact that, at a 60% equity allocation, almost all of the surplus volatility arises from the volatility of
equities. The "flatness" also illustrates an inherent problem in traditional
surplus optimizations. While an "optimal" solution may always be found,
there is a wide range of suboptimal portfolios offering virtually equivalent surplus protection. These "suboptimal" portfolios may be more attractive from other vantage points, for example, in the context of
asset-only performance.

IMPACT OF THE EQUITY ALLOCATION AND FUNDING RATIO

In this section, we show how the funding ratio and the equity allocation
affect the risk-adjustment. As a first example, we plot the funding ratio
risk-adjustment against the equity percentage for two different durations
when the nominal funding ratio is 140% (see Exhibit 7).

An all-bond portfolio with a 4.64-year duration (the current duration
of the Salomon Brothers Broad Investment-Grade Bond Index[SM]) will
have surplus risk because of the 2.5-year mismatch relative to the 7.1-

EXHIBIT 7
FUNDING RATIO RISK-ADJUSTMENT VERSUS EQUITY ALLOCATION
(FUNDING RATIO = 140%)

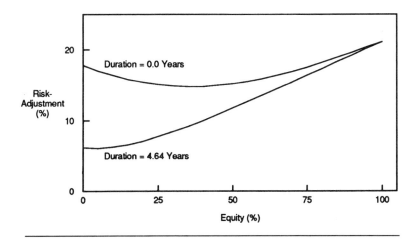

year immunizing duration. An all-bond portfolio with a 0-year duration (cash equivalents) will have even more surplus risk because of the greater duration gap. Consequently, the risk adjustment is greater for the 0-year duration portfolio.

The addition of equity affects the risk-adjustment in rather different ways, depending on the magnitude of the duration gap. For 4.64-year duration bonds, equity additions lead to ever larger risk-adjustments. However, at a 0-year duration, the portfolio already has equity-like volatility because of the greater gap relative to the 7.1-year immunizing duration. The replacement of a small proportion of 0-year duration bonds with equity leads to a decline in surplus volatility because the positive duration of equity leads to a narrowing of the asset/liability duration gap. This volatility decrease is reflected in a lower risk-adjustment. At larger equity percentages, equity becomes the dominant component of surplus risk, and the required funding ratio risk-adjustment rises toward the 21.1% level of an all-equity portfolio.

To see the effect of the funding ratio, we compare the risk-adjustment for a plan with a 100% funding ratio to a 140% funded plan (see Exhibit 8). Although the bond duration is 4.64 years in both cases, the duration mismatch is greater for the 100% funding ratio because of the longer immunizing duration (10 years versus 7.1 years). Consequently, the all-bond portfolio with a 100% funding ratio requires a greater adjustment for surplus risk.

High funding ratios reflect a greater proportion of assets to liabilities. Consequently, at higher funding ratios, the riskiness of the assets has a more pronounced impact on the risk-adjustment. As the equity allocation increases, the risk-adjustment tends to grow more rapidly for plans with higher funding ratios.[10]

IMPACT OF RISK TOLERANCE

To this point, our risk-adjustment calculations have been arbitrarily based on the tenth percentile surplus return. More risk-averse plan sponsors may decide to focus on a lower percentile return (for example 5%, or a 95% assurance level) and accept the resulting greater risk-adjustment.

---

[10] A different perspective on the impact of the equity allocation on a fund's shortfall risk is provided in Zvi Bodie, "Shortfall Risk and Pension Fund Asset Management," *Financial Analysts Journal*, May/June 1991.

EXHIBIT 8
RISK-ADJUSTMENTS AT DIFFERENT FUNDING RATIOS
(DURATION = 4.64 YEARS)

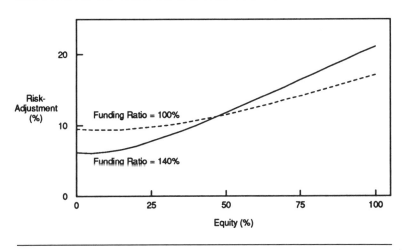

However, more risk-tolerant sponsors may focus on higher percentile returns and take a smaller "haircut."

Insight into the effect of a sponsor's risk-tolerance can be gained by comparing the funding ratio risk-adjustment for a range of shortfall probabilities and funding ratios (see Exhibit 9). These cases are based on a constant benchmark allocation of 60% equity and 40% bonds with a 4.64-year duration.

In Exhibit 9, at all funding ratios, we observe a substantial sensitivity to changes in the shortfall probability. For example, with a 100% funding

EXHIBIT 9
FUNDING RATIO RISK-ADJUSTMENT
(60% EQUITY/40% BOND PORTFOLIO)

	Risk-Adjustment			
	Shortfall Probability			
Funding Ratio	*5%*	*10%*	*15%*	*38%*
100%	16.8%	12.5%	9.6%	0.7%
120	17.4	12.8	9.7	0.4
140	18.5	13.6	10.2	0.1
160	20.0	14.6	10.9	(0.1)

ratio, the risk-adjustment increases by 4.3% (from 12.5% to 16.8%) when the shortfall probability decreases from 10% to 5%. However, the risk-adjusted surplus is less sensitive to the funding ratio than it is to the sponsor's risk tolerance. For example, at a 10% shortfall probability, there is only a 2.1% difference between the risk-adjustment for a 100% funding ratio and a 160% funding ratio.

At higher shortfall probabilities, we can see the effects of greatly relaxed risk tolerance. For example, a 38% shortfall probability approximates the asset-only risk/return trade-off that is imbedded in the market, given our assumption of a 5% equity premium. Because the added return roughly provides the required compensation, there is no need for a risk-adjustment at this shortfall probability. This is the risk tolerance that is implied by the conventional practice of viewing a portfolio as providing a fixed funding assurance, regardless of its asset allocation.

CONCLUSION

In this chapter, we have defined the risk-adjusted surplus of a pension fund based on a one-year horizon. Many would argue that a one-year test, although appropriate in certain narrow circumstances, is irrelevant and indeed inimical to the development of sound pension funding and investment policies.

To frame this view persuasively, we can use the example of a large public employee retirement system — one of the longest-term undertakings in the realm of finance. One can argue that such a system should adopt an investment policy that maximizes long-term return and establish a contribution policy that is consistent with long-term return expectations. The system's investment and actuarial status should be reviewed periodically, not to respond to or anticipate each flutter in the markets, but to see whether the long-term outlook has changed fundamentally to an extent that demands restructuring. A temporary dip in the funding ratio below 100% is virtually a non-event, unlike the catastrophic impact that a comparable event would have on a bank or an insurance company. Short-term pension fund volatility, therefore, should be tamed by the passage of time, not by compromising the pursuit of long-term return.

This appealing stance reflects a large part — but not all — of the plan sponsor's responsibilities. It fails to reflect the need for prudent contingency planning and the fact that volatility is not evanescent but persistent. Consider the case of a plan sponsor who seeks to justify a lower contribution level by proposing a high-return 100% equity portfolio for a fully funded public plan with $100 million in assets and liabilities. It is easy for the sponsor to dismiss a one-year calculation that shows that the new risk-adjusted surplus is in fact a deficit of $17.1 million. It would be more difficult to dismiss an analogous calculation that produced a similar deficit over 20 years. Although we have not formulated a 20-year definition of risk-adjusted surplus in this chapter, simulations indicate significant potential deficits even over a period of decades.[11]

We would not argue that the risk adjustment that takes the plan from fully funded status with an immunization strategy to a deficit when equity is introduced necessarily makes equity exposure imprudent. No single point on the continuum from full immunization to 100% equity is right for all sponsors, but risk-adjusted surplus offers a means of comparing various points on the continuum in the light of a particular sponsor's risk tolerance.

In practice, many plan sponsors might be tempted to use the higher expected return from equities to justify an increased discount rate, without considering the downside possibilities. They would thereby lower their stated liability and *increase* the reported surplus. In our view, tying a higher surplus and therefore a lower contribution stream to a riskier investment strategy is a step that should be taken only with due consideration for potentially disappointing results. The risk-adjusted surplus can be useful as an approximate measure of the potential disappointment.

---

[11] Insight into the relationship between short- and long-term risk can be found in Martin L. Leibowitz and Terence C. Langetieg, "Shortfall Risks and the Asset Allocation Decision," *Journal of Portfolio Management,* Fall 1989.

CHAPTER 11

Tax Consequences of Trading

ROBERT D. ARNOTT
PRESIDENT
CHIEF INVESTMENT OFFICER
FIRST QUANDRANT CORP.

Much capital and intellectual energy has been invested over the years in assessing the appropriate investment disciplines for the tax-exempt client. Remarkably little effort has been expended on *differentiating* the appropriate treatment of the taxable investor. In fact, we find that tax consequences have a great deal of impact in reshaping optimal investment practices. This has a bearing both on the management of assets for wealthy individuals and on the substantial taxable corporate assets which are subject to active management.

Perhaps the most important consequence of taxation is that turnover presupposes "alpha"[1] — for certain asset classes, a large alpha. In a tax-exempt portfolio however, such as a pension fund or endowment, every basis point of excess return or alpha after trading costs falls straight to

---

[1]Alpha is the excess return, earned by active management, over and above the return for passive management with similar risk.

the bottom line. In a taxable portfolio, however, every trade incurs a tax liability on the *full* cumulative capital appreciation, appreciation which might otherwise be permitted to grow tax-free. In essence, trading shifts the tax burden from income-only to total return. This means that *effective* trading costs for taxable investors are many times greater than the corresponding costs for tax-exempt investors.

This challenge of trading in taxable portfolios is very subtle. It does not affect all asset classes equally. Asset classes which deliver the bulk of their total return in income, with comparatively little from capital appreciation, are largely unaffected. This is not to say that trading is "free" in these markets, but there is no large hidden trading cost due to tax consequences for these markets. Additionally, the tax consequences of trading will not affect all trades equally. If a trade which realizes a gain can be offset against a loss, then the trade is "free," at least with respect to tax consequences.[2]

The asset allocation consequences of taxation are obvious, absent trading. For the taxable investor, tax-exempt bonds dominate taxable bonds. Assets that earn most of their long-term return through capital gains (e.g., venture capital, stocks or real estate) dominate markets that earn fully taxable income (e.g., commercial paper). Trading has a subtle effect, however, in that it robs the investor of these very tax benefits of capital appreciation. Even at relatively low levels of turnover, the capital gains on stocks, or other investments where capital gains are an important part of the return, begin to incur full taxation.

Accordingly, the taxable investor should favor tax-free investments (e.g., municipal bonds), tax-deferred investments (e.g., real estate, stocks or tax-favored IRA and Keogh portfolios), and should shun turnover on assets which earn capital gains (e.g., stocks). Active management is still possible. For active management, there are important tax benefits to "overlay" strategies with futures or options, which earn alpha, on an *untraded* foundation of stocks which earn capital gains. In this fashion, the capital gains can accumulate, with tax consequences deferred indefinitely; these deferrals reduce the net present value of the tax consequences substantially.

---

[2]Taxable losses can, for both personal and corporate investors, be offset against gains in other years, and visa versa. Also, for individual investors, a modest loss can be realized and offset against other income. Accordingly, one need not be obsessive about matching gains against losses in each trade, or even each year. But matching is required in the long run to avoid tax consequences.

WHY SHOULD INVESTMENT MANAGERS CARE ABOUT TAX CONSEQUENCES?

Most investment capital is taxable. Of the $9 *trillion* in liquid, investable stock and bond assets in the United States at year-end 1990, just over 30% is tax-exempt. Pensions, foundations and endowments are an important part of the investment world. But corporate reserves, insurance company reserves, and mutual funds are all institutionally managed *taxable* assets. Their combined value exceeds that of the conventional tax-exempt asset base. Personal wealth, including institutionally managed trust assets, is also a large pool of assets.

Managing taxable assets in the same fashion as tax-exempt assets is irresponsible. It robs the client of the wealth accumulation that can result from a more responsible policy. In essence, the investment manager for such assets should always ask whether a realized gain can be offset with a realized loss (and *both* must be perceived to be profitable trades in their own right). In cases where a gain cannot be offset, it will be taxed; the investment manager should have a clear understanding of the tax consequences and the *implied alpha*[3] of the trade.

Even the management of *tax-exempt* assets can be enhanced if we are aware of the tax-motivated trades that can lead to pricing opportunities.

- For example, a sale motivated by tax considerations can create a buy opportunity for the tax-exempt investor. Both investors may be acting intelligently, even optimally, and each investor funds excess return for the other.

- Furthermore, tax-induced year-end trades can lead to opportunities for tax-exempt investors. These trades are typically sub-optimal for taxable investors (they generally reflect poor planning early in the year); but they create impressive opportunities for tax-exempt investors. Such year-end trades are so prevalent that the strongest observed "January effect" is the tendency for the unsuccessful stocks of one year to rebound in January, following the tax-motivated drubbing they receive in December.

---

[3]The implied alpha is the excess return which must be earned on a trade in order to realize an improved long-term after-tax return.

It is beyond the scope of this chapter to explore the interplay between tax-induced trading and tax-exempt investing, but it merits consideration. In essence, *all* investors should care what motivates the taxable investor.

A PRIMER ON TAX CONSEQUENCES

Let us suppose that we are handling investments for a corporation with a marginal tax rate of 48% or a wealthy individual with a tax rate of 40%.[4] What are the investment implications if we buy an investment, hold it for a year, then sell? What will we have at the year-end? As Exhibit 1 shows, the consequences depend on the nature of the investor. The corporate client, eligible for a 70% exclusion on dividend income for stock investments, gets 64%[5] of the total return for stocks; the individual investor, despite a lower tax rate, gets a lower 60% of the total return. The dividend exclusion is clearly a valuable tax break. For taxable bonds,

EXHIBIT 1
SIMPLE TAX CONSEQUENCES, ONE-YEAR HOLDING PERIOD

Investment	Expected Total Return	Paid as Income	Expected Capital Gain	After-Tax Return Personal	After-Tax Return Corporate
Venture Capital	15.0%	0.0%	15.0%	9.0%	7.8%
Common Stocks	10.0%	3.5%	6.5%	6.0%	6.4%
Real Estate	8.0%	5.0%	3.0%	4.8%	4.2%
Taxable Bonds	8.0%	8.0%	0.0%	4.8%	4.2%
Tax Exempt Bds	6.0%	6.0%	0.0%	6.0%	6.0%

---

[4]The top combined federal/state/local tax rate for New York City individuals and corporations in 1991 is 40.05% and 47.6%, respectively. Other locations lead to slightly lower figures, but do not materially affect the conclusions.

[5]If the total return on stocks includes 3.5% from dividends and 6.5% from appreciation, then the corporate investor earns (after tax) 52% of the 6.5% capital appreciation, or 3.38%, plus 70% of the dividends (due to the exclusion), or 2.45%, plus 52% of the remaining 30% of the dividends, or 0.55%. This yields an after-tax total return of 6.38%, or 64% of the pre-tax total return. On the total return of 10% from dividends and appreciation, the individual investor simply pays tax of 40%, leaving 6% for after-tax return, or 60% of the pre-tax total return.

corporations and individuals keep 52% and 60% of the pretax total return, respectively.

Simply put, the long-term total return on bonds is *expected* to closely match the income generated by the investment, and their long-term expected capital gain will, over time, typically average roughly zero. For stocks, venture capital and real estate, a meaningful part of the total return is expected to be earned in capital gains. Consequently, the investor with differential tax treatment on income and capital gains may see sharply different asset class preferences than the investor with equal treatment. Also, we can see that the benefits of tax-exempt investments are considerable. In this example, if we do not expect a large risk premium for stocks vis-a-vis tax-exempt bonds, then the return benefits for equity ownership can easily disappear entirely.

Thus far, our observations have been simple, even to the point of being simplistic. Now, let us consider the alternative case in which we *never* trade. Then capital gains can build indefinitely without taxation. This means that the portion of total return attributable to appreciation is earned with no taxes whatsoever, as illustrated in Exhibit 2.

A comparison between these approaches suggests that each corporate transaction in Venture Capital must surely require 7.2% *annual* value-added over simply holding the current investments. This figure comes from the difference between the 15% realized by the corporate investor who holds a venture capital investment indefinitely, and the 7.8% realized by the corporate investor who sells, and pays the tax, after one year. The corresponding required value-added from trading would be 3.3% and 1.4% for stocks and real estate, respectively.

EXHIBIT 2
SIMPLE TAX CONSEQUENCES, INFINITE HOLDING PERIOD

				After-Tax Return	
	Expected	Expected			
	Total	Paid as	Capital		
Investment	*Return*	*Income*	*Gain*	*Personal*	*Corporate*
Venture Capital	15.0%	0.0%	15.0%	15.0%	15.0%
Common Stocks	10.0%	3.5%	6.5%	8.6%	9.5%
Real Estate	8.0%	5.0%	3.0%	6.0%	5.6%
Taxable Bonds	8.0%	8.0%	0.0%	4.8%	4.2%
Tax Exempt Bds	6.0%	6.0%	0.0%	6.0%	6.0%

Since these figures are for after-tax returns, one might even argue that the implicit *pretax* alpha (annual value-added) for trades in these markets are roughly 14%, 6%, and 3%, respectively. Why so large? Because the one-year investor in venture capital must realize a 29% pre-tax return in order to achieve the same 15% after-tax return earned by the buy-and-hold investor; thus, the pretax alpha from active management must be 14%! Conversely, one might construe this as the implicit tax-induced *trading cost* associated with trades in these asset classes, over and above direct costs such as commissions, fees or market impact.

Indeed, neither a one-year horizon nor an infinite horizon is realistic. Investments are not, and *should* not be, held forever. Even if they were, the Venture Capital return cited in the example would converge after only a few years to a common stock return, as would the compounded after-tax rate of return. The bonds would expire and the real estate (unless raw land) would crumble.

One fact which is obvious in these two exhibits is that the 100%-turnover investor and the no-turnover investor have the same expected compounded returns for bonds (the same is true for tax-exempt bonds).[6] The reason is simple. In asset classes where the expected long-term return equals the income, there are no long-term tax consequences. This is not to say that trading is "free." Rather, there are no subtle hidden tax consequences. On a short-term basis, of course one can realize gains or losses for bonds; accordingly, on a short-term basis, one cannot ignore taxes. But taxes are not nearly so serious a problem for these asset classes.

Why not carry this analysis to its logical conclusion? Why not stop trading? The answer is simple. Some turnover is inevitable. Income is reinvested. Some trading is forced due to takeovers, bankruptcies, and so forth. Consequently, a more relevant analysis is to ask how much excess return one must achieve to yield the same after-tax return at various levels of turnover. Our analysis seeks to answer this question.

Furthermore, no investor's horizon is infinite. Alas, we do not live so long. Even "investors" who should act as a perpetuity, such as foundations, and endowments, do not behave accordingly, because they are governed by individuals with career and life expectancies. Therefore, we

---

[6]This analysis would not apply to "original discount" bonds (e.g., zero-coupon bonds), for which income must be accrued and taxed.

use a 20-year horizon for our analysis, which is as long as most investors are likely to look ahead.[7]

METHODOLOGY

Our method is simple and deterministic.[8] It is illustrated in Exhibit 3, which explores the case of an individual in the 40% tax bracket who realizes a market return of 10%. This return is based on a dividend income of 3.5% and capital appreciation of 6.5%. Further, the individual is a passive investor, who makes *no* trades bearing tax consequences. Accordingly, this investor reinvests all after-tax income and allows capital gains to accumulate tax-free.

In the first year, the investor receives income of $3.50 on each initial $100 unit share, pays $1.40 in tax, and reinvests the remaining $2.10 at a market price which has now risen to $106.50. This $2.10 buys .0197 shares, boosting the total shares held to 1.0197. The purchase price of $106.50 also boosts the average cost basis to $100.13. This pattern is repeated until, in year number 20, this investor holds 1.4778 shares at an average cost basis of $137.85.

After 20 years, the assets have grown to 520.7% of initial value, for an apparent return of fully 8.6% (compared to 10% for the tax-exempt investor). At first glance this strategy looks quite good; we seem to have captured the full theoretic return of the infinite-horizon investor. Unfortunately, if we wish to *realize* their gains, then we must pay $126.80 in tax for each $100 in starting value. This tax burden is 40% of the price difference between the final index of $352.36 and the cost basis of $137.85, multiplied by the 1.4778 shares that are now held. Our *true* after-tax return is 7.10%, realized after a 20-year investment horizon. This is still a nice increment over the 6% after-tax return for the active trader, but a substantial decrement over the theoretic return for the infinite-horizon investor.

Based on this analysis, we might surmise that 100% turnover reduces the long-term compounded rate of return for a stock market investment

---

[7]It is well worth noting that, for individual investors, mortality carries its own "benefits." The cost basis for investments is reset upon death. This *magnifies* the importance of tax consequences on trading. Indeed, if we take account of the revisions in cost basis, the "infinite horizon" case has more merit than we might initially suppose.

[8]We also ran a stochastic study based on two of these examples, introducing market volatility. Results were essentially identical to the deterministic findings.

EXHIBIT 3
ANALYSIS OF TAX CONSEQUENCES OF ACTIVE MANAGEMENT
Case 1. Buy & Hold, with Resale After 20 Years

High-Bracket Individual Investor
ASSUMPTIONS:

Market Total Return	10.00%	Alpha from Active Mgt.	0.00%
Dividend Yield/Coupon	3.50%	Marginal Tax Rate	40.00%
Capital Appreciation	6.50%	Dividend Exclusion	0.00%
Annual Turnover	0.00%	Long-Term Gains Rate	40.00%

Year	Cost Basis	Index Level	Units Held	Income	Realized Gains	Less Tax	Cumul Value	Tax-Free Growth
1991	100.00	100.00	1.0000				100.00	100.00
1992	100.13	106.50	1.0197	3.50	0.00	1.40	108.60	110.00
1993	100.39	113.42	1.0398	3.80	0.00	1.52	117.94	121.00
1994	100.79	120.79	1.0603	4.13	0.00	1.65	128.08	133.10
1995	101.34	128.65	1.0812	4.48	0.00	1.79	139.10	146.41
1996	102.05	137.01	1.1026	4.87	0.00	1.95	151.06	161.05
1997	102.91	145.91	1.1243	5.29	0.00	2.11	164.05	177.16
1998	103.95	155.40	1.1465	5.74	0.00	2.30	178.16	194.87
1999	105.16	165.50	1.1691	6.24	0.00	2.49	193.48	214.36
2000	106.56	176.26	1.1921	6.77	0.00	2.71	210.12	235.79
2001	108.16	187.71	1.2156	7.35	0.00	2.94	228.19	259.37
2002	109.97	199.92	1.2396	7.99	0.00	3.19	247.82	285.31
2003	112.00	212.91	1.2640	8.67	0.00	3.47	269.13	313.84
2004	114.26	226.75	1.2890	9.42	0.00	3.77	292.27	345.23
2005	116.77	241.49	1.3144	10.23	0.00	4.09	317.41	379.75
2006	119.54	257.18	1.3403	11.11	0.00	4.44	344.70	417.72
2007	122.58	273.90	1.3667	12.06	0.00	4.83	374.35	459.50
2008	125.92	291.70	1.3937	13.10	0.00	5.24	406.54	505.45
2009	129.56	310.67	1.4212	14.23	0.00	5.69	441.51	555.99
2010	133.53	330.86	1.4492	15.45	0.00	5.18	479.48	611.59
2011	137.85	352.36	1.4778	16.78	0.00	6.71	520.71	672.75

Ending Value after Final Sale							393.91	672.75
Implied Annualized Return							7.10%	10.00%

EXHIBIT 4
SIMPLE TAX CONSEQUENCES, 20-YEAR HOLDING PERIOD

Investment	Expected Total Return	Expected Paid as Income	Capital Gain	After-Tax Return Personal	Corporate
Venture Capital	15.0%	0.0%	15.0%	12.3%	11.6%
Common Stocks	10.0%	3.5%	6.5%	7.1%	8.1%
Real Estate	8.0%	5.0%	3.0%	5.2%	4.6%
Taxable Bonds	8.0%	8.0%	0.0%	4.8%	4.2%
Tax Exempt Bds	6.0%	6.0%	0.0%	6.0%	6.0%

by 1.1% (when compared with the investor who turns over the portfolio only once at the end of 20 years). As a result, this manager must expect to earn a 1.1% annualized excess return on each trade.

This interpretation of the data is flawed. As Exhibit 5 demonstrates, the investor who incurs 100% turnover must earn an alpha of 1.89% to realize the same 7.1% after-tax return as the passive investor with a 20-year horizon. Indeed, the required alpha rises to a surprising 4.5% if we want our 100% turnover strategy to match the mythical infinite-horizon passive investor! Can active management add 1.9% (or 4.5%) in incremental returns? For some investment managers in some market cycles, of course, the answer is "yes." But most cannot add this kind of value, particularly after various direct costs,[9] such as commissions, market impact for trades, and management fees.

In Exhibit 6, we carry through on this analysis to assess the annualized alpha required to merit various levels of turnover, as compared with the 20-year horizon investor. The final column indicates the implied alpha that the 100% turnover investor must expect in order to match the theoretical return of the mythical infinite-horizon investor. This last column is only of value as a curiosity, since tax law changes, government changes and other sweeping changes make an infinite horizon impractical.[10]

---

[9]See Robert D. Arnott and Wayne H. Wagner, "The Measurement and Control of Trading Costs," *Financial Analysts Journal,* November/December 1990.

[10]As long as the restatement of cost basis upon death is allowed under tax law, this column may be a useful reflection of the alpha required to justify active trading for wealthy individuals.

EXHIBIT 5
ANALYSIS OF TAX CONSEQUENCES OF ACTIVE MANAGEMENT
Case 2. 100% Turnover; Enough Alpha to Match Buy & Hold

High-Bracket Individual Investor
ASSUMPTIONS:

Market Total Return	10.00%	Alpha from Active Mgt.	1.89%
Dividend Yield/Coupon	3.50%	Marginal Tax Rate	40.00%
Capital Appreciation	6.50%	Dividend Exclusion	0.00%
Annual Turnover	100.00%	Long-Term Gains Rate	40.00%

Year	Cost Basis	Index Level	Units Held	Income	Realized Gains	Less Tax	Cumul Value	Tax-Free Growth
1991	100.00	100.00	1.0000				100.00	100.00
1992	108.29	108.39	0.9884	3.50	8.39	4.76	107.13	111.89
1993	117.37	117.48	0.9766	3.75	9.08	5.13	114.74	125.19
1994	127.21	127.33	0.9650	4.02	9.73	5.50	122.88	140.07
1995	137.88	138.01	0.9535	4.30	10.42	5.89	131.59	156.72
1996	149.45	149.59	0.9421	4.61	11.16	6.31	140.93	175.35
1997	161.98	162.14	0.9309	4.93	11.95	6.75	150.93	196.20
1998	175.57	175.73	0.9198	5.28	12.80	7.23	161.64	219.52
1999	190.30	190.47	0.9088	5.66	13.71	7.75	173.11	245.62
2000	206.26	206.45	0.8980	6.06	14.68	8.30	185.39	274.81
2001	223.56	223.77	0.8873	6.49	15.72	8.88	198.55	307.48
2002	242.31	242.54	0.8767	6.95	16.84	9.51	212.63	344.03
2003	262.63	262.88	0.8663	7.44	18.03	10.19	227.72	384.93
2004	284.66	284.93	0.8559	7.97	19.31	10.91	243.88	430.69
2005	308.54	308.83	0.8457	8.54	20.68	11.69	261.18	481.89
2006	334.42	334.73	0.8356	9.14	22.15	12.52	279.71	539.17
2007	362.47	362.81	0.8257	9.79	23.72	13.40	299.56	603.27
2008	392.87	393.24	0.8158	10.48	25.41	14.36	320.81	674.98
2009	425.82	426.22	0.8061	11.23	27.21	15.37	343.57	755.22
2010	461.54	461.97	0.7965	12.03	29.14	16.47	367.95	845.00
2011	500.25	500.72	0.7870	12.88	31.21	17.63	394.06	945.45

Ending Value after Final Sale							393.91	945.45
Implied Annualized Return							7.10%	11.89%

EXHIBIT 6
IMPLIED "ALPHAS" AT VARIOUS LEVELS OF TURNOVER

Investor	Marginal Tax Rate	Assumptions Dividend Exclusion	Cap Gains Tax Rate
Individual #1	40%	-none-	40%
Individual #2	40%	-none-	20%[1]
Corporate #1	48%	70%	48%
Corporate #2	48%	-none-[2]	48%

"Alpha," in Basis Points, to match 20-yr Investor (Annual Turnover)

Investor	After-Tax Stock Return	5%	10%	25%	50%	100%	To Match Infinite Horizon
Individual #1	7.10%	34[3]	61	114	157	190	448
Individual #2[1]	7.90%	60	106	195	262	310	428
Corporate #1	8.05%	44	81	159	225	282	630
Corporate #2	6.42%	42	75	147	205	253	645

[1]This is included in the event that Congress ever reinstates a tax break on Capital Gains.
[2]Certain corporate stock investments, such as certain types of taxable VEBA trusts, may not generate the dividend exclusion.
[3]For example, an annual excess return of 34 basis points at 5% annual turnover is required to match the results for a 20-year Buy-and-Hold Strategy.

In essence, we find that higher turnover must generate a higher alpha to cover hidden tax costs. This alpha must be net of all direct trading costs and management fees. However, this alpha does not rise linearly with turnover. The first 10% of turnover each year bears a hidden tax consequence nearly as large as the next 40%.

WHAT TRADES CREATE TAX CONSEQUENCES?

For taxable accounts, is this a prescription for passive management (e.g., index funds) and a proscription on active management? No, However, it is a caution on casual active management. If we do not believe active management can add substantially to returns (history is disheartening on this score), then we must become passive or, at least, *very* tax-conscious. In this context, passive need *not* mean index fund management. Rather it means managing trades in a fashion which realizes negligible capital gains.

For the manager of taxable assets, trades can be broken into two classes, those that bear tax consequences and those that do not. The former consists of all trades in which net capital gains are realized. The latter consists of all trades in which there are no net realized capital gains. The expected long-term average capital gain on most fixed income instruments is roughly zero; accordingly, we must focus our primary attention on investments, such as stocks, in which a meaningful portion of the long-term expected total return is earned in the form of capital gains.

Clearly, the passive strategy for the taxable investor is one in which trades deemed attractive are subject to a secondary screen. They must also have a possible "pair" to neutralize tax consequences. If an investment is held at a profit, and is now deemed vulnerable, we cannot sell it without first:

a. finding a correspondingly attractive sale held at a loss, *or*
b. determining that the trade carries rewards which exceed the hidden tax costs. This requires a new trading objective. The objective is no longer to maximize reward per unit of risk. It is to maximize *after-tax* reward per unit of risk.

"Overlay" strategies, intended to deliver alpha without disrupting underlying holdings, represent another category of trading which bears esssentially no hidden tax consequences. For example, the use of futures and options hedging or arbitrage strategies, or the use of "swaps" to reshape the return attributes of the portfolio, will not disrupt the accumulation of capital appreciation in the underlying stock holdings. Accordingly, these can be attractive active management strategies for taxable portfolios.

Such overlay strategies typically generate gains and losses which are realized, for tax purposes, in the year in which they are generated. Therefore, one might suppose that these strategies are unattractive for the taxable investor. On the contrary, if they are overlaid on a portfolio which is designed to accumulate capital gains tax free, then their gains or losses represent little more than alpha. They need not affect or impede the tax-free accumulation of gains in the underlying assets

With overlay strategies, we find that the tax consequence is limited to direct taxation of alpha. If the strategy is profitable, then the alpha incurs a tax, and the after-tax portion of the alpha flows directly to the bottom line. If the alpha is negative, the loss creates a credit which can free up the manager to trade one or another underlying asset in the portfolio. In either event, the tax consequence is related solely to the alpha, and not to the total return on the underlying portfolio. In other words, the alpha is taxable, but the unrealized capital gains on the underlying portion of the portfolio is not.

It is beyond the scope of this paper to further explore the tax benefits of such overlay strategies. Still, it is interesting to note that, despite the lack of hidden trading costs or hidden tax consequences to taxable investors, overlay strategies have remained chiefly popular with tax-exempt investors.

SUMMARY

Most institutional investing for taxable investors is handled similarly to the investing for tax-exempt investors. This is an error and in most cases a serious error. Such investing should be done with an eye carefully focused on the tax consequences of trading and an awareness of hidden trading costs, over and above the costs of commissions and market impact.

The easy solution to these problems is for the manager of a taxable portfolio is passively manage any asset classes, such as stocks, which earn much of their return from capital appreciation. A naive response to this puzzle is to index the assets and simply reinvest income as needed. This need not mean matching an index like the S&P 500. Rather, it means designing a portfolio which we are not likely to wish to trade. For example, a "tilted" portfolio favoring low price/book, or small stocks might be constructed. Income and pairs trades can be used to rebalance, as needed.

There are other solutions. The preferred alternative, which is desireable if the investor has skill in choosing individual investments, is to treat each trade as an optimization[11] puzzle. Instead of seeking to maximize return per unit of risk, we must seek to maximize after-tax return (net of all hidden tax and trading consequences) per unit of risk. Typically, this will mean "pairs" trading, in which we match a capital gain against a capital loss.

Each trade has a return consequence that we can estimate. If it is a compelling trade, this takes the form of a large pretax expected alpha. If less compelling, the expected alpha is correspondingly less. Each sale incurs a taxable gain or loss. If we have a holding at a large profit, then we must find many holdings at losses to offset against that large gain. We would not want to execute that trade for a modest expected alpha. Ironically, the same holds for potential sales held at a large loss. Such trades create an important risk: if we cannot offset them against gains before the grace period for such offsets expires, then we lose the tax benefits of the realized loss. Consequently, the asset management process should maximize the expected *after-tax* alpha by focusing on pairs trades, offset against one another. Except in unusual circumstances, one should shun unmatched trades.

Optimization can be used to maximize after-tax alpha by directly controlling for tax consequences. The result is sharply reduced turnover, which falls further with the passage of time. However, if an investor has skill in identifying superior investment opportunities, this can yield improved after-tax returns with negligible tax consequences.

---

[11]Optimization is a mathematical technique, more precisely known as "quadratic programming," which seeks to maximize return at any level of risk or, conversely, to minimize risk at any level of return. The implications of our research is that the optimization should be constrained to match gains against losses.

SECTION TWO

Tactical Asset Allocation – Theory and Practice

CHAPTER 12

Tactical Asset Allocation: A Review of Current Techniques

CHARLES H. DuBois
MANAGING DIRECTOR
CHANCELLOR CAPITAL MANAGEMENT, INC.

TAA may be a recent addition to the lexicon of the investment business, but it is, in some respects, old-fashioned market timing adorned with a presumably more respectable name. In this sense then, TAA (market timing) has been around for a long time. It has often been dismissed as not only difficult to implement, but also risky with little likelihood of adding consistent value over the long term. However, despite the skepticism often expressed as to the potential of "timing" techniques, TAA has been gaining increasing acceptance in the marketplace. What are the reasons for this new-found respectability?

Importance

Most investors recognize that when a market moves in a particular direction, most of the individual securities comprising that market will move in the same direction. Reasonably diversified portfolios will almost certainly move in the same general direction as the overall market. Typically 85–95% of an equity portfolio's variability can be explained by general equity market movements. Only the remaining 5–15% of variability can be explained by the difference in a portfolio's exposure to common macroeconomic factors and/or specific industry or company developments. Consequently, the most effective way of meaningfully impacting returns is by changing exposures to the overall markets.

For most investors, risk relates to the chances of losing money. Money will be lost most often in a bear market. Since TAA strategies address overall market exposure and typically make very sizable changes in asset exposure levels, they potentially offer a much greater opportunity to reduce down-market risk than do most conventionally managed portfolios.

Lackluster Results of Traditional Management

Conventional "active" investment managers have underperformed the major averages. This result has increased interest in other "active" strategies, such as TAA, that may improve returns and has reduced concerns that TAA strategies may be giving up important returns by being "passive" in other dimensions. While TAA techniques are not necessarily restricted to using "passive" market proxies, most have taken this route. Such vehicles as index funds, financial futures, and Treasury bonds are the most widely used instruments.

Low Transaction Costs, Available Liquidity

One of the principal historical drawbacks of TAA was the cost of transacting, particularly as asset size increased. Costs included not only commissions and fees but also the marketmaker's spread and market impact (the additional spread that might be necessary to satisfy a larger order). About 25–40% of the historical value-added of the more active TAA strategies could have been lost as a consequence of the transaction costs associated with trading in the traditional stock and bond markets.

Today, however, costs have been reduced in a number of ways. The list includes lower commissions, the use of index funds, and, most significantly, the availability of high volume futures markets for both stocks and bonds. Currently, transaction costs of TAA implementations appear to be less than a tenth of those that existed, say, 10 years ago. Hence, a significant impediment to the viability of TAA strategies has been largely eliminated for today's TAA managers.

The relatively high liquidity and low transaction costs inherent in most TAA approaches have largely eliminated asset size as a deterrent to performance. Many traditional active investment managers who invest in individual securities find that with larger size comes less flexibility, higher transaction costs, and reduced investment returns. For these reasons, and independent of other considerations, TAA can be a particularly attractive strategy for large multi-billion dollar portfolios. Indeed, for very large ($10 billion and over) portfolios the application of TAA techniques may be the only practical way of adding significant value over time with any "active" investment strategy.

Credible, Systematic, and "Fact-Based" Techniques

The TAA strategies which have gained the most popularity in the marketplace have been both quantitative and (primarily) "fact-based."[1] With a quantitative approach, information that can form the basis for decision making is systematically organized. Examples of quantitative procedures used for TAA are asset class comparisons based upon expected return levels, econometrically derived forecasts, and simple composites of several market indicators. With a "fact-based" approach, only currently available information is used. In contrast, a "forecast-based" process is dependent upon a forecast of future developments. An example of a fact-based variable would be the current level of interest rates. An example of a forecast-based variable would be the projected rate of GNP growth.

Today's most popular strategies, being both quantitative and fact-based, simply observe the current status of one or more variables and make decisions accordingly. It's been said, "Forecasting is difficult, particularly when it concerns the future." Since a procedure in which objectively observing existing data is used to make decisions is obviously "easier" than one which requires forecasts and/or subjective judgments, confidence in the process is greatly enhanced.

Of course, it is critical that there be a positive relationship between the status of such indicators and subsequent market performance for such a decision-making framework to add value. On this score, there appears

---

[1] I credit George Richvalsky, then with Richvest Management, Inc., with coining the term "fact-based," as opposed to "forecast-based."

to be both theoretical and empirical support for the types of variables being used for today's fact-based techniques. Subsequent sections of this chapter will address the conceptual and statistical underpinnings of some of these variables.

Quantitative fact-based methods also have the advantages of being compatible with performing historical simulations and the application of disciplined implementation procedures. A disciplined approach to setting asset exposure levels is made feasible when systematic techniques are used to determine the outlooks for the financial markets involved. The discussion below elaborates on these two merits of today's TAA strategies.

Availability of Historical Simulations

While making investment decisions based upon qualitative assessments of future developments can be effective (it is certainly popular), such a procedure obviously does not lend itself to historical simulation. One way around this problem is to use a more quantified "forecast-based" technique which specifies the historical relationships between the decision-making variables being considered and actual asset class performance. Indeed, such a forecast-based approach will often demonstrate excellent historical results based upon the relationship of market returns to coincident and/or future economic and financial variables. However, in order to add value, an ability to forecast these variables with reasonable accuracy is necessary. Since the task of forecasting variables such as corporate profits or inflation rates can be nearly as difficult as the primary objective of forecasting stock and bond prices themselves, a forecast-based approach, no matter how innovative, exhaustive, or disciplined, can be subject to serious uncertainty as to future results.

In contrast, quantitative fact-based methods have the advantage of not requiring forecasts of economic or financial data. Consequently, historical simulations can be performed with relatively high credibility, since the historical information being used is only that which was available at the time that historical decisions were being made.

Such simulations, by covering differing economic and market environments over a significant period of time, can help establish the historical accuracy and consistency of a particular TAA methodology. These simulations can also play a key role in establishing reasonable expectations for future returns and aid in evaluating "real-time" experience as it develops. For example, during the inevitable periods of sub-par performance, it is reassuring to demonstrate that the shortfall is well within the bands of an historical experience which was quite good overall.

In sum, while there is no substitute for "real-time" results, the availability of the perspective provided by simulated historical results can be an important aid in establishing the credibility of any "fact-based" process.

Disciplined Implementation Procedures

Even if a sufficient degree of satisfaction and comfort is reached with respect to forecasting accuracy (the hard part), there remains the problem of converting forecasts into above-average returns for actual portfolios. Without sufficient rigor in implementation, there is a real danger of not fully capturing the predictive ability of the forecasting technique. Fortunately, the quantitative nature of most of today's most popular forecasting approaches lends itself to the development of a systematic linkage between the readings of a forecasting procedure and actual market exposures. These "rules of the game" usually also cover investment vehicles, "neutral" benchmarks, ranges of exposures, aggressiveness of implementation, frequency of rebalancing, and so on. Relative to less well-defined processes, imposing such a disciplined approach increases confidence in a number of ways:

- The speed and efficiency of decision making is greatly enhanced.
- Objectivity is increased. One of the possible drawbacks of traditional market timing is the subtle intrusion of our emotions and biases which, too often, are unduly influenced by recent market movements or by economic or political events which may already be reflected in current market prices.
- Communication between manager and client is improved. For example, the status of, and reason for, current asset exposures can be easily communicated. Performance attribution can also be reviewed in a straightforward manner.

In short, investment professionals who are attracted to disciplined forecasting techniques will want the same systematic thinking applied to achieving and reporting results. The attractiveness of TAA strategies can be increased if such issues are adequately addressed by those involved in this process.

"Real-Time" Track Records

Last, but not least, have been the encouraging results of those who have used disciplined TAA strategies. The earliest advocates of such techniques have been active for almost 20 years, with actual funds in some cases being managed for fully 15 years, with impressive results. Other "quantitative" TAA managers have apparently also been quite successful in adding value for their clients. Thus, in addition to the historical simulations referred to previously, favorable real-time results over a fairly long period of time have significantly enhanced the reputation of TAA disciplines.

Investment Implications

The increased interest in TAA appears to be soundly based. As with all investment strategies there will be difficult periods — TAA forecasting techniques have been, and always will be, far from perfect. However, even a moderate amount of forecasting ability, properly implemented, can produce returns well above average. Thus, for those willing to commit their time and thought to developing appropriate procedures and realistic objectives, the potential rewards should be well worth the effort.

VALUATION APPROACHES TO TACTICAL ASSET ALLOCATION

Assets should generally be purchased when cheap and sold when expensive — this statement meets with little debate. Most investors would also agree that any useful "valuation" technique should make sense and possess demonstrable and significant predictive accuracy. However, agreement is not as clear-cut as to which measures of value, if any, best meet these criteria. Consequently, this section will review and analyze the application of specific valuation concepts to forecasting stock and bond returns.

Risk Premium or Spread Technique

Today's most widely used TAA valuation method is the "Risk Premium" or "Spread" approach. This approach simply compares expected return proxies for the markets involved and makes decisions accordingly.[2] For example, if the expected return of equities, as compared to bonds, appears to be above average, an above-average allocation to stocks *vis-a-vis* bonds would be indicated. The asset classes most frequently used are equities, long-term bonds and Treasury bills.

The acceptance of this approach has in part been due to its straightforward rationale. What could be more direct and sensible than to increase or decrease relative exposure to an asset class as the expected relative return increases or decreases? An investor who does so is presumably coolly and systematically taking advantage of the periodic opportunities offered by the emotional swings of the financial markets. In contrast, a less straightforward "market timing" approach probably would not have been accepted as quickly or as broadly as has been the case for the Risk Premium technique.

Derivations The expected returns used for the Risk Premium approach are typically determined as follows:

Equities: Creating an expected return for equities is equivalent to determining the equity market discount rate or cost of equity capital. While entire books have been devoted to the determination of the cost of equity, relatively simple approaches can achieve very satisfactory results without sacrificing theoretical appeal. The most popular approaches to calculating an expected equity return fall into the "bottoms-up" and "top-down" categories:

- *"Bottoms-up"*: This return is an average (usually "market-value" weighted) of individual company returns and hence comes from the "bottoms-up."

  The individual company returns are usually derived from a dividend discount model and hence are a function of current stock prices and estimates of future earnings and dividends. Larger investment organizations can obtain such estimates from internal security analysts. Others without such resources can obtain the necessary projections from a number of data sources. The previous section noted that most TAA approaches are primarily "fact-based," that is, they do not require estimates or projections of future events.

---

[2]William Fouse, then with the Wells Fargo Bank, is credited with being the first to derive and use a formal "Premium" approach to Tactical Asset Allocation.

The principal exception is in this case, where the expected return for equities is determined from the "bottoms-up" based on forecasts for future earnings and dividend growth.

- *"Top-down"*:   Individual company analysis can be foregone when using data and assumptions for the overall market and economy to arrive at a "top-down" expected equity return.

Some "top-down" approaches simply add an estimate of future earnings or dividend growth to the current dividend yield of the overall market to arrive at an expected return. This technique has strong conceptual appeal since it can be demonstrated that the expected long-run return of the equity market at any point in time is equal to the market's dividend yield plus the future growth rate of earnings or dividends.

A second popular method is to invert the equity market's price-to-earnings ratio to create an "earnings yield." While an earnings yield is theoretically equivalent to an expected return only under special circumstances,[3] it has been a reasonable proxy for expected return.

With either of these "top-down" approaches (yield plus growth or earnings yield), there are a relatively large number of choices available with respect to calculating the more difficult-to-determine variables, i.e., future growth for the former calculation and market earnings for the latter.

"Bottoms-up" or "top-down?" The primary advantage of the "bottoms-up" approach is that it reflects the current expectations of actual people in contact with real companies, as opposed to the more theoretical top-down calculation. Consequently, the proponents of the "bottoms-up" approach point out that since expectations determine prices, a measure of the actual expectations of market participants should be the preferred method of calculating an expected return.

However, despite the appeal and popularity of the "bottoms-up" technique, the advantages of the "top-down" calculation should not be ig-

---

[3]Through manipulation of the "Gordon-Shapiro" equation, where Price equals Dividends divided by: the Discount Rate (Expected Return) minus the Growth Rate, it can be shown that the Earnings/Price ratio equals Expected Return when Payout Ratios are 100% or, more realistically, when Return on Equity equals the Discount Rate. Manipulation of the same equation also demonstrates that Expected Return equals Dividend Yield plus the Growth Rate, as asserted in the preceding paragraph.

nored. First, because of the nature of the input requirements of the "bottoms-up" approach, the earliest available data are from the early 1970s. While evaluating such data up to the current time is certainly meaningful, a mechanically derived "top-down" return can be constructed as far back as desired, thus providing additional insight with respect to the effectiveness of an approach. In addition, a "top-down" approach can be performed by one person. If that person is unavailable, another can perform the same calculation. By contrast, the "bottoms-up" approach may require greater resources with less continuity. Finally, it can be argued that the "top-down" technique, being "fact-based" rather than "forecast-based," may be less biased and more consistent over time. For example, security analysts appear to show a substantial lag, often measured in years, in revising their nominal growth rates for changes in secular inflation expectations.

In any case, regardless of the approach used to generate an expected equity return, the results have and will differ somewhat over the short run, but be broadly similar over the long run. This latter assumption is dependent on any bias in a particular calculation being either persistent or random and not being systematically related to economic or market cycles in a counterproductive way. This assumption appears to be valid for most methods used to calculate the expected equity market return.

Bonds: In contrast to the many variations used to construct an expected equity return, the proxy for an expected bond return is usually the yield-to-maturity of a current coupon bond. Typically, an issue with a long maturity is used, with Treasury bonds often preferred.

The current yield-to-maturity of a bond can differ significantly from the return actually realized, even if held to maturity, because of reinvestment of the coupon income at interest rates that differ from current levels. Nevertheless, the implicit assumption that reinvestment yields will be equal to current yields appears to be a reasonable and practical assumption with respect to expectations at a point in time.

Cash: The "cash" return is the return available from fixed-income securities with relatively short maturities, usually 3–12 months. Three-month Treasury bill yields are typically used to represent cash returns because of their short maturities, "risk-free" credit status, and historical data availability. In actual practice, short-term funds may be invested in private credit market instruments that carry higher yields than Treasury bills. However, the historical studies reviewed in this chapter will use

3-month Treasury bills and, consequently, will interchangeably refer to "cash" and "bills."

Historical Analysis — Definitions The previous section indicated a number of choices available for deriving expected returns. Therefore, before presenting the past record of the Risk Premium approach, I will first specify the definitions of the expected returns used for the analyses to be presented in this chapter:

Equities: Because it is conceptually equal to expected return and possesses an empirical record as good or better than other choices, the yield plus growth approach is used to determine the expected equity return. This expected return is the sum of the current annualized yield of the S&P 500 plus the expected annual growth rate of earnings or dividends. The expected nominal growth rate, in turn, is the sum of inflation expectations and real growth expectations.

Inflation expectations are defined as an annualized 20-quarter exponentially weighted moving average of the GNP implicit price deflator, with an adjustment factor for the recent trend in wholesale prices. An exponential moving average is simply a fancy way of expressing the fact that more recent observations are weighted more heavily in the calculation than distant observations. The adjustment for trend in the more sensitive wholesale price index attempts to correct for the tendency of the reported GNP deflator to lag changes in current expectations. The overall result is a mechanically derived number that does an excellent job of tracking the survey-based measures of longer-term "embedded" or secular inflation rates.

As suggested by Estep and Hanson,[4] real growth expectations are assumed to be somewhat below the average assumption when inflation expectations are high, and somewhat above average when inflation expectations are low. The average expectation for real growth is assumed to be 2.8% annually.

Bonds: The expected return for bonds is defined as the current yield-to-maturity of a 20-year current coupon Treasury bond.

---

[4]Tony Estep and Nick Hanson, "The Valuation of Financial Assets in Inflation," in Frank J. Fabozzi (editor), *The Institutional Investor Focus on Investment Management*, Cambridge, MA: Ballinger Publishing, 1989.

Bills: The expected return for T-bills is equal to the bond-equivalent yield of a 3-month Treasury bill.

Thus, the "Risk Premiums" used to determine relative asset class attractiveness are:

- Stocks/Bills Risk Premium — Expected return for equities minus expected return for Treasury bills.
- Bonds/Bills Risk Premium — Expected return for bonds minus expected return for Treasury bills.
- Stocks/Bonds Risk Premium — Expected return for equities minus expected return for bonds

Results — Stocks/Bills Risk Premium   Exhibit 1 shows the historical results of the Stocks/Bills Risk Premium, as defined above, for forecasting subsequent returns of stocks versus bills. The first column shows historical ranges of the Stocks/Bills Risk Premium. The next column indicates the number of month-end observations that have occurred within the specified ranges over the 1951–89 period. Shown in the next three columns are the average realized equity returns (versus bills) for each Premium range. Results are shown for the subsequent 1-, 3- and 12-month periods. The final three columns indicate the percentage of observations within each range that were followed by positive excess returns for the 1-, 3- and 12-month periods.

Exhibit 1 tells us that very high Stocks/Bills Risk Premiums of above 10% have occurred on only 10 occasions over this period, on a monthly basis. Subsequent to these very favorable readings, stocks have returned well above the historical average, with the 12-month equity return averaging a handsome 26% excess over the bill return. Stocks outperformed bills 80% of the time (8 out of 10) for the subsequent 1 month and 3 month periods while, for the 12-month period, stocks outperformed bills in every case. Following this example, the returns and probabilities of positive returns for other Risk Premium ranges can be readily observed. Overall, Exhibit 1 demonstrates the quite meaningful differences in future returns that have been associated with different levels of this straightforward measure of equity market attractiveness.

Similar data could be presented for the Bonds/Bills Risk Premium and Stocks/Bonds Risk Premium. However, "Information Coefficients" provide a more concise way to discuss the effectiveness of the Risk

EXHIBIT 1
STOCKS/BILLS PREMIUM* AND SUBSEQUENT PERFORMANCE STOCKS
VS. BILLS 1951–1989

Premium Range	# Mo. Obs.	Avg. Subsequent Excess Return			Probability of Positive Excess Return		
		1 mo.	3 mo.	12 mo.	1 mo.	3 mo.	12 mo.
> 10	10	2.5%	6.8%	26.1%	80%	80%	100%
8–9.9	64	1.9	4.8	16.7	66	78	89
6–7.9	102	0.5	2.0	6.1	57	63	63
5–5.9	64	0.7	1.6	4.8	61	70	67
4–4.9	107	0.4	1.8	2.7	60	64	62
2–3.9	96	(0.1)	(1.4)	2.8	48	42	60
< 2	25	(1.8)	(1.7)	(6.9)	32	36	40
	468	0.5	1.5	5.7	57	61	66

*Long-term expected equity return minus 3-month T-bill yield.

Premium indicators, as well as other forecasting measures to be subsequently reviewed. While "Information Coefficients" allow us to summarize a considerable amount of information briefly, the tradeoff is that detailed information, such as that shown in Exhibit 1, will not be presented. (However, the appendix includes graphs of the key measures covered in this chapter versus the relevant market indexes. Historical perspective can be obtained from these.)

Information Coefficients   What matters, of course, are the subsequent returns associated with various levels of a forecasting variable. However, this chapter will evaluate the predictive accuracy of forecasting techniques reviewed by showing the "Information Coefficients" or "ICs" between a forecasting variable and subsequent returns.[5] The IC is simply a correlation coefficient between forecasts and outcomes. If there were a perfect relationship between an indicator reading and subsequent returns, the IC would be 1.00. An IC of –1.00 would be perfectly terrible

---

[5]Keith Ambachtsheer, of Keith P. Ambachtsheer & Associates, Inc., had much to do with popularizing the "IC" concept. He has written a number of articles on the subject; for example, see: "Where Are the Customers' Alphas?" *Journal of Portfolio Management,* Fall 1977, pp. 52–56.

(of course, such a perverse relationship, and large negative ICs in general, could be made useful by inverting the forecasting variable, assuming a solid rationale existed for doing so). An IC of 0.00 or in the vicinity of 0.00 would be consistent with the efficient market hypothesis; that is, no significant relationship between forecasts and actual subsequent returns exists.

ICs have a number of merits. First, they summarize a considerable amount of information, thereby vastly simplifying analysis and the presentation of results. Second, ICs provide perspective on the degree of forecasting power that a technique possesses on a linear scale of 0 (no forecasting power) to 1 (perfect forecasting power). This insight is often not achieved with return analyses. Third, if the ICs of two or more forecasting approaches are known, along with their correlations, it is a relatively easy matter to calculate how well the approaches should work in combination. Without this ability determining the value of combining techniques would be a particularly thorny problem. Finally, ICs also lend themselves to tests of statistical significance. Therefore, the "luck or skill" question can be addressed.

Exhibit 2 provides a reference to establish the significance of the ICs to be reviewed in this chapter. For simplification purposes, presenting this exhibit is preferable to constantly indicating the significance level of all of the ICs to be reported. The data are based upon the standard Student's "t" Distribution. For example, in Exhibit 4 the 1-month IC of the Stocks/Bills Risk Premium is .18 for the 1951–89 period. Therefore, this IC is significant at the 99.99% level, since .18 is above .17.

Although the exhibits containing IC data in this chapter show the ICs of a forecasting technique generally increasing over time, the 1-month ICs actually have the most relevance because active TAA strategies recognize that the long term is a series of short terms. Consequently, for TAA strategies which respond quickly to changing conditions (by rebal-

EXHIBIT 2
MONTHLY IC LEVEL NECESSARY FOR SIGNIFICANCE LEVEL

Period Covered in Analysis	90%	95%	99%	99.9%	99.99%
1951–65	.10	.13	.17	.23	.27
1966–89	.08	.10	.14	.18	.21
1951–89	.06	.08	.11	.14	.17

ancing, say, monthly), shorter-term predictive accuracy is, in effect, being compounded over time to achieve optimal long-term results. For example, it can be demonstrated that a TAA process which rebalances monthly and possesses a 1-month IC of .29 will deliver stronger performance than a process that capitalizes on a forecasting technique that has a 1-year IC of 1.00, i.e., a perfect 1-year forecaster![6] For these reasons, most of the subsequent evaluation of predictive accuracy will focus on the 1-month results.

However, the 3-month and 12-month results still play an important role in the evaluation of TAA strategies and, therefore, are included in many of the initial exhibits reviewing predictive accuracy. The 3-month results would be of most significance to those who make the TAA decision on a quarterly basis. This may be a reasonable assumption for many investment committees. Longer-term results, 12 months or longer, are useful for two reasons. First, a technique that was effective over 1 month or 3 months, but not over 12 months, would probably require large and frequent changes in asset allocation. This could not only unsettle clients and managers but also, through higher transaction costs, reduce returns. Second, most of the methods being used for TAA, such as the various "valuation" techniques, are considered longer-term approaches to forecasting the financial markets. Therefore, relatively high ICs over longer time horizons validate the conceptual underpinnings of these forecasting methods.

It was previously noted that what count are returns. One way of demonstrating the relationship between ICs and returns is shown in Exhibit 3. Exhibit 3 indicates the annualized added return that can be expected for particular percentile ranges of a forecasting variable with a 1-month IC level of .10. Since the relationship between added return and the IC level is linear, returns associated with other 1-month IC levels can then be readily determined. For example, assume that our forecasting technique for stocks versus bills possesses a 1-month IC of .20. Exhibit 3, which refers to data for an IC of .10, indicates that if such a forecasting variable were currently in the 6th to 15th percentile of its historical range,

---

[6]Return variability increases approximately with the square root of time, e.g., if 1-month stock market volatility is 4%, then expected annual volatility would be about 14% ($4 \times \sqrt{12}$). Consequently, ICs should increase with the square root of time in order to maintain a *constant* degree of value-added, excluding transaction costs. The 1.00 1-year IC cited in the text is just under $.29 \times \sqrt{12}$.

EXHIBIT 3
RELATING ICs TO RETURNS

Status of Current Forecast within Historical Range of Observations	1-Month IC of .10 Theoretical Annualized Expected Return (Relative to Avg. Return) 1951–89		
Percentile Range	*Stocks/Bills*	*Bonds/Bills*	*Stocks/Bonds*
1– 5%	10.2%	6.3%	10.8%
6–15	6.5	4.1	6.9
16–35	3.5	2.2	3.5
36–65	0.0	0.0	0.0
66–85	(3.5)	(2.2)	(3.5)
86–95	(6.5)	(4.1)	(6.9)
96–100	(10.2)	(6.3)	(10.8)
Memo:			
Average Excess Return	5.8	(0.6)	6.4
Standard Deviation	4.2	2.6	4.4

The return standard deviation shown is monthly.
All other return data are annualized.

then stocks, on average, should outperform bills by about 13.0% (6.5 x 2) annually[7] over the historical average return spread during the periods for which such a forecast would be in effect.

---

[7]The derivation of, for example, the 6.5% shown in Exhibit 3 and the 13.0% referenced in the text was based upon:

  a. An historical (1951/89) standard deviation of 1-month returns for stocks versus bills of 4.17.

  b. In the normal distribution, the forecast in the 6th to 15th percentiles represent observations which, on average, are 1.3 standard deviations above a mean forecast.

  c. If we were clairvoyant and possessed a 1-month IC of 1.00, our expected monthly excess return, in this example, would be 1.3 standard deviations above the mean return or 4.17 times 1.3 = 5.42%.

  d. However, since the assumed IC of Exhibit 3 is .10, not 1.00, the expected monthly excess return is 5.42% times .1 or 0.54%.

  e. 0.54% can be annualized by multiplying by 12 = 6.5%, the number shown in the exhibit. (We can multiply by 12 because the 0.54% is a logarithmic excess return — see footnote 8).

  f. For an IC of 0.2, the expected relative performance would be twice as large as the result for a 0.1 IC, or 13.0%.

Exhibit 3 contains comparable information for the remainder of the forecast spectrum for stocks versus bills. Similar information is provided for bonds versus bills and stocks versus bonds. These theoretical returns provide insight into the return significance of ICs reviewed in this chapter. Actual realized returns have, for practical purposes, closely matched these theoretical returns.

Results   Exhibit 4 shows ICs for the Stocks/Bills, Bonds/Bills and Stocks/Bonds Risk Premiums versus the comparable excess returns for the subsequent 1, 3 and 12 months.[8] The results are based upon monthly data from 1951 to 1989 (since performance was measured for periods of up to 12 months subsequent to the forecasts, the market returns used extended to the end of 1990). Results are also shown for the 1951–65 and 1966-89 periods. Beginning in 1966, the U.S. economy and the financial markets have experienced significantly greater volatility than was the case over the generally calm 1951–65 period. Thus, the mid-sixties represents a useful division of results.

The ICs for the Risk Premium measures have been generally positive. In fact, there has been a positive correlation between Premium levels and subsequent returns. The 1-month IC's all fall in the same very significant area of .15 to .21, with the exception of the Bonds/Bills Risk Premium and the Stocks/Bonds Risk Premium for 1951–65 (zero IC and .09 IC, respectively). The 3-month and 12-month ICs are generally even higher. However, since they represent overlapping observations, their statistical significance is somewhat reduced.

Additional insight is gained from the average annualized rate of excess return associated with each 1% change in the level of the Risk Premium forecasts (shown at the bottom of Exhibit 4). For example, a 1% increase (decrease) between the expected return for stocks and the T-bill yield has resulted in actual subsequent returns of stocks versus bills increasing (decreasing) by 4.0% annualized.[9]

---

[8]In all of the analyses presented in this chapter, the natural logarithms of relative wealth ratios were used to represent subsequent excess returns, rather than simple arithmetic differences. This procedure properly treats, for example, a relative gain of 100% as having the same economic significance as a relative loss of 50%.

[9]This result was determined from a simple regression of Premium levels versus subsequent 1-month excess returns.

EXHIBIT 4
PREMIUM APPROACH INFORMATION COEFFICIENTS

1 Mo. Horizon	Stocks/Bills[a]	Bonds/Bills[b]	Stocks/Bonds[c]
1951–65	.16	.00	.09
1966–89	.17	.16	.15
1951–89	.18	.15	.15
3 Mo. Horizon			
1951–65	.27	(.03)	.17
1966–89	.20	.24	.23
1951–89	.27	.22	.25
12 Mo. Horizon			
1951–65	.50	(.06)	.39
1966–89	.19	.41	.34
1951–89	.37	.37	.43

Actual Subsequent 1-Month Return Difference (Annualized)
For Each 1% Difference of Premium Forecast

	Stocks/Bills	Bonds/Bills	Stocks/Bonds
1951–85	4.0%	3.6%	3.7%
Memo:			
Premium-Avg.	5.5	1.0	4.4
Std. Dev.	2.3	1.3	2.2

[a]Expected equity return minus T-bill yield versus excess returns of stocks to bills.
[b]Treasury bond yield minus T-bill yield versus excess returns of bonds to bills.
[c]Expected equity return minus Treasury Bond yield versus excess returns of stocks to bonds.

Investment Implications

In sum, the information provided in Exhibit 4 offers strong statistical support for the Risk Premium approach. There have been significant and profitable historical relationships between straightforward measures of relative market attractiveness and subsequent relative market returns.

"True" Long-Term Value—The Expected Real Return Approach

The Risk Premium approach seems sensible and has proven results. However, one conceptual criticism has been that the expected returns used for both stocks and bonds are long-term expected returns, while the return used for the "cash" alternative, such as the 3-month Treasury bill yield, is for the very short term. This short-term yield does not necessarily, and often clearly does not, represent investor expectations for "cash" returns over a longer time horizon. Hence, in this sense, the Stocks/Bills and Bonds/Bills Risk Premiums may be good measures of current competitive pressures but may not represent comparable long-term expected return differentials. (This is not to say that the Risk Premium approach is not superior — more on that issue later.) Therefore, this section will review the construction and forecasting record of "true" long-term value measures for stocks and bonds.

Investors are compensated for the risks they take by being provided with "real" returns, i.e., returns after inflation. Consequently, in theory, the long-term real return being offered by an asset class should be the basis for determining whether or not an asset is attractively priced.

Expected real returns, as was the case for expected nominal equity return, are not directly observable. Consequently, for the purpose of analysis, we should seek to construct reasonable estimates of real return expectations.

Definitions:

1. *Expected Real Equity Return*—the expected long-term equity return (identical to the yield plus growth formulation described in the previous section) minus the expected rate of inflation. As previously noted, inflation expectations are defined as an annualized 20-quarter exponentially weighted moving average of the GNP deflator, with an adjustment factor for the recent trend in wholesale prices.
2. *Expected Real Bond Return or Real Bond Yield*—the yield-to-maturity of a current coupon 20-year maturity Treasury bond minus the expected rate of inflation.

These comparisons differ from the Premium analysis by examining expected nominal returns for stocks and bonds relative to inflation expectations instead of Treasury bills. The results, then, will vary because of differences between the estimates of long-term inflation rates and Treasury bill yields.

This section will include no analysis for stocks versus bonds *per se* since a real return comparison for stocks versus bonds is identical to the nominal return comparisons of the previous section.

Results Exhibit 5 shows the ICs between the Expected Real Equity Return and the subsequent performance of stocks versus bills and between the Expected Real Bond Return (Real Bond Yield) and the future returns of bonds versus bills. The 1-, 3- and 12-month time horizons are included.

As was the case with the Premium analysis, the results are encouraging. The ICs indicate that both stocks and bonds have offered significantly more reward when long-term real returns appear high than when they appear low. Each 1% change in the Expected Real Return for equities has, on average, resulted in a 7.6% (annualized) change in the performance differential between stocks and bills. For bonds, a less dramatic but still meaningful 2.5% of annualized return of bonds versus bills has been associated with each 1% change in the Real Bond Yield.

The ICs also tell us that stock market excess returns have generally been somewhat more accurately forecasted with the Stocks/Bills Premium indicator over 1 month and 3 months (these results are presented in Exhibit 4) than with the Expected Equity Real Return. The Expected Real Equity Return appears to be more effective for the longer time horizon of 12 months. With respect to forecasting bonds versus bills, the Real Bond Yield possesses the same or greater effectiveness than the Bonds/Bills Risk Premium indicator over both the full horizon and the more recent 1966–1989 span. The 1951–1965 span had negligible inflation, so the Real Bond Yield turns out to be less useful than the Bonds/Bills Risk Premium over that span.

The final section of this chapter provides an attempt to reconcile and utilize the theoretical and empirical differences between the Risk Premium approach to valuation and the Real Return valuation measures.

Traditional Measures of Stock Market Valuation

Most investors in the equity market do not use the types of valuation measures which have just been discussed. Therefore, the relationship of more traditional measures of stock market "value" merits a comparison with the valuation techniques reviewed in this chapter.

252   DuBois

EXHIBIT 5
REAL RETURN APPROACH INFORMATION COEFFICIENTS

1 Mo. Horizon	Stocks/Bills[a]	Bonds/Bills[b]
1951–65	.11	.05
1966–89	.14	.18
1951–89	.14	.15
3 Mo. Horizon		
1951–65	.19	.08
1966–89	.25	.32
1951–89	.24	.25
12 Mo. Horizon		
1951–65	.41	.13
1966–89	.48	.57
1951–89	.47	.45

Actual Subsequent 1-Month Return Difference (Annualized)
For Each 1% Difference of Real Return Forecast

	Stocks/Bills	Bonds/Bills
1951–89	7.6%	2.5%
Memo:		
Real Return-Avg.	6.9	2.5
Std. Dev.	0.9	1.8

[a]Expected equity return minus expected inflation versus excess returns of stocks to bills.
[b]Treasury bond yield minus expected inflation versus excess returns of bonds to bills.

The most popular stock market valuation measures are those which relate stock prices to the earnings, dividends or book values underlying these prices. All of these indicators attempt to determine the *absolute* attractiveness of the equity market, not the relative attractiveness to alternatives. Therefore, these indicators are analogous to the Expected Real Equity Return calculation of the previous section, as they attempt to determine if the return the investor is receiving is commensurate with the normal risks of stock market investing.

The close relationship between the Expected Real Return of the equity market and these traditional valuation measures can be demonstrated statistically:[10]

Expected Equity Real Return Correlation with:

S&P 500 Earnings to Price Ratio	S&P 500 Dividends to Price Ratio	S&P 400 Book Value to Price Ratio
.79	.94	.83

The predictive ability of these traditional indicators can also be quantified and compared to the Real Return measure:

1 Month "ICs"—Stocks vs. Bills

Exp. Equity Real Return	S&P 500 Earnings to Price Ratio	S&P 500 Dividends to Price Ratio	S&P 400 Book Value to Price Ratio
.14	.06	.11	.10

The straightforward conclusions are that conventional indicators of value are not only highly related to the Expected Real Return indicator, but also possess generally significant but somewhat less predictive accuracy than the real return methodology. Consequently, it can be demonstrated that these traditional valuation techniques offer no additional predictive accuracy to that already possessed by the Expected Real Return variable. This conclusion holds true for other variations of these traditional value indicators, such as techniques that relate stock prices to various measures of "economic" earnings, "cash flow," or "replacement cost" book value. Therefore, the sole measure used in this chapter to determine the absolute attractiveness of the equity market will continue to be the Expected Real Return indicator, due to its theoretical appeal and empirical validity.

A once widely followed and still popular measure of the *relative* attractiveness of stocks versus *bonds* compares the dividend yield of the equity market to long-term bond yields. The conceptual problem with this dividend yield/bond yield "spread" is that the bond yield represents a total return while the dividend yield ignores the returns from equity ownership which result from the growth of dividends. This problem

---

[10]This is based upon monthly data from 1951 to 1989. Earnings are trailing for 12 months. Dividends are based upon the current annual rate. Book/Price ratio is for the S&P 400 index since book values for the S&P 500 are not available.

becomes very clear during periods of changing long-term inflation expectations. For example, if a 1% increase in the expected inflation rate were to occur, bond yields would increase by 1%, everything else being equal. The expected long-term nominal returns from equity ownership would also increase by about 1%, as the higher expected long-term inflation would result in a higher rate of expected nominal dividend growth. As a result, the spread between the current dividend yield and current bond yields would widen by 1%, creating a misleading "deterioration" in the relative attractiveness of the equity market. On this score, relative to history, the stock/bond yield spread has been significantly favoring bonds for most of the past 20 years. Thus, this observation is principally a reflection of higher inflation rates relative to history, rather than a fundamental change in the relative appeal of stocks versus bonds.

The expected equity return used for the analyses presented in this chapter resolves this problem by focusing on expectations of *total* return for the equity market. This total return can then be properly compared to a bond yield, resulting in the Stocks/Bonds Return Premium previously analyzed. Empirically, this Stocks/Bonds Return Preimum outperforms the dividend yield/bond yield spread for forecasting subsequent stock versus bond performance. The comparative 1-month ICs are .15 versus .12 for the 1951–89 period. In addition, no improvement in effectiveness is obtained by considering the traditional dividend yield/bond yield spread in combination with the Stocks/Bonds Return Premium.

In short, on both conceptual and empirical grounds, the conventional yield comparison between stocks and bonds can be safely discarded in favor of the types of measures used in this chapter.

Investment Implications

It has been demonstrated that both the Risk Premium and Real Return valuation techniques have a significant level of historical predictive ability. Of the two, the Premium approach has been generally superior for forecasting stocks versus bills, except for the one important exception previously cited. The Real Return technique has performed the same or moderately better than the Premium measure for forecasting bonds versus bills. Traditional measures of stock market valuation offer no additional information to that which can be obtained by using the Risk Premium and Real Return valuation measures.

In the next section, business cycle factors which can play an important role in TAA strategies will be reviewed. Then the relationship between, and combinations of, valuation and cyclical factors will be analyzed as to their implications for TAA techniques. Finally, the possible value of "sentiment" and "technical" variables will be reviewed.

CYCLICAL CONSIDERATIONS FOR TACTICAL ASSET ALLOCATION

Investment practitioners have long recognized that the cycles in stock and bond prices are often not only closely linked, but are also tied, in important ways, to the cyclical behavior of overall economic activity and the associated responses taken by the nation's fiscal and monetary policymakers. "The stock market leads the economy by six months," is one maxim. "The Federal Reserve writes the market letter for Wall Street," is another. Consequently, while previous sections discussed and evaluated concepts of value as they related to stock and bond performance, this section will review variables related to the cyclical forces which importantly and regularly impact stock and bond prices.

Historical Perspective

As an introduction, Exhibits 6 and 7 demonstrate the cyclical relationships between interest rates, stock prices and economic activity over the past 38 years. Exhibit 6 documents the dates of the troughs and peaks. Exhibit 7 shows the leads or lags of the sequential cyclical events of Exhibit 6.

It is generally recognized that the cyclical swings of stock prices typically lead major changes in the level of economic activity. Exhibit 7, column 1, indicates that the stock market bottoms have led the trough in economic activity in every case, with the median lead being about 6 months. Column 4 shows that the stock market's median lead at economic peaks has been somewhat longer, averaging about 9 months. Columns 2 and 5 indicate that the troughs and peaks in the economy have been closely associated with troughs and peaks in interest rates. On average, interest rates have modestly lagged the concomitant swings in economic activity. Continuing through the cycle, columns 3 and 6 demonstrate that interest rates have always led (with the exception of one tie) the opposite turn of the stock market. That is, rising interest rates have preceded stock market peaks while interest rates have usually been falling prior to stock market bottoms. It is important to note that a relatively long period of

EXHIBIT 6
STOCK MARKET, ECONOMIC ACTIVITY, INTEREST RATES, CYCLICAL TROUGHS AND PEAKS 1952–1990

(1) Stock Market Trough[1]	(2) Economy Trough[2]	(3) Interest Rate Trough[3]	(4) Stock Market Peak	(5) Economy Peak	(6) Interest Rate Peak
9–53	5–54	8–54	8–56	8–57	10–57
12–57	4–58	4–58	7–59	4–60	1–60
10–60	2–61	5–61	2–66	9–66	9–66
10–66	6–67	1–67	12–68	12–69	5–70
5–70	11–70	3–71	1–73	11–73	8–74
10–74	3–75	12–76	2–80	1–80	2–80
3–80	7–80	6–80	11–80	7–81	10–81
8–82	11–82	11–82	10–83	6–84	5–84
7–84	5–86	4–86	7–90	7–90	9–90

[1] Stock market peaks and troughs are based upon weekly average prices of the S&P 500. The major stock market peaks of December 1961 and August 1987 have not been included because they were not primarily associated with cyclical factors, i.e., they did not accompany or precede an economic recession or significant slowdown. The 1962 market decline was caused by a combination of overvaluation and supply/demand imbalances related to high levels of investor optimism and speculation in 1961. Although the 1987 market decline was preceded by higher long-term interest rates (short-term rates increased only moderately), the primary causes appeared to be the same as in 1962, overvaluation and speculation.
[2] Economic peaks and troughs are based upon the official designations of the National Bureau of Economic Research, with two exceptions. The "growth recessions" from 9–66 to 6–67 and from 6–84 to 5–86 have not been classified as recessions. The data used for these economic peaks and troughs are the author's own.
[3] Interest rate peaks and troughs are based upon weekly average yields of 20-year Treasury Bonds.

EXHIBIT 7
LEADS (LAGS) OF SEQUENTIAL EVENTS OF EXHIBIT 6

(Months)

Exhibit 6 columns	(1)	(2)	(3)	(4)	(5)	(6)	(7)	(8)
Cycle[a]	(1)–(2) Market Trough to Econ. Trough	(2)–(3) Econ. Trough to Yield Trough	(3)–(4) Yield Trough to Market Peak	(4)–(5) Market Peak to Econ. Peak	(5)–(6) Econ. Peak to Yield Peak	(6)–(1) Yield Peak to Market Trough	(1)–(3) Market Trough to Yield Trough	(4)–(6) Market Peak to Yield Peak
9/53–12/57	8	3	24	12	2	2	11	14
12/57–10/60	6	0	15	9	(3)	9	6	6
10/60–10/66	4	3	57	7	0	1	7	7
10/66–5/70	8	(5)	23	12	5	0	3	17
5/70–10/74	6	4	22	10	9	2	10	19
10/74–3/80	5	21	38	(1)	1	1	26	0
3/80–8/82	4	(1)	5	8	3	10	3	11
8/82–7/84	3	0	11	8	(1)	2	3	7
7/84–10/90	22	(1)	51	0	2	1	21	2
Mean	7.3	2.7	27.3	7.2	2.0	3.1	10.0	9.2
Median	6.0	0.0	23.0	9.0	2.0	2.0	7.0	7.0
Std. Dev.	5.4	7.0	16.8	4.4	3.3	3.5	7.8	6.1

[a]Stock market trough to trough.

rising interest rates, averaging about 23 months, has elapsed before stock prices have finally peaked. In contrast, the stock market has usually turned up quite quickly after interest rates have begun to fall, with the median lead being about 2 months. Finally, columns 7 and 8 have been added to show the lead of the stock market relative to interest rates. Column 7 is simply the sum of columns 1 and 2 while column 8 is the sum of columns 4 and 5. With the exception of one tie, the troughs and peaks of the stock market have always led, over this period, the troughs and peaks of the interest rate cycle.

A large number of other relationships and observations can be derived from Exhibit 7. For example, adding the means of columns 2, 3 and 4 (averaging 37 months) and columns 1, 5, and 6 (12 months) gives us the average length of economic contractions and expansions, respectively, over this period. Or, in each of the 8 cycles, stocks spent more time rising when interest rates were in a cyclical upswing (column 3) than when interest rates were falling (column 7)! Columns 3, 6, 7 and 8 are probably of most relevance to stock and bond market strategists. These suggest that observing one market may provide some insight with respect to the outlook for the other. More on this later.

These relationships are, of course, not new. As long ago as 1913, Wesley Mitchell documented such standard cyclical patterns.[11] Since then an enormous amount of business cycle research has been accomplished, much of it under the auspices of the National Bureau of Economic Research. The purpose of Exhibits 6 and 7 is not to provide any new insights but to reaffirm and update the basic relationships, especially those concerning the financial markets, as they have existed over the recent past.

Causes and Effects

Why are these cyclical relationships and patterns observed? Let's start with the situation when the economy begins to recover from its recession lows (column 2 of Exhibit 6). The stock market, having anticipated the turn in economic activity, is already up substantially from its cyclical bottom. Interest rates are low and liquidity is abundant reflecting relatively low credit demands, price pressures which are still easing, and a Federal Reserve which is pursuing an expansionary monetary policy.

---

[11]Wesley C. Mitchell, *Business Cycles*, University of California-Berkeley Press, 1913.

Some of this excess liquidity finds its way into financial assets, thus providing one important reason why bonds are still performing reasonably well while the stock market is continuing to move ahead briskly.

However, as the recovery continues and slack in the economic and financial systems is reduced, some upward pressure on interest rates will occur. The increase in the price of money occurs as a consequence of increased credit demands, moderately higher inflation expectations, or, typically, a combination of the two.

This initial increase in interest rates is not necessarily negative for stock prices. It is simply the monetary response to stronger economic activity and associated improvements in pricing flexibility which, in turn, will improve corporate profitability. In addition, concerns about the economy have not yet completely disappeared and the Federal Reserve, while not as generous as earlier, is providing sufficient liquidity to sustain economic growth. Hence, stock prices continue to move forward, although the rate of gain is not as strong as that which occurs when interest rates are falling. In contrast with bonds, which are often falling in price, relative equity returns usually continue to be favorable at this stage of the cycle.

As the economic expansion continues, demands for credit become more vigorous reflecting the inventory and investment needs created by the stronger levels of economic activity, reduced availability of resources, and more optimistic assessments of the future. In addition, upward pressure on prices may increase to more worrisome levels. Consequently, the cyclical rise in interest rates becomes more pronounced. At about this time, the Federal Reserve with inflationary pressures replacing economic growth as its principal concern, will attempt to cool the economy by adopting a policy of monetary restraint that, over the short-term, will only accentuate the increase in interest rates.

It is during this latter phase of the economic expansion that the environment becomes hostile for stock prices. The increases in interest rates and related phenomena which occur at this stage are negative for stock prices for a number of reasons:

First, the strong economy, in combination with a more restrictive monetary policy, has eliminated any of the excess liquidity which helped boost the equity market earlier in the cycle. Hence, a key support to stock prices has been removed from the scene.

Second, increases in the costs of labor, materials and money, combined with lower productivity increases (inherent to the latter stage of an economic expansion) cause unit labor costs to move up significantly. These increases typically cannot be completely offset by price increases. Sales growth is also slowing as a result of physical constraints and the level of overall economic activity, which the authorities are slowing down. The combination of reduced profit margins and less ebullient sales causes corporate profits to level off, if not decline – a negative for stocks.

Third, future business investment in plant and equipment will be reduced by the higher interest rates, as well as the associated reduction in profitability. Since business investment is the cornerstone of future corporate earnings, this development is also a negative for the stock market.

Fourth, and perhaps most importantly, the combination of reduced investments (plant, equipment, inventories, construction, consumer durables, etc.), a maturing economic expansion and monetary restraint, will typically cause the imbalance that leads to an overall economic slow-down, and, in most cases, an outright recession. Such a development will obviously have a harsh impact on both corporate profits and stock prices.

Fifth, and moving closer to the markets themselves, the increase in interest rates will reduce the competitive position of the equity market and, therefore, significantly reduce the demand for stocks. At the same time, carrying costs are increasing for those who have purchased equities with borrowed funds, such as the millions of investors with debit balances in their "margin" accounts.

Finally, if the equity market does not materially decline, at least for a while, the increase in interest rates will increase the relative exposure to stocks vis-a-vis bonds in investors' portfolios, thereby reducing any need to increase equity exposure or creating a reason to reduce equity exposure. The increase in interest rates will also decrease the present value of pension fund liabilities, everything else being equal, thereby reducing funding needs. Since pension fund flows typically have an important impact on the market's supply and demand equations, any reduction in these flows will lower the demand for equities.

For some or all of these reasons stock prices, often trading more narrowly and erratically for the previous several months, will peak. Economic activity will still be strong and the expectations of business-men and a number of economists may still be rosy. Nevertheless, the seeds of an economic slowdown will have been planted, and stock prices will begin to decline.

When business activity does begin to slow, interest rates will some-times begin to fall coincidentally. However, if inflation pressure persists or a stringent monetary policy remains in place during the early stages of the economic decline, interest rates will peak somewhat after the peak in economic activity. The stock market, now worried about the clear decline in the economy, will still be falling and bonds will outperform stocks.

As the decline in output continues, the flip-side of the phenomena, which occurs at the latter stages of an economic upswing, will begin to exert a positive influence on the prospects for the economy. In addition, the normal secular forces of growth will be an important aid in arresting the downswing in economic activity. Consequently the stock market, beginning to see the light at the end of the tunnel, stops going down. A move by the Federal Reserve to aggressively promote economic growth will, at this point, send stock prices soaring. Subsequently as the economy recovers, the cycle begins anew.

This brief review of the classical description of the business cycle and the related behavior of the financial markets is, of course, a simplification, in that:

1. On a micro scale, the experiences of specific industries will differ importantly from cycle to cycle.
2. On a macro basis, the characteristics of each cycle can be significantly affected by events specific to that cycle, such as wars, financial crises, or unusual monetary or fiscal policy actions.
3. Secular forces can create a more permanent change to the nature of the cycle. For example, income stabilization policies that began to exert their full force by the 1950s have considerably reduced, as compared with earlier cycles, the amplitude of the cyclical fluctuations of consumer income and related variables.
4. More recently, the cyclical behavior of the economy has become increasingly influenced by the "globalization" of economic forces and the increased focus of policymakers on such forces.

For these and other reasons, the leads and lags among various economic and financial market turning points, as observed in Exhibit 7, are quite variable and, on some occasions, nonexistent. Nevertheless, the regularity of the ebbs and flows of business and financial market cycles, as Exhibit 7 clearly demonstrates, continues to be generally operative.

Practical Implications

While such information is of obvious interest to students of cyclical behavior, is it useful to the investment practitioner looking for insights into where the financial markets may be headed?

In one sense, no. The leads and lags documented in Exhibit 7 as just noted, are variable and can be quite long. In addition, the peaks and troughs are only observable well after the fact. Consequently, an understanding of normal cyclical behavior doesn't assure an ability to forecast current market behavior.

However, a recognition of the normal cycle is essential to providing perspective to the daily diet of market and economic information that the investor attempts to digest. An appreciation for typical cyclical behavior also can be particularly useful from time to time. For instance, if the blanks of the following paragraph are filled with the respective words listed below the paragraph, then the market strategist usually has valuable information at the times that the specific situation exists:

If_____ have been _____ meaningfully and _____ have not yet begin to significantly _____, then it is unlikely that _____ have yet _____.

a. stock prices, falling, interest rates, fall, stock prices, bottomed;
b. interest rates, falling, stock prices, rise, interest rates, bottomed;
c. stock prices, rising, interest rates, rise, stock prices, peaked;
d. interest rates, rising, stock prices, fall, interest rates, peaked.

For example, during 1985, 1986 and early 1987, condition "c" existed. Stock prices were rising while interest rates were either falling or leveling off. A pronounced cyclical increase in interest rates did not occur. Therefore it was unlikely, from a cyclical perspective, that stock prices had peaked. For market analysts who fretted about the equity market for a number of reasons over this period, this simple observation provided useful information which might have improved results.

By the late spring of 1987, interest rates were finally increasing and condition "d" was in place. Consequently, the interest rate increase should have continued as long as stock prices had not fallen significantly. Recognition of this pattern proved to be valuable, for when it was finally the time to buy bonds (October 19, 1987), the stock market had indeed fallen sharply.

As a recent example, condition "b" was in effect during the fall of 1990. The recession-induced decline in interest rates was unlikely to end until the stock market had rallied meaningfully. Long-term interest rates then declined until mid-February 1991. At this point, the very strong stock market rally which began in mid-January 1991 had rendered condition "b" no longer operative, and instead indicated condition "c" was back in force. That is, stock prices were unlikely to decline in an important way until interest rates increased significantly.

Of most importance, understanding cyclical forces leads to the recognition that interest rates and related phenomena are importantly related to changes in the economy and the financial markets. These relationships are either because of direct causality or because of their relationship with other factors which are causal. The observed historical leads and lags, *per se*, are not critical, assuming that differences in lead/lag relationships among cycles can be explained by differences among the causal variables. What is relevant to the market forecaster is the strength of the relationship between such "causal" variables and future market behavior. The following analysis addresses this need.

Composite Cyclical Indexes

It is well known, and supported by Exhibit 7, that movements in stock prices usually precede changes in economic activity. Therefore, in order to forecast changes in stock prices, it will do us little good to observe what is occurring with respect to current economic activity. Rather, in order to forecast stock prices we must study events which precede (with a longer lead time than stock prices) turning points in the economy.

The previous discussion indicated that measures of liquidity, interest rates, Federal Reserve policy, and so on, play an important leading role with respect to stock prices. Therefore, we can construct a Cyclical Equity Index that combines measures of these types of variables—4 indicators in all.

In contrast, bond prices respond quickly and, in some cases, almost definitionally to changes in various pressures in the economic and financial system (with stock prices, as noted, being affected later). Consequently, we can integrate proxies for current economic, financial, and inflation pressures, along with a measure of the prospective change in these pressures, to create a Cyclical Bond Index.

Exhibit 8 shows the results of using these composite indexes to forecast subsequent returns. The format is similar to that used for the "value"

EXHIBIT 8
CYCLICAL APPROACH INFORMATION COEFFICIENTS

	Cyclical Equity Index[1]	Cyclical Bond Index[2]	Equity Index Minus Bond Index[3]
1 Mo. Horizon			
1951–65	.23	.19	.16
1966–89	.25	.28	.26
1951–89	.25	.24	.22
3 Mo. Horizon			
1951–65	.40	.31	.30
1966–89	.34	.38	.30
1951–89	.36	.34	.28
12 Mo. Horizon			
1951–65	.59	.34	.44
1966–89	.29	.52	.17
1951–89	.44	.45	.21

[1] Cyclical Equity Index versus excess returns of stocks to bills.
[2] Cyclical Bond Index versus excess returns of bonds to bills.
[3] Cyclical Equity Index minus Cyclical Bond Index versus excess returns of stocks to bonds.

measures in the previous section. The 1-, 3-, and 12-month "ICs" are shown for forecasting stocks versus bills, bonds versus bills, and stocks versus bonds.

Generally speaking, the predictive ability of the Cyclical Indices is higher than that of the "valuation" approaches discussed in the prior section, particularly for the low-inflation years 1951–1965. The key 1-month ICs for the Cyclical Indexes are higher in every case than the 1-month ICs for either the Risk Premium or Real Return measure. While the approximate translation from ICs to returns was previously discussed, it is worth noting that when, for example, the Cyclical Equity Index was quite positive (top 10% of all observation) stocks subsequently out-performed bills by 28% annualized, while when the Cyclical Equity Index was negative (bottom 10%), stocks subsequently underperformed bills by 24% annualized.

It is worth recalling that these results were based upon information known at the time the Cyclical Indexes were constructed. No forecasts were being made. The Cyclical Indices were created by merely observing the "facts" as they existed at a point in time. However, knowing what has occurred in the recent past can often provide considerable information with respect to what may occur in the future.

Investment Implications

In sum, the rationales and results presented in this section strongly indicate that measures of cyclical conditions should be considered for use in TAA strategies.

COMBINING VALUATION AND CYCLICAL INDICATORS

The rationales and records of valuation and cyclical variables potential to add value to TAA strategies was evaluated in the previous discussion. We can now review the relationships between these 2 major classes of variables and the resulting implications for TAA techniques.

Exhibits 9, 10 and 11 summarize the key results. The 1-month ICs for the Risk Premium, Real Return and Cyclical measures discussed in preceding sections are shown for the periods of interest. Exhibits 9, 10 and 11 cover this information for forecasting stocks versus bills, bonds versus bills, and stocks versus bonds, respectively.

The information provided by Exhibit 9 indicates that each of the three individual approaches are significantly related to the subsequent returns of stocks versus bills. As previously noted, the Cyclical Indices have been the most effective predictors of future return. Over the 1951–89 period, the stocks versus bills forecasting accuracy of the Cyclical Index is approximately 45% greater than that of the Risk Premium indicator. The Risk Premium technique, in turn, demonstrates 20% higher predictive capability than has the Expected Real Return methodology.

It might be expected that "value" indicators provide a market outlook that is useful separately from the message of the cyclical variables. If this were true, the use of the two techniques in combination would provide better results than those obtained by using the cyclical indicators alone. The facts bear this out.

We first consider the Risk Premium methodology in this context for stocks versus bills. Exhibit 9 shows that the combination of the Cyclical Equity Index and the Risk Premium indicator adds only slightly to the results of the cyclical indicators alone. The primary reason for this result

EXHIBIT 9
STOCKS VERSUS BILLS SUMMARY

Forecasting Excess Returns—Stocks vs. Bills

Technique	1-Month ICs		
	1951–89	*1951–65*	*1966–89*
Risk Premium–Exp. Equity Return minus T-bill Yield	.17	.16	.17
Real Return–Exp. Equity Return minus Inflation	.14	.11	.14
Cyclical Bond Index	.25	.23	.25
Combinations			
Risk Premium, Real Return	.19	.16	.21
Risk Premium, Cyclical	.26	.24	.26
Real Return, Cyclical	.28	.24	.30

Correlations Between Techniques

	1951–89	*1951–65*	*1966–89*
Risk Premium, Real Return	.52	.92	.06
Risk Premium, Cyclical	.37	.30	.39
Real Return, Cyclical	.01	.12	(.09)

can be found among the correlations shown at the bottom of the exhibit. The Risk Premium indicator has a positive .37 correlation with the Cyclical Index. Therefore, its ability to add value to the cyclical approach, given that its predictive value is lower than the Cyclical Index in the first place, is limited.

Now the Risk Premium indicator for stock versus bills is equal to the expected equity return minus the current T-bill yield. T-bill yields are, of course, very sensitive to the cyclical forces which impact interest rates. Hence, movements of T-bill yields are related to movements of the Cyclical Equity Index. This perhaps obvious observation is, then, the cause of the positive correlation between the Premium indicator and the Cyclical Equity Index.

As noted earlier, one criticism of the Risk Premium technique is that it combines a measure of long-term expectations (in this case, the expected equity return) with a cyclical short-term return (the T-bill yield), and consequently, is not a measure of "true" long-term value. It can now

EXHIBIT 10
BONDS VERSUS BILLS SUMMARY

Forecasting Excess Returns—Bonds vs. Bills

	1-Month ICs		
Technique	1951–89	1951–65	1966–89
Risk Premium–Bond Yield minus T-bill Yield	.15	.00	.16
Real Return–Bond Yield minus Inflation	.15	.05	.18
Cyclical Bond Index	.24	.19	.28
Combinations			
Risk Premium, Real Return	.19	.04	.22
Risk Premium, Cyclical	.24	.19	.28
Real Return, Cyclical	.28	.20	.31

Correlations Between Techniques

	1951–89	1951–65	1966–89
Risk Premium, Real Return	.23	(.12)	.27
Risk Premium, Cyclical	.56	.50	.65
Real Return, Cyclical	(.02)	.03	.14

be seen that this "shortcoming" can be a virtue, since changes in the T-bill yield act as a (perhaps suboptimal) useful proxy for the cyclical factors which importantly impact equity market performance. On the other hand, because of this cyclical sensitivity, the Risk Premium measure does not appear to add material value to cyclical factors. Therefore, it would appear to be of little interest to those *directly* addressing cyclical conditions with indicators such as those used in the Cyclical Equity Index.

In contrast, the Expected Real Equity Return indicator possesses lower predictive content than the Risk Premium indicator, but, being a more valid measure of "true" long-term value, it is relatively uncorrelated with cyclical indicators of the equity market. Because of this lack of correlation, combining the Real Return measure with the Cyclical Equity Index results in about a 12% increase in effectiveness (combined IC of .28 versus .25 for Cyclical alone). Therefore, in this context, the notion that

EXHIBIT 11
STOCKS VERSUS BONDS SUMMARY

Forecasting Excess Returns—Stocks vs. Bonds

Technique	1-Month ICs		
	1951–89	*1951–65*	*1966–89*
Risk Premium–Exp. Equity Return minus Bond Yield	.15	.09	.15
Cyclical–Cyclical Equity Index minus Cyclical Bond Index	.22	.16	.26

Combination			
Risk Premium, Cyclical	.29	.19	.33

Correlations Between Techniques

	1951–89	1951–65	1966–89
Risk Premium, Cyclical	(.17)	.01	(.19)

valuation and cyclical variables should be combined makes no apparent sense.

Exhibit 10 summarizes the data on bonds versus bills. Here the same conclusion that was reached for stocks versus bills can also be made and for the same reasons. That is, the Cyclical Bond Index has been the most useful for forecasting bonds versus bills for the 1951–89 period. The Risk Premium indicator is correlated with the Cyclical Index and no value is added by combining the Premium indicator with the Cyclical Index. However, the effectiveness of the Cyclical approach is increased by about 16% by adding the Real Return indicator to the Cyclical Bond Index.

In Exhibit 11, the results of combining valuation and cyclical variables to forecast the relative returns of stocks versus bonds are reviewed. The cyclical measure of stock to bond attractiveness is simply the Cyclical Equity Index minus the Cyclical Bond Index. The 1-month IC data indicate that historically the cyclical factors have been about 50% more effective than the Risk Premium valuation indicator for forecasting future returns of stocks versus bonds.

Since short-term yields do not play a role in the Stock/Bond Risk Premium indicator, one would expect little correlation between the Risk Premium indicator and the cyclical measure of stock to bond attractiveness. In fact, the correlations have been negative for the 1951–89 and 1966–89 periods. Because of this independence, the addition of the Risk Premium valuation indicator to the Cyclical Index increases stock versus bond predictive ability by over 30% for the 1951–89 period.

This Stocks/Bonds Risk Premium measure of value is the expected Equity Return minus the long-term bond yield. In this case, the Risk Premium indicator is equivalent to a Real Return indicator since inflation expectations are included in both the Expected Equity Return (as calculated) and the nominal bond yield (implicitly).

The conclusion drawn from Exhibits 9 through 11 is that the best results are achieved by combining the cyclical indicators, which are the most powerful, with independent measures of "true" long-term value. The historical weights, derived from standard regression analyses, which should be applied to these cyclical and valuation indicators to achieve the best results are detailed in Exhibit 12. It is impressive to see that, regardless of the period covered or the returns being forecast, the results

EXHIBIT 12
"VALUATION" VERSUS "CYCLICAL" RELATIVE IMPORTANCE

| | *Forecasting Stocks versus Bills* | | |
	1951–89	*1951–65*	*1966–89*
Valuation[1]	35%	26%	38%
Cyclical[2]	65%	74%	62%

| | *Forecasting Bonds versus Bills* | | |
	1951–89	*1951–65*	*1966–89*
Valuation[3]	38%	20%	37%
Cyclical[4]	62%	80%	63%

| | *Forecasting Stocks versus Bonds* | | |
	1951–89	*1951–65*	*1966–89*
Valuation[5]	44%	36%	41%
Cyclical[6]	56%	64%	59%

[1] Expected Equity Return minus Expected Inflation.
[2] Cyclical Equity Index.
[3] Bond Yield minus Expected Inflation.
[4] Cyclical Bond Index.
[5] Expected Equity Return minus Bond Yield.
[6] Cyclical Equity Index minus Cyclical Bond Index.

are quite similar, with the cyclical measures comprising anywhere from 56% to 80% of the total forecasting weight.

Investment Implications

If value is defined by the Expected Real Return being offered by stocks or bonds, then the cyclical environment for stocks and bonds is largely independent of valuation considerations. Consequently, adding the two approaches versus using the cyclical indicators alone increases overall predictive accuracy by 12% to 30%. As a rule of thumb, the cyclical outlook should be considered about twice as important as valuation levels for determining the near-term outlook for the financial markets.

Other Concepts to Consider

The use of cyclical monetary and economic variables in combination with measures of value is one example of how a purely valuation-based process can be improved by including other types of variables. The motivation for considering other approaches is twofold: first, to increase the level of predictive ability, thereby improving investment returns; and, second, to increase the diversification of the forecasting process, thereby increasing the consistency of investment returns. The result of such improvements should be fewer periods of underperformance and/or a lower average magnitude of underperformance when shortfalls occur. Such motivations have caused many TAA managers to not only add business cycle variables to their valuation process, but also to extend their strategies to include factors related to "sentiment" or "technical" conditions. A brief review of the usefulness of these types of variables in forecasting the stock market is presented in the following section.

Sentiment

It has been said that the cycles of the markets are related to the cycles of business overlaid with the cycles of investor greed and fear. The psychological component of returns present in all markets are addressed in the "sentiment" category. A number of TAA investment processes use variables related to measures of investor sentiment. The majority of sentiment indicators are an attempt to measure the attitudes and actions taken by various groups of market participants. Examples in the U.S.

stock market are the magnitude of public put option buying, the level of institutional cash holdings, and the status of a variety of surveys measuring investor opinions.

The theory that such measures provide utility is based upon the principle that as investors become increasingly optimistic (pessimistic) in their expectations about the future course of prices, the probability of a market decline (advance) is increased. This, of course, is the doctrine of "contrary opinion."

There are good reasons why such perverse tendencies are consistently observed. It is axiomatic that when the majority of investors are, or have been, bullish on a market, they will be relatively fully invested. Therefore, they possess a somewhat limited capacity to continue buying. Prices tend to fall as even "good news" has little effect upon prices, since already committed investors cannot act further upon the "good news." "Bad news," however, will precipitate some selling, causing prices to fall.

Conversely, when investors are pessimistic and have structured their portfolios to reflect their cautious outlook, there exist, again in a relative sense, few remaining potential sellers. There is, however, an important source of market demand since higher cash reserves will eventually be committed to the market as more favorable conditions appear to market participants.

Such reasoning suggests that "contrary" indicators should play a meaningful role in stock market forecasting. An analysis of several such measures supports this contention.

Technical

Some TAA investment managers use a limited number of "technical" indicators to improve overall effectiveness and diversity. Technical indicators are defined as those based solely upon measures of market prices or volume and the myriad of relationships that can be derived from such statistics. There are, of course, a vast array of technical theories and indicators. A sampling of the menu would include measures of relative strength, money flows, breadth, divergence, overbought-oversold, presumably repetitive cycles, chart patterns, new highs and new lows, upside/downside volume, volume confirmation, etc. Some have been personalized, e.g., Arms Index, Elliot waves, Gann squares, McClellan oscillator, etc. Examples of technical variables actually used by some TAA processes are measures of market volatility, market momentum (trend following or "mean-reversion"), and market breadth and consistency.

Advocates of the technical approach assert that the "action" of a market itself often offers a clue to its future behavior. This occurs because the status of many technical indicators reflects how underlying supply and demand conditions for a market are changing.

As is true with all indicators, including those previously mentioned, technical measures have to possess two initial requirements for use in a TAA process: (1) an understandable rationale, and (2) a good track record. Some technical indicators fail to meet the first requirement.

While many technical measures do possess a plausible rationale, the second requirement, a demonstrated record of predictive content, is often lacking. This occurs for two reasons: (1) many technical variables cannot be defined objectively, and (2) many which can be rigorously defined are found, after testing, to be devoid of significant predictive content. (The debate about their usefulness, though, will never be fully resolved, as advocates of many technical indicators will warn that they require "interpretation.")

Despite these problems, there are a number of technical variables which have an understandable rationale, can be objectively measured, and possess a documented track record. Since they represent an additional way of viewing the market outlook, such measures can be considered by TAA investment managers.

Combining Concepts

Exhibit 13 shows data summarizing the possible benefits of including sentiment and technical variables in addition to the valuation and cyclical indicators previously discussed. The data pertain to stocks vs. bills for the 1966–89 period.

The Sentiment group is a composite of four variables measuring institutional and individual actions, attitudes, and speculation. The Technical Composite consists of four indicators measuring momentum and "divergence" within the market. The Valuation and Cyclical concepts are represented respectively by the Expected Real Return and Cyclical Equity Index.

In Exhibit 13, the upper half shows the ICs with subsequent one-month excess returns for each of the four broad categories and their correlation to each other. It can be seen that the historical one-month predictive abilities of the Sentiment and Technical Composites, taken alone, have

EXHIBIT 13
VALUATION, CYCLICAL, SENTIMENT, TECHNICAL
FORECASTING EXCESS RETURNS—STOCKS VS. BILLS
1-MONTH HORIZON—1966–89

	ICs with 1 Month Excess Returns	Correlation Matrix for Indicators			
		V	C	S	T
Valuation (V)	.14	1.00			
Cyclical (C)	.25	(.09)	1.00		
Sentiment (S)	.23	.50	.04	1.00	
Technical (T)	.22	(.03)	.46	.15	1.00

Combined Models					
	ICs with 1 Month Excess Returns	Relative Importance			
		V	C	S	T
V	.14	100%			
V + C	.30	38	62		
V + C + S	.34	14	53	33	
V + C + S + T	.35	14	39	29	18

been higher than for valuation and nearly as high as the cyclical indicators. The correlation matrix shows that the Sentiment group has been highly correlated with the Value variable. That is, when stocks have been "cheap" investors typically have been pessimistic, and, when stocks have been "expensive" investors generally have been optimistic. Since valuation levels reflect, in part, investor expectations, perhaps this result should not be too surprising.

The other relatively high correlation is between the Technical and Cyclical Composites. This relationship reflects the tendency of technical conditions to be "strong" at the same time that interest rates are falling, the Federal Reserve is accommodative, etc., and for the technical environment to often be weak when money is tight and interest rates are increasing.

The lower part of Exhibit 13 shows the buildup of forecasting ability as valuation measures are enhanced by the addition of the Cyclical, Sentiment and Technical Composites. While the added value of the sentiment and technical variables (to the valuation and cyclical variables previously analyzed) has been limited by the positive correlations discussed in the immediately preceding paragraphs, the overall increase in effectiveness is on the order of 17%, a material increase. Furthermore, the increase in process diversification reduces its reliance on any single technique. This reduces risk not only in a fundamental intuitive sense but also, in the actual implementation of the forecasts and actual portfolio variability versus an objective.

The optimal weights for each group for this period are also shown. When all four categories of variables are analyzed at the same time, the Cyclical group obtains the highest weighting (39%), followed by Sentiment (29%), Technical (18%) and Valuation (14%). This result demonstrates that valuation levels, over the short-run, can be the least important factor affecting subsequent returns.

Investment Implications

Sentiment and technical variables are useful forecasters of future market direction. They appear to deserve a place in a comprehensive Tactical Asset Allocation forecasting process.

SUMMARY

Tactical Asset Allocation, for a variety of reasons, is here to stay. The approach to TAA that has gained the most credence and popularity has been based upon straightforward comparisons of expected return proxies for the markets involved. This "Risk Premium" technique has been quite effective for the practitioners that have used it.

For the purpose of forecasting stocks versus cash or bonds versus cash, the Premium approach has demonstrated significant predictive ability. Valuation measures that derive an expected real rate of return by subtracting an expected inflation rate from an expected long-term return for stocks and bonds have also been effective, but have not shown as much forecasting accuracy as the Risk Premium technique. For comparing stocks to bonds, the Risk Premium approach is equivalent to the Real Return technique and has also been quite effective historically.

Traditional measures of stock market valuation, such as ratios of stock prices to earnings, dividends or book value, or of stock yields to bond yields, have been either inferior and/or redundant with the Risk Premium and Real Return valuation measures reviewed in this chapter and, therefore, offer no additional value-added.

The cyclical swings of business and credit conditions are closely tied to the cycles of stock and bond prices. Variables that attempt to measure cyclical conditions have demonstrated shorter-term predictive ability greater than that of the Risk Premium or Real Return valuation techniques for both stocks compared to bills, bonds versus bills, and stocks versus bonds.

The Risk Premium valuation approach for stocks to bills and bonds to bills is actually more related to the cyclical variables than to the Real Return valuation indicators. This is a consequence of the cyclically sensitive T-bill yield being used in the Premium calculation. In contrast, the Expected Real Return valuation approach for stocks versus bills and bonds versus bills is essentially independent of cyclical conditions. Consequently, a combination of the Cyclical Index with the Real Return variables results in the most effective combination of cyclical and valuation factors.

For comparing stocks to bonds, where the Real Return variable is equivalent to the Premium indicator, a combination of the Cyclical Indexes with Real Return comparisons has also been quite useful.

Historically, the best results have been achieved when the Cyclical Indices were weighted approximately twice as heavily as the Real Return valuation measures.

Sentiment indicators measure the actions and attitudes of investors and are used in a "contrary" manner. Technical factors measure a market's "internal" condition which, in turn, can reflect how underlying supply and demand conditions are evolving.

Composites of selected sentiment and technical variables were found to be useful alone and to add predictive value and diversification to the TAA predictive process.

CONCLUSION

Many of today's TAA strategies are based solely upon "valuation" techniques. Others, however, also use measures of the "cyclical" environment. Some have added "sentiment" and "technical" factors. This chapter has demonstrated the generally significant forecasting ability of each of these approaches. For those who focus entirely or heavily upon valuation, this chapter also suggests that an increased consideration of other types of variables may offer the opportunity for further increases in the effectiveness of TAA strategies.

APPENDIX

Exhibits A-1 to A-10 graphically portray the recent history of the principal forecasting tools reviewed in this chapter. The definition of the forecast variable for each exhibit is given below:

Exhibit	Label on Chart	Definition
A-1	Stock/Bills Expected Return Premium	Expected Equity Return minus T-bill Yield
A-2	Expected Real Equity Return	Expected Equity Return minus Expected Inflation
A-3	Cyclical Equity Index	Composite of 4 Cyclical Equity Indicators
A-4	Bonds/Bills Expected Return Premium	Treasury Bond Yield minus T-bill Yield
A-5	Expected Real Bond Return	Treasury Bond Yield minus Expected Inflation
A-6	Cyclical Bond Index	Composite of 4 Cyclical Bond Indicators
A-7	Stock/Bonds Expected Return Premium	Expected Equity Return minus Treasury Bond Yield
A-8	Cyclical Stocks/Bonds Index	Cyclical Equity Index minus Cyclical Bond Index
A-9	Equity Sentiment Index	Composite of 4 Sentiment Indicators
A-10	Equity Technical Index	Composite of 4 Technical Indicators

The historical performance of the relevant index is shown with each indicator history. For example, the indicators designed to forecast equity market performance are shown versus an index of the relative performance of stocks versus T-bills.

Stock returns are equal to total returns for the S&P 500. Bond returns are represented by total returns from 20-year Treasury bonds. Three-month Treasury bill returns represent the "bill" returns.

The exhibits have the following in common:

1. The top half depicts the relative performance index. The scale is logarithmic with December 1965 = 1.
2. The bottom half shows the value of the forecasting variable. For the Premium and Real Return comparisons, the actual Risk Premiums and Real Returns are shown. In contrast, for ease of understanding and comparison, each of the Cyclical and Composite

Indices has been constructed with a mean of 0 and a standard deviation of 5.

3. Indicator data are plotted for month-end from January 1965 to November 1991. The relative return indices are shown monthly through December 1991.

4. Generally, these charts offer pictorial support to the analyses performed in the text. While all of the histories could be reviewed extensively, comments are restricted to the equity market with respect to real return valuation (Exhibit A-2) and the cyclical environment (Exhibit A-3), the purpose being to give the reader a general appreciation which can be applied to the other charts.

Comments on Exhibits A-2 and A-3

Valuation is important (Exhibit A-2). Stocks were clearly overvalued prior to the major bear markets of 1973–74 and 1987. The years 1974 and 1982 represent periods of undervaluation that led to major bull markets. On the other hand, valuation can be of limited use at times. The important 1981–82 bear market began from a period of apparent "fair" valuation. The 1970–72 and the recent 1990–92 bull markets did not begin in a particularly undervalued condition. As can be seen, apparent overvaluations or undervaluations can persist for a long time, and even worsen, before being corrected. Stocks became overvalued in 1971 and 1986, yet the markets rolled on for 12–24 months. Conversely, the undervaluations of the late 1970s persisted for many years.

It can be seen from Exhibit A-3 that cyclical conditions can explain much that valuation cannot. The overvaluations of 1971–72 and 1986–87 were not corrected until the cyclical environment had deteriorated. Similarly, the undervalued markets of 1974 and 1982 did not soar until cyclical conditions had turned for the better. The bear market that began in late 1980 from a "fairly valued" condition was accompanied by very hostile cyclical forces. The favorable cyclical environments of 1970 and 1991 led to bull markets that were quite strong, despite the fact that they were not, to begin with, particularly cheap. The point, of course, is that despite the demonstrated importance of valuation levels, overall cyclical conditions can often explain much of stock market behavior that absolute valuation levels cannot.

EXHIBIT A1

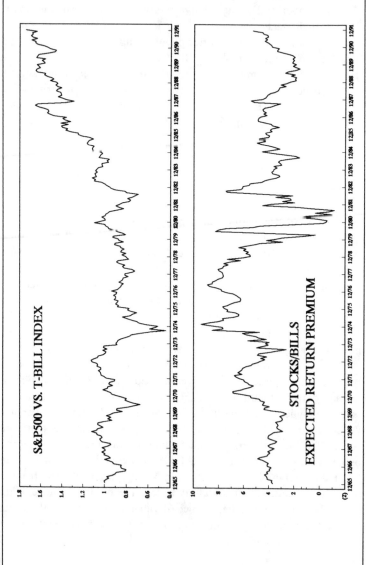

EXHIBIT A2

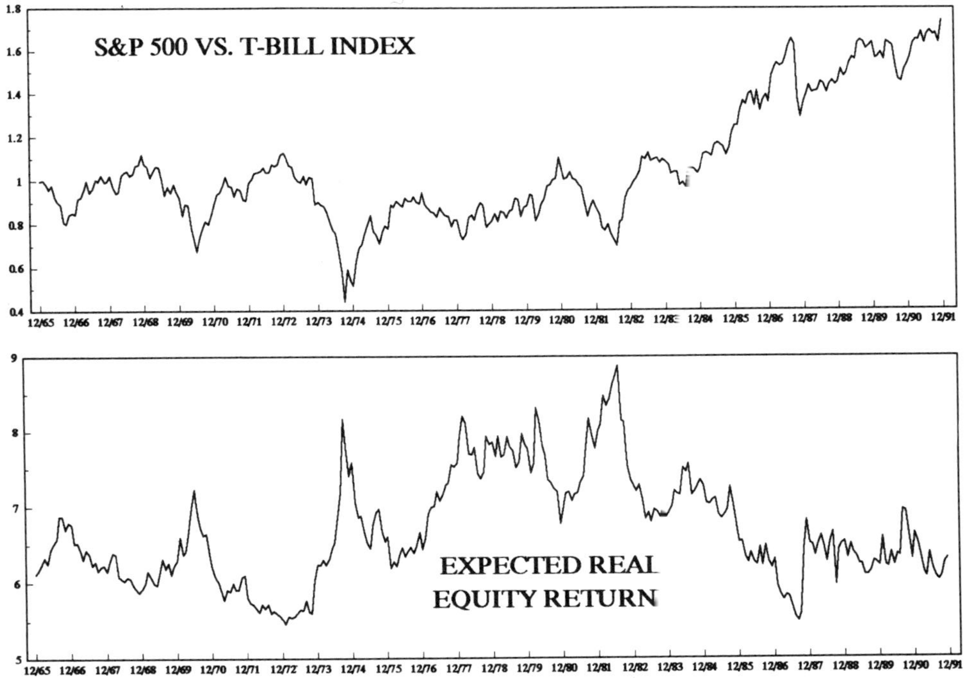

S&P 500 VS. T-BILL INDEX
1.8
1.6
1.4
1.2
1
0.8
0.6
0.4
12/65 12/66 12/67 12/68 12/69 12/70 12/71 12/72 12/73 12/74 12/75 12/76 12/77 12/78 12/79 12/80 12/81 12/82 12/83 12/84 12/85 12/86 12/87 12/88 12/89 12/90 12/91
EXPECTED REAL
EQUITY RETURN
9
8
7
6
5
12/65 12/66 12/67 12/68 12/69 12/70 12/71 12/72 12/73 12/74 12/75 12/76 12/77 12/78 12/79 12/80 12/81 12/82 12/83 12/84 12/85 12/86 12/87 12/88 12/89 12/90 12/91

EXHIBIT A3

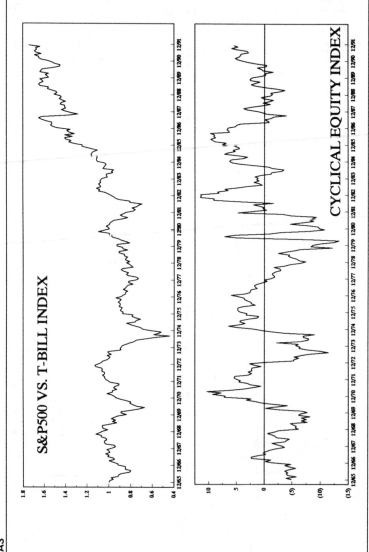

S&P500 VS. T-BILL INDEX

CYCLICAL EQUITY INDEX

EXHIBIT A4

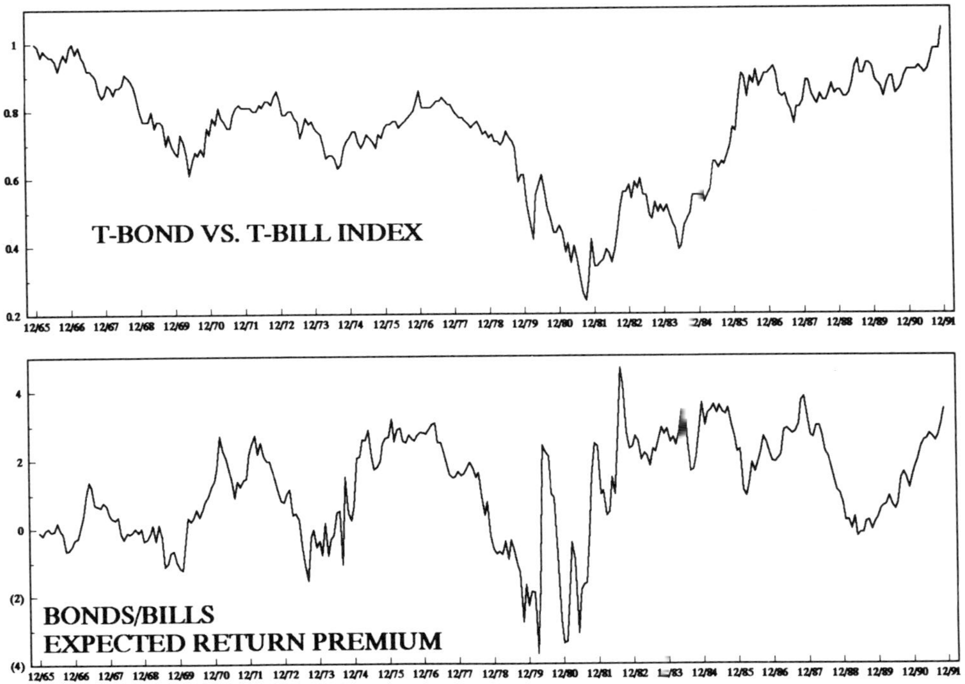

T-BOND VS. T-BILL INDEX
1
0.8
0.6
0.4
0.2
12/65 12/66 12/67 12/68 12/69 12/70 12/71 12/72 12/73 12/74 12/75 12/76 12/77 12/78 12/79 12/80 12/81 12/82 12/83 12/84 12/85 12/86 12/87 12/88 12/89 12/90 12/91
BONDS/BILLS
EXPECTED RETURN PREMIUM
4
2
0
(2)
(4)
12/65 12/66 12/67 12/68 12/69 12/70 12/71 12/72 12/73 12/74 12/75 12/76 12/77 12/78 12/79 12/80 12/81 12/82 12/83 12/84 12/85 12/86 12/87 12/88 12/89 12/90 12/91

EXHIBIT A5

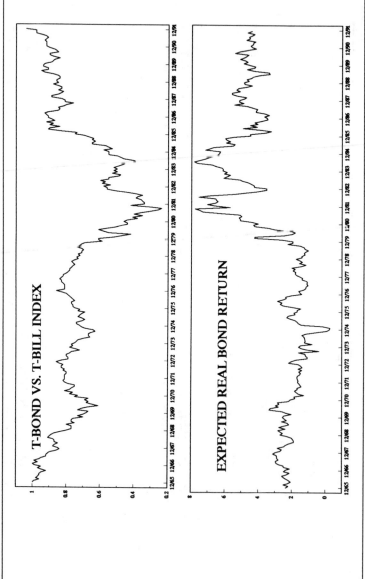

EXHIBIT A6

T-BOND VS. T-BILL INDEX
1.2
1
0.8
0.6
0.4
0.2
12/65 12/66 12/67 12/68 12/69 12/70 12/71 12/72 12/73 12/74 12/75 12/76 12/77 12/78 12/79 12/80 12/81 12/82 12/83 12/84 12/85 12/86 12/87 12/88 12/89 12/90 12/91
CYCLICAL BOND INDEX
10
5
0
(5)
(10)
(15)
12/65 12/66 12/67 12/68 12/69 12/70 12/71 12/72 12/73 12/74 12/75 12/76 12/77 12/78 12/79 12/80 12/81 12/82 12/83 12/84 12/85 12/86 12/87 12/88 12/89 12/90 12/91

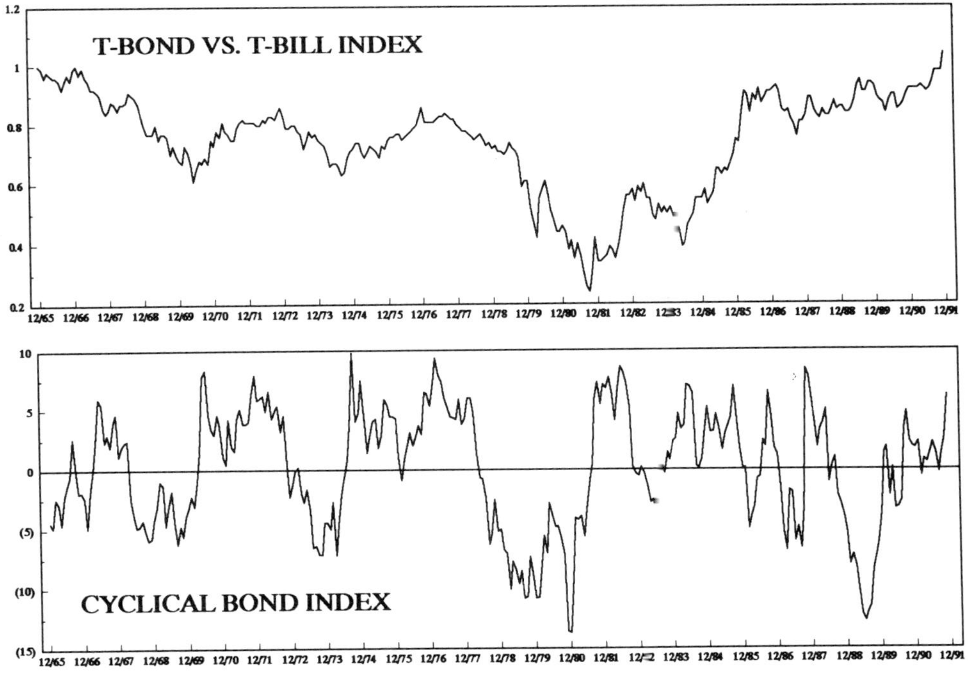

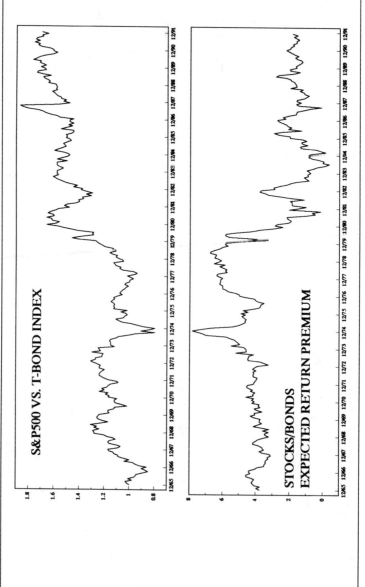

S&P500 VS. T-BOND INDEX

**STOCKS/BONDS
EXPECTED RETURN PREMIUM**

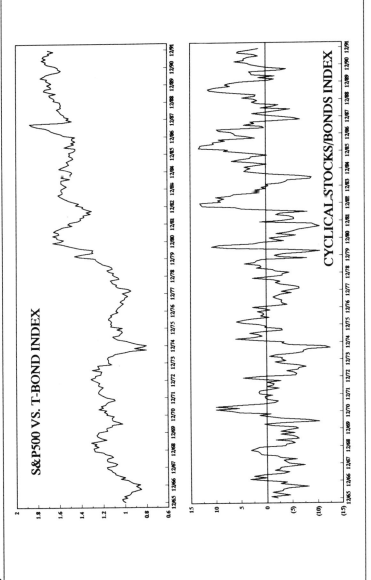

EXHIBIT A9

S&P500 VS. T-BILL INDEX
1.8
1.6
1.4
1.2
1
0.8
0.6
0.4
12/65 12/66 12/67 12/68 12/69 12/70 12/71 12/72 12/73 12/74 12/75 12/76 12/77 12/78 12/79 12/80 12/81 12/82 12/83 12/84 12/85 12/86 12/87 12/88 12/89 12/90 12/91

EQUITY SENTIMENT INDEX
10
5
0
(5)
(10)
12/65 12/66 12/67 12/68 12/69 12/70 12/71 12/72 12/73 12/74 12/75 12/76 12/77 12/78 12/79 12/80 12/81 12/82 12/83 12/84 12/85 12/86 12/87 12/88 12/89 12/90 12/91

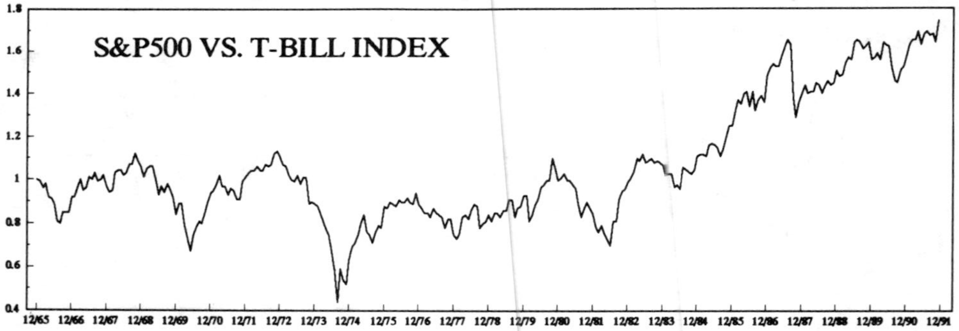

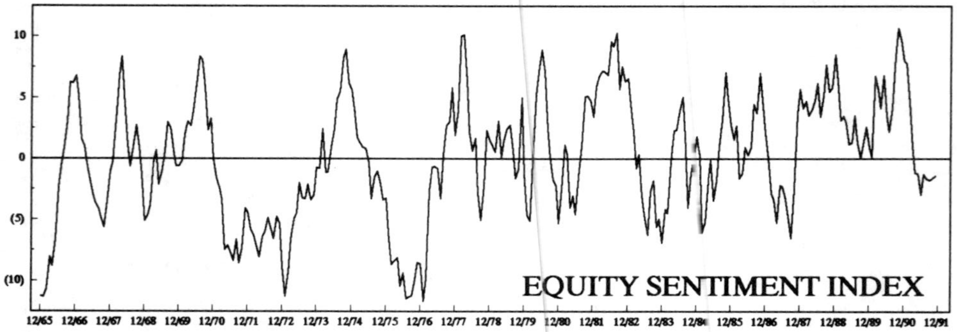

EXHIBIT A10

S&P500 VS. T-BILL INDEX
1.8
1.6
1.4
1.2
1
0.8
0.6
0.4
12/65 12/66 12/67 12/68 12/69 12/70 12/71 12/72 12/73 12/74 12/75 12/76 12/77 12/78 12/79 12/80 12/81 12/82 12/83 12/84 12/85 12/86 12/87 12/88 12/89 12/90 12/91

EQUITY TECHNICAL INDEX
10
5
0
(5)
(10)
(15)
12/65 12/66 12/67 12/68 12/69 12/70 12/71 12/72 12/73 12/74 12/75 12/76 12/77 12/78 12/79 12/80 12/81 12/82 12/83 12/84 12/85 12/86 12/87 12/88 12/89 12/90 12/91

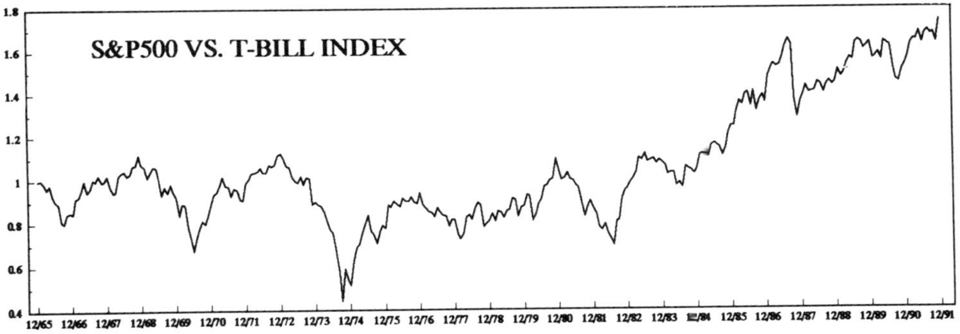

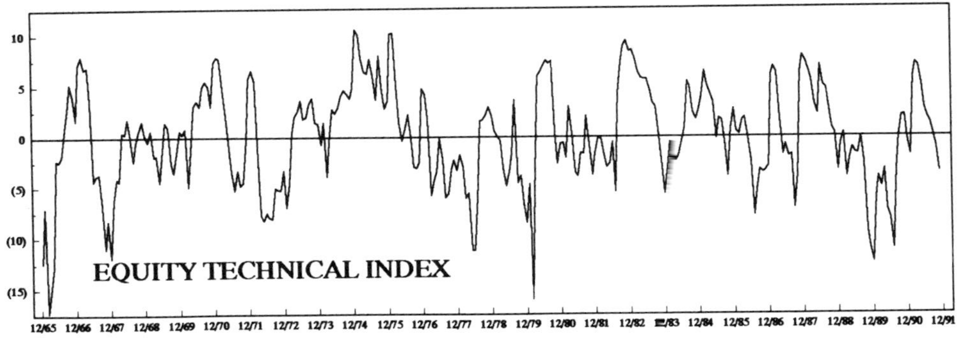

CHAPTER 13

Asset Allocation — Reward and Diversification

JEREMY J. EVNINE

IRIS FINANCIAL ENGINEERING AND SYSTEMS, INC.

Current conventional wisdom would have it that a pension sponsor wishing to put money into a tactical asset allocation (AA) fund should centralize his decision and have only one tactical asset allocation manager. Clearly, no one would expect a sponsor to take the same attitude toward stocks selection or asset class selection. Why then for asset allocation? Indeed, the same paradigm that we use to solve the stock selection problem can be used to solve the AA selection problem — namely, the twin concepts of added value, and added diversification.

In the case of stock selection, the added value is expected return, and the lack of perfect correlation across stocks is the reason to diversify, rather than putting all funds in the stock with the highest expected return. In the case of AA funds, the measure of value can be taken as the implied look-back option supplied by a successful fund, and the lack of correlation of successful timing across funds can be used as a measure of diversification.

The next section provides an overview of the problem at hand and the methodology we use to analyze it. The following section discusses the concept of the value of an AA fund. The third section analyzes the effect of diversification across AA funds. The last section concludes.

OVERVIEW

Tactical asset allocation funds, or market timing funds, have presented investors with the greatest temptation, and with the greatest frustration as well. While a mispriced security can provide an investor with an opportunity to make more profit without more risk, the mispricings are usually found in assets with little market depth. Occasionally, persistent mispricings in traded assets with deep markets may allow large amounts of money to be made, such as was the case with the S&P 500 and the Treasury Bond futures contracts. But these opportunities diminished in size as more investors lined up to take advantage of them. By contrast, if one could truly discover a mispricing of one entire asset class relative to another, one could invest extremely large sums in such a timing strategy. Moreover, since such mispricings could only be discovered by an understanding of the macroeconomy, rather than violations of technical relationships (such as the cost-of-carry formula for stock index futures), one might hope these opportunities would persist for relatively long periods of time.

Unfortunately, it has been rather difficult to tell whether an AA fund was successfully doing its purported job or not, since the standard Capital Asset Pricing Model-based performance measurement methods break down in the case of a market timing fund. The CAPM states that if:

$$R_i = R_f + \beta(R_m - R_f) + e_i$$

where

R_i is the period return on stock i,

R_f is the period riskless rate,

R_m is the period return on the market portfolio, and

β is the coefficient which suggests the sensitivity of stock to market moves,

then the expectation of e_i is zero.

If β, the stock's beta relative to the market portfolio, is known, then an excess return of $\beta(R_m - R_f)$ can be obtained without skill, simply by taking an appropriate mix of cash and the market portfolio. Holding stock i in other than its capitalization weight is only justifiable if an investor knows that the expectation of e_i is different from zero. Thus, microforecasting is concerned with seeking out stocks whose residual has non-zero expectation, and then over- or under-weighting them relative to the market portfolio. If the null hypothesis is that the residuals have normal distribution with zero mean, then statistics with the t-distribution can be constructed to test the hypothesis of no forecasting ability.

In market timing, however no stock need ever be held in other than its capitalization weights. When the stocks, as a class, are favored, wealth is moved out of some other asset class (e.g., money market funds, bonds) and into, say, the market portfolio or a proxy for it. Hence, investors may change their beta by moving money in or out of stocks, but never attempt to seek for non-zero mean residuals. This makes the CAPM of little value as a means to evaluate investment performance.

Over the last few years, AA funds have become more common, to the point where they may be viewed as commodities, rather like index funds. Those investors wishing to engage in market timing via these AA funds have therefore been faced with a decision as to how they should allocate their money across these funds.

The argument in indexing has been to centralize money into a single fund, on the grounds that many of these funds were very similar and had the same objective (e.g., track the S&P 500 index), and therefore economies of scale dictated that money not be spread around many similar funds. Typically, the deviations from the intended results in index funds are small, and most funds are affected by the same phenomena in the same way (e.g., tenders, mergers, changes in index composition). The same type of reasoning seems to have spilled over into AA funds, where there may be many funds which seek to achieve the same objective; for example, to time between the stock and bond, or the stock, bond and cash markets. However, since different funds may well use different signals to generate the allocation decision, the arguments for centralization should not be expected hold. A model based on a dividend discount model for stocks may fail, where one based on an analysis of equity risk premia, or on an individual's intuition, may succeed. Or vice versa.

Given two tactical AA funds, most investors will find themselves obliged to treat each fund as an indivisible asset. They must simply decide how much wealth to allocate to each fund. If it were possible to combine the timing models from each fund into a single model, then it might be possible to create a "super fund," in which all the best ideas behind the most successful AA funds were combined. If so, this would obviate the need to consider the problem at hand, since all wealth would probably best be placed in the one "superfund." However, most investors will not be able to do this, and even if they had access to the paradigms underlying the models that had proved successful, it might not be at all clear how to combine different methodologies to create the single "super fund."

This being the case, a paradigm is needed that will allow investors to decide how to allocate money across AA funds. Such a paradigm can be found by looking at the paradigm used by some AA funds themselves: namely, the twin concepts of relative value and diversification.

For stocks, the measure of value is the expected period return. The risk is that there may be a residual return around this expected value, which is quantified as the variance of the stock's return. Diversification stems from the imperfect correlation of one stock with another. For example, suppose stock A has an expected return of 15% and standard deviation (square root of variance) of 25%, while stock B has an expected return of 13% and a standard deviation of 24%, on an annualized basis. Suppose further that the correlation coefficient of stock A with stock B is 0.5. Then, if we divide our money equally between stocks A and B, our portfolio will have an expected return of:

$$E = 0.5(15\%) + 0.5(13\%) = 14\%$$

The standard deviation of our portfolio will be:

$$s = \sqrt{(0.5)^2(0.25)^2 + 2(0.5)(0.5)(0.25)(0.24)(0.5) + (0.5)^2(0.24)^2}$$

$$= 21.2\%$$

Thus, even though we have sacrificed 1% of expected return by including stock B in our portfolio, we have reduced our risk by almost 4%. Most investors would agree that this risk/reward tradeoff is a desirable one to be able to measure, and then to make.

VALUE

The method of quantifying the value added by a market timing fund owes its origins to the work of Henriksson and Merton.[1] The general concept is to map the timing decisions of the AA fund into two components. The first is a static mix, which represents the allocation decision in a particular market environment, and the second is a look-back option to change the static mix to some other mix, in the event that a different market environment comes to pass.

By way of example, consider an AA fund which times between the stock and the bond markets by allocating money between a stock fund and a bond fund at the beginning of the month, and revisiting the decision at the beginning of the next month. A perfect market timer would always put 100% of this money into the asset class which was destined to outperform the other. This could be viewed as a static position of 100% in the bond fund (corresponding to an environment in which bonds outperform stocks), together with an option to exchange the bonds for stocks at the end of the month, in the event that stocks outperform bonds. One would pay very little to a manager for assuming a static mix, since that can be achieved without any timing skill. By contrast, the exchange option has positive value. Since the timer is essentially adding the exchange option without paying for it in the market, his added value is the value of the monthly exchange option, and this can be valued using modern option pricing theory.

In reality, no AA fund achieves perfect timing, nor do most funds take extreme positions in the asset classes. Generally a two-way fund such as the one described above would shift its exposure to the asset classes gradually, as one asset class was perceived to have better prospects than the other. In this case, the returns to the asset allocation model can be fit to the following model:

$$R_{aa2} = a + (w_sR_s + w_bR_b) + b \max (R_s - R_b, 0) + e$$

[1]Roy D. Henriksson and Robert C. Merton, "On Market Timing and Investment Performance, II. Statistical Procedures for Evaluating Forecasting Skills." *Journal of Business,* 54, July 1981, and; R. Merton, "On Market Timing and Investment Performance, I. An Equilibrium Theory of Value for Market Forecasts," *Journal of Business,* 54, July 1981.

subject to

$$w_s + w_b = 1$$

where

1. *R* denotes (one plus) the returns on the 2-way AA fund, stocks and bonds, respectively
2. *w* represents the investment weights in stocks and bonds, respectively
3. *a* and *b* are constants
4. *e* denotes a residual, or "plug."

The coefficients *a, b* and the *w*'s can be estimated, post factum, by linear regression methods. This model says that the AA returns are equivalent to those achieved by assuming a static mix w_s, w_b, which provides the return when bonds outperform stocks, plus *b* options to exchange bond return for stock return, when stocks outperform bonds. For a perfect timer, $w_s = 0$, $w_b = 1$, and $b = 1$. Note that to fit this model, we do not need to know the forecasts of the allocator; we only need to know the returns on the fund and the returns to the underlying asset classes. Thus, even the "non-quant" armed only with a spreadsheet package with linear regression, and the return series, can fit the above model. In practice, we substitute $1 - w_s$ for w_b, and rewrite the equation as:

$$R_{aa2} - R_b = a + w_s(R_s - R_b) + b\,[\max\,(R_s - R_b,\,0)] + e$$

We now estimate w_s and b directly by linear regression. Evnine and Henriksson[2] describe how this methodology was applied to one such AA fund, for which the estimated coefficients were:

$$a = -0.34\%,\ b = 0.424,\ w_s = 41.83\%,\ w_b = 58.17\%$$

The R^2 from their regression was 87%, and the standard error of the residual was 1.17%. The interpretation is that the AA fund was equivalent to taking a fixed position of 41.83% in stocks and 58.17% in bonds when

---

[2]Jeremy J. Evnine and R. Henriksson, "Asset Allocation and Options," *Journal of Portfolio Management*, 14 , Fall 1987.

bonds outperform stocks, and paying 34 basis points for an option to exchange 42.4% of the bonds for stocks when stocks outperform bonds. The exchange option was valued using a model by Margrabe,[3] and found to be worth 1.797%. Thus, the value added by the market timing ability of this particular fund could be estimated at:

$$- 0.34 + (0.424) (1.797) = 0.39\% \text{ / month}$$

By repeating this procedure for several AA funds, an investor can produce value measures for each fund which are directly comparable.[4]

This methodology is not limited to AA fund that time between only two markets. For example, Evnine and Henriksson also consider a fund that allocates across three asset classes: stocks, bonds and cash. In this case, the returns to the AA fund are modeled as coming from:

1. a fixed cost (a);
2. a constant stock/bond/cash mix, when cash is expected to outperform stocks and bond;
3. a number (b) of options to exchange the cash return for the maximum of the returns to stocks and bonds; and
4. a residual (e).

This can be written as:

$$R_{aa3} = a + (w_sR_s + w_bR_b + w_cR_c) + b[\max (R_s - R_c, R_b - R_c, 0)]$$

Note that:

$$\max (R_s - R_c, R_b - R_c, 0) = \max [\max (R_s, R_b) - R_c, 0]$$

so the implicit option is indeed an option on the maximum of the stock and bond returns, with a strike price equal to one plus the cash return.

---

[3] William Margrabe, "The Value of an Option to Exchange One Asset for Another." *Journal of Finance*, 33, March 1978.

[4] Henriksson examined a large number of mutual funds that claimed to be engaged in market timing, and, using the above methodology, found very little evidence of successful market timing. R. Henriksson, "Market Timing and Mutual Fund Performance: An Empirical Investigation," *Journal of Business*, 57, January 1984. However, Weigel, "The Performance of Tactical Asset Allocation," *Financial Analysts Journal*, September/October 1991, finds that a majority of TAA managers do possess timing ability.

Using regressions, Evnine and Henriksson obtained the following estimates:

a = − 0.34%, b = 0.3844
fixed stock/bond/cash mix = 38.16% / 7.18% / 54.76%

The regression had an R^2 of 80%, and the standard error of the residual
was 1.48%. The interpretation of the results is similar to that of the 2-way
fund, only in this case the option is harder to value, since it is an exchange
option on the maximum of two asset returns. Stulz has provided a framework for evaluating options on the maximum of two assets,[5] Using his
model, Evnine and Henriksson estimated the value of the option on the
maximum of the stock and bond returns at 2.447% per month. From this,
the added value of the AA manager could be valued at:

− 0.34 + (0.3844) (2.447) = 0.60% / month

   Since a static asset mix can be obtained without engaging in market
timing, an investor is in reality paying an asset allocation manager to
provide him with these exchange, or look-back options; the quantity of
options and the value of each option are, therefore, the determining
components of the value to the allocation decision.
   It is important to realize that the analysis outlined above was designed
as a performance measurement tool, not as a prediction tool. It is by its
nature backward-looking, and it should not be assumed that the equivalence between the fund and an exchange option that has been established
historically is necessarily a good predictor of a future equivalence between the fund's performance and an exchange option. This is similar to
the problem of using historical mean returns as predictors of future
expected returns. They tend to do an extremely poor job. However, in
the case of stocks, there are alternative methodologies for predicting
future expected returns, such as dividend discount models for individual
stocks, or an examination of the behavior of risk premia for the stock
market as a whole, or even an investor's intuition. There is, as yet, no
methodology for trying to predict the future number of exchange options
implicit in a tactical asset allocation fund, so an investor may have no
alternative to using the estimated value for the coefficient b in the above

---

[5]Rene Stulz, "Options on the Minimum or the Maximum of Two Risky Assets: Analysis
and Applications," *Journal of Financial Economics*, 10, July 1982.

model, and then using judgmental override to arrive at a prediction for the future value of b.

A valuation model is required to price the implicit exchange option. Margrabe's model values an exchange option between two risky assets, and is therefore appropriate to value an option to exchange bonds for stocks. If the allocation decision is between a single risky asset class and riskless cash (e.g., Treasury bills), then the Black-Scholes model is an appropriate valuation model.[6] Stulz's model values an option to exchange riskless cash for the maximum of two risky assets, and is therefore appropriate to value the exchange option implicit in asset allocation between, say, stocks, bonds and riskless cash. If the third asset class is also risky, Stulz's model may be generalized in the way that Margrabe's model generalizes that of Black-Scholes. In any event, the Black-Scholes or Margrabe models are simple to implement, requiring only univariate normal distribution values, and are frequently available in standard packages. The Stulz model requires bivariate normal distribution, which is not generally available and for which there is no readily simple approximation.

All of the above models assume that the risky assets in question follow a (joint) lognormal diffusion process. If it is felt that other stochastic processes better describe the behavior of asset prices (such as a jump process, or a jump diffusion process), then other models are available to value the exchange option. For example, real estate might be felt to be inadequately valued by a Black-Scholes model, either because real estate prices may not be well modeled by the required lognormal process, or because the friction in trading real estate asset may preclude valuation by no-arbitrage arguments. This makes the option substantially more difficult to value. However, it should be noted that when comparing two tactical asset allocation funds that allocate across the same asset classes, the implicit option may not need to be valued at all, since it will be the same for both funds. It may be sufficient to compare the coefficients b for the two funds to obtain an adequate comparison of the two funds.

Models to evaluate exchange options between a greater number of asset classes would be extremely complex, and while the correspondence between an asset allocation fund and an implicit exchange option can readily be estimated (as above), the option value would be quite hard to estimate.

---

[6]Fischer Black and Myron Scholes, "The Pricing of Options and Corporate Liabilities," *Journal of Political Economy*, 81, May/June 1973.

Whichever option valuation model is used to value the implicit exchange option, forward-looking inputs will be required. The most important inputs are the volatilities of the asset classes relative to one another. For example, in the case of asset allocation between stocks and bonds, we need the standard deviation of the difference of the logarithmic returns between stocks and bonds. In the case of an option to exchange riskless cash for the better of stocks and bonds, we need the volatilities of stocks and bonds, as well as the correlation between them. Interest rates will not be required as inputs to the valuation model. Since we are exchanging one return for another, the present value of the strike price, in a Black-Scholes sense, is exactly $1. If cash is one of the asset classes, then the interest rate appearing in either the Black-Scholes or Stulz model is precisely one plus the return to cash, which is known in advance. However, since the strike price appears in both models discounted back to the present, the interest rate will disappear form the formula. Neither do we need to worry about dividend forecasts, since if we allocate wealth to stocks, we will collect the dividends; so the exchange option is, in a sense, dividend-protected.

Volatility is the single most important input into the valuation model that cannot be directly observed. In a backward-looking analysis, we can use the actual realized volatility, measured either from daily returns intra-month, or from monthly returns, which are more likely to be easily obtainable. On a forward-looking basis, we will need to use a prediction of volatility. It should be clear intuitively that the added value of a successful asset class timer is greater when the relative volatility across asset classes is greater.

Finally, then, the investor has in hand the estimated values of the coefficients a and b in the model described above. He then applies any judgmental override which he feels appropriate. This may be indispensable if the fund in question has insufficient performance history to generate meaningful historical estimates of a and b. Next, using forward looking inputs, the investor values the implicit exchange option. He then multiplies this value by his forward-looking estimate of the coefficient b, adds the estimate of the coefficient a, and this is his valuation measure.

DIVERSIFICATION

The model used above for returns to an AA strategy express these returns as:

AA return = fixed cost

    + static mix return

    + exchange option return

    + residual return

The static mix is neutral, in the sense that it contributes neither to the risk nor reward of the timing attempts. Any investor can assume a constant mix at virtually no cost (over and above the transaction costs of, say, monthly rebalancing). The value of the AA strategy comes from the fixed cost and the value of the exchange option. The risk in the AA strategy stems from the residual return. This has, by construction, a mean of zero, but may be positive or negative. Its value represents the amount by which the AA return differs from that of a static mix and an exchange option. If it were identically zero, then the investor would know for certain that his return would correspond exactly to that obtained from a static mix and an exchange option, and the value of that strategy is known. To the extent that the residual has a large variance around zero, this represents risk to the strategy.

If the investor's attitude towards risk were known, in the sense that he had a known risk aversion parameter, then the certainty equivalent of the risk in the residual could be computed and subtracted from the value of the exchange option. This would have the effect of making the added value of the AA manager slightly lower than it would be in the absence of residual risk.[7]

However, if the investor has the opportunity of investing in several similar AA funds, for which the residuals are not too highly correlated, then the risk in the residual can, to some extent, be diversified away. Consider the stock/bond and stock/bond/cash AA funds above that were analyzed by Evnine and Henriksson. If an investor places all of his funds in the 2-way AA fund, he obtains options worth 0.39% per month, plus a residual investment with a standard deviation of 1.17% per month. If he places all his fund in the 3-way AA fund, he obtains options worth 0.60% per month, plus a residual investment with a standard deviation of 1.48% per month.

An analysis of the fitted residuals in the regressions of the 2-way and 3-way strategies yields the result that the correlation of the two sets of

---

[7]See Evnine and Henriksson.

residuals is 0.62. Thus, we expect some possibility of diversifying the residual risk. Suppose that an investor places two-thirds of this wealth in the 3-way AA strategy, and one-third of this wealth in the 2-way strategy. The added value in the mixed strategy due to exchange options is:

$$(2/3) \ (0.60) + (1/3) \ (0.39) = 0.53\% \ / \ month$$

The variance of the residual from this mixture is given by:

$$(2/3)^2 \ (1.48)^2 + 2 \ (2/3) \ (1/3) \ (1.48) \ (1.17) \ (0.62) + (1/3)^2 \ (1.17)^2$$

which is $1.603\%^2$. Hence, the standard deviation of the residual is 1.27% per month. If the residuals had a zero correlation, then the standard deviation of the residual of the mixed portfolio would have been 1.06% per month; and if the correlation were -0.3, the residual of the mixture would have a standard deviation of 0.95% per month.

The same principle that guides us in stock selection can be made to work here, too. We do not place all our funds into the single stock with the highest expected return, since the risk involved in such a strategy is unnecessarily high. By placing some of our funds into stocks with lower expected return, we will reduce the "value" (expected return) of our portfolio, but this will be more than compensated for by the reduction in risk that stems from the fact that the stock returns are imperfectly correlated. This is the paradigm that underlies the Markowitz selection model,[8] and also underlies the arguments above for choosing between AA funds.

This leads naturally to the question: How well do the residuals form different AA funds correlate with each other? While the modeling of the covariance of stock returns has received a great deal of attention over the last 20 year, the same cannot be said of asset allocation funds. The two funds considered above had a fairly high correlation because they were managed by the same firm and used identical methodologies, the only difference being that the 3-way strategy included cash as an additional asset. On the other hand, the fact that the two strategies were not timing identical asset classes probably reduced the correlation somewhat.

---

[8]Harry Markowitz, "Portfolio Selection," *Journal of Finance*, 7, March 1952.

In general, many AA models use the yield-to-maturity on fixed-income assets as a proxy for the expected return on those assets. There are many models that use some form of a dividend discount model to obtain an expected return on stock. All models of this type will probably produce residuals that correlate fairly highly with one another. However, strategies that use macroeconomic models or subjective inputs to produce the asset allocation decision will probably correlate less highly with models of the first type. If histories of the strategies under consideration are available, then the regressions described may be run and the residuals explicitly computed. In this case, the correlations and standard deviations of the residuals can all be computed from the output of the same regressions. If histories are unavailable, then guesses must be made as to the degree of diversification that will be obtained from mixing strategies.

Let us assume that we now have in hand both the valuation measures of all the AA funds in our investable universe, and the standard deviations and correlation coefficients of the residuals from the look-back option model. How should we then allocate our wealth across the AA funds in our universe? A pure mean/variance approach may be misleading. The AA funds do not comprise all the available funds in which we may place our wealth. In particular, if we choose a particular portfolio of AA funds, we will implicitly obtain the corresponding portfolio of static mixes that make up the first half of the look-back option model specification. But the resultant static mix may be combined, if desired, with a completeness fund to obtain a static mix of the investor's choice. This latter may stem from a strategic asset allocation decision, choice of normal portfolio, and so on.

The real tradeoff is between the added value in the portfolio of implicit options, which has positive "utility," and the variance in the portfolio's residual, which has negative "utility." Rather than attempting a formal optimization, a better approach may simply be to examine potential combinations of the tactical AA funds, and to compare the net value of look-back options, and variance of the portfolio residual around the option mapping, until the highest level of comfort is obtained. This will allow an investor to take into consideration such factors as trust in the look-back option as a suitable description of an AA fund, the amount of money to be given to any one manager, or to any one type of AA strategy, and so on. Even if hard numbers are difficult to come by, the intuition suggested by the Markowitz selection model can still be useful in determining how to allocate funds across asset allocation managers.

CONCLUSION

We have shown that the concepts underlying the Markowitz selection model may be useful in determining how to allocate wealth across asset allocation funds. In place of expected return, the measure of value is the value of implicit exchange, or look-back, options provided by a successful timing strategy. This is the paradigm suggested by Henriksson and Merton to evaluate market timing models. The residual from their model is the risk that the investor would like to diversify away, if possible, and this may be achieved by spreading wealth across different funds, particularly those that use different methodologies to generate the allocation decision.

CHAPTER 14

Asset Allocation Using Futures Markets

ROGER G. CLARKE
CHIEF INVESTMENT OFFICER
TSA CAPITAL MANAGEMENT

The area of active or tactical asset allocation has attracted enormous interest in recent years. The objective in active asset allocation is performance. The intent is to shift the asset mix in response to changing patterns of opportunity which are available in the markets.

In one sense, active asset allocation is comparable to equity sector rotation, except that instead of rotating among the economic sectors of the equity market, portfolio exposure is rotated among the sectors of the capital markets or asset classes. This strategy involves a disciplined, quantitative structure for measuring the likely available returns on the major asset classes, typically stocks, bonds and cash. Active asset allocation is designed to exploit shifts in the relative attractiveness among these asset classes.

A shift in the asset mix in a portfolio can be done by buying and selling the actual underlying assets in the portfolio or by buying and selling futures contracts. Only within the last decade have the futures markets been well developed enough in financial futures to accommodate major volume for trading.

Nature of a Futures Contract

Basically, a futures contract is an agreement for the purchase or sale of an item with the price established up front but with settlement delayed to a future date. The concept behind a futures contract is one that we use all the time. For example, the terms of purchase at a car dealership are often quite similar to a futures contract. The car dealer may not have on the lot the exact car the buyer wants. The buyer can purchase the car at an agreed price but may have to await delivery of the car until some future date. If car prices go up, the buyer will benefit because the agreed price for the car will be less than the subsequent current market price at the time of delivery. These terms are similar to those of a futures contract. The buyer may have to post a small down-payment or deposit in order to ensure the car dealer that the buyer will follow through with the purchase of the car. However, actual payment for the car does not take place until the car is delivered.

Equity index and financial futures contracts work in a similar manner. The contracts have standardized provisions similar to those specifying the color, style and other options on a car. This package of standard features can then be traded on organized exchanges. They are highly liquid because one futures contract looks exactly like another. A small performance bond or initial margin is deposited at the contract origination date. No actual cash changes hands in the purchase or sale of a futures contract at the beginning except for this small deposit. However, unlike our car example, any change in the price of stocks or bonds over time is settled on a daily basis. This process of settling daily gains and losses is called "marking to market." The daily settlement requires that money be transferred between the investor and the broker each day to reflect these gains or losses and reduces the accumulation of large unrealized losses that may cause one of the parties to default on the obligation.

The important thing about futures contracts is that the futures price moves directly with the underlying price of the commodity which is linked to the futures contract. This is what makes the futures contract an important investment instrument. The futures price is kept highly correlated with the cash price of the underlying instrument because of the arbitrage possibilities that are created if the futures price deviates to a great extent. As a result, transactions in the futures markets can be used as a substitute for actually buying and selling the underlying assets. This close correlation between the futures price and the underlying cash instrument is illustrated in Exhibit 1 where we have plotted the price of

EXHIBIT 1
S&P 500 FUTURES VS. S&P 500 INDEX—MARCH 1991–MAY 1991

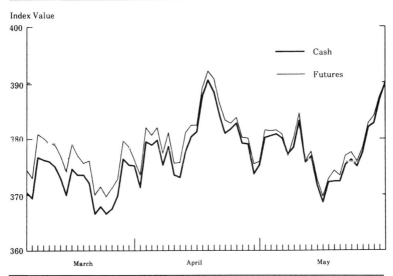

Index Value

the futures contract on the S&P 500 against the S&P 500 index. The futures price does deviate from the index itself, but these deviations are generally too small to be profited from in any systematic way.

To illustrate the investment exposure that an investor can achieve through the use of the futures market, consider the following example, with January 2, 1991, prices. Suppose an investor has a current portfolio worth $100 million, and that the S&P 500 index is at 326.45. Each index point on the S&P 500 is worth $500. Consequently, each futures contract has a dollar equity exposure of 500 times the value of the index, or an equivalent value of $163,225 (with the index at 326.85). The number of contracts needed for equivalent equity exposure of a $100 million portfolio would be approximately 613 futures contracts.

Exhibit 2 illustrates the investment impact that futures contracts would have on an equity portfolio, compared to a straight $100 million equity investment in the index. The S&P 500 index on January 2, 1991, stood at 326.45 and finished the month of January at 343.93. This movement in the S&P 500 index during the month of January would have led to an increase in a $100 million equity portfolio of $5,354,572. The purchase of 613 futures contracts would have led to a total dollar gain of $5,455,700. Though the futures contracts do not track the movement in

EXHIBIT 2
EQUITY EXPOSURE THROUGH FUTURES

Current Portfolio Value:		$100,000,000
Current S&P 500 Index:		326.45
$/Contract		x 500
		$163,225
Contracts Needed for	100,000,000	
Equivalent Exposure	————	= 613 contracts
	163,225	

	S&P Future	S&P Index	Equity Portfolio
Jan. 31, 1991	344.65	343.93	$105,354,572
Jan. 2, 1991	326.85	326.45	100,000,000
Net Point Gain	17.80	17.48	
$/Contract	x 500		
Total Gain/Contract	$8,900		
# of Contracts	x 613		
Total $ Gain	$5,455,700		$5,354,572

the S&P 500 index exactly, the percentage differences are usually small. This tight linkage between the movement in the underlying commodity and the future is what makes the futures contract useful for investment purposes. If the futures price were not so tightly linked and it could drift aimlessly away from the cash price, futures contracts would not be very helpful for managing asset allocation.

It is the possibility of arbitrage which keeps the S&P 500 futures closely linked to the S&P 500 index. If the futures price is too high relative to the S&P 500 index, an investor will have an incentive to borrow money, buy a market basket of stocks resembling the S&P 500 and sell the overpriced S&P 500 futures contract. During the life of the futures contract the investor would reap the rewards of any changes in the price of the stock plus the accumulated dividends from the stocks. At the expiration of the futures contract the futures price will converge to the price of the stocks. Consequently, the investor is completely protected against the price movement in the stocks that have been purchased because the short futures position offsets the long cash position. The investor is then left with the dividends which accrue on the underlying stocks less the interest paid on the money borrowed initially to purchase the stocks. This spread between dividends accrued and interest paid determines the fair price of the futures.

If the futures price deviates too far from this fair price, an investor can earn above-market rates with little risk. This is the arbitrage process which keeps the S&P 500 future closely linked to the performance of the S&P 500 index. If the futures price is too high relative to its fair value, an investor can sell the future and buy stocks and earn an above-market interest rate. On the other hand, if the futures price is too low relative to its fair value, an investor can effectively borrow at below-market rates by selling stocks and buying the undervalued futures. The fair pricing of the futures contract on the S&P 500 is illustrated in Exhibit 3 using the data in Exhibit 2 and assuming that the annualized interest rate and dividend yield are 6.0 and 3.2%, respectively. With 73 days left to expiration, the fair price of the futures contract would be $328.30.

Advantages of Implementation Using Futures Contracts

The principal disadvantage of active asset allocation without the use of futures is the size of transaction costs. Transaction costs often fall in a fairly wide range for stocks and bonds. Let's suppose that transaction costs are 100 basis points for equities and half that for bonds. Tactical asset allocation will likely produce turnover amounting to perhaps 100% per annum. This means that an asset allocation discipline must add 75 basis points per annum or is not worth employing. Most tactical asset allocation disciplines do indeed offer rewards several times that. Therefore, tactical asset allocation does not require the use of futures. It can be implemented effectively and very profitably without resorting to the use of futures.

What about implementation through futures? As Exhibit 4 suggests, the merits of using futures in asset allocation are considerable. First, the commissions on a futures trade are trivial. A $20 round-trip commission for purchase and subsequent sale of approximately $160,000 worth of exposure in the stock market will represent less than 2 basis points. Liquidity is typically excellent and market impact is usually small, adding no more than 5 to 10 basis points. Instead of an asset allocation

EXHIBIT 3
FAIR PRICING OF S&P 500 FUTURES CONTRACT

$$F = I(1 + (r-d)n/365)$$

F = Fair price of the S&P 500 futures contract
I = Price of the S&P 500 Index
n = Number of days until expiration of the future
r = Annualized riskless interest rate with maturity of *n* days
d = Annualized dividend yield on the S&P 500 stocks

The fair price of the futures contract with 73 days to expiration, a risk-less rate of 6.0%, a dividend yield of 3.2% and with the index at 326.45 would be:

$$F = 326.45(1+(.06-.032)73/360)$$
$$= 328.30$$

---

discipline having to add 75 basis points, it need only add 10 to 20 basis points to cover the transaction costs.

Second, these markets are very deep and liquid. Stock index futures generally trade over $8 billion each day. Bond futures are one of the most liquid markets in the world, routinely trading over $30 billion daily. As such, a $100 million asset allocation shift of broad market exposure can be executed in minutes with relative ease and little market impact.

For example, Exhibit 5 illustrates the growth in equity index futures in recent years relative to the dollar volume of equities traded on the New York Stock Exchange. Stock index futures were first introduced in 1982. By 1983, the average daily dollar volume traded in equity index futures surpassed that traded on the NYSE itself. Now the stock index futures trade approximately twice the volume of the stocks in the NYSE.

EXHIBIT 4
ASSET ALLOCATION IMPLEMENTATION—ADVANTAGES OF USING FUTURES

1. Reduce transaction costs
2. Easy adjustment of market exposure; rapid execution
3. Same-day settlement; simultaneous trades
4. No disruption of underlying asset management
5. Stabilizes portfolio income stream
6. Potential for favorable mispricing

EXHIBIT 5
NEW YORK STOCK EXCHANGE VS. S&P 500 FUTURES DOLLAR VOLUME
(DAILY AVERAGE: MAY 1982–DECEMBER 1990)

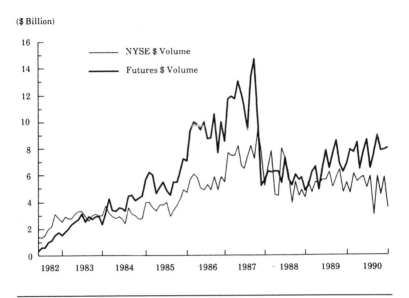

Third, futures permit simultaneous trades. If investors want to sell $100 million worth of bond exposure and buy $100 million worth of stock market exposure without using futures, they can eliminate the bond exposure in minutes, since the Treasury markets are highly liquid. However, on the equity side, they may have to carefully craft a buy program consistent with their investment management disciplines and have their trading desk and brokers work the order carefully – all of which can take extra time.

To some extent this is mitigated if the trades are managed through index funds, where a program trade can be effected quickly. But, even with index funds, the manager can run into a problem with the differences in settlement times. The stocks generally settle in five days, while Treasury bonds settle in a day. This means that there could be $100 million completely unexposed to the market for four days in order to synchronize settlement dates. Investors can make a $100 million shift in their asset mix in minutes using futures without any concern for settlement timing or other operational difficulties.

Fourth, a shift in mix implemented by futures is not disruptive to the management of the underlying assets. If investors want to sell $100 million in stocks and buy $100 million in bonds, they will have to carefully design a sell program which will not alter the characteristics of the equity portfolio in unintended ways. This alone can take some time. They then have to execute the trade, carefully working the order in conformity with available liquidity. Then they have to do the same thing on the bond side. The whole process could take several days. With futures, the underlying stock and bond portfolios are not disrupted. Indeed, the futures strategy can be implemented without concerning the underlying asset manager.

This separation of the futures positions from the asset managers has another advantage. If the active asset managers are outperforming the index, the use of futures will permit the investor to fully capture the value added within the asset classes. The futures only reflect the index return, while the assets are earning the index return plus something extra. Thus, any excess returns stay with the portfolio. However, the reverse is also true: any underperformance within the asset classes relative to the index also stays with the portfolio.

Fifth, for organizations where income is a consideration, the use of futures does not disrupt the income stream. If the portfolio is shifted from stocks into bonds, the income will rise, which is nice. If a few months later it is shifted back to stocks, the income will drop, which might be an unpleasant dose of reality. With the use of futures, the underlying asset mix need not change, and the income stream generated by those assets need not change either. However, the value of the futures will fluctuate as the markets move, resulting in gains and losses on the futures positions; but these changes might be considered more as realized capital gains than as income. When accounted for in this way, the income can remain stable though the asset mix is shifting.

Sixth, the futures may be favorably mispriced. If a futures trading strategy uses the futures mispricing as a part of the decision rule, a strategy can be designed which benefits from any ongoing pattern of futures mispricing. From time to time futures do stray from the fair value vis-a-vis the underlying assets.

Let's look a little closer at the issue of futures mispricing. Research suggests that many times the futures are favorably mispriced when tactical asset allocation shifts are made. But thus far, they have rarely been unfavorably mispriced to an extent which would justify the transaction costs of making an asset allocation shift via the stock and bond markets.

In short, the mispricing has been highly advantageous for most conventional tactical asset allocation processes.

Much of the reason why mispricing usually favors asset allocation trades is because most tactical asset allocation disciplines are inherently contrarian. It is often a buy low, sell high discipline. When equities sag, equity exposure is typically boosted. This usually happens at a time when, due to the drop in the stock market, there is a good deal of pessimism and the futures are underpriced *vis-a-vis* fair value. Equity exposure is often cut after significant market rallies. This is typically a period of euphoria in which the futures are overpriced *vis-a-vis* fair value. In short, asset allocation disciplines, because they are contrarian, often reap some benefit from futures mispricing.

Consider the following two illustrations of the asset allocation decision. In the example in Exhibit 6, we accomplish asset allocation by using the underlying assets. In this case, we start with the portfolio of $50 million of equity and $50 million of bonds. If we wanted to shift the asset allocation mix to 60% equity and 40% bonds, we would sell $10 million worth of bonds and buy $10 million of equity exposure. The

EXHIBIT 6
ASSET ALLOCATION SHIFT USING UNDERLYING ASSETS

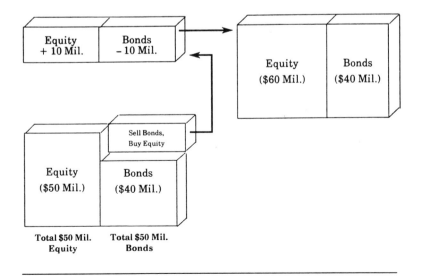

resulting portfolio would be shifted to $60 million in equity exposure and $40 million in bonds.

Next consider the asset allocation shift using futures. First, the use of futures requires a liquidity reserve in order to fund the margin requirements for the futures positions. In the example in Exhibit 7, we begin with a portfolio totaling $100 million, composed of $45 million worth of equity, $45 million worth of bonds and $10 million in cash equivalents. The cash reserve is used as collateral for the futures positions. In order to accomplish the asset allocation shift, we must buy $15 million worth of equity exposure and sell $5 million worth of bond exposure. With these futures transactions, equity exposure in the portfolio would total $60 million. This is achieved by having $45 million of equity exposure in the underlying stocks and $15 million of equity exposure through the futures market. The bond exposure in the portfolio would be reduced to $40 million from the initial $45 million by the short position of $5 million worth of bond futures. As a result of the futures transactions, the total portfolio exposure has been changed to 60% equities and 40% bonds, while underlying assets have been left in place.

It is important to understand how the cash reserve is accounted for. Futures are priced such that when the futures contract is combined with

EXHIBIT 7
ASSET ALLOCATION SHIFT USING FUTURES

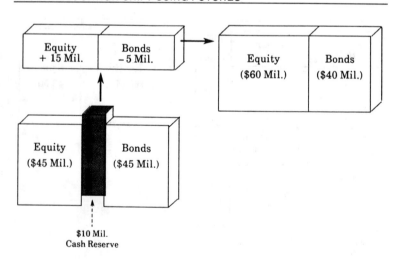

an equivalent amount in cash reserves, the combination behaves as if it were invested in the equity or bond index. Consequently, the $10 million in cash plus $10 million in equity futures will behave as if it were invested in the equity index. The short position of $5 million in bond futures creates an additional $5 million in synthetic cash (the combination of the $5 million short futures position and $5 million of the long bond position will behave as if it were cash). This additional $5 million cash created synthetically supplies the cash base needed for the rest of the $15 million equity futures position. In short, it is the combined investment in cash reserves plus the futures contracts which behave like the underlying assets. To count the cash again in the portfolio would double count the investment exposure.

Disadvantages of Implementation Using Futures Contracts

Though having important advantages, the use of futures for asset allocation does have some disadvantages, as noted in Exhibit 8. In the first place, even though the use of futures often allows for favorable mispricing, there is the potential for unfavorable mispricing. These periods of unfavorable mispricing will increase the cost of the asset allocation move using futures relative to making the shift using the underlying assets. However, the mispricing would have to be quite severe before it would actually be more advantageous to trade the underlying securities. With current arbitrage activity it is unlikely that such levels would occur very often.

A second disadvantage of using futures involves the potential tracking error between the underlying assets and the futures contract. Even if there is no mispricing of the futures contract, the underlying portfolio

EXHIBIT 8
ASSET ALLOCATION IMPLEMENTATION–DISADVANTAGES OF USING FUTURES

1. Risk of unfavorable mispricing.
2. Tracking error between the futures and the portfolio.
3. Liquidity reserve required to accommodate margin requirements.
4. Daily back office work required to mark to market.
5. Replaces active asset returns with index-like performance on the liquidity reserve.
6. Disruption of asset management to raise cash if the liquidity reserve is depleted.

may have somewhat different characteristics than the equity market index or fixed-income security tied to the futures. Most managers will try to duration-match the futures position with the underlying fixed-income assets or beta-match the equity index futures with the equity portfolio, but this will not be a perfect fit. The differential performance between the futures and the actual portfolio could be positive or negative and is referred to as *tracking error.*

A third disadvantage of using futures for asset allocation arises because of the back office work which is required on a daily basis to mark the futures positions to market. Any gains and losses in the futures contracts are required to be settled daily; this requires transfers of funds between the investor and the broker. This daily back office work requires constant attention and can sometimes be bothersome.

A fourth disadvantage of using futures is that a cash liquidity reserve is necessary to accommodate the margin requirements and daily settlement of the futures positions. Funding this liquidity reserve often forces the investor to liquidate some assets currently invested in stocks and bonds. Though the underlying reserve is invested in cash equivalents, a full investment exposure can be achieved by buying equity index or bond futures to overlay the cash position. This replaces the active asset returns which might be had from investing in actual stocks and bonds with index-like performance tied to the futures contracts. To the extent that active asset management can add value relative to the index, this differential return is sacrificed because of the necessity to fund the liquidity reserve and achieve full exposure indirectly using a futures overlay.

A final disadvantage of using futures also occurs because of the daily marking to market which forces the fund to realize the daily gains and losses. If the asset allocation decision is wrong and the differential market returns are substantial, the cash reserve can be depleted fairly quickly. If the futures positions are to be maintained, the cash reserve must be replenished. This infusion of cash usually requires some liquidation of underlying assets. Selling assets to raise cash will now affect the managers of the underlying assets and may interrupt their investment strategies.

CALCULATING THE FUTURES POSITIONS FOR ASSET ALLOCATION SHIFTS AND RISK ADJUSTMENTS

Once an asset allocation policy is decided, and the portfolio exposure is determined, this exposure must be translated into an appropriate number of futures contracts. In this section we discuss the process to calculate the number of futures contracts necessary to alter the portfolio mix and adjust its risk characteristics.

Equity Exposure

Consider an underlying equity portfolio combined with n_s equity index futures contracts. The sensitivity of the portfolio to a change in the equity index can be represented as:

$$\Delta E = \left[\frac{E\beta_S}{I_S} + n_S\, \beta_F \right] \Delta I_S \tag{1}$$

where:

$E \quad = A_S V_O =$ The value of the current equity portion of a portfolio

$V_O =$ The total value of the portfolio

$A_S =$ The actual proportion of equity in the portfolio

$\beta_S =$ The current beta of the equity in the portfolio relative to I_S

$I_S \quad =$ The \$ value of the equity futures index (typically \$500 times the index)

$n_S \quad =$ The number of equity futures contracts

$\beta_F =$ The beta of the equity futures contract

$T_S \quad =$ The target proportion of equity in the portfolio

$\beta_T =$ The target beta of the portfolio relative to I_S

Equating the response of the combined equity portfolio and the futures contracts to that of a target portfolio with desired beta β_T gives:

$$\Delta E = \left[\frac{A_S\, V_O\, \beta_S}{I_S} + n_S\, \beta_F \right] \Delta I_S = \frac{T_S\, V_O\, \beta_T\, \Delta I_S}{I_S} \tag{2}$$

Solving for the appropriate number of equity futures contracts results in:

$$n_S = \frac{V_O}{I_S \beta_F} (T_S \beta_T - A_S \beta_S) \tag{3}$$

By rearranging terms this equation can be rewritten as:

$$n_S = \frac{V_O \beta_S}{I_S \beta_F} (T_S - A_S) + \frac{V_O T_S}{I_S \beta_F} (\beta_T - \beta_S) \tag{4}$$

The first term represents the number of futures contracts needed to change the current asset mix to the recommended mix at the current beta. The second term represents the number of futures contracts needed to change the recommended equity mix to the target beta from its current beta.

For example, assume an equity portfolio has the following parameters:

$V_O = \$100,000,000$

$A_S = .45$

$\beta_S = 1.0$

$I_S = \$125,000$

$\beta_F = 1.0$

$T_S = .50$

$\beta_T = 2.0$

The number of equity futures contracts needed to alter the portfolio exposure would be:

$$n_S = \frac{100,000,000(1.0)}{125,000(1.0)} (.50 - .45) + \frac{100,000,000(.50)}{125,000(1.0)} (2.0 - 1.0)$$

$$= 40 + 400$$

$$= 440 \text{ contracts}$$

Changing the mix of the current portfolio from 45% equity to 50% equity would require 40 contracts to be purchased. Another 400 contracts would be required to change the resulting portfolio beta from 1.0 to 2.0 as illustrated in Exhibit 9.

Debt Exposure

The interest rate sensitivity of a bond portfolio which contains n_B bond futures contracts would be:

$$\Delta B = -BD_B^* \Delta i - n_B D_F^* F\Delta i_F \tag{5}$$

where:

B $= A_B V_O =$ The value of the current bond portion of a portfolio

V_O = The total value of the portfolio

A_B = The actual proportion of bonds in the portfolio

D_B^* = The modified duration of the bonds in the portfolio

F = The \$ value of the bond futures contract

n_B = The number of bond futures contracts

D_F^* = The modified duration of the bond future

T_B = The target proportion of bonds in the portfolio

D_T^* = The modified duration of the target portfolio

i = The current yield to maturity on the bonds in the portfolio

i_F = The current yield to maturity on the bond futures index

Equating the response of the target portfolio of desired duration D_T^* to the bond portfolio combined with the futures contracts gives:

$$\Delta B = -A_B V_O D_B^* \Delta i - n_B D_F^* F\Delta i_F = -T_B V_O D_T^* \Delta i \tag{6}$$

Solving for the appropriate number of bond futures contracts results in:

$$n_B = \frac{V_O}{D_F^* F} (T_B D_T^* - A_B D_B^*) \left[\frac{\Delta i}{\Delta i_F} \right] \tag{7}$$

By rearranging terms this equation can be rewritten as:

$$n_B = \left[\frac{V_0 \, D_B^*}{D_F^* \, F} (T_B - A_B) + \frac{V_0 \, T_B}{D_F^* \, F} (D_T^* - D_B^*) \right] \left(\frac{\Delta i}{\Delta i_F} \right) \tag{8}$$

The first term represents the number of futures contracts needed to change the current bond position to its recommended mix at its present duration. The second term represents the number of contracts needed to change the recommended bond proportion from the current duration to the target duration.

For example, assume a bond portfolio has the following parameters:

V_O	= \$100,000,000
A_B	= .45
D_B^*	= 5.0 years
F	= \$90,000
D_F^*	= 9.0 years
T_B	= .50
D_T^*	= 10.0 years
$\Delta i / \Delta i_F$	= 1.0

The number of bond futures contracts needed to alter the portfolio exposure would be:

$$n_B = \frac{100,000,000(5.0)}{90,000\,(9.0)} (.50 - .45) + \frac{100,000,000(.50)}{90,000\,(9.0)} (10.0 - 5.0)$$

$$= 31 + 309$$

$$= 340 \text{ contracts}$$

The results indicate that 31 bond contracts would be required to increase the mix of the current bond position from 45 to 50% at the current duration of 5 years. An additional 309 contracts would be required to increase the resulting portfolio's duration from 5 to 10 years resulting in a net position of 340 bond contracts needed to create the combined position. The complete set of transactions to alter both the portfolio mix and its risk characteristics is shown in Exhibit 9.

EXHIBIT 9
RISK ADJUSTMENTS USING FUTURES

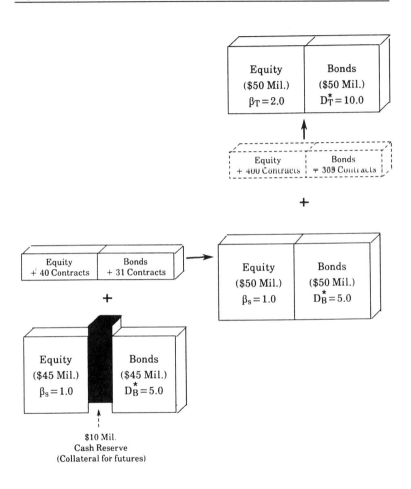

MEASURING PERFORMANCE OF ACTIVE
ASSET ALLOCATION STRATEGIES

Anyone involved in the evaluation of active asset allocation strategies can find performance measurement a perplexing issue. Standards of comparison are difficult to come by. The issue is further complicated by the fact that the mode of implementation often differs from manager to manager. Some use futures, others use index funds, while still others use a combination of the two. Typically, the value-added by an active asset allocation strategy is measured by comparing its performance to that of a passive benchmark mix, which is regularly rebalanced. Though this sounds simple enough, there are subtleties to consider, particularly where futures are involved.

Though not a panacea for the complexities of asset allocation performance measurement, the formulas below do provide a straightforward way of evaluating the strategy's effectiveness. The first section reviews the return components of the asset allocation portfolio. The second explains how to calculate the value added by a futures overlay relative to a passive benchmark portfolio mix.

Portfolio Return Components

The return for the total portfolio can be segregated into the return on the underlying assets plus the return from futures activity related to asset allocation shifts.

$$R_P = R_A + R_F \qquad (9)$$

where:

R_P = Return on Portfolio

R_A = Return on Underlying Assets

R_F = Return from Futures Activity

= F/I

F = Total Dollar Futures Gains or Losses

I = Initial Value of Investment Portfolio

The benchmark return $R*$ is the standard against which the performance of the portfolio is measured to evaluate whether the active asset shifts have added value relative to a passive buy and hold strategy.

The asset and benchmark returns can be further broken down into their components using the following symbols:

	Target Mix	Benchmark Mix	Physical Asset Mix	Physical Asset Returns	Benchmark Returns
Stocks	T_S	B_S	A_S	R_S	R_S^*
Bonds	T_B	B_B	A_B	R_B	R_B^*
Cash	T_C	B_C	A_C	R_C	R_C^*

$$R_A = A_S\,R_S + A_B\,R_B + A_C\,R_C \tag{10}$$

$$R^* = B_S\,R_S^* + B_B\,R_B^* + B_C\,R_C^* \tag{11}$$

The total return on the underlying assets is given by the actual proportion of the portfolio in each class of assets times the return on the respective asset class. The benchmark return is given by the normal or benchmark proportion in each asset class times the respective benchmark return.

Components of Value Added

The term *value added* (VA) is defined as total portfolio return less the return for the benchmark of the portfolio, or,

$$VA = R_P - R^* \tag{12}$$

where:

VA = *Value added* for the portfolio

R_P = Total portfolio return

R^* = Benchmark return

For example, if the portfolio returns 3.9% and the benchmark returns 2.2%, the *value added* would be 1.7%.

$$VA = 3.9 - 2.2$$
$$= 1.7\%$$

Substituting the components of each return into the value added equation and rearranging terms gives the *value added* as:

322   Clarke

$$VA = R_P - R^*$$
$$= R_A + R_F - R^*$$
$$= [A_S (R_S - R_S^*) + A_B (R_B - R_B^*) + A_C (R_C - R_C^*)]$$
$$+ R_F - [R_S^* (B_S - A_S) + R_B^* (B_B - A_B) + R_C^* (B_C - A_C)] \qquad (13)$$

The first set of terms represents the *value added* by the management of the underlying assets held at their actual mix in the portfolio. The second set of terms represents the *value added* by active asset allocation. The returns reflect the total gains from futures activity less those incurred as a result of first adjusting the portfolio mix from its actual asset mix to its benchmark mix. This difference represents the active bet made by the asset allocation decision and assumes that the futures generate index-like returns equal to the benchmark.

To illustrate the *value added* calculations, consider a $50,000,000 portfolio with the following data and a benchmark of 50% equity and 50% bonds:

	Target Mix	Benchmark Mix	Physical Asset Mix	Physical Asset Returns	Benchmark Returns
Stocks	.60	.50	.80	11.00	10.00
Bonds	.40	.50	.10	−3.00	−1.00
Cash	.00	.00	.10	5.00	5.00

$$R_F = -1,350,000/50,000,000 = -2.7\%$$

The components of total *value added* would be:

$$VA = 0.6 + (-2.7-(-3.9))$$
$$= 1.8\%$$

The *value added* from the management of the underlying assets is 0.6% while the *value added* from active asset allocation is 1.2% (−2.7 − (−3.9)). The sum of these two components gives a *value added* for the entire portfolio of 1.8%. Notice that the total futures activity resulted in a net cash drain of −2.7%. However not all of this is due to active asset allocation. Indeed, the cash drain due to rebalancing to the benchmark mix amounts to −3.9%. The net effect of the two actually gives a positive value added by active asset allocation equal to 1.2%.

The gains from futures activity can be approximated by a fixed weighting of index returns if the target mix is held constant over the measurement period. The returns from futures activity could be represented as:

$$R_F = (T_S - A_S)R_S^* + (T_B - A_B)R_B^* + (T_C - A_C)R_C^* \qquad (14)$$

The return from futures activity is that earned by shifting the actual portfolio mix to its target mix from its actual mix with the incremental shift yielding index-like returns. Substituting (14) into (13) gives a slightly altered form of the *value added* equation:

$$VA = [A_S(R_S - R_S^*) + A_B(R_B - R_B^*) + A_C(R_C - R_C^*)]$$
$$+ [R_S^*(T_S - B_S) + R_B^*(T_B - B_B) + R_C^*(T_C - B_C)] \qquad (15)$$

The first set of terms again represents the *value added* by the management of the underlying assets held in their actual mix in the portfolio.

The second set of terms reflects the *value added* from active asset allocation. They are generated by the index returns of the futures as the portfolio is shifted from its benchmark mix to its recommended or target mix. The only difference between the two representations of total *value added* in (13) and (15) lies in this term. Using the actual returns from futures activity gives a more accurate measure of value added if the target portfolio mix varies over the measurement period. Otherwise, equation (15) gives a reasonable approximation.

Using the data from our previous example and assuming that the target mix has been held constant, gives the total *value added* as:

$$VA = 0.6 + 1.1$$
$$= 1.7\%$$

In this case the estimate of *value added* from active asset allocation using a constant target mix is slightly less (1.1% versus 1.2%) than that calculated using the actual futures gains.

Futures Returns and Cash Flows

The total returns from futures activity are due to two different effects. The first effect comes from the active asset allocation decision and reflects returns generated by the difference between the target asset mix and the benchmark mix. The second effect captures returns caused by any difference between the mix of physical assets used in the portfolio and the benchmark mix of the asset allocation portfolio. These two parts can be seen by decomposing the total return from futures activity as follows (assuming that the target mix is held constant over the measurement period):

$$R_F = [(T_S - B_S)R_S^* + (T_B - B_B)R_B^* + (T_C - B_C)R_C^*]$$
$$+ [(B_S - A_S)R_S^* + (B_B - A_B)R_B^* + (B_C - A_C)R_C^*] \qquad (16)$$

The first group of terms reflects the returns from the active bet on asset allocation. The returns from this part of the strategy will be positive if asset allocation is adding value. Positive value added implies positive cash flows into the portfolio as the futures are marked to market.

The second group of terms reflects the returns from the rebalancing needed to bring the effective mix of the portfolio to its benchmark position before any active asset allocation bets are taken. For a portfolio whose physical asset mix is close to its benchmark mix, this latter term will generally be small and have little impact on cash flows from futures activity.

However, if the actual underlying portfolio mix deviates substantially from the benchmark mix, the size of futures positions required to bring the portfolio to its benchmark position can be large. If index returns in the market are also large, the cash flows into or out of the portfolio can be considerable. These cash flows do not reflect either *value added* or lost since they are offset by unrealized gains or losses in the underlying physical assets. Substantial cash flows from this segment can be troublesome, however, since they can be large enough to distort the cash flows from value added by asset allocation and give the impression that *value added* is different than it really is.

As an illustration, consider the following example:

	Target Mix	Benchmark Mix	Physical Asset Mix	Benchmark Returns
Stocks	.60	.50	.80	10.00
Bonds	.40	.50	.10	−1.00
Cash	.00	.00	.10	5.00

The total returns from futures activity split into its two parts would be:

$$K_F = [(.60 - .50)(10.0) + (.40 - .50)(-1.0) + (.0 - .0)(5.0)]$$
$$+ [(.50 - .80)(10.0) + (.50 - .10)(-1.0) + (.0 - .10)(5.0)]$$
$$= 1.1 - 3.9 = -2.8\%$$

The active asset allocation decision has added 1.1% to the performance of the portfolio against the benchmark of 50% equity/50% bonds. However, the actual mix of underlying assets is overweighted in equity relative to the benchmark so that the cash flow from the futures positions has subtracted 3.9% due to the rebalancing. This 3.9% cash drain from futures positions would be offset by unrealized gains in the overweighted equity position held as actual assets so that no actual net loss has occurred from the rebalancing. Nevertheless, the net cash flow from futures activity would be negative amounting to 2.8% of the portfolio value even though the *value added* from active asset allocation is positive. This negative cash flow can give the impression that asset allocation has not added value. In addition, if the futures margin reserve is to be maintained at a certain level, some cash would need to be transferred to the reserve to replenish it. This could be accomplished by realizing some of the gains in the equities which are overweighted relative to the benchmark mix.

SUMMARY

The growth of the futures markets in the last decade has provided a rapid and low-cost alternative to implement tactical asset allocation. Though futures are easy to implement, they do have some disadvantages. One of the biggest disadvantages is the potential tracking error between the investor's portfolio and the specific indices underlying the futures.

The use of futures to implement tactical asset allocation also requires the use of a cash reserve to service margin requirements. Because the physical assets may not be held in a mix equal to the benchmark against which tactical asset allocation is compared, some of the cash flows from the futures are not attributable to asset allocation. This requires a careful specification of what part of the futures returns are used to rebalance the portfolio before any active positions are taken in order to evaluate the *value added* by active asset allocation.

CHAPTER 15

A Disciplined Approach to Global Asset Allocation*

ROBERT D. ARNOTT
PRESIDENT
CHIEF INVESTMENT OFFICER
FIRST QUADRANT CORP.

ROY D. HENRIKSSON
SENIOR VICE PRESIDENT
KIDDER PEABODY, INC.

INTRODUCTION

Does a disciplined approach to active asset allocation lend itself to export? Can the methods developed for the allocation of United States assets be applied in overseas markets? Yes. Our preliminary empirical results suggest that the same tools that have proven so profitable in the United States have value in the international arena.

---

*Updated from *Financial Analysts Journal,* May/June 1989.

The development of a global strategy for tactical asset allocation is a challenging task, if only because the most profitable strategy is to focus on the least comfortable asset class. With an objective measure of prospective market returns, one can determine the relative market outlook for various asset classes, and that outlook can provide valuable guidance on asset allocation. The markets provide an objective measure of prospective returns. We *know* the yield for cash equivalents. We *know* yields-to-maturity for bonds. We can estimate the approximate earnings yield or dividend discount model rate of return for equities. Comparisons of these measures have been used with great success to profit from the relative performance of stocks, bonds, and cash in the United States.[1] Other information, regarding, for example, recent inflation or the economic environment, included in a disciplined manner, may provide additional insight into the return prospects for each asset class.[2]

Past efforts to globalize the asset allocation decision have fallen prey to several kinds of errors. One common misconception about global markets is that something is fundamentally wrong when one market trades at several times the price/earnings ratio of another. Such differences cannot be attributed merely to differences in accounting: even after these are factored out, the residual difference between the ratios can still be very large. Nevertheless, there is nothing in investment theory to suggest that price/earnings differences between markets are any more symptomatic of disequilibrium than are differences in bond yields.

This observation leads to a rather simple conclusion for evaluating equity markets in global asset allocation: it is not appropriate to compare the earnings yield in one country with its counterpart in another. Rather, one should compare the earnings yield (or some other equity return measure) in one country with the cash or bond yields in the *same* country, thereby providing a measure of the equity risk premium in that country. These equity risk premia may then be readily compared *across* national boundaries.

---

[1] See Jeremy Evnine and Roy Henriksson, "Asset Allocation and Options," *Journal of Portfolio Management*, Fall 1987.

[2] For U.S. investors, this approach to asset allocation is detailed in Robert D. Arnott and James N. von Germeten, "Systematic Asset Allocation," *Financial Analysts Journal*, November/December 1983. See also Chapter 12 in this book.

Such comparisons can provide direct and objective measures of relative opportunities both within and between countries. There is no reason that equity risk premia should be the same in different countries. The economic risks of each country may be different. However, changes in the relative risk premia between two equity markets can provide a measure of changes in relative valuation and potentially of changes in the relative attractiveness of the two markets. Thus, these risk premium changes can suggest abnormal relative opportunities within a country, and can provide a framework for asset allocation with a truly global perspective. Such a framework enables comparisons among Japanese stocks, German bonds, and United States cash.

FUNDAMENTALS OF ASSET ALLOCATION

Pricing in any market reflects the collective judgments of all the participants in that market. By basing a measure of future asset class returns on current indications of relative opportunity, one capitalizes on this information. The assumption underlying such a model is that financial markets demand different rates of return from different asset classes.

The sophisticated investor must continually ask a critical asset allocation question: in the prevailing market environment, which assets merit emphasis? The natural tendency is to choose the comfortable answer, the answer that minimizes anxiety. The comfortable answer, however, is rarely the profitable answer. Few managers were aggressively cutting United States equity holdings in early 1973 or mid 1987. Few managers were doing the opposite in late 1974, late 1990, or after the 1987 crash. While these may not have been comfortable strategies, they certainly would have been profitable.

A discipline for asset allocation can provide a reasoned basis on which to resist with confidence the comfortable answers when pursuit of a contrarian strategy would be most rewarding. This chapter describes a discipline that, in essence, allows the market to indicate what future returns will be. The asset allocation decision can then be based, as it should be, primarily on the relative attractiveness of returns from the various asset classes. The allocations will change only with changing prospects for those returns.

UNLOCKING MARKET OUTLOOK

This disciplined approach to asset allocation rests on four assumptions.

1. *Prospective long-term returns for various asset classes are directly observable in the markets.* We know the yield on cash; we know the yield-to-maturity on long bonds; and the capital markets provide some crude but objective measures of long-term prospects for equities. These take the form of earnings yield, dividend yield, or consensus-based dividend discount models.
2. *These returns reflect the consensus view of all market participants of the relative attractiveness of asset classes.* For example, if calculated equity returns are high relative to bond returns, then the market is implicitly demanding a substantial equity risk premium. Such a premium suggests that investors are uneasy about equities.
3. *These relative returns tend to exhibit normal (or equilibrium) levels.* On average over time, bonds *should* yield more than cash and stock returns should exceed either.
4. *As future relative returns stray from their normal levels, market forces pull them back into line.* Such adjustments create an asset allocation profit mechanism.

Even if one disregards the third and fourth assumptions and assumes no equilibrating mechanism in the markets, a disciplined approach to asset allocation can still work. If long-term equity return prospects rise by 100 basis points relative to other asset classes, the investor will expect to earn 100 basis points of excess return per year, even if there is no tendency to return to equilibrium. Nevertheless, the equilibrating mechanism has been the source of the impressive long-term profits achieved by many tactical asset allocation practitioners.

For example, suppose the equity risk premium is 100 basis points higher than its equilibrium level relative to long bonds. Then either long bond yields should rise 100 basis points or stock earnings yield should fall 100 basis points in order to restore equilibrium. These adjustments require a price move in either stocks or bonds amounting to *many times* the 100-basis-point disequilibrium. While this equilibrating mechanism is not essential for successful active asset allocation, it plays a key role in providing the substantial profits that such strategies have delivered.

WHY DO CONVENTIONAL GLOBAL COMPARISONS FAIL?

As we noted earlier, one of the most obvious errors in global asset allocation is to compare such measures of the return on equities as dividend yields or price/earning ratios across national boundaries. Such comparisons are as meaningless as directly comparing yields for bonds or cash between countries! It may be useful to analyze why direct comparisons fail in the bond markets in order to understand why they also fail for equity valuations.

Equilibrium theory explains differences in bond yield by citing long-term inflation rate differences and currency shifts. If 10-year government bonds yield 10% in one country and only 5% in another, there can still be effective yield parity if the currency in the high-yield country should erode 5% per year *vis-a-vis* the currency in the low-yield country. Such a differential would result in a 40% currency depreciation over the course of a decade. Currency moves of this magnitude are so common as to be routine. There is no evidence to suggest that international interest-rate differences run contrary to equilibrium theory.

The same analysis applies to rates of return in the dividend discount model. If the dividend discount model rate of return is 15% for one country and 10% for another, the difference in *nominal* returns can be fully justified by an expectation of long-term 5% annual currency divergence. The investor from the low-return country seeking to capture the superior performance offered the high-return country would expect to forfeit the differential performance through currency depreciation. Similarly, if the investor were to seek protection against this currency erosion by hedging in the foreign exchange markets, she would find the foreign exchange forward markets priced to take away much, if not all, of the excess returns.

Price/earnings ratios historically have tended to be rather closely correlated with dividend discount model rates of return. Hence, the same argument can be applied to price/earnings comparisons. There is nothing in equilibrium theory to suggest that it should be inappropriate for $100 to buy $5 per year of earnings in one country and $10 per year in another. If we suppose the currency of the high-price/earnings country to appreciate relative to the currency of the low-price/earnings country, the book value, sales, and currency-adjusted earnings of companies in the low-price/earnings country will all diminish when measured in the currency of the high-price/earnings country.

For price/earnings ratios, there are several factors other than currency risk that cloud the comparison of one country with another:

- accounting principles differ,
- growth opportunities differ,
- economic risks differ, and
- differences in political climate or stability will influence investors' perceptions of future cash flows.

All of these considerations, and other less influential ones, could justify substantial differences in earnings yields, *even in the absence of currency considerations.*

In general, there is no theoretical support for the common argument that countries with low price/earnings ratios, low price-to-cash-flow, or low price-to-book-value ratios present inherently more attractive investment opportunities than their high multiple counterparts. The appropriate comparison will be much more complex, as it must take into account the many factors that affect the equilibrium relations of prices and earnings.

RETURNS AND PRICE/EARNINGS RATIOS

It is true that the empirical evidence shows a weak tendency for countries with low price/earnings ratios to offer higher return prospects than countries with high ratios. There is nothing wrong with this. However, differences in price/earnings ratios can arise not only from currency depreciation or interest rate differentials, but also from greater growth prospects or higher risks. In the absence of market barriers, differences in equilibrium expected returns should result from differences in risk. A riskier market will require a higher expected return, which will be accompanied by a lower price/earnings ratio.

Because P/E ratios *should* differ across countries, it might seem that the best way to compare equity markets in different countries is to compare the equity risk premia offered in those countries. Regardless of any price/earnings ratio differences, if the *equity risk premium* in one country is higher than another, we might argue that the higher risk premium implies a better investment opportunity.

Even here, however, there is a potential pitfall. The *equilibrium* relation in one country between earnings yield and bond or cash yields (and, hence, the normal equity risk premium in that country) might be higher or lower than in another. Thus, since different growth rates, accounting standards, or political and economic climates can justify different equilibrium relationships, even equity risk premia cannot be directly compared.

This observation leads to the final step in the comparative analysis. If the equity risk premium is measured in any one country and compared with the normal equity risk premium for that country, an *abnormal equity risk premium* can be detected. This abnormal equity risk premium is an indication of how far the equity markets of a given country have strayed from equilibrium, either above or below the normal reward opportunities. The abnormal risk premia *can* be directly compared across international boundaries.

GLOBAL ASSET ALLOCATION AND CURRENCY SELECTION: TWO SEPARATE DECISIONS

The kind of framework we have described makes no naive assumptions about the normal relations between price/earnings ratios across international boundaries, and it makes no assumptions inconsistent with equilibrium theory. Importantly, such a framework separates the currency forecast from the forecast for asset class returns, and thus presents the investor with an array of fully hedged investment alternatives. Forecasts of hedged asset class returns can be developed directly from measurements of risk premia. These can then be supplemented with independent forecasts of currency returns.

Distinguishing asset class expectations from currency expectations is important because it achieves two often contradictory objectives: it broadens the set of investment alternatives and simultaneously simplifies the evaluation of those alternatives. If asset class decisions are based on fully hedged (local currency) return expectations, the resulting structure will give approximate equivalence among cash equivalents around the globe, since the forward markets are largely driven by this arbitrage. This is graphically illustrated in Exhibit 1.

This structure leads to direct comparability of the asset classes and to variance and covariance measures that are independent of the home currency. The currency decision can then be made separately, based on whether the incremental return associated with an attractive currency would justify the incremental risk associated with lifting the hedge. In

EXHIBIT 1

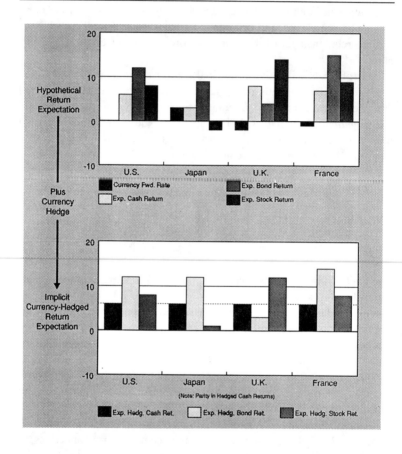

fact, the appropriate "no-forecast" allocation for investors will be fully hedged since the two-sided nature of the currency market makes it un- likely that the normal expected return from unhedged positions is suffi- cient to justify bearing the additional risk.

THE DECOUPLING OF ASSET ALLOCATION AND CURRENCY SELECTION

This view of the global capital markets clearly suggests that the currency decision and the asset allocation decision can and should be made independently. It is worth asking whether history supports this view. Exhibits 2 and 3 summarize the historical return and volatility of international equities. In examining historical data, we should note that historical returns tend to be poor indicators of future returns and that historical volatility tends to be a better, but still imprecise (witness October 1987), indicator of future volatility. Therefore, while it is not appropriate to scrutinize the individual numbers, the general pattern of the results is quite important.

During the five-year period ending 1990, a hedged strategy sharply impaired the performance of a global portfolio. The reason is clear: the dollar fell relative to other world currencies far more than the forward rates used for hedging would have suggested. However, the results over a longer horizon are somewhat more encouraging. It would seem that the dollar outpaced forward-rate expectations early in the past decade by nearly as much as it underperformed later in the decade.

The unhedged volatilities of individual equity markets around the world, denominated in U.S. dollars, all substantially exceed the volatility of the United States market. The correlations among the world's markets, however, are low enough that the volatility of the world market, even on an unhedged basis, over spans of five and ten years, was slightly lower than that of the United States.

By hedging, the investor is exposed only to the volatility of each market in local currency terms (and the very modest currency risk of the unknown change in asset value over the hedging interval). The empirical evidence supports the assertion that this second source of risk is quite small; thus, market risk may be effectively decoupled from currency risk, and the results are striking. Over any historical time span, most individual world equity markets still exhibit somewhat more volatility than the United States market. With the exception of Italy, however, their ten-year volatilities have been only moderately above that in the United States.

The hedged world portfolio consistently exhibits nearly 10% less volatility than the unhedged world portfolio. Even though historical correlations are slightly higher among hedged equity returns than among unhedged equity returns, the lower volatilities of the hedged returns more than offset the diminished opportunity for risk reduction through diver-

EXHIBIT 2
ANNUALIZED TOTAL RETURN OF INTERNATIONAL EQUITIES (%)

	1-Year*		3-Year		5-Year		10-Year	
	Unhedged	Hedged	Unhedged	Hedged	Unhedged	Hedged	Unhedged	Hedged
France	(15.0)	(24.6)	16.3	15.9	18.5	10.9	13.1	16.2
Germany	(9.3)	(18.9)	18.4	18.5	12.6	3.1	19.2	17.4
Italy	(22.3)	(30.5)	(2.0)	(1.8)	7.8	0.5	7.6	10.6
Japan	(37.0)	(39.1)	(3.5)	2.2	20.3	13.8	20.8	18.2
U.K.	3.5	(12.4)	7.2	7.5	14.3	9.0	12.3	16.2
U.S.	(3.1)	(3.1)	14.1	14.1	13.1	13.1	13.9	13.9
World	(19.1)	(22.9)	5.9	8.5	16.9	12.5	16.4	16.0

*Through 12/90. MSCI index data; First Quadrant currency data.

EXHIBIT 3
ANNUALIZED VOLATILITY OF INTERNATIONAL EQUITIES (%)

	3-Year*		5-Year		10-Year	
	Unhedged	Hedged	Unhedged	Hedged	Unhedged	Hedged
France	26.0	24.3	27.3	25.4	25.9	22.8
Germany	27.9	23.9	27.7	26.3	24.4	22.1
Italy	22.5	20.4	28.5	27.3	27.6	26.9
Japan	29.1	25.0	29.7	25.0	25.2	20.3
U.K.	20.0	17.3	23.2	21.8	22.2	19.4
U.S.	14.1	14.1	18.8	18.8	16.6	16.6
World	17.2	15.8	18.5	17.4	15.9	14.6

*Through 12/90. MSCI index data; First Quadrant currency data.

sification. This result holds true even though the United States market represents a large portion (between 35% and 60%, depending on the year) of the world market! In other words, hedging reduces risk even more sharply than this data might suggest. When compared with a simple United States equity investment, the risk reduction ranges up to 13%, again despite the fact that the United States is a large part of the index.

What are the costs and rewards of hedging? Exhibit 4 gives some insight into the penalty that risk extracts from returns. Suppose one believed that all the world's markets offered an expected return of 12%. Then an investment solely in the United States market, with its average volatility of 15%, might be expected to deliver a compounded geometric return of 10.9%. If that risk can be reduced by a fifth (from 15% to 12%) through the use of a global hedged portfolio, then the geometric return will rise by 40 basis points to 11.3%.

In the wake of October 1987, if a higher standard deviation is assumed, the penalty of risk is greater still. This result follows without making any assumptions at all about active management or ability to select countries or markets. Currency hedging on the forward markets is quite inexpensive, costing far less than this very real penalty of risk. If the disciplines described in this chapter can be used effectively to select the world's better performing markets, then the reward of hedged international investing is greatly enhanced, because the penalty of currency risk is avoided. If a high currency standard deviation is assumed, the penalty of risk is greater still.

We would not advocate the automatic use of a currency hedge. If the investor believes a certain foreign currency will perform much better than its forward rates, a hedge is not necessarily desirable. Clearly, over the past five years, the falling dollar would have caused a currency hedge for United States investments overseas to be costly. In the absence of a

EXHIBIT 4
THE PENALTY OF RISK

Average Return	Standard Deviation	Geometric Return
12%	10%	11.5%
12%	12%	11.3%
12%	15%	10.9%
12%	20%	10.0%
12%	25%	8.9%

confident view on foreign currency strength, however, a currency hedge not only significantly reduces the risk of global investing, but in so doing also improves long-term expectations.

STAGE I MODELING:
DO OBJECTIVE MEASURES OF VALUE MATTER?

The expected return on bonds can be represented by their yields-to-maturity; the expected return on cash is cash yield. Equity valuation presents a more difficult problem. Ideally, it calls for a measure of the net present value of future cash flows. In a practical international context, however, normalized earnings yields prove to be the most manageable and consistent indicator of stock performance.[3] To fully calculate total returns for equity completely, it is necessary to add a measure of sustainable growth. The addition of economic variables to the regressions indirectly but effectively introduces such a measure.

None of these measures differs conceptually from those now widely employed in similar models in the United States. In general, remarkably few changes were required to adapt a United States model to the markets of other countries.

In a Stage I asset allocation model, one assumes that objective measures of prospective relative return (or value) are positively correlated with subsequent actual relative returns. Is the equity risk premium versus bonds (stock earnings yield minus bond yield) positively correlated with the subsequent relative performance of stocks versus bonds? Is the equity risk premium versus cash (stock earnings yield minus cash yield) positively correlated with the subsequent relative performance of stocks versus cash? Is the bond maturity premium (bond yield minus cash yield) positively correlated with the subsequent relative performance of bonds versus cash? If the answers to all these questions are affirmative, a Stage I model will be profitable. In essence, a Stage I model assumes that there is an equilibrating mechanism between asset classes, whereby unusual market conditions give rise to unusual subsequent relative performance.

Exhibits 5, 6, and 7 give univariate regression coefficients of 15 different countries for Stage I asset allocation. In each instance, we are testing the relation between objective measures of the prospective return

---

[3]See also Robert D. Arnott and Erik H. Sorensen, "The Equity Risk Premium and Stock Market Performance," Salomon Brothers Inc, July 1987, later published in the *Journal of Portfolio Management*, Summer, 1988.

EXHIBIT 5
STOCK EARNINGS YIELD MINUS BOND YIELD

Coefficient of Regression with Subsequent Asset
Class Relative Performance

	Stock/Bond	Stock/Cash	Bond/Cash
Australia	−0.23	−0.76	−0.53
Austria	1.09	0.98	−0.11
Belgium	0.24	0.19	−0.05
Canada	0.33	0.28	−0.05
Denmark	0.05	−0.18	−0.23[1]
France	0.16	−0.05	−0.21[2]
Germany	0.46	0.29	−0.16
Italy	0.04	−0.05	−0.10[2]
Japan	1.39[1]	1.36[1]	−0.03
Netherlands	1.64[2]	0.97[2]	−0.67[1]
Spain	2.90[2]	2.79[2]	−0.11
Sweden	0.79	0.44	−0.34
Switzerland	0.86[1]	0.88[1]	0.02
U.K.	1.36[2]	0.80	−0.54
U.S.A.	0.36	0.10	−0.26
Average	0.76[2]	0.54	−0.22[2]

[1]Significant at 5% level
[2]Significant at 1% level
Note: The data covers various time periods. For most countries, data is included from December 1972 through February 1987; for Australia, Austria, Japan, Spain, Sweden, and the U.K., however, data beginning in September 1979 or July 1981 were included.

differences and the subsequent realized return differences over a one-month horizon.

In order to understand the information in the exhibits better, consider the regression coefficient for Japan in the Stock/Bond column of Exhibit 5. In this exhibit, the equity risk premium is measured against bonds (stock earnings yield minus bond yield). In the Stock/Bond column, this risk premium measure is regressed against the subsequent excess returns of stocks over bonds. The resulting regression coefficient is 1.39. In other words, for every 100-basis-point change in the Japanese stock/bond risk premium (stock market earnings yield minus 10-year bond yield), there

EXHIBIT 6
STOCK EARNINGS YIELD MINUS CASH YIELD

Coefficient of Regression with Subsequent Asset
Class Relative Performance

	Stock/Bond	Stock/Cash	Bond/Cash
Australia	−0.30	−0.32	−0.03
Austria	0.25	0.42	0.16[1]
Belgium	0.11	0.18[1]	0.07[1]
Canada	0.17	0.22	0.05
Denmark	0.03	0.01	−0.03
France	0.56[1]	0.95[2]	0.40[2]
Germany	0.27	0.35[1]	0.08
Italy	0.12	0.32	0.20[2]
Japan	1.77	1.64[1]	−0.13
Netherlands	0.60[2]	0.61[2]	0.01
Spain	0.68	0.72	0.04
Sweden	0.43	0.24	−0.18
Switzerland	0.16	0.28	0.12[2]
U.K.	0.34	0.14	−0.18
U.S.A.	0.30[1]	0.37[2]	0.07
Average	0.36[2]	0.41[2]	0.04

[1]Significant at 5% level
[2]Significant at 1% level

is an average of 139 basis points difference in the relative performance of stocks versus bonds over the subsequent month.

At first glance, this number might seem extraordinary. How can a 100-basis-point change in the risk premium translate into more than 100 basis points in the subsequent month's performance? The answer is found in the leverage inherent in the capital markets. Suppose the earnings yield was 4% at a time when the 10-year bond yield was 6%. A 100-basis-point rally in stocks would depress the earnings yield by only 4 basis points (from 4.00% to 3.96%). A 100-basis-point rise in bonds would depress 10-year bond yields by only about 13.5 basis points (from 6.00% to about 5.865%). A relative performance difference of 139 basis points in a single month, stemming from a 100-basis-point stock/bond disequilibrium, could reduce the disequilibrium either by 5.5 basis points

EXHIBIT 7
BOND YIELD MINUS CASH YIELD

	Coefficient of Regression with Subsequent Asset Class Relative Performance		
	Stock/Bond	*Stock/Cash*	*Bond/Cash*
Australia	−0.47	−0.44	0.03
Austria	0.08	0.43	0.36^2
Belgium	0.12	0.23^1	0.12^2
Canada	−0.02	0.25	0.28^1
Denmark	−0.16	0.24	0.26^1
France	0.20	0.54^2	0.34^2
Germany	0.19	0.42^1	-0.22^2
Italy	0.04	0.28^1	0.24^2
Japan	−0.72	−0.81	−0.09
Netherlands	0.26	0.53^2	0.27^1
Spain	−0.48	−0.34	0.14
Sweden	−0.01	0.00	0.01
Switzerland	−0.02	0.14	0.16^2
U.K.	−0.04	−0.12	−0.06
U.S.A.	0.22	0.52^2	0.30^1
Average	−0.05	0.12	0.17^2

[1] Significant at 5% level
[2] Significant at 1% level

from a change in the stock earnings yield or by 18.6 basis points from a change in bond yields. Neither comes close to closing the 100 basis point disequilibrium.

The striking finding in Exhibit 5 is that the equity risk premium versus bonds serves as a predictor for the subsequent relative returns of stocks versus bonds in 14 of the 15 countries tested, five of them with statistical significance. The average link between the stock/bond disequilibrium and subsequent stock/bond relative performance is a strong one: every 100 basis points of measured disequilibrium translates into 76 basis points of relative performance in the subsequent month! Intriguingly, this variable is also quite powerful in suggesting future bond behavior, as can be seen in the Bond/Cash column. In 14 of the 15 countries tested, if the equity risk premium is abnormally high, the subsequent bond market performance is adversely affected relative to cash.

Exhibit 6 suggests that the equity risk premium versus cash (stock earnings yield minus cash yield) is a good indicator of stock excess returns versus cash in 14 of the 15 countries tested. The stock/cash risk premium is also indicative of the relative performance of stocks versus bonds in 14 of the 15 countries tested.

Finally, Exhibit 7 suggests that the slope of the bond market yield curve is a powerful indicator of subsequent bond performance relative to cash. If the yield curve is unusually steep (that is, if bond yields are high relative to cash yields), the outlook is good for fixed-income returns. This relationship is statistically significant for over half of the countries tested.

This finding for the slope of the bond market yield curve flies in the face of conventional wisdom. The conventional wisdom is that a steep yield curve suggests a likelihood of rising yields. If this were true, then a steep yield curve would correspond to weak bond results relative to cash. The empirical evidence is quite persuasive in refuting this view. While the relationship is not invulnerable to error, a steep yield curve tends to correspond to stronger returns on bonds than on cash.

The implication of these three tests is relatively straightforward: market-implicit rate of return matters. If the equity risk premium is unusually high, it follows that most investors are averse to equities. The investor with the courage to bear that risk will tend to be rewarded. If the bond market maturity premium is high, most investors are evidently averse to interest rate risk. The investor willing to bear that risk reaps reward.

STAGE II MODELING:
A CHANGING EQUILIBRIUM

Recent studies of capital markets behavior suggest that the equilibrium relationships between asset classes can change.[4] An obvious question is whether it makes sense to employ a process in which current market conditions are measured against recent, rather than long-term, equilibria.

In order to test the effects of a changing equilibrium, Exhibits 8, 9, and 10 adopt a short-term definition of equilibrium. These exhibits, rather

---

[4]See Arnott and Sorensen, "Equity Risk Premium Review; Reflections on the Risk Premium," Salomon Brothers Inc, February 16, 1988.

EXHIBIT 8
24-MONTH TREND IN STOCK EARNINGS YIELD MINUS BOND YIELD

| | Coefficient of Regression with Subsequent Asset Class Relative Performance | | |
	Stock/Bond	Stock/Cash	Bond/Cash
Australia	−0.48	−0.70	−0.22
Austria	0.11	0.24	0.13
Belgium	0.36	0.28	−0.09
Canada	0.44	0.75[1]	0.31[1]
Denmark	0.08	0.13	0.05
France	1.18[1]	1.57[2]	0.38[1]
Germany	0.66	0.02[1]	0.26
Italy	0.14	0.47	0.33[2]
Japan	4.16[1]	3.16	−0.99
Netherlands	1.32[2]	1.00[2]	−0.33
Spain	2.58[2]	2.42[1]	−0.16
Sweden	1.00	0.78	−0.23
Switzerland	0.96	1.39[1]	0.43[2]
U.K.	1.22[2]	0.82	−0.34
U.S.A.	0.49	0.84[2]	0.35
Average	0.95[2]	0.94[2]	−0.01

[1] Significant at 5% level
[2] Significant at 1% level

than comparing the current risk premium with a long-term equilibrium relation, compare the current risk premium with the average value over the most recent 24-month period. For example, to measure the United States stock/bond disequilibrium for January 1987, the equity risk premium against bonds (stock earnings yield minus bond yield) is averaged over the period January 1985 through December 1986. The risk premium that existed at the beginning of January 1987 is compared with this 24-month average. Any difference is then viewed as a disequilibrium suggesting relative opportunities between stocks and bonds.

As Exhibits 8, 9, and 10 show, this approach actually worked better than the Stage I approach for most countries. The improvement is especially noticeable for the stock/bond and stock/cash relationships as the regression coefficient increases in 11 of the 15 countries. A Stage I

EXHIBIT 9
24-MONTH TREND IN STOCK EARNINGS YIELD MINUS CASH YIELD

Coefficient of Regression with Subsequent Asset
Class Relative Performance

	Stock/Bond	Stock/Cash	Bond/Cash
Australia	−0.26	−0.26	0.00
Austria	−0.20	0.00	0.19^2
Belgium	0.08	0.14	0.05
Canada	0.11	0.30	0.20^1
Denmark	0.04	0.33^1	0.29^1
France	1.28	1.61^1	0.34^2
Germany	0.32^1	0.50^2	0.18^1
Italy	−0.04	0.18	0.22^2
Japan	2.11^1	1.90^1	−0.22
Netherlands	0.55^2	0.62^2	0.07
Spain	3.07^1	2.97^1	−0.10
Sweden	0.22	0.16	−0.08
Switzerland	0.24	0.41^1	0.17^2
U.K.	0.16	0.06	−0.07
U.S.A.	0.39^1	0.61^2	0.22
Average	0.47^1	0.60^2	0.10

[1]Significant at 5% level
[2]Significant at 1% level

approach, based on the naive assumption of static equilibrium relationships, has merit and can add value. But an approach that recognizes the potential for changes in equilibrium may lead to better predictive power.

REAL INTEREST RATES

In a study published in 1983,[5] the trend in real interest rates (defined as Treasury bill yields minus 12-month CPI inflation) was found to be a powerful factor in the performance of the United States capital markets.

[5]Arnott and von Germeten, "Systematic Asset Allocation," *Financial Analysts Journal,* November/December 1983.

EXHIBIT 10
24-MONTH TREND IN BOND YIELD MINUS CASH YIELD

	Coefficient of Regression with Subsequent Asset Class Relative Performance		
	Stock/Bond	*Stock/Cash*	*Bond/Cash*
Australia	−0.38	−0.34	0.05
Austria	−0.54	−0.14	0.40[2]
Belgium	0.01	0.10	0.08[2]
Canada	−0.05	0.19	0.24
Denmark	−0.02	0.24	0.26[1]
France	−0.04	0.28	0.32[2]
Germany	0.27	0.45[1]	0.19[1]
Italy	−0.12	−0.04	0.08
Japan	0.30	0.64[1]	0.34
Netherlands	0.37	0.60[2]	0.23
Spain	−0.60	−0.50	0.10
Sweden	0.63	0.69	0.06
Switzerland	0.21	0.41	0.20[2]
U.K.	−0.10	−0.11	−0.01
U.S.A.	0.40[1]	0.60[2]	0.20[1]
Average	0.02	0.20	0.18[2]

[1]Significant at 5% level
[2]Significant at 1% level

The results in Exhibit 11 reaffirm that relationship. These results suggest that a rise in real interest rates in the United States leads to a substantial flight of money out of stocks. The result is significant at the 1% level, and every 100-basis-point rise in real interest rates translates into a one-month performance penalty of 50 basis points for stocks versus bonds.

As we seek to broaden this research, however, we find the relationships between real interest rates and the markets are not consistent around the globe. We find statistical significance for only three countries (albeit highly significant for each): the United States, West Germany, and the Netherlands. Elsewhere, the relation is spotty and inconsistent at best.

EXHIBIT 11
24-MONTH TREND IN REAL CASH YIELD

Coefficient of Regression with Subsequent Asset
Class Relative Performance

	Stock/Bond	Stock/Cash	Bond/Cash
Australia	−0.21	−0.11	0.10
Austria	0.69	0.47	−0.22
Belgium	0.00	−0.03	−0.03
Canada	−0.18	−0.16	0.01
Denmark	0.08	−0.01	−0.09
France	0.03	−0.08	−0.11
Germany	−0.40[1]	−0.54[2]	−0.14
Italy	−0.03	0.02	0.04
Japan	−0.76	−0.35	0.40
Netherlands	−0.42[2]	−0.46[2]	−0.04
Spain	−0.88	−0.86	0.02
Sweden	−0.29	−0.01	0.28
Switzerland	0.01	0.00	−0.01
U.K.	−0.16	0.16	0.35
U.S.A.	−0.50[2]	−0.43[2]	0.07
Average	−0.20	−0.16	0.04

[1]Significant at 5% level
[2]Significant at 1% level

In short, CPI inflation appears to have only limited merit for active asset allocation decisions in the global arena.

Does this mean that the results for the United States, West Germany, and the Netherlands are spurious, stemming from random noise in the data? Or does it mean that in these countries the relations between markets and real interest rates are especially powerful? Statistical tools cannot answer these questions. Nevertheless, we are skeptical about such inconsistent relations, which do not stand up to a global evaluation. We are inclined to ignore models, such as the trend in real yields, that show only intermittent statistical significance.

EXHIBIT 12
STOCK RETURN VARIANCE

	Coefficient of Regression with Subsequent Asset Class Relative Performance		
	Stock/Bond	Stock/Cash	Bond/Cash
Australia	−0.33	0.77	1.01
Belgium	0.65[1]	0.88[2]	0.23[2]
Canada	2.00[1]	2.48[2]	0.47
Denmark	0.14	0.60	0.46
France	−0.47	−0.84	−0.37
Germany	0.22	0.44	0.22
Italy	0.36	0.37	0.02
Japan	1.00	1.13	0.13
Netherlands	0.73	1.04	0.32
Sweden	2.40	2.88[1]	0.48
Switzerland	0.25	0.28	0.04
U.K.	−0.18	−0.25	−0.11
U.S.A.	1.27[1]	1.83[2]	0.56
Average	0.62[1]	0.89[2]	0.27[2]

[1] Significant at 5% level
[2] Significant at 1% level

STAGE III MODELING:
THE INFLUENCE OF THE MACROECONOMY

Capital markets do not exist in a vacuum. Asset values do not rise and fall of their own accord. Rather, they embody the views of the investment community about future macroeconomic prospects. In a world where the judgments of millions of investors shape market pricing patterns, it might seem reasonable to assume market efficiency and to assume that the macroeconomy cannot provide useful guides to future capital market performance. If the consensus views of investors fairly reflect macro-economic factors, then the markets should be fairly priced to reflect this kind of objective information. The empirical evidence shows this may not be the case.

Several macroeconomic factors appear to be somewhat predictive of the subsequent performance of various assets. We studied the following variables:

* stock return variance,
* rate of change in retail sales,
* rate of change in producer prices,
* levels of employment, and
* rate of change in unit labor costs.

Each of these variables was tested by regression analysis in which the data were appropriately lagged to reflect reporting delays that differ from country to country. The results were surprisingly significant.

Stock return variance simply represents the volatility of stock market performance over the preceding six months. A Salomon Brothers study in April 1987 found this variable to be a powerful indicator of future stock market performance in the United States. Past volatility and subsequent reward (stock excess returns versus bonds) are positively correlated in 10 of the 13 countries tested and stock excess returns versus cash are related to market volatility in 11 of the 13 countries. This consistency suggests that stock market volatility has global relevance.

One might think that the rate of change in retail sales is a useful indicator of economic activity, and hence an indicator of equity prospects. Unfortunately, the evidence in Exhibit 13 suggests that retail sales are fully discounted in securities prices, as the regression coefficients display no consistent directional patterns. In fact, retail sales are significantly positively correlated with West German stock performance and significantly negatively correlated with United Kingdom equity performance. These results would not earn the confidence of any sensible investor.

The rates of change for producer prices give more promising results. Whereas the results in Exhibit 11 suggested that real yields, based on CPI inflation, are of limited value, inflation as measured in producer prices, as shown in Exhibit 14, turns out to be consistently useful. In every country tested, an acceleration in PPI inflation translates into a subsequent erosion of bond performance. In 6 of the 13 countries, the relation was statistically significant; in 5 of the 13 countries, it was significant at the 1% level.

EXHIBIT 13
PERCENTAGE CHANGE RETAIL SALES

Coefficient of Regression with Subsequent Asset
Class Relative Performance

	Stock/Bond	Stock/Cash	Bond/Cash
Australia	0.00	0.02	0.01
Belgium	0.02	0.02	0.00
Canada	0.14	−0.09	−0.23
Denmark	0.04	0.07	0.03
France	0.04	−0.05	−0.09
Germany	0.34[1]	0.37[2]	0.03
Italy	0.00	0.00	0.00
Japan	0.34	0.12	−0.23
Netherlands	0.02	0.05	0.03
Sweden	−0.01	−0.05	−0.03
Switzerland	0.07[2]	0.07[1]	0.00
U.K.	−0.62	−0.77[1]	0.14
U.S.A.	0.31	−0.09	−0.39[1]
Average	0.05[1]	−0.03	−0.08

[1]Significant at 5% level
[2]Significant at 1% level

Acceleration in PPI inflation also has a bearing on stock market performance. Accelerating PPI inflation depresses subsequent stock market performance versus cash in 9 of 13 countries. Five of 13 coefficients are statistically significant, and each of the significant coefficients is negative. In short, although CPI inflation appears nearly irrelevant, PPI inflation acted as a depressant on both stocks and bonds.

The final two tests gave consistent and intriguing results. The first of them, Exhibit 15, is a test of unemployment. If unemployment is above average, both stocks and bonds achieve better subsequent rewards. The relation is slightly more consistent for bonds than it is for stocks: for bonds the relationship holds in every country except Canada, whereas for stocks it fails to hold in three countries. However, the average impact on stocks was greater than the average impact on bonds. All of the

EXHIBIT 14
PERCENT CHANGE PRODUCER PRICE INDEX

Coefficient of Regression with Subsequent Asset
Class Relative Performance

	Stock/Bond	Stock/Cash	Bond/Cash
Australia	0.13	0.08	−0.06
Belgium	−0.43	−0.55[1]	−0.12
Canada	2.34	1.43	−0.91
Denmark	0.06	0.13	−0.47
France	−0.14	−0.34	−0.20[2]
Germany	−0.98	−1.91[2]	−0.92[2]
Italy	0.02	0.75	−0.73[2]
Japan	0.46	0.45	−0.01
Netherlands	−0.62	−0.87[1]	−0.25
Sweden	−0.90	−1.36	−0.46
Switzerland	−1.45[2]	−1.81[2]	−0.35[2]
U.K.	0.17	−0.60	−0.78
U.S.A.	−0.18	−1.08[2]	−0.90[2]
Average	−0.08	−0.55	−0.47[2]

[1]Significant at 5% level
[2]Significant at 1% level

statistically significant results point to stronger capital markets performance when unemployment is above average than when unemployment is below average.

Finally, if people are working and are well paid, unit labor costs can rise rapidly (Exhibit 16). Here we find a relationship even more consistent than the one with unemployment rates. Rising unit labor costs hurt stock market performance in each country where this statistic is available. Bonds are hurt by rising unit labor costs in all but one country (Canada) in which this data is available.

Evidently, the capital markets and the workforce operate at cross purposes. Crudely stated, if the worker is happy, the investor will be sad, and vice versa.

EXHIBIT 15
UNEMPLOYMENT

Coefficient of Regression with Subsequent Asset
Class Relative Performance

	Stock/Bond	Stock/Cash	Bond/Cash
Australia	−0.96	−0.16	0.80
Belgium	0.15[1]	0.23[2]	0.08[2]
Canada	−0.11	−0.24	−0.13
Denmark	−0.42[1]	−0.07	0.36
France	0.46	0.96[1]	0.49[1]
Germany	0.26[2]	0.39[2]	0.12[1]
Japan	0.05	0.06	0.02
Netherlands	0.12	0.21	0.09
Switzerland	1.92	2.09	0.16
U.K.	0.02	0.23	0.22
U.S.A.	0.33	0.69[2]	0.35
Average	0.17	0.40	0.23[2]

[1] Significant at 5% level
[2] Significant at 1% level

EXHIBIT 16
PERCENTAGE CHANGE UNIT LABOR COSTS

Coefficient of Regression with Subsequent Asset
Class Relative Performance

	Stock/Bond	Stock/Cash	Bond/Cash
Belgium	−0.40	−0.51	−0.11
Canada	−0.08	−0.06	0.02
Denmark	0.37	−0.30	−0.67
France	−1.18	−2.03[1]	−0.84
Germany	−0.31[2]	−0.30	0.01
Italy	−0.23	−0.40	−0.17[1]
Netherlands	−0.46	−1.16[1]	−0.70
Sweden	0.09	−0.04	−0.13
U.K.	0.47	−0.02	−0.54
U.S.A.	0.06	−0.44	−0.50
Average	−0.17	−0.53[2]	−0.36[1]

[1] Significant at 5% level
[2] Significant at 1% level

CONCLUSION

The most telling conclusion of this research is that the relationships successfully applied to asset allocation strategies in the United States also have promise for other countries around the globe. Although statistical significance was sometimes elusive, the consistency of the results from one country to another is ample grounds for encouragement about the merit of these investment tools.

What about the investor who wants to take a disciplined approach to asset allocation on a global basis? The evidence would suggest that such a disciplined approach is not only intuitively appealing, but also profitable.

CHAPTER 16

International Asset and Currency Allocation

ADRIAN LEE
VICE PRESIDENT
J. P. MORGAN INVESTMENT MANAGEMENT INC.
LONDON

The focus of this chapter is on the international asset allocation issues that confront U.S. investors. These are:

1. International assets versus domestic assets.
2. International equities versus international fixed income.
3. Foreign currency exposure versus foreign asset exposure.

We will show that, when an investor considers the full opportunity set of all the world's capital markets, both equities and fixed income, his risk/reward preference as revealed by domestic asset allocation choices should also be reflected in international asset allocation choices. In other words, an investor with a balanced domestic portfolio is likely also to prefer a balanced international portfolio.

It will also be shown that, in international investment, it is appropriate to separate long-run asset allocation decisions from long-run currency allocation decisions. This suggests that investors will inevitably enhance their risk/return opportunity set by *separately* making two kinds of international allocation decisions — one concerning asset exposure and one concerning currency exposure. When these allocations differ, the use of continuously hedged international portfolios is implied.

In fact, we will conclude that, in general, it may be more appropriate for a U.S. investor's *normal* international equity and fixed-income portfolios to be defined as fully hedged or partially hedged. Only under perverse assumptions about long-run currency surprises should an international investor's *normal* portfolio be exposed to foreign currency.

We will use the results of the last 13 years to illustrate the effects of these choices in the past and we shall outline a framework for how these decisions can be addressed optimally in the future.

INTERNATIONAL CAPITAL MARKET RETURNS AND RISKS

The world's investable capital markets, excluding cash and real estate, comprise some $19 trillion as of December 1990. This forms the universe for an institutional investor (see Exhibit 1). The world fixed-income

EXHIBIT 1
WORLD CAPITAL MARKETS

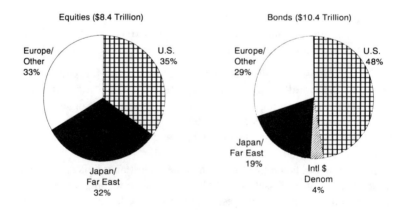

Equities ($8.4 Trillion)

Europe/Other 33%
U.S. 35%
Japan/Far East 32%

Bonds ($10.4 Trillion)

Europe/Other 29%
U.S. 48%
Japan/Far East 19%
Intl $ Denom 4%

Sources: Morgan Stanley Capital International, Salomon Brothers Inc.

markets total some $10.4 trillion, while the world equity markets total $8.4 trillion. The U.S. markets comprise less than half the total of world markets in both the case of fixed-income and equities.

The non-U.S. markets have offered significant opportunities for U.S. investors over the last 13 years. These opportunities can be seen in the form of return enhancement and risk reduction.

RETURN ENHANCEMENT

Exhibits 2 and 3 show the returns in U.S. dollars from investing in international equity and fixed-income markets over the last 13 years. For both equities and fixed-income securities, non-U.S. markets have yielded significantly higher returns than their U.S. equivalents. A market weighted average of all non-U.S. equity markets returned 17.5% per annum in U.S. dollars compared with 12.9% per annum from the U.S.

EXHIBIT 2
INTERNATIONAL EQUITY MARKETS
RETURNS IN U.S. DOLLARS 1978–1990

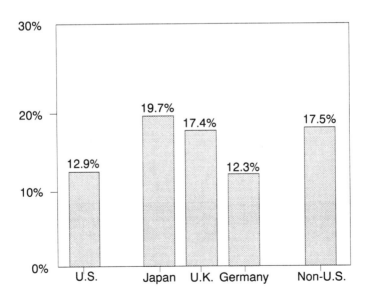

EXHIBIT 3
INTERNATIONAL FIXED-INCOME MARKETS
RETURNS IN U.S. DOLLARS 1978–1990

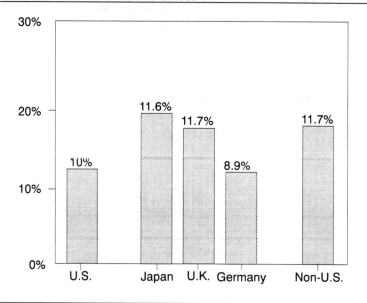

equity market. Similarly, non-U.S. fixed-income markets returned 11.7% compared to the U.S. fixed-income return of 10.0%.

RISK REDUCTION

While the non-U.S. capital markets offered the U.S. investor significant return opportunities, they did so without increasing risk. In fact, the U.S. investor's total portfolio risk was reduced through the use of non-U.S. markets. Exhibits 4 and 5 show the annualized standard deviation of U.S. dollar return from the international markets over the period 1978–1990. While individual international equity and fixed-income markets are significantly more risky than their U.S. equivalent, a diversified portfolio of non-U.S. equities or non-U.S. fixed-income securities is not significantly more risky than the equivalent domestic market. For example, a market weighted average of non-U.S. equity markets had an annual standard deviation of dollar return of 19.5% per annum compared with 16.2% per annum for the U.S. equity market.

EXHIBIT 4
INTERNATIONAL EQUITY MARKETS
STANDARD DEVIATION OF RETURNS IN U.S. DOLLARS   1978–1990

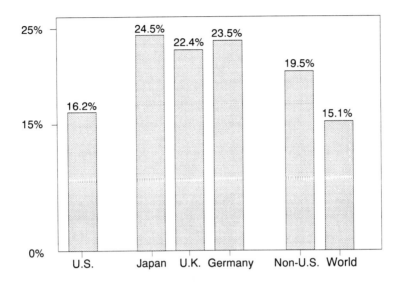

EXHIBIT 5
INTERNATIONAL FIXED-INCOME MARKETS
STANDARD DEVIATION OF RETURNS IN U.S. DOLLARS   1978–1990

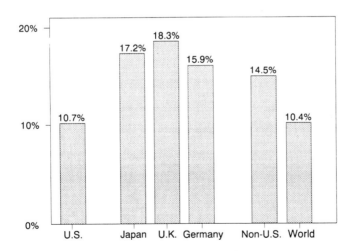

This diversification *between* international markets is significant for both equities and fixed-income securities. It is important to bear in mind that international investment for any investor, U.S. or otherwise, always offers two tiers of diversification: first, diversification out of the domestic market; second, diversification across the many markets outside the domestic market.

In assessing the risk of international investment, the relevant measure is not total risk of the international markets, but their contribution to the overall risk of the investor's portfolio. From this perspective, international investment offers risk *reduction* in addition to the return opportunities described above. For both international equities and fixed-income securities, a capitalization weighted world portfolio of U.S. and non-U.S. markets is less risky than the U.S. market alone. This shows that diversification into international markets in fact reduces a U.S. investor's total portfolio risk.

INTERNATIONAL ASSET ALLOCATION

Exhibit 6 illustrates the returns and risks to various asset allocation decisions over the period 1978–1990. The line joining USS and NUSS shows returns and risks to a portfolio ranging from 100% U.S. equities up to 100% non-U.S. equities. The line USB, NUSB shows portfolios ranging from 100% U.S. fixed-income to 100% non-U.S. fixed-income. The line NUSB, NUSS shows all combinations of international fixed-income securities and international equities.

Exhibit 6 shows (1) that international equities and fixed-income securities add value when compared with their domestic counterparts, and (2) that they offer diversification among themselves (see frontier of the shaded area). This is the third tier of international diversification—across international equity and fixed-income.

From an asset allocation perspective, it is appropriate to consider the full spectrum of all international assets simultaneously when identifying an investor's portfolio risk/reward tradeoff. In other words, the more traditional domestic/international allocation question is more appropriately addressed in the context of simultaneous allocations across all four asset classes—U.S. equities, U.S. fixed-income, international equities and international fixed-income securities.

Of critical importance to this asset allocation problem is the correlation of diversification characteristics of all asset classes simultaneously. Exhibit 6 also gives these correlations for the period 1978–1990.

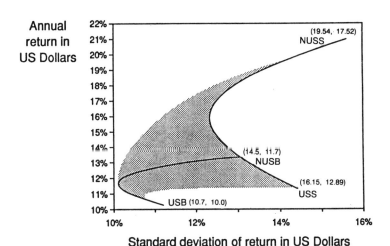

Standard deviation of return in US Dollars

Correlations

U.S. stocks (USS)	1.00			
U.S. bonds (USB)	.33	1.00		
Non-U.S. stocks (NUSS)	.38	.22	1.00	
Non-U.S. bonds (NUSB)	.04	.36	.68	1.00

When an investor considers these four asset classes simultaneously in an optimization context, it is likely that his risk preference, as revealed by his domestic stock/bond allocation, will also be reflected in his international stock/bond allocation. In other words, say that in the absence of international investment, an investor was prepared to accept a target risk level of 12% as revealed by a 60/40 stock bond allocation; then, when international assets are allowed into the universe, the optimal portfolio at the same risk level will include both international stocks and bonds. A balanced U.S. investor is likely also to be a balanced international investor.

The exact proportions of such optimal portfolios will inevitably depend on the future expectations for risk, return and covariance. Examples

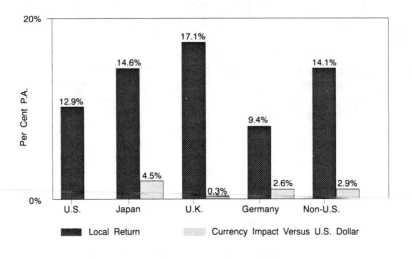

of such optimal portfolios using *ex ante* equilibrium assumptions are discussed at a later stage.

U.S. investors considering such asset allocation issues are often concerned with the relatively high correlation between international equity and international fixed income. This high correlation results from both asset classes sharing very similar currency exposure — a Japanese equity and a Japanese bond imply identical exposure to the Yen.

In order to appropriately identify asset allocation policies in global investment, it is important first to separate international asset allocation issues from international currency allocation. Indeed, we shall show in the next section that the risk/reward opportunity set for a U.S. investor is greatly enhanced by considering these allocations separately, and that the high correlations of international equities and bonds can be greatly reduced when asset and currency decisions are separated.

SEPARATION OF ASSETS AND CURRENCIES — HEDGED INTERNATIONAL PORTFOLIOS

Returns to a U.S. investor in international markets derive from two separate sources of return — local asset return and currency appreciation (depreciation) versus the U.S. dollar. The local and currency returns to U.S. investment in international equities and fixed-income securities are shown in Exhibits 7 and 8.

EXHIBIT 8
INTERNATIONAL FIXED-INCOME MARKETS
LOCAL AND CURRENCY RETURNS 1978–1990

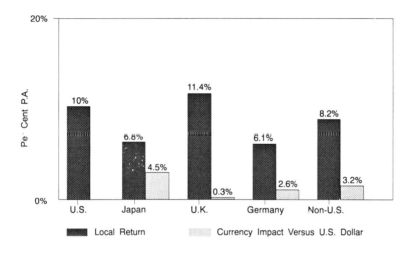

The contribution of currency return to total return has been unsystematic; for some markets it has been positive and for others negative; for diversified portfolios or non-U.S. markets it has been small.

In contrast, however, the contribution of currencies to investment risk is significant and systematically positive. Exhibits 9 and 10 separate the total risk (standard deviation of return) of international equities and fixed-income markets into risk from local return volatility and currency volatility versus the U.S. dollar. Total risk is given by the outlined bar, and component risks are given by the inner bars. It can be seen that currency risk is approximately equal to 70% of the local risk of equity markets and more than 200% of the risk of local fixed-income markets. The total risk as indicated by the outlined bar is not equal to the addition of the two component risks, because standard deviations are not additive, due to the correlations of local asset and currency returns. These correlations are indicated also in Exhibits 9 and 10.

The correlations are consistently small especially for international equities. This observation, combined with the fact that currency risk is

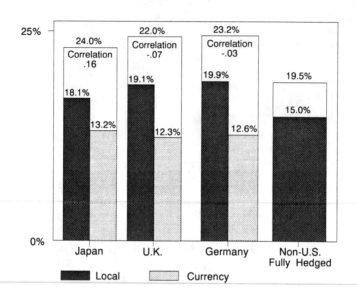

EXHIBIT 9
INTERNATIONAL EQUITY MARKETS
LOCAL AND CURRENCY RISKS 1978–1990

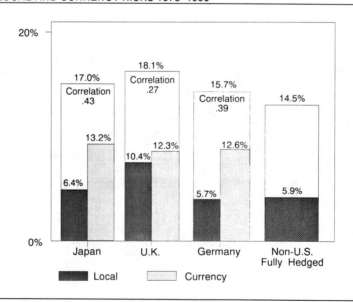

EXHIBIT 10
INTERNATIONAL FIXED-INCOME MARKETS
LOCAL AND CURRENCY RISKS 1978–1990

a significant source of investment risk in international portfolios, suggests:

1. Currency risk should be managed and not simply assumed in international investment.
2. Currency exposure decisions should be managed separately from asset exposure decisions.

HEDGED INTERNATIONAL INVESTMENT

International portfolios that have exposure only to local asset return can be constructed by hedging the currency exposure of the underlying foreign asset back into the dollar. The risks of such hedged portfolios of all non-U.S. markets is also given in Exhibits 9 and 10. These risks show that hedged portfolios, with only exposures to international assets and not currencies, can avoid the significant currency risks associated with international investment.

Return to a fully hedged foreign investment is equal to:

local asset return + forward premium/discount[1]

Exhibit 11 plots the risks and returns to the full spectrum of asset and currency allocation choice over the period 1978–1990 — U.S. stocks, U.S. bonds, non-U.S. stocks, non-U.S. bonds, non-U.S. stocks fully hedged and non-U.S. bonds fully hedged.

It can be seen that the returns to fully hedged international equities and bonds for the period 1978–1990 were roughly equivalent to their dollar-adjusted equivalent. *Ex post* the hedged and unhedged returns will differ by the "surprise currency" depreciation beyond that anticipated in the forward premium. In other words, unhedged investment will outperform hedged investment only if currency appreciation is greater than that anticipated by the forward premium.

Including fully hedged portfolios in the universe of choice greatly enhanced the risk/reward opportunity set to the U.S. investor. In fact, hedged international equities and bonds dominated their unhedged equivalents in terms of return and risk; this is so because hedged portfolios had similar returns to unhedged portfolios but significantly reduced risks.

---

[1] Forward premium = U.S. short-term rate – foreign short-term rate.

366   Lee

EXHIBIT 11
INTERNATIONAL EQUITY AND BOND MARKETS
RETURNS AND RISK 1978–1990

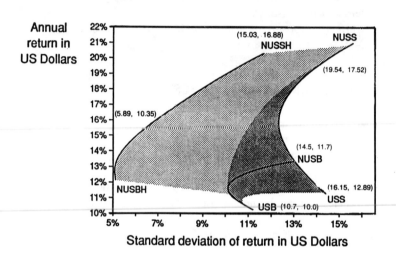

Standard deviation of return in US Dollars

Correlations

U.S. stocks (USS)	1.00					
U.S. bonds (USB)	.33	1.00				
Non-U.S. stocks (NUSS)	.38	.22	1.00			
Non-U.S. bonds (NUSB)	.04	.36	.68	1.00		
Non-U.S. stocks hedged (NUSSH)	.53	.14	.80	.17	1.00	
Non-U.S. bonds hedged (NUSBH)	.22	.51	.48	.67	.36	1.00

Also, and importantly, hedged international equities and bonds are significantly less correlated than their unhedged counterparts, –.36 versus .75, thus improving diversification between international equities and bonds. This addresses the concern raised earlier of the relatively high correlation between international bonds and equities, due to their shared currency exposure.

Hedged international portfolios have equivalent diversification characteristics to unhedged portfolios, as can be seen from the correlations of returns in Exhibit 11.

Currency exposure in international portfolios is not itself the source of international diversification. It can be shown that diversification of unhedged international investment, as measured by correlation of domestic asset return with combined return of foreign local asset and currency, can be broken down as follows:

$$R_{a+c,u} = \left(R_{a,u}\frac{S_a}{S_{a+c}}\right) + \left(R_{c,u}\frac{S_c}{S_{a+c}}\right)$$

a = foreign asset local returns
c = foreign currency returns
u = domestic asset returns
R = correlation coefficient
S = standard deviation (risk)

This says that the unhedged correlation is the weighted average of local asset correlation with the domestic asset and the correlation of the foreign currency with the domestic asset. The weights are given by the respective ratios of asset risk and currency risk to total risk.

It can be shown that hedging will not reduce diversification unless

$$\frac{R_{c,u}}{R_{a,u}} < \frac{S_{a+c} - S_a}{S_c}$$

In other words, unless $R_{c,u}$ is small and the increase in risk associated with currency exposure is large, hedging will not reduce diversification. Empirically the impact of hedging on diversification has been minimal.

However, the appropriate way to evaluate the impact of hedging is by examining its effect on total portfolio risk, i.e., its marginal impact on the risk of a portfolio of U.S. and international assets. The chapter appendix shows the condition under which hedged international investment will reduce total portfolio risk when compared with unhedged international investment. *The combined impact of diversification and international risk reduction associated with hedging has always been to reduce total portfolio risk for a U.S. investor.*

LONG-RUN INTERNATIONAL ASSET ALLOCATION – A FRAMEWORK FOR A GENERALIZED SOLUTION

In order to identify appropriate optimal asset allocation strategies, the asset allocation problem should be separated into *domestic assets, hedged foreign assets* and *currency*. Solutions to optimal allocations should then be sought simultaneously with all assets: In this context, currency can be thought of as a separate asset class or exposure and uncoupled from its traditional overlap with international assets. Conceptually, optimal currency exposure can be less than, or indeed greater than, international asset allocations.

Optimization theory would suggest allocations to foreign currency in proportion to its expected return and inversely proportional to its variance and covariance with all other assets. (See Appendix B for theoretical framework).

In this framework of *hedged assets* and *currency,* "expected currency return" refers to currency appreciation in excess of the forward premium. This we refer to as "currency surprise." The expected currency return should also be adjusted in practice by the transaction cost required to hedge currency exposure. Appendix C outlines the sources of transaction costs and estimates for each source.

Exhibits 12 and 13 show optimal asset and currency exposure and the associated hedge ratios for a range of assumptions, allocations and risk levels. It was assumed that hedged international assets return the equivalent of their domestic counterpart and historical risks and covariances over the last 13 years were used.

A range of transaction costs were used and three alternative assumptions for surprise currency return are given.

a. Zero expected currency returns. This is equivalent to assuming that currency markets are "efficient": the expected future spot rate equals the current forward rate.

b. Zero compound returns. This is equivalent to a zero long-run return assumption and implies a positive expected arithmetic return equal to half the variance of currency. It is also consistent with Seigel's paradox as it applies to currency. This refers to the fact that the return to a U.S. investor and foreign investor in any given scenario never sum to zero because of the way spot rates are expressed. See Appendix D for an example of this.

EXHIBIT 12
OPTIMAL CURRENCY EXPOSURE AS % OF PORTFOLIO

10% International Equity Allocation

Overall Equity Allocation

		40%		60%		70%	
	Transaction Costs	% Currency	Hedge Ratio	% Currency	Hedge Ratio	% Currency	Hedge Ratio
Zero expected currency return	0%	−16	100	−14	100	−13	100
	.05%	−15	100	−13	100	−12	100
	.10%	−14	100	−12	100	−10	100
	.15%	−13	100	−10	100	−8	100
Zero compound currency return	0%	−2	100	4	60	10	0
	.05%	−1	100	5	50	11	0
	.10%	0	100	6	40	13	0
	.15%	0	100	7	30	15	0
Tactical expectation +2% pa	0%	16	0	40	0	50	0
	.05%	16	0	41	0	51	0
	.10%	16	0	41	0	51	0
	.15%	17	0	42	0	52	0
−2% pa	0%	−51	100	−64	100	−71	100
	.05%	−51	100	−64	100	−70	100
	.10%	−51	100	−65	100	−70	100
	.15%	−51	100	−65	100	−70	100

EXHIBIT 13
OPTIMAL CURRENCY EXPOSURE AS % OF PORTFOLIO

10% International Equity, 10% International Bonds

| | | Overall Equity Allocation | | | | | |
| | | 40% | | 60% | | 70% | |
	Transaction Costs	% Currency	Hedge Ratio	% Currency	Hedge Ratio	% Currency	Hedge Ratio
Zero expected currency return	0%	−17	100	−15	100	−14	100
	.05%	−16	100	−13	100	−12	100
	.10%	−15	100	−12	100	−11	100
	.15%	−14	100	−11	100	−9	100
Zero compound currency return	0%	−3	100	4	80	10	50
	.05%	−2	100	5	75	12	40
	.10%	−1	100	7	66	13	35
	.15%	0	100	8	60	14	30
Tactical expectation +2% pa	0%	16	20	35	0	50	0
	.05%	16	20	36	0	50	0
	.10%	17	15	36	0	50	0
	.15%	17	15	36	0	50	0
−2% pa	0%	−50	100	−70	100	−80	100
	.0	−50	100	−70	100	−80	100
	.1	−50	100	−70	100	−80	100
	.15%	−50	100	−70	100	−80	100

c. Tactical expectation. While it may appear theoretically and empirically that the long run currency return is zero, it has been true that currency returns have often been persistently positive or negative through extended periods of time. In other words, currency can be tactically forecasted and managed.

The results in Exhibits 12 and 13 suggest several conclusions about optimal asset and currency allocations.

1. Optimal currency allocation is rarely if ever equal to optimal international asset allocation. Nor is optimal currency exposure related to the size of international allocations.
2. Therefore, no one optimal hedge ratio exists. The optimal hedge ratio depends on the risk preference of the investor, overall asset allocation and the size of the international asset allocation, the last factor suggesting that hedge ratios should be higher the higher the international allocation.
3. If currency is assumed to have a zero expected arithmetic return, then optimal currency exposure is in fact negative and 100% hedged international investment is appropriate at all levels of transaction costs. This negative exposure exists because of currency's positive covariance with other assets, particularly U.S. bonds.
4. If currency is expected to have a zero compound return, then optimal currency exposure is higher for more aggressive plans (about 10%) and lower for less aggressive plans (0%). For a typical plan, optimal currency exposure may be about 6%, suggesting a 40% hedge ratio for 10% international associations, a 60% hedge ratio for a 20% international allocation.
5. Optimal hedge ratios in an overall plan context are very sensitive to tactical expectations. A plus or minus 2% expectation changes the hedge ratio forecast 0% to 100%. This reinforces the need for tactical currency management.

SUMMARY AND CONCLUSIONS

On the basis of past data and optimization of *ex ante* expectations, we can conclude:

1. Investment in both international equities and fixed income in significant percentages will raise returns and reduce risks for U.S. investors.

2. There are significant benefits to separating long run international asset allocation decisions from long run currency decisions.

3. International investment may be more appropriately defined as being on a fully hedged or partially hedged basis, and the hedge ratio should be identical to the context of overall asset allocation.

APPENDIX A

The appropriate question in evaluating the case for hedged international investment is whether or not the risk of a diversified portfolio using hedged foreign securities is lower than that of a diversified portfolio using unhedged foreign investment.

Assume the diversified portfolio is split $w\%$ domestic, $1 - w\%$ foreign. The risk of a hedged diversified portfolio is given by:

$$\text{VAR}\left(\frac{u}{w} + \frac{a}{1 - w}\right) \tag{1}$$

Risk of unhedged diversification is given by:

$$\text{VAR}\left(\frac{u}{w} + \frac{a + c}{1 - w}\right) \tag{2}$$

Total portfolio risk reduction is given by:

$$\text{VAR}\left(\frac{u}{w} + \frac{a + c}{1 - w}\right) - \text{VAR}\left(\frac{u}{w} + \frac{a}{1 - w}\right) \tag{3}$$

$$= \frac{\text{VAR}(u)}{w^2} + \frac{\text{VAR}(a + c)}{(1 - w)^2} + \frac{2\,\text{COV}(u, a + c)}{w(1 - w)}$$

$$- \left[\frac{\text{VAR}(u)}{w^2} + \frac{\text{VAR}(a)}{(1 - w)^2} + \frac{2\,\text{COV}(u, a)}{w(1 - w)}\right]$$

$$= \frac{1}{(1 - w)^2}\,[\text{VAR}(a) + \text{VAR}(c) + 2\,\text{COV}(a, c)] +$$

$$\frac{2}{w(1 - w)}\,[\text{COV}(u, a) + \text{COV}(u, c)] - \frac{\text{VAR}(a)}{(1 - w)^2} - \frac{2\,\text{COV}(u, a)}{w(1 - w)}$$

$$= \frac{1}{(1 - w)^2}\,[\text{VAR}(c) + 2\,\text{COV}(a, c)] + \frac{2}{w(1 - w)}\,\text{COV}(u, c)$$

$$= \frac{1}{(1 - w)^2}\,\left[S_c^2 + 2R_{a,c}\,S_a\,S_c\right] + \frac{2}{w(1 - w)}\,R_{u,c}\,S_u\,S$$

> 0, unless $R_{c,a}$ or $R_{u,c}$ are significantly negative.

Unless there is a significantly *negative* correlation between currency appreciation and the local or domestic asset, hedged foreign investment reduces total portfolio risk over unhedged investment.

Historically, these correlations have been consistently non-negative. For U.S. and Japanese equities for 1970–1986, the empirical results are as follows, where $w = .5$. from equation (1):

$$= \frac{(.108)^2}{4} + \frac{1}{2} \times .108 \left[.197 \times .08 + .158 \times .04 \right]$$

$$= .016$$

or hedging reduced the standard deviation of the diversified portfolio from 19% to 14.2% per annum.

How negative do these correlations have to be to justify unhedged investment on a risk equivalent basis?

Using the data for 1970–1986 again and assuming the correlation between local asset and currency is zero, then the yen should have a $-.34$ correlation with the U.S. equity market. The equivalent number for bonds is $-.57$.

APPENDIX B

Optimal Currency Exposure

- Markowitz optimization theory suggests that optimal currency exposure, in general is given by:

$$\mu' \, v_c^{-1} \, (\mu' \, v^{-1} \, \mu)^{-1}$$

Where v_c^{-1} is the column of the inverse covariance matrix relating to the covariance of currency with all assets,

μ is the vector of expected returns of all assets, and

v is the covariance matrix of all assets and currency.

- An interesting example of the general solution is where currency is uncorrelated with all assets. In this case optimal currency exposure is given by:

$$\frac{\text{Expected Return to Currency}}{\text{Variance of Currency}} \times \frac{\text{Portfolio Variance}}{\text{Portfolio Expected Return}}$$

APPENDIX C

Transaction Costs for Passive Hedging

- Sources of transactions cost include:
  a. Spot spread on initial hedge,
  b. Forward spread on rollovers,
  c. Cash flow-related transaction cost at rollover, and
  d. Market impact.

- Estimates for normal trading volumes:
  a. 3.5 – 6.0 basis points once off
  b. 10.0 – 15.0 basis points per annum for monthly rollover,
      3.0 – 7.0 basis points per annum for semi-annual rollover
  c. Depends on cash management approach, rollover periodicity, and opportunity costs. Is probably zero if overall net cash flow to investor is positive, or if a cash balance is held and futures are purchased to regain asset exposure.
      Monthly rebalancing with a zero cash balance implies 14 basis points per annum.
      Quarterly rebalancing with a zero cash balance implies 8 basis points per annum.
  d. Should be minimal.

APPENDIX D

Seigels Paradox and Equilibrium Currency Returns

Currency return U.S. investor $\quad = \dfrac{S_t}{S_{t+1}} - 1 = R_t - 1$

Currency return NON-U.S. investor $= \dfrac{S_{t+1}}{S_t} - 1 = \dfrac{1}{R_t} - 1$

Aggregate currency return $\quad\quad = R_t + \dfrac{1}{R_t} - 2$

$$\text{But, } E\left(\frac{1}{R_t}\right) > \frac{1}{E(R_t)}, \text{ iff Var}(R_t) > 0$$

Therefore, aggregate currency return > 0

An example:

	U.S. Currency Return	Foreign Return	Currency Aggregate
Currency Appreciation	+10%	−9.09%	0.91%
Currency Depreciation	−10	11.11	1.11
Expected Return	0	1.01	—

SECTION THREE

Active Asset Allocation —
What Are the Risks?
Should It Work?

CHAPTER 17

Asset Allocation Could Be Dangerous to Your Health: Pitfalls in Across-time Diversification*

PAUL A. SAMUELSON
INSTITUTE PROFESSOR EMERITUS
MASSACHUSETTS INSTITUTE OF TECHNOLOGY

The most recent god that failed has been asset-allocation strategy. This claims to be able to detect at any time whether equity investors are to be well rewarded or poorly rewarded for taking on risks. By giving low weight to equities when they are prone to do poorly and high weight when prone to do well, asset-allocation techniques are seen to be a variant of "timing" methods.

Asset allocators' finest hour came just before the October 1987 world-wide crash when they kept their devotees from losing 23% of portfolio value in a brief time period. Recent success in Wall Street breeds customers; during 1988–1989 many converts of the asset-allocators rue-

---

*This chapter is a lightly altered version of my piece of the same title in *Journal of Portfolio Management*, Spring 1990.

fully missed the high total returns garnered by stocks here and abroad. Whether the 1990s will compensate cannot now be known.

In my 1989 survey reflecting on the surprising efficiencies of speculative markets and the historical successes of indexers, I pointed out how costly it can be to act like a market timer when in fact you lack ex-ante and ex-post ability to discern over- and under-valuation of the market as a whole. See Samuelson [1989].

In particular I mentioned the case of an MIT professor who in one year went back and forth 16 times between all-equities and zero-equities. Since no load was charged for the switches and since no academic fool could be so unlucky as to have been wrong every time in his moves, one, at first careless thought, might suspect that he had done himself little harm: whereas his complacent colleagues stayed all year long half-and-half in stocks and fixed-principal assets, this professor would seem to have achieved his half-and-half mix by *across-time diversification* (so to speak, Monday-Wednesday-Friday in stocks and Tuesday-Thursday-Saturday in bonds).

As argued in Samuelson [1989], this evaluation would indeed be a careless underestimation of the inefficiency of *across-time diversification*. Because the point occasioned some correspondence with practical investors and is in any case important in its own right, I present here a terse demonstration of the costliness in a random-walk model of *across-time diversification* in comparison with optimal *at-each-time diversification* for rational investors who seek to maximize the expected value of terminal utility of wealth and who possess specified constant relative risk aversion.

I must not pretend to prove too much. *If you do have timing ability, flaunt it!* (See Chapter 19.) But in the absence of Napoleonic pretensions to clairvoyance, your rational flauntings are more likely to involve switches of a few percent in your equity fraction around some optimal intermediate level, rather than the swings from 100% in stocks to 10% in stocks that characterized many asset-allocation systems in the last two years.

ASSUMPTIONS

Suppose safe cash has a constant total return. Let a specified portfolio of equities have a total return that is a random variable whose outcomes can be better or worse than cash in each period: posit the null hypothesis that each period's distribution of total returns is independent of any other's (a random walk). Begin with my having the logarithmic utility proposed by Daniel Bernoulli in 1738, $U(W)=\log W$, where W is terminal wealth after T periods from now.

It is well-known, as in Merton [1969] or Samuelson [1969], that if I am a rational maximizer of such declared expected utility, I shall do best *if I myopically put the same w_t fraction of my portfolio into equities during every period.* For every w_0,

$$w_T^* = w_{T-1}^* = \ldots = w_1^* \tag{1}$$

For expositional simplicity, let $w_t^* = \dfrac{1}{2}$.

The arithmetic mean, or expected value of the dollar outcomes of the portfolio that is 100% in stocks must be greater than safe-cash's outcome of $1+r$ — else I'd hold none of that risky equity portfolio. What interests Bernoulli, however, is its geometric mean (G.M.). This can be less than or greater than $1+r_0$. Call it Case 1 when G.M. of stocks alone = $1+r_1$ >$1+ r_0$, and Case 2 when $1+r_1 < 1+r_0$. Write $1+r_{1\,2}$ for the G.M. of the 50–50 portfolio.

Consider twins: A always puts 50–50 into stocks and cash; B, half the time, and with no serendipity with respect to "timing," puts 100% into stocks and the other half puts all into cash.

It is important to realize that the geometric mean of the 50–50 portfolio is greater than "the greater of the G.M. of cash or the G.M. of pure-stocks." Why? Because that is what is meant when we say that I as a Bernoulli utilitarian will maximize $E\{\log W\}$ by selecting as my fractional equity share, w_t^*,

$$0 < w_t^* = \frac{1}{2} < 1 \tag{2}$$

Then, recognizing that the log of the G.M. is the $E\{\log W\}$, we write

G.M. of cash < G.M. of 50–50 > G.M. of pure stocks   (3)

This can be rewritten as

$$1 + r_0 < 1 + r_{1/2} > 1 + r_1 \tag{3a}$$

$$1 + r_{1/2} > 1 + \text{Max}(r_0, r_1) > 1 + \frac{1}{2}(r_0 + r_1) \tag{3b}$$

We can now describe how badly or well people will fare pursuing different strategies, assuming each starts out with the same initial wealth. The *certainty equivalent* for an investor in cash only will grow like

$$W_0 (1 + r_0)^t, t = 1,2,...,T \tag{4}$$

Perhaps think of this as 3%, with $1 + r_0 = 1.03$.

The *certainty equivalent* for a Bernoulli who rashly holds only stocks will grow like

$$W_0 (1 + r_1)^t, t = 1,2,...,T \tag{5}$$

This certainty equivalent is the amount of safe wealth that gives him as much expected utility as his lucrative-but-risky stocks-only portfolio would give. Perhaps set it at 4%, or 1.04.

The *certainty equivalent* for the rational non-timer grows better than either of the above, growing like

$$W_0 (1 + r_{1/2})^t > W_0 \text{Max}[1 + r_0, 1 + r_1]^t \tag{6}$$

The left side of (6) is the growing amount of safe wealth that just matches his expected utility from holding the optimal proportion of stocks. For a numerical example suppose it to be 6%, with $1 + r_{1/2} = 1.06$.

The delusioned timer who embraces across-time diversification on a 50–50 basis has a certainty equivalent that grows like

$$W_0 [(1 + r_0)(1 + r_1)]^{1/2 \, t} < W_0 (1 + r_{1/2})^t \tag{7}$$

Since the G.M. of 1.03 and 1.04 is 1.035, the left-hand side grows only like $(1.035)^t$: its shortfall from $(1.06)^t$ is the penalty inherent in across-time diversification.

You may wonder whether I have stacked the deck against across-time diversification? After all, my w_t^* of $\frac{1}{2}$ picked $\frac{1}{2}$ because it was truly the best fraction to pick. Why stick the across-time diversifier with this *same* 50–50 fraction? Surely, let him pick the *best fraction of the time* to be solely in stocks: call it v^*, with $1-v^*$ being the fraction of time to be solely in cash:

$$v^* \underset{<}{\overset{>}{=}} w_t^* = \frac{1}{2}$$

When Robert Merton and I each analyzed how to select optimal v^*, we both were surprised to discover the solution is a Bang-Bang one. Either v^* is 0 or 1 depending upon whether $1+r_0 > 1+r_1$ or $1+r_1 > 1+r_0$! (In our numerical example, $1.04 > 1.03$ and $v^* = 1$.)

In a white-noise process of a random walk, it is never mandatory to diversify *across* time. Your best *across-time* diversification is to stay always in the pure strategy that is maximal in *its* E{log W}! If that seems like folly, so much the worse for trying to time in a random-walk model.

Now, it can be verified that you still stand to average out worse even with your best v^*, since (6) showed that your certainty equivalent now grows like

$$W_0 \left[\text{Max}[1 + r_0, 1 + r_1]\right]^t < W_0 (1 + r_{1/2})^t \quad \text{QED} \tag{8}$$

In our example, $W_0(1.04)^t < W_0(1.06)^t$. Thus, even in the best Bang-Bang solution you are losing one-third of your obtainable 6% certainty equivalent!

GENERALIZATIONS

Everything said here about Bernoulli logarithmic utility holds qualitatively when we replace log W by $W^{1/2}$ or by $-W^{-1}$, or $-W^{-2}$,..., or W^{γ}/γ with $0 \neq \gamma < 1$. Thus, for $-W^{-1}$ we speak of the *harmonic mean* instead of the *geometric mean* — and likewise for the properly defined γ *mean*. A brief Mathematical Appendix gives details.

In all cases you will pay dearly in expected utility terms for a fancied (but false) ability to time. It is not merely that you fail to garner the better *mean* return, but as well you pay the bitter price of losing risk-reducing diversification. It is a corollary that a system that has modest true ability to "time" will bring you less final net benefit to the degree that it involves some bad side effects of *across-time* diversification.

CAVEATS

Suppose you correctly recognize that what you face is *not* a white-noise process but rather a red-noise process showing "mean reversion" and detectable negative autocorrelation à la Summers-Poterba [1988] or Fama-French [1988]. Then, as described in the Tobin-*fest* paper of Samuelson [1991], your w_{t+1}^* will be optimally lower when your w_t^* is optimally higher. For the w_t^*'s to oscillate out of the (.40, .60) interval around $\frac{1}{2}$, would presuppose a Markov process that is very red indeed.

The danger in the dividend-discount models that the asset-allocator tends to appeal to is that *their very appearance of scientific objectivity seductively leads to the hubris of believing in the wisdom of vast swings in equity holdings.*

Even a modest ability on the part of a would-be timer to recognize occasions when the mean returns of stocks are high and when they are low can be rationally indulged *on a small scale* despite the present chapter's strictures concerning induced riskiness-costs. Why? Because any w_t near to the optimal w_t^* is almost as good as w_t^*, for the reason that all smooth maxima are virtually horizontal curves with a shortfall from the maximum that has the extreme smallness associated with the square of $(w_t - w_t^*)$. When this evil is small, it is overweighed by any true ability to discern an improvement in the mean of equities, an ability that brings you benefit that varies with the first power of $(w_t - w_t^*)$. The logic of this paragraph, alas, cannot justify the broad swings in the equity fraction that so many asset-allocation systems recommend. When the asset allocators go back to the drawing boards, they can benefit from this paragraph's analysis by putting the strong burden of proof against each further recommended change in $w_t - w_t^*$. (Remark: Sometimes practical men say that they don't know their own $U(W)$ function. I agree that, if you don't know where you want to go, it becomes rather pointless to discuss how best to go there. However, not knowing whether my $U(W)$ is $-1/W$ or $-1/W^2$ cannot justify my acting as if I were indifferent to risk. Wherever you are between the two cases of the previous sentence, my warnings apply.)

After the surgeon general has warned that cigarettes can be dangerous to your health, honesty compels few qualifications since there are less pyrrhic ways of avoiding overweight. The case against timing is less conclusive in principle since the strong evidence in favor of *micro*efficiency of security markets lacks power as a proof of the *macro*efficiency of general stock levels.

Thus, Chapter 19 does deduce a limited efficacy for timers in a Markov process where the probability of a rise in general equity prices in the period ahead is weakly reduced by a rise in last period's prices — the "red noise" departure from white noise probabilities. It similarly deduces a role for timing in a fundamentalist's model involving an invariant probability distribution for the S&P around a postulated exogenous geometric trend.

All the more important becomes the present chapter's warning against the pitfalls intrinsic to *across-time diversification.* The optimal variations in equity fractions that I deduced for the prudent timer were moderate. Why?

Consider the case when I operate without fire insurance on my house. Most times I notice no cause for regret. But actually the clock of risk is always running against me. Always? Yes, even though on rainy days with lightning-free skies, and when the children and help are away on vacation, my amount of fire insurance might rationally be lightened. Once I have the hubris to program for each day a variable coverage of fire insurance, human nature is all too likely to dull my recognition of the ominous clock of risk that is always running against the uninsured in some degree. That week when the timer garners a capital gain by undiversifying his portfolio, does he realize that he should debit, against his gain in mean, the insidious rise in riskiness that was inseparably involved?

The would-be timer needs the message of this chapter more than agnostics do. For it will keep to the forefront of his benefit-cost calculus the increasing riskiness inherent in *sizeable across-time departures from diversification* — for what I have called euphemistically *across-time di-*

versification is more accurately to be dubbed *across-time deviations from diversification.* The easier part of being a timer is judiciously selling before peaks. The harder part is being sure to buy back before the market has already reachieved its earlier peak.

REFERENCES

Fama, E.F. and K.R. French, "Permanent and Temporary Components of Stock Prices," *Journal of Political Economy* 96, 1988, pp. 246–73.

Merton, R.C., "Lifetime Portfolio Selection under Uncertainty: The Continuous-Time Case." *Rev. Econ. Statist.,* 51(3), August 1969, pp. 247–57.

Poterba, J.M. and L.H. Summers, "Mean Reversion in Stock Returns: Evidence and Implications," *Journal of Financial Economics* 22, 1988, pp. 27–59.

Samuelson, P.A., "The Judgment of Economic Science on Rational Portfolio Management: Indexing, Timing, and Long-Horizon Effects," *Journal of Portfolio Management,* Fall 1989, pp. 4–12.

_____ "Longrun Risk Tolerance When Equity Returns Are Mean Regressing: Pseudoparadoxes and Vindication of 'Business Man's Risk,'" *Macroeconomics, Finance and Economic Policy: Essays in Honor of James Tobin,* W. Brainard, W. Nordhaus and H. Watts (eds.) Cambridge, MA: MIT Press, 1991.

_____ "Longrun Risk Tolerance in a Fundamentalist Model of Equities," MIT Working Paper, June 1988.

MATHEMATICAL APPENDIX

1. Cash is assumed to have a safe total return of r_0 in each period. Each dollar invested in the common stock has a total return in each period that is the random variable $X_t - 1$, where ($\ldots, X_{t-1}$, $X_t, X_{t+1}, \ldots$) are identically and independently distributed:

$$\text{Prob}[X_t \leq x] = P(x); P(x) \equiv 0, x < 0 \tag{A1}$$

$$E[X_t] > 1 + r_0 = R \tag{A2}$$

$$\text{Var}[X_t] > 0, P(R-) > 0 \tag{A3}$$

2. One-period maximization involves

$$\text{Max}_w E\{U[W_0(1-w)R + W_0wX_1]\}$$

$$= E\{U[W_0(1-w^*)R + W_0w^*X_1]\} \tag{A4}$$

$$= \bar{e}(w^*)$$

where w^* is the unique root for w of

$$0 = E\{U'[W_0(1-w)R + W_0wX_1]W_0[X_1 - R]\} \tag{A5}$$

For $1 > \gamma \neq 0$ and $U(W) = W^\gamma/\gamma$, we write w^* as w_γ. For $U(W) = \log W$, we write w^* as w_0 and can verify that $w_\gamma \to w_0$ as $\gamma \to 0$. Note that as γ falls from 1, w_γ declines, reaching 0 as $\gamma \to -\infty$. For $\gamma \leq 0$ and $P(0) > 0$, $w_\gamma < 1$.

For $1 > \gamma \neq 0$, the *certainty equivalent* that is as good as having $\bar{e}(w)$ can be written as

$$W_0(1 + r_w[\gamma]) = \gamma[\bar{e}(w)^{1/\gamma}] \tag{A6}$$

$$W_0(1 + r_0) < W_0[1 + r_{w\gamma}[\gamma]] > W_0(1 + r_1) \tag{A7}$$

3. For time-independent processes,

$$E[Z_1 \ldots Z_T] = E[Z_1] \ldots E[Z_T] \qquad (A8)$$

Therefore, for $T \geq 2$ and $\gamma \neq 0$, our multi-period maximization can be shown to reduce to myopic behavior, with

$$(W_0^\gamma/\gamma) \quad \underset{w_1 \ldots w_T}{\text{Max}} \quad E\left\{ \prod_1^T [R + w_t X_t - w_t R]^\gamma \right\}$$

$$= (W_0^\gamma/\gamma)[E\{[R + w_\gamma X - w_\gamma R]^\gamma\}]^T = \bar{e}(w*)^T \qquad (A9)$$

$$> (W_0^\gamma/\gamma)(\text{Max}[R^\gamma, E\{X^\gamma\}])^T \qquad (A10)$$

The optimizing *certainty equivalent* will grow like

$$W_0\{1 + r_{w\gamma}[\gamma]\}^t, t = 1, 2, 3, \ldots, T \qquad (A11)$$

4. The maximization problem for the *across-time* diversifier becomes bang-bang, taking the following form:

For $\gamma \neq 0$ and $0 \leq v \leq 1$,

$$(W_0^\gamma/\gamma) \underset{v}{\text{Max}}[(R^{\gamma T})^{(1-v)}(E\{X^\gamma\}T)^v]$$

$$= (W_0^\gamma/\gamma)[\text{Max}(R^\gamma, E\{X^\gamma\})]^T \qquad (A12)$$

From the inequalities of (A7) and (A10), the *across-time diversifier* clearly does worse than the non-timer, with *certainty equivalent* of

$$W_0[\text{Max}[1 + r_0, 1 + r_1]]^T < W_0\{1 + r_{w\gamma}[\gamma]\}^T \qquad (A13)$$

For the Bernoulli case, where $\gamma \rightarrow 0$, (A9) and (A12) are replaced by

$$\log W_0 + TE\{\log[R + w_0X - w_0R]\}$$
$$> \log W_0 + T \, \text{Max}[\log R, E\{\log X\}] \qquad (A14)$$

5. Asset allocators have the possibility of being helpful when we replace probabilistic *independence* (or the weaker *martingale* process) by *red-noise mean reversion* or *negative* autocorrelation. Now (A1) is replaced by

$$\text{Prob}\{(p_{t+1} - p_t)/p_t \leq x \mid p_t = y\} = P(x \mid y) \qquad (A15)$$

$$\partial P(x \mid y)\partial y > 0, \ (\partial / \partial y)E\{(p_{t+1} - p_t)/p_t \mid p_t = y\} < 0 \qquad (A16)$$

Somehow the asset allocators are supposed to have knowledge from dividend discounting models of (A16)'s inequalities that other investors do not have or do not believe in. What evidence would convert us to that view? Finally, even if (A16)'s inequalities have the indicated signs, unless their quantitative magnitudes are believed to be substantial, only modest variations of w_t^* around w_γ would be justifiable.

CHAPTER 18

Does Tactical Asset Allocation Work?

ROGER G. CLARKE
CHIEF INVESTMENT OFFICER
TSA CAPITAL MANAGEMENT

MEIR STATMAN
PROFESSOR AND CHAIRMAN
DEPARTMENT OF FINANCE
SANTA CLARA UNIVERSITY

INTRODUCTION

The underlying premise of tactical asset allocation is that there are reliable leading indicators to security returns. If so, knowledge of today's level of the leading indicators can be used to forecast tomorrow's security returns. But are there reliable leading indicators of security returns? Can the leading indicators be put to use in tactical asset allocation? What are the effects of transactions costs? And what are the pitfalls of overconfidence? We will try to answer these questions.

Consider first the concept of leading indicators in its familiar setting, the series of leading indicators of economic activity compiled by the

Department of Commerce. A recent article by Paul Duke in *The Wall Street Journal* noted that the index of leading indicators rose 0.8% in May of 1991 following increases in April and March.[1] "It looks as though the economy probably hit bottom in April and started to grow in May," said Michael Penzer, an economist with the Bank of America in San Francisco..."Four months of increases seem to pretty much confirm that we are seeing a recovery," he said. "From here, it's onward and upward."

The money supply is one of the leading indicators of economic activity in the Department of Commerce Index, but is it also a leading indicator to stock prices? Milton Friedman and Anna Schwartz (1963) found that in the period from 1867 to 1960 increases in the growth rate of money supply preceded expansions in economic activity by about 8 months while declines in the growth rate of money supply preceded contractions in economic activity by about 20 months. Money supply can be a leading indicator to economic activity because economic activity cannot change instantaneously in reaction to changes in monetary policy. It takes considerable time to plan and execute capital investment programs, and it takes considerable time to scale down capital investment programs. But there is no equivalent argument for changes in security prices in reaction to changes in money supply, since security prices can change instantaneously. Indeed, an index of stock prices is one of the leading indicators of economic activity in the Department of Commerce series.

The possibility of instantaneous changes in security prices in response to new information implies that in an efficient market there should be no leading indicators to security prices. Still, market efficiency is a hypothesis, not an established fact, and researchers have tested whether changes in money supply serve as a leading indicator to stock prices. Early studies by Sprinkel (1964) and Keran (1971) supported the hypothesis that changes in money supply can be used to forecast stock prices. However, more recent studies by Cooper (1974) and Rozeff (1974, 1975) indicated that changes in stock prices lead changes in money supply and that changes in money supply *cannot* be used to forecast changes in stock prices.

The findings of Cooper and Rozeff are, of course, consistent with the semi-strong version of the market efficiency hypothesis. The logic behind the semi-strong hypothesis is that the public availability of leading indicators of security prices draws investors who eliminate the usefulness

---

[1]"Leading indicators of the economy advance in May," *The Wall Street Journal*, July 1, 1991.

of the indicators as they capitalize on the indicators through trading. The logic of efficient markets is the logic of learning. Investors might not recognize the value of a leading indicator for a while, but in time at least some investors learn the value of a leading indicator, use it, and eliminate its value through their use.

But what if investors fail to learn? And what if investors who do learn are unable to eliminate the effects on security prices of investors who fail to learn? Psychologists have identified several classes of cognitive errors and noted that they are common and resistant to learning. (For a collection of some of the most important work see Kahneman, Slovic and Tversky (1982).) Shefrin and Statman (1990) focused on two broad classes of cognitive errors, base rate underweighting and probability mismapping, and showed the particular biases that might be reflected in security prices when investors commit these errors.

Investors who underweight base rates assign too much weight to recent observations and too little weight to more distant ones. Solt and Statman (1988) provided an example of base rate underweighting. They showed that writers of investment advisory newsletters tend to become more optimistic about the prospects of the stock market following in-creases in stock prices and more pessimistic after decreases. The behavior of writers of investment newsletters is consistent with a pattern where recent returns receive too much weight and therefore recent trends are extrapolated. Solt and Statman also showed that there is no relationship between forecasts in investment newsletters and subsequent changes in stock prices. The persistent use of investment newsletters in face of the evidence that they do not work is one of the many pieces of evidence suggesting that cognitive errors in financial markets are common and resistant to learning.

A recent study of Stumpp and Scott (1991) found that changes in real money supply are not useful as a leading indicator of stock prices. Stumpp and Scott wondered why investment strategists continue to use money supply as a leading indicator to stock prices in light of its poor track record and suggested that "One explanation, see Solt and Statman (1988), is that belief in the indicator has to do with errors in cognition" (P. 40).

The studies by Solt, Statman, Stumpp and Scott showed that some investors fail to learn that the leading indicators they rely on are false. *But that does not imply that there are no good leading indicators.* Many examples of reliable leading indicators exist. Ferson and Harvey (1991) found that dividend yield, the differential between the yields of invest-

ment grade and junk bonds and the differential between yields of one-
and three-month Treasury Bills are reliable leading indicators of stock
and bond prices. Engel and Hamilton (1990) found evidence of nonlinear
serial dependence in changes of exchange rates. This implies that past
changes in exchange rates can be used to forecast future changes. Similarly, Chance (1990) reported that the ratio of the volume of put options
to calls could be used to forecast stock prices.

Reliable leading indicators of security returns exist but they are far
from perfect. Ferson and Harvey noted that the adjusted R^2 of a regression of realized returns on the leading indicators in their study exceeded
4% in each of 25 portfolios and exceeded 10% in 16 of the portfolios.
Of course, 10% is a long way from 100%. How can tactical asset allocators use imperfect indicators? When should tactical asset allocation
switch from stocks to cash? This is the topic of the next section.

The Value of Imperfect Leading Indicators

Tactical asset allocators in our example choose cash (e.g., Treasury bills)
or stocks (e.g., the S&P 500), aiming to invest in the one with the highest
return.[2]

To simplify, we assume that a leading indicator, I_t, is available today
(time t), containing information about stock returns in the coming period,
S_{t+1}. We can write the relationship between the leading indicator and
future stock returns as:

$$S_{t+1} = \overline{S} + \beta I_t + e_{t+1} \tag{1}$$

where:

S_{t+1} = the return on stocks in the coming period, t+1

I_t = the value of the leading indicator at time t,

e_{t+1} = the residual or error term,

$\overline{S}$ = the long-run mean return on stocks, and

β = the sensitivity of stock returns to changes in the leading
          indicator

We assume that the return on cash, C, is 7.0% and the long-run
expected return on stocks, $\overline{S}$, is 15.5%, implying a risk premium of

---

[2]The model and the discussion related to it are taken from Clarke, FitzGerald, Berent and
Statman (1989).

8.5%.[3] We use 20.5% as the standard deviation of the return on stocks. For simplicity, we normalize the leading indicator so that its mean is zero and its standard deviation is one. We also assume that the leading indicator, stock returns and the error term are normally distributed.[4]

How much information about future stock returns does the leading indicator contain? The amount of information is measured by the correlation between the leading indicator at time t and the return on stocks over the following period $t + 1$. The expected return on stocks for a given level of the leading indicator can be written as:

$$\text{Expected } (S_{t+1} \mid \text{given } I_t) = \overline{S} + \beta I_t = \overline{S} + \frac{\rho \sigma_s}{\sigma_I} I_t \tag{2}$$

where:

ρ = the correlation coefficient between I_t and stock returns in period $t + 1$,

σ_s = the standard deviation of stock returns (σ_s = 20.5), and

σ_I = the standard deviation of the leading indicator (σ_I = 1.0).

A correlation coefficient of zero implies that the leading indicator contains no information about future stock returns. In that case, the expected stock return is always at its mean of 15.5%, regardless of the level of the leading indicator. This is evident from Equation (2):

$$\text{Expected } (S_{t+1} \mid \text{given } I_t) = 15.5 + \frac{0.0 \times 20.5}{1.0} I_t$$

$$= 15.5$$

The case where the leading indicator contains no information is an important case. Note that the expected return on stocks where the leading indicator contains no information is its mean, 15.5%. The 15.5% figure is, of course, higher than the 7.0% expected return on cash so rational tactical asset allocators with no information never switch to cash. Early

---

[3]The risk premium and standard deviation figures were adopted from *Stocks, Bonds, Bills and Inflation* yearbooks from Ibbotson Associates, Chicago.

[4]The assumption of normality is not critical for the results. Other distributional assumptions could be used, but normality puts the computations into a familiar framework.

studies by Sharpe (1975), Jeffrey (1984) and Chua and Woodward (1986) that cast doubt on the usefulness of tactical asset allocation were constructed on the implicit assumption that tactical asset allocators without information switch from stocks to cash. Thus, while they established the case against asset allocators who follow suboptimal rules, they did not establish a case against asset allocators using rational, optimal rules.

Consider now the case where the leading indicator contains some, but not perfect, information about future stock returns. This is the case, for example, when the correlation between the leading indicator and future stock returns is 0.3, (and the R^2 is 0.09). Equation (2) shows that the expected stock return increases by 6.15% as the leading indicator increases by one:

$$\text{Expected } (S_{t+1} \mid \text{given } I_t) = 15.5 + \frac{0.3 \times 20.5}{1.0} I_t$$
$$= 15.5 + 6.15\, I_t,$$

Asset allocators choose stocks when the expected stock return exceeds the cash return. When the correlation is 0.3, expected stock returns exceed cash returns when the leading indicator exceeds a normalized level of –1.38. Asset allocators would therefore choose stocks when the leading indicator exceeds –1.38 and cash when the leading indicator falls below that level:

$$\text{Expected } (S_{t+1} \mid \text{given } I_t) \geq c$$
$$15.5 + \frac{0.3 \times 20.5}{1.0} I_t \geq 7.0$$
$$I_t \geq -1.38$$

Figure A illustrates the relationship between conditional expected stock returns and the leading indicator for correlations of 0.3 and 0.5. Note that imperfect information makes rational tactical asset allocators cautious as they consider a switch from stocks to cash. Asset allocators wait until the leading indicator drops to –0.83 before switching from stocks into cash when the correlation is 0.5 but when information is

FIGURE A
EXPECTED STOCK RETURNS CONDITIONAL ON THE LEADING
INDICATOR WHERE THE CORRELATIONS BETWEEN THE
LEADING INDICATOR AND STOCK RETURNS ARE 0.3 AND 0.5.

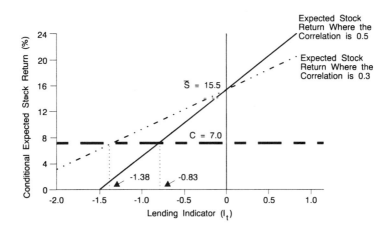

worse, at a correlation coefficient of 0.3, asset allocators wait until the leading indicator drops to −1.38 before switching.

The Risk and Returns of Asset Allocation

Tactical asset allocators who have information switch from stocks to cash when the expected return on cash exceeds that of stocks. Of course, the information is imperfect and some switches will result in losses. How does the use of imperfect information affect the risk and return of the portfolios of tactical asset allocators?

We can investigate the risk and return of tactical asset allocators' portfolios through simulation. Tactical asset allocators in our example follow a rule whereby all funds are invested in stocks if the expected stock return, given the leading indicator, exceeds the cash return; otherwise, all funds are invested in cash.

Consider first the case where the correlation between the leading indicator and stock returns is 0.3. If the leading indicator is 0.1, should an asset allocator choose stocks or cash? The expected return on stocks, given a leading indicator of 0.1, is:

$$\text{Expected } (S_{t+1} \mid \text{given } I_t = 0.1) = 15.5 + \frac{0.3 \times 20.5 \times 0.1}{1.0}$$

$$= 16.1$$

The conditional expected return on stocks is 16.1% which is higher than the 7.0% cash return, so stocks are chosen. Of course, the actual stock return is not likely to be identical to the expected return. The standard deviation of conditional stock returns when the correlation co-efficient is 0.3 is:[5]

$$\sigma_e = \sigma_s \sqrt{1 - \rho^2}$$
$$= 20.5 \sqrt{1 - 0.3^2}$$
$$= 19.6$$

We proceed in the simulation by picking an actual stock return, given the leading indicator, from a normal distribution with a mean of 16.1% and a standard deviation of 19.6%. For example, imagine that the actual stock return picked is 14%.

In summary, the simulation proceeds in three stages. The first stage involves the generation of a value of the leading indicator from its specified distribution. The second stage involves the calculation of an

---

[5]We know from Equation (1) that the variance of stock returns is related to the variance of I_t and the variance of the residual by:

$$\sigma_s^2 = \beta^2 \sigma_I^2 + \sigma_e^2$$

$$= \rho^2 \sigma_s^2 + \sigma_e^2$$

$$\sigma_e^2 = (1 - \rho^2) \sigma_s^2$$

The variance of the residual must decline as the correlation between stock returns and I_t, increases so that the variance of stock returns remains constant. Note that the residual variance (or "noise") declines as information (or correlation) increases.

expected return on stocks conditional on the leading indicator. Stocks are chosen if the conditional return on stocks exceeds the return on cash; otherwise cash is chosen. If cash is chosen, the process ends and the asset allocator receives the cash return. However, if stocks are chosen, the third stage involves the generation of an actual stock return from a distribution with the conditional expected stock return and standard deviation.

We repeated the three-stage process 40,000 times, so that we have 40,000 monthly returns for the asset allocator's portfolio. The mean annualized return on the portfolio, when the correlation coefficient is 0.3 is 21.4%, a 5.9% "value added" over the 15.5% mean return on stocks. Exhibit 1 reveals that increases in information, or correlation, lead to an increase in the mean return of the asset allocator's portfolio. The mean portfolio return in our example reaches 46.8% when the correlation is a perfect 1.0.[6]

EXHIBIT 1
RISK AND RETURN OF AN ASSET ALLOCATOR'S PORTFOLIO
(SWITCHING ALLOWED ONCE A MONTH)

(1)	(2)	(3) = (2)–15.5	(4)	(5) = (2)/(4)	(6)
Correlation Between the Leading Indicators & Stock Returns	Mean Annual Return of Asset Allocator's Portfolio	Value Added by Asset Allocator, Relative to Buy- and Hold-Stock Portfolio	Standard Deviation of Annual Return on Asset Allocator's Portfolio	Ratio of Mean to Standard Deviation	Percentage of Periods When Asset Allocator's Portfolio is Invested in Stocks
0.0	15.5	0.0	20.5	0.76	100.0
0.1	16.0	0.5	19.4	0.82	86.1
0.2	18.5	3.0	17.9	1.03	70.8
0.3	21.4	5.9	17.2	1.24	64.9
0.4	24.8	9.3	16.6	1.49	60.6
0.5	28.5	13.0	16.3	1.75	58.6
0.6	31.7	16.2	15.8	2.00	56.8
0.7	34.9	19.4	15.6	2.24	56.1
0.8	38.7	23.2	15.2	2.55	55.7
0.9	42.8	27.3	14.8	2.89	54.4
1.0	46.8	31.3	14.3	3.27	54.2

[6]The value of perfect information has been compared to the value of a put option on the stock portfolio by Merton (1981). In a sense the goal of the asset allocator is to create the same pattern of returns but pay as little as possible for the put option.

The impact of using information by tactical asset allocators extends beyond increases in expected returns. Tactical asset allocation can also reduce risk, as reflected both in a lower variance and in a positive skewness in the distribution of returns. The lower variation implies that asset allocation reduces the deviations of returns from their mean. The positive skewness implies that large deviations, when they occur, are likely to be "good." In other words, large deviations are more likely to come because returns are higher than the mean than because returns are lower than the mean. An asset allocator is likely to hold stocks when stocks increase sharply and hold cash when stocks decline sharply.

Consider the case where the correlation is 0.3 and monthly switching is allowed. The expected return on the asset allocator's portfolio is 21.4%, 5.9 percentage points higher than the 15.5% return on stocks. Moreover, the standard deviation of the returns on the asset allocator's portfolio is 17.2%, 3.3 percentage points lower than the standard deviation of the stock returns. Finally, while the return distribution of a stock portfolio is symmetric, the returns on the asset allocator's portfolio are skewed to the right, as Figure B illustrates.[7]

What can we say, then, about the effectiveness of tactical asset allocation? We know that the effectiveness of asset allocation increases with the level of information available to a asset allocator. That, by itself, is not surprising. More surprising is the fact that relatively modest amounts of information add considerable value. A 0.3 correlation (R^2 of 0.09) brings an expected annual return that is 5.9 percentage points higher than the expected return available to one who buys and holds stocks when monthly changes in the portfolio are allowed.

The Effect of Transaction Costs

So far we have assumed that asset allocators can switch from stocks to cash and back without incurring transaction costs. How does the analysis change once transaction costs are recognized?

We estimated the expected return and standard deviation of an asset allocators' portfolio, assuming two levels of transaction costs. The first

---

[7]The single decision rule used here always places the asset allocator in stock or cash. Other decision values could also be used which gradually draw the investor into cash as information becomes more negative on stock returns. For example, using a mean/variance decision framework produces returns with a slightly different mean and variance but displays the same general characteristics of larger return and smaller variance than the buy and hold strategy.

FIGURE B
THE DISTRIBUTION OF RETURNS ON AN ASSET ALLOCATOR'S
PORTFOLIO WHERE THE CORRELATIONS BETWEEN A LEADING
INDICATOR AND STOCK RETURNS ARE 0.0 AND 0.3.

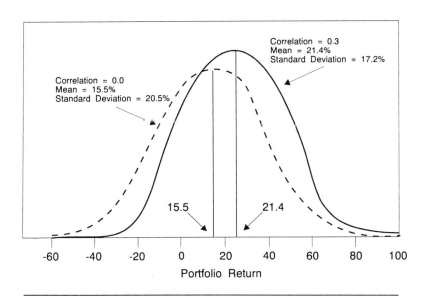

level, 0.1% per one-way transaction represents the range of transaction costs when futures contracts are used to switch from one asset to another. The second level, 1.0%, represents the range of transaction costs when physical assets are used. A switch from cash to stocks occurs only if the conditional expected return on stocks exceeds that of cash by an amount that is at least equal to the one-way transaction cost. A similar criterion applies to switches from stocks to cash. Exhibit 2 compares these expected returns with those obtained without transaction costs.

Consider again the case of a 0.3 correlation coefficient. Recall that value added by asset allocation with monthly revisions and without transaction costs is 5.9%. The 0.1% transaction cost reduces the value added to 5.5%. However, the 1.0% transaction cost reduces the value added considerably, from 5.9 to 1.2%.

EXHIBIT 2
EFFECT OF TRANSACTION COSTS ON THE VALUE ADDED BY AN ASSET ALLOCATOR (MONTHLY SWITCHING)

Correlation Between the Leading Indicator and Stock Returns	Value Added by an Asset Allocator When Transaction Costs Are		
	0.0%	0.1%	1.0%
0.0	0.0	0.0	0.0
0.1	0.5	0.2	0.0
0.2	3.0	2.4	0.1
0.3	5.9	5.5	1.2
0.4	9.3	8.8	3.4
0.5	13.0	11.9	6.4
0.6	16.2	15.6	9.5
0.7	19.4	19.2	12.9
0.8	23.2	22.6	16.8
0.9	27.3	26.4	20.0
1.0	31.3	30.7	23.4

The Dangers of Overestimating the Available Amount of Information

Construction of tactical asset allocation models involves the possibility that some variables are there because their "noise" is mistaken for information. In other words, it is possible that some variables that contain no information about future security returns are included because, by chance, they have had a high correlation with future security returns during the time period used in the construction of the model. Wise tactical asset allocators attempt to mitigate against this danger by choosing only variables that are based on a rationale extending beyond high correlations. Still, it is likely that precautions are insufficient, and asset allocators should always be aware that the true amount of information in their models is probably not as high as the historical R^2 indicates.

Imagine that the true correlation between the leading indicator and subsequent stock returns is 0.3, but that an asset allocator concludes, erroneously, that the correlation is higher, say, 0.5. An asset allocator who makes no allowance for overestimation makes suboptimal decisions. Specifically, he sometimes chooses to invest in cash when an investment in stocks is the optimal choice.

The nature of the error can be illustrated by revisiting Figure A. An asset allocator estimates the expected return on stocks based on the line represented by a correlation of 0.5, while the true expected return is the line represented by a correlation of 0.3. The error is costless when the leading indicator exceeds −0.83, because, in that case, stocks are the optimal choice for either correlation. Similarly, the error is costless when the leading indicator falls below −1.38, because in that case cash is the optimal choice for either correlation. However, when the leading indicator is between −1.38 and −0.83, the optimal choice is stocks, and the asset allocator errs by choosing cash.

How costly is the error that results from overestimating correlations? Exhibit 3 provides several cases. For example, the value added by an asset allocator who estimates a 0.3 correlation correctly is 5.5%, assuming a one-way transaction cost of 0.1% and monthly switching. The value added drops slightly to 5.4% when the 0.3 true correlation is overestimated as 0.5. The overestimation of the amount of information available to an asset allocator is especially expensive when transaction costs are high. For example, an asset allocator who has no information, but who overestimates the information and assumes that the correlation is 0.5, can expect to lose 4.0% per year when the one-way transaction cost is 0.1% and over 8.0% per year when the one-way transaction cost is 1.0%.

Performance of Tactical Asset Allocators

Simulations suggest that modest amounts of information in leading indicators can lead to useful tactical asset allocation and empirical evidence suggests that leading indicators exist. But has tactical asset allocation worked in practice? Weigel (1990, 1991) studied the real time performance of nine tactical asset allocators. He found that the returns of the

EXHIBIT 3
EFFECT OF MISESTIMATION OF CORRELATION ON VALUE ADDED BY AN ASSET ALLOCATOR (MONTHLY SWITCHING; 0.1% TRANSACTION COST)

True Correlation	*Value Added When Estimated Correlation Is:*					
	0.0	*0.1*	*0.2*	*0.3*	*0.4*	*0.5*
0.0	0.0	−1.3	−3.1	−3.8	−4.7	−4.0
0.1	0.0	0.2	0.5	−1.1	−0.8	−1.2
0.2	0.0	1.8	2.4	2.2	2.0	2.2
0.3	0.0	3.3	5.3	5.5	5.7	5.4
0.4	0.0	4.9	8.1	8.4	8.8	8.2

EXHIBIT 4
QUARTERLY EXCESS RETURNS COMPARED TO MANAGERS
BENCHMARK PORTFOLIOS

Manager	Excess Returns
3	.33
4	.50
6	.07
7	−.01
10	.24
11	.21
13	−,19
14	.48
15	.01
Average	.18

majority of asset allocators exhibited the positive skewness associated with successful tactical asset allocation and that nearly all achieved returns higher than those of their stated benchmark portfolio. However, caution should be exercised in the interpretation of Weigel's results since the longest of the series covers the period from 1980 to 1989.

CONCLUSION

Asset allocation models look very much like econometric models of the economy, but that look is deceiving. Models of the economy are designed to reveal the true relationships between variables that describe the state of the economy, such as the GNP, money supply and security returns. However, tactical asset allocation models are designed to reveal errors investors make in mapping the relationship between future security returns and public information about variables such as the GNP and money supply. As noted earlier, forecasting models of security returns are possible only if investors commit systematic cognitive errors as they map the relationship between public information and future security returns. In the absence of cognitive errors security prices would be efficient in the semi-strong sense and tactical asset allocation would be futile.

Variables in a typical tactical asset allocation model are often classified into three groups: value variables, economic variables and sentiment variables. Economic variables are useful if investors are slow to incorporate economic information into security prices. For example, it is possible that investors do not fully incorporate into security prices information about unemployment for a month after that information becomes public. Value variables and sentiment variables are attempts to benefit from the tendency of investors to overreact. Investors tend to expect continuation of trends, becoming more optimistic after rises in security prices. Sentiment variables recognize that the optimism of investors might prevail for some short run, as investors create "bubbles." Value variables are a recognition of the fact that while "bubbles" might be created in the short run, a contrarian view is likely to prevail in the long run.

Tactical asset allocation models allow asset allocators to exploit the cognitive errors of other investors. Equally important is the protection from cognitive errors that models offer to asset allocators. Tactical asset allocators without information who aim for the highest expected return should always stay with the asset class that has the highest expected returns, even when the choice seems uncomfortable and contrary to their intuition (e.g., holding stocks after a decline in stock prices). Moreover, asset allocators with information should be aware not only of the fact that the information they have is imperfect but also of the likelihood that the historical R^2 of their model is probably an exaggerated measure of the amount of information they truly have. That means that asset allocators and their clients should not be surprised by long dry spells and that tactical asset allocators should base their allocations on a more humble assessment of information than indicated by the R^2. All this implies that tactical asset allocation should be used with knowledge and caution. Still, evidence suggests that there are leading indicators to security returns and that tactical asset allocators can incorporate them into models that add value to their clients.

REFERENCES

Chance, D. M., "Option Volume and Stock Market Performance," *Journal of Portfolio Management,* Summer 1990.

Chua, J.H. and Woodward, R.S., "Gains from Stock Market Timing," *Monograph Series in Finance and Economic,* Monograph 1986-2, Salomon Brothers Center, New York University.

Clarke, R.G., FitzGerald, M.T., Berent, P. and Statman, M., "Market Timing with Imperfect Information," *Financial Analysts Journal,* November/December 1989.

Cooper, R.V.L., "Efficient Capital Markets and the Quantity Theory of Money," *Journal of Finance,* 29, No. 3, June 1974.

Engel, C. and Hamilton, J.D., "Long Swings in the Dollar: Are They in the Data and Do Markets Know It?"*The American Economic Review,* September 1990.

Ferson, W. E. and Harvey, C. R., "The Variation of Economic Risk Premiums," *Journal of Political Economy,* Vol 99. No 21, 1991.

Friedman, M.J., and Schwartz, A.J., "Money and Business Cycles," *Review of Economics and Statistics,* 45. No. 1, (Supplement) February 1963.

Jeffrey, R.H., "The Folly of Stock Market Timing," *Harvard Business Review,* July/August 1984.

Kahneman, D. and Slovic, P. and Tversky, A., "Judgment Under Uncertainty: Heuristics and Biases," *Cambridge: Cambridge University Press,* 1982.

Merton, R., "On Market Timing and Investment Performance: I. An Equilibrium Theory of Value for Market Forecasts." *Journal of Business,* July 1981, pp. 363–406.

Rozeff, M.S., "Money and Stock Prices: Market Efficiency and the Lag Effect of Monetary Policy," *Journal of Financial Economics,* 1, No. 3, September 1974.

Sharpe, W., "Likely Gains from Market Timing," *Financial Analysts Journal,* March/April 1975.

Shefrin, H. and Statman, M., "The Equilibrium Consequences of Particular Errors by Noise Traders," Santa Clara University, *Working Paper,* 1991.

Solt, M.E., and Statman, M., "How Useful is the Sentiment Index?" *Financial Analysts Journal,* September/October 1988.

Sprinkel, B.W., *"Money and Markets: A Monetarist View,"* Homewood, Ill.: Richard D. Irwin, 1971.

Stupp, M. and Scott J., "Does Liquidity Predict Stock Returns?" *Journal of Portfolio Management,* Winter 1991.

Weigel, E., "The Value Added to Tactical Asset Allocation: An Empirical Assessment," Frank Russell Research Commentary, February 1990.

Weigel, E., "The Performance of Tactical Asset Allocation," *Financial Analysts Journal,* September/October 1991.

CHAPTER 19

At Last, A Rational Case for Long-Horizon Risk Tolerance and for Asset-Allocation Timing?

PAUL A. SAMUELSON
INSTITUTE PROFESSOR EMERITUS
MASSACHUSETTS INSTITUTE OF TECHNOLOGY

1. As you grow older and the time horizon of your investing shortens, should you rationally cut down on your exposure to lucrative but risky equities?
2. And, when you are young with many chances ahead to recoup any transient losses, can you afford to take a "business man's risk?"
3. College endowments and portfolios of permanent foundations, expecting to be operating and growing virtually forever, can they, by the same logic, largely ignore short-run riskiness and invest heavily in common stocks with high average mean returns, relying on "diversification over time and the cancellations of repeated chances in the Law of Large Numbers?"
4. After stocks have extraordinarily risen in value, should you rationally lighten up on them? After they have been languishing unusually long in price level, should you time your portfolio choices by

leaning against the wind in the general direction of taking on extra fractional share of equities?

These are old and basic questions. The conventional wisdom gives them an affirmative answer:

> Long-horizon investors allegedly can, *ceteris paribus*, tolerate more risk and thereby garner higher mean returns.
>
> The rational age-specific pattern of asset allocation allegedly involves, as you age, some tapering down of equities relative to lower-variance assets.
>
> Thus, although CREF is careful not to express judgments about optimal strategies for its professorial participants to follow, readers of TIAA-CREF's many publications could be forgiven for tacitly presuming that it is more normal at advanced ages to shift from the equities of CREF to the bonds and nominal-principal investments of TIAA and CREF than vice versa.
>
> Contending that markets do not go one way indefinitely, contrarians counsel that investors downplay equities when their price/earnings ratios have become high and their Tobin-q-ratio has run way past unity. Practical investing counselors endorse "timing" in principle while admitting that experience turns up little documentation that would-be timers have fared well.

Like so much that belongs to the conventional wisdom, this described dogma has not as yet earned the imprimatur of science. Thus, when Samuelson [1969] was motivated to investigate rational life-cycle investing for those who maximize expected utility and who possess constant-relative-risk aversion, there emerged the surprising theorem that your uncle with few years to go should hold exactly the same fraction of wealth in risky (*random-walk*) stocks as he did when young and as you do now. This mandate that rational investors should be *myopic*, ignoring the length of their time horizon, is a specific denial of the conventional wisdom.

HOW TIME ADDS TO RISK

How is such a nihilistic result possible? Here are relevant considerations.

Repeated investing over many periods does not cause risk to wash out in the long run. Insurance companies do not eliminate total risk by insuring more and more ships. As shown in my discussion of fallacies of interpreting the Law of Large Numbers (Samuelson 1963), each new independent risk adds to the *absolute total* of risk. But *total absolute* risk grows as the *square root* of the number of *independent* ships insured and not in proportion to their numbers. It is the *subdividing* of risk by bringing in new members to the insuring syndicate that, together with bringing in of new independent ships, does reduce the *relative* riskiness per dollar. ($\sqrt{N}$ does grow with N; but making the denominator in Total Riskiness/Total Number of Insurers be proportional to N, does produce $\sqrt{N}/N$ which does decline like $1/\sqrt{N}$ toward zero.)

The diversification over time which a pension fund or young person achieves when investing over many periods thus cannot cancel out or effectively reduce the dispersion of wealth outcomes that occurs at distant dates in the future.[1]

In Chapter 17, it is demonstrated that, if the probabilities that stocks and bonds are subject to in successive periods are broadly independent, the twin who is half the time in stocks and half the time in bonds will experience over a lifetime a demonstrably worse risk-adjusted return than the twin who is always 50% in each. (Of course, if you have a magic demon that tells you when bonds will soar and when stocks will zoom, then you and the Tooth Fairy should follow Will Rogers' formula for being a perfect timer by only buying securities that are going to appreciate.)

A LOOPHOLE UNDER MEAN-REGRESSION?

All the above applies to equity markets that are truly *random walks*. Now that Poterba and Summers (1987), Fama and French (1988), Modigliani and Cohen (1961), Tobin and Brainard, and other observers are providing

---

[1]There is a misleading spurious parallel between the decline of N/N with time horizon and the decline with $\sqrt{N}$ of the variance of a portfolio's *mean* annual return with N. For independent probabilities, Variance {log (mean annual return)} $\to 0$ as $1/\sqrt{N} \to 0$. However, the dispersion of my terminal year's log Wealth, Var{logW_N}, does rise with N in proportion to N and *ceteris paribus* that does lower my Exp {$U_N(W_N)$}.

evidence that — *over long periods of time, epochs of strong equity returns tend to be followed by epochs of weak, and vice versa* — at long last I am able to deduce some *rational* basis for the conventional wisdom according to which long investing horizons do call for more equity exposure than short horizons do.

> Theorem: For a *white-noise* process of a random walk, where percentage price changes of stocks tomorrow are truly independent of yesterday's changes, would-be timers are shooting themselves in the leg. So to speak they lose two ways: in geometric mean return and in volatility of return.
>
> By contrast, when white noise is replaced by *red noise* so that the next several-years' return is negatively auto-correlated with the last several-years' return, then lower fractional shares in equities should follow upon higher fractional shares. Indeed, when the process involves *violet noise,* meaning that next week's expected change in price is positively correlated with last week's change, you should be a timer in the style of a momentum trader — piling on to any price trends (and helping to make them worse?).

Samuelson (1991) confirmed that the spirit of the above theorem holds for a fundamentalist's model that goes beyond a red-noise process involving a Markov matrix that makes serial correlations of price changes be negatively autocorrelated. Such Markov processes still have the dubious implication that, if we wait long enough, *real* stock prices can wander anywhere with one GM share being worth less than a peanut or more than the annual GNP.

Also, suppose you have rational reason to believe that real stock prices tend to be in an invariant percentage probability spread around some exponential real time trend. Such a fundamentalist model entails optimal portfolio choice by cautious people that is more risk tolerant for the long horizon than for the short. And it does imply that the canny timer should lighten up on stocks when they have risen above trend and load up when they have fallen behind trend. Clearly as such a fundamentalist contrarian timer, you must belong to an elite minority — for if everyone shared your Bayesians, the S&P-500 would not be going through its Shiller-Keynes gyrations.

I have spelled out the mathematical derivation at the May 1988 Tobin Colloquium at Yale, held to honor James Tobin on the occasion of his

Seventieth Anniversary. See Samuelson (1991) for details. Here I shall merely sketch the nature of the argument.

When equity return rates of one 5-year period are *negatively corre-lated* with those of the last such period, my Tobin-fest essay demonstrated that extreme runs tend to be self-cancelling, making the wealth outcomes at the end of a long horizon bunch up around their middle in comparison with the log-normal outcomes of the *random walk.* Paradoxically, such a bunching around the middle does not compel all risk averters to plunge more heavily into equities. For risk-averse investors who maximize Ex-pected value of their utility, which happens to be the logarithm of wealth (à la 1738 Daniel Bernoulli), *the time horizon turns out not to matter at all* — both in the Poterba-Summers *rebound* model and the *random-walk model.*

However, the bulk of the empirical evidence, cross-sectional and from time series, is that real-life investors are *more risk averse* than Bernoulli. Instead of having a utility function like log(Wealth), their behavior is better rationalized if we hypothesize for them something like

$$U(W) = -1/W \text{ or } -1/W^2$$

When I calculate for $(-1/W)$ the 1-period and 2-period optimal equity shares in the *rebound* case, I deduce that the longer time horizon does mandate some greater tolerance for lucrative but risky stocks. QED. The intuitive reason for the result is that a bad outcome for my equities in a pre-ultimate period just ahead is not so bad since it shifts the odds towards a remunerative rebound, a consideration that relieves equity exposure of some of its abhorrent riskiness.

There is also deduced to be a case for being a *market timer,* reducing equity share after a boom epoch and raising it after bear markets. How-ever, following a crash year like 1987, there is probably already an excessive fad for "asset allocation" models that try to "time." In the present age of capital-gains taxation at full marginal rates, the burden of proof has shifted against turnover. One should also ponder over the final caution in my Tobin paper:

> A final caveat may be in order warning against overtouting this deductive qualitative result. Since it takes a long time to duplicate statistical samples of long-term epochs, our confi-dence in the strength of the *rebound* [red-noise] deviation from the *random walk* must be guarded. Moreover, the size

of the alleged effect, particularly after we discount for the possible one-time nature of the 1920–1945 swings of the Great Depression and World War II, may not be too great quantitatively. For these reasons, a certain caution toward the new results would seem prudent.

REFERENCES

Fama, E.F. and French, K.P., "Permanent and Temporary Components of Stock Prices," *Journal of Political Economics* 96, No. 2, 1988, pp 246–273.

Poterba, J.M. and Summers, L., "Means Reversion in Stock Returns: Evidence and Implications," Cambridge, MA: NBER, March 1987.

Samuelson, P.A., "Lifetime Portfolio Selection by Dynamic Stochastic Programming," *Review of Economics and Statistics* 51(3), August 1969, pp. 239–46; Reprinted in *Collected Scientific Papers of Paul A. Samuelson* Vol. III, R. Merton (ed.), Chapter 204, pp. 883–90.

_____, "Risk and Uncertainty: A Fallacy of Large Numbers," *Scientia*, 6th series, 57th year, April/May 1963, pp. 1–6; Reprinted in *Collected Scientific Papers of Paul A. Samuelson*, Vol. I, J.E. Stiglitz (ed.), Chapter 16, pp. 153–158.

_____, "Longrun Risk Tolerance When Equity Returns are Mean Regressing: Pseudoparadoxes and Vindication of 'Businessman's Risk'," in Brainard, W., Nordhaus, W., and Watts, H. (eds.), *Macroeconomics, Finance and Economic Policy: Essays in Honor of James Tobin.* Cambridge, Mass.: MIT Press, 1991.

_____, "Asset Allocation Can Be Dangerous To Your Health: Pitfalls in Across-time Diversification," *Journal of Portfolio Management*, 16, 1990, pp. 5–8.

Shiller, R., "Stock Prices and Social Dynamics," *Brookings Papers on Economic Activity*, 1986, pp. 457–498.

Tobin, J. and Brainard, W. L., "Asset Markets and the Cost of Capital," in *Economic Progress, Private Values and Public Policy: Essays in Honor of William Fellner,* eds. R. Nelson and B. Balassa, 1977; Amsterdam, North-Holland, pp. 235–262. Reprinted in Tobin, J., *Essays in Economics: Theory and Policy,* Cambridge, Mass., The MIT Press, 1982.

INDEX

A

Accounting principles, 332
Accumulated Benefit Obligation
See Projected
ABO, 26, 27, 29–31, 35, 41, 170,
178–179
  balance with incremental
  PBO, 35–40
Across-time diversification
  pitfalls, 381–391
Active asset allocation
  risks, 379–416
  strategies, 49
    performance measurement,
    319–325
    temptations, 51–53
Allocation. *See* No-forecast
Allocation model. *See* N-asset,
  Two-asset
  extension
    multiple scenarios, 148–154
    risk-of-loss, 145–148
    short/long term, 154–159
ALPHA, 102, 108–112
AMEX stock, 156
Analysis. *See* Regression, Risk,
  Tactical

Arms index, 271
Asset
  See Allocation categories,
    Capital
  evaluation, 22
  owner identification, 10–12
  requirements
    balancing surplus shortfall
    requirements, 185–187
  risk-adjusted
    shortfall definition, 203–206
  risk-free, 13
  variable asset class, 171
  variable-income, 39
Asset allocation (AA)
  See Active, Allocation, Currency,
    Futures, Global, Going,
    Integrated, International,
    Policy, Tactical
  checklist, 98–103
  danger, 381–391
  decoupling, currency selection,
    335-343
  diversification, 289–302, 381–
    391
  dynamic strategies, 3–4, 5–6
  fundamentals, 329
  futures markets, 303–326

417